PETROGLYPHS, PICTOGRAPHS, AND PROJECTIONS

Petroglyphs, Pictographs, and Projections

NATIVE AMERICAN ROCK ART IN THE CONTEMPORARY CULTURAL LANDSCAPE

Richard A. Rogers

THE UNIVERSITY OF UTAH PRESS
Salt Lake City

The Defiance House Man colophon is a registered trademark of The University of Utah Press. It is based on a four-foot-tall Ancient Puebloan pictograph (late PIII) near Glen Canyon, Utah.

Library of Congress Cataloging-in-Publication Data

Names: Rogers, Richard A. (Richard Alleyne), 1965, author.
Title: Petroglyphs, pictographs, and projections : Native American rock art in the contemporary cultural landscape / Richard A. Rogers.
Description: Salt Lake City : University of Utah Press, [2018] | Includes bibliographical references and index. |
Identifiers: LCCN 2017052551 (print) | LCCN 2017059376 (ebook) | ISBN 9781607816195 () | ISBN 9781607816188 (cloth)
Subjects: LCSH: Rock paintings—North America. | Petroglyphs—North America. | Appropriation (Art) | Commodification. | Culture and tourism. | Kokopelli (Pueblo deity) | Indians of North America —Antiquities.
Classification: LCC GN799.P4 (ebook) | LCC GN799.P4 R67 2018 (print) | DDC 709.01/13—dc23
LC record available at https://lccn.loc.gov/2017052551

For

my mother, Valery Lee Morse

and

my father, Ronald Alleyne Rogers

CONTENTS

FIGURES

Color Plates

following page 216

Acknowledgments

This book has been two decades in the making, and many people have contributed to its genesis, development, and completion. I thank the following individuals and institutions for their contributions:

All of those who have spent time with me visiting and discussing rock art sites, and who have otherwise supported my interest in rock art and the examination of its contemporary interpretation and use: Barb White, Joseph Wilhelm, Jeanne Padgett Wilhelm, Christine Stephenson, Joe and Nancy Jordan, Bern Carey, Carly Long, and many more. I am especially indebted to Joseph Wilhelm for years of conversations in which many of the ideas in this book were birthed and to Christine Stephenson for bringing my work deeper into archaeology.

Kelley Hays-Gilpin for her germinal work on gender and rock art, making my forays into that topic much easier; for her research into Kokopelli, flute players, and their phalluses (or lack thereof), which brought a level of clarity (amidst great ambiguity) to that topic in a way that many others have failed to do; and for supporting my research in a multitude of other ways.

Janna Jones and Mark Neumann, colleagues in the School of Communication at Northern Arizona University, for reading early drafts and bearing with me as I worked to produce narratives not just linear arguments.

Mark Neumann for companionship and assistance in finding the site depicted in the David Muench photograph discussed in chapter 8 and for showcasing my work in online publications.

Carly Long, my partner and colleague, for assistance photographing the Klare Spring interpretive sign in Death Valley National Park, the "Indian blanket" pictograph in Fremont Indian State Park, the "Disney" panel in Joshua Tree National Park, and the "World's Largest Kokopelli" in Camp Verde, as well as for her invaluable role in producing the two maps created for the book.

Christine Oravec and Joe Brame for showing me sites around St. George, including ones that became central to some of the arguments in this book, and for Chris's early influences on my development as a scholar and her later encouragement to continue my work with rock art.

Lance Diskan for sending me countless photographs of Kokopelli kitsch, Emilly Borthwick-Wong for sending a photograph of the Cocao-pelli t-shirt, Bobby Stead for the petroglyph magnet pictured in Figure 5.9, and all the other students over the years who have gifted me specimens of Kokopelli kitsch.

Daniel McCarthy for his insights on the "Disney" panel in Joshua Tree National Park, Alleyne Rogers for his assistant with Latin usage, and Catherine Fowler for discussing Paiute shamanism.

Liam Brady, Don Christensen, Sara Hayden, Tom Nakayama, and John Sloop as well as the anonymous reviewers of the four previously published essays on which this book is partially based (see below).

The Department of Anthropology at Northern Arizona University for the opportunity to teach a course on the archaeology of rock art, which helped me synthesize the field in broader terms as opposed to my specific lines of interest, and my students in ANT 355 for putting up with a nonarchaeologist teaching a class on the archaeology of rock art.

Jeremy Haines, Jeanne Shofer, Peter Pilles, and others on the archaeological staff at the Coconino National Forest for their instruction and support of my archaeological endeavors.

Jannelle Weakly at the Arizona State Museum; Daisy Njoku at the National Anthropological Archives, Smithsonian Institution; Shawn San Roman at the Museum of Northern Arizona; Jonathan Pringle and Jess Vogelsang at Special Collections and Archives, Cline Library, Northern Arizona University; and Leigh Kuwanwisiwma at the Hopi Cultural Preservation Office for assistance with some of the images used in the book.

Reba Rauch and the University of Utah Press for their assistance in making this a better book and for providing the opportunity to symbolically return to my alma mater.

Northern Arizona University for two sabbaticals (2005–2006 and 2012–2013) and the NAU Office of the Vice President for Research for two Scholarly and Creative Activity grants (2014–2015 and 2017–2018) in support of this project.

While these and many others have made invaluable contributions to this book, I alone am responsible for the errors of fact, interpretation, and judgment contained herein.

Finally, my thanks to Carly and Marley for their patience during the final months of finishing the manuscript, and Winona (Winnie) and Angell (Ainge) for their companionship and lap-warming.

Four of the chapters in this book are expansions, revisions, and updates of previously published articles. The following chapters are based on these prior publications:

Chapter 4: Rogers, Richard A. 2007. From Hunting Magic to Shamanism: Interpretations of Native American Rock Art and the Contemporary Crisis in Masculinity. *Women's Studies in Communication* 30:78–110.

Chapter 5: Rogers, Richard A. 2007. Deciphering Kokopelli: Masculinity in Commodified Appropriations of Native American Imagery. *Communication and Critical/Cultural Studies* 4:233–255.

Chapter 6: Rogers, Richard A. 2009. "Your Guess Is as Good as Any": Indeterminacy, Dialogue, and Dissemination in Interpretations of Native American Rock Art. *Journal of International and Intercultural Communication* 2:44–65.

Chapter 7: Rogers, Richard A. 2007. Overcoming the Preservation Paradigm: Toward a Dialogic Approach to Rock Art and Culture. In *American Indian Rock Art*, Vol. 33, edited by Don D. Christensen and Peggy Whitehead, pp. 53–66. American Rock Art Research Association, Tucson, Arizona.

CONNECTIONS, CHASMS, AND CONTEXTS

Rock art is the predominant but contested term used in Anglo-America to refer to petroglyphs and pictographs, images pecked into or painted on (respectively) rock surfaces. In the context of the United States, the term specifically implies images made long ago by Native Americans, generally excluding marks on rock made by Westerners or in recent times. Over the last three decades, Native American rock art has become increasingly visible in a variety of venues, including parks, monuments, museums, galleries, coffee-table books, souvenir stores, housing developments, and academic publications.

My interest in rock art started in what seemed to be a happenstance sort of way, but, not coincidentally, it closely followed the increased visibility of rock art in the United States. In my first years of spending time in the desert Southwest, especially southern Utah, I began to encounter rock art in the course of exploring what I perceived as largely natural landscapes. In subsequent years, I continued to encounter rock art as an unintended result of my wanderings across the Colorado Plateau, Great Basin, and elsewhere in the greater Southwest, including both *in situ* images and, far more frequently and inescapably, reproductions of rock art in museums and visitor centers, on recreational and commercial signage, and in souvenir shops and art galleries. Only later did my hiking, camping, and backpacking trips change focus, become driven by the goal of finding, appreciating, and photographing—in effect, "collecting"—rock art.

While my initial encounters with rock art may have been happenstance, my and others' interest in ancient marks on rock is anything but. As I hope this book will demonstrate, this interest is deeply

1

embedded in social structures, cultural politics, and webs of meaning spun by and from entities ranging from Hollywood to the Southwest tourism industry, from archaeology to evolutionary theory, from the landscapes in which rock art occurs to the New Age commodity machine, from the precontact indigenous peoples who produced the rock art to contemporary Native Americans.

Connections and Chasms

My first encounter with rock art "in the wild," as I like to say, occurred while exploring the Needles District of Canyonlands National Park in southeastern Utah. I recall stopping at Newspaper Rock, a state-managed roadside attraction just outside the park boundary. This amazing panel has hundreds of petroglyphs (pecked images) on a single, large, beautiful rock face. However, I do not recall any particularly potent response to that experience, and my memories are clouded by later visits to the same Newspaper Rock (a name given to several rock art sites in the Southwest and beyond). What I do vividly remember is later that same day, after driving down a long, sandy road inside the park, hiking up to a sandstone ridge that contained a natural window with a spectacular view to the south. Next to that window was a series of handprints, made by covering a hand with paint and pressing the palm and fingers against the rock face. I knew nothing about rock art and little about Southwest archaeology—only vague impressions gleaned from interpretive signs in parks and monuments across the Four Corners area, mostly about the mysterious disappearance of the "Anasazi." I had no idea that the sandy road had brought us within a few hundred feet of dozens of outstanding pictographs. I had no idea that the Colorado Plateau, the Great Basin, and much of the rest of the American West is literally peppered with rock art sites ranging from a single pecked image on a basalt boulder to multitudes of painted images spread across a sandstone alcove the length of a football field.

I was transfixed by these ancient handprints. They seemed personal, individualized, leaving a mark not just of an abstract culture ("Anasazi," "Basketmaker," "Fremont," or the like) but of a living, breathing human. While rock art images in general tempt us with a fantasy of connecting to the thought worlds of their makers, handprints (see Plate 1) are a direct imprint, a material copy, of another human, one of a radically different culture and time, but another human, readily recognizable to me, recalling finger painting as a child and making a similar handprint, albeit with manufactured paint on paper. Those traces of my childhood are long gone, but the handprints remain, be they eight hundred or eight thousand years old. I was there, looking through that stone window at the remarkable landscape beyond, standing in the same place that these others—ancient and, to me, quite alien, abstract, but now also familiar and concrete—had also stood, taking in a view that these others had also, so long ago.

Over twenty years later, as a fully committed rock art enthusiast and researcher, I visited Fremont Indian State Park in central Utah to experience the park's rock art and examine how it is presented to the public. Standing at "point of interest #12" on the driving tour of the park, I looked through a short metal pipe fixed in place next to a picnic table, the pipe helping me visually locate a large pictograph on a cliff face on the other side of Clear Creek Canyon (see Plate 2). Between me and the pictograph were not only several hundred yards of space containing the bottom of the canyon and the stream that runs through it, but Interstate 70, a four-lane, divided highway with a constant flow of traffic. A nearby interpretive sign identified the large, rectangular design as an Indian blanket. My experience of this pictograph, unlike the handprints in Canyonlands, was not dominated by a sense of connection to its makers. Viewing the image through a fixed metal pipe, the highway manifesting a petroleum-fueled and mobile America that bombarded my senses and materially separated me from the image, and a square metal interpretive sign telling me what the image meant all contributed to a sense of profound distance. Despite my knowledge of rock art and archaeology, despite my excitement at seeing new sites and images, my experience was one of alienation, an acute awareness of the unbridgeable gaps of time and culture between myself and those who produced the image, and of the imposition of those alienations by my culture, as physically manifested in the viewing pipe, the highway, and the constant traffic.

My experiences of the handprints and the blanket pictograph manifest the dialectical tensions that both drive and confound the desire for connection, the urge to bridge enormous gaps of time and culture. The desire to connect is driven by those very gaps, paralleling the multitude of alienations that characterize many people's experiences of modernity. Rock art is valued for the possibilities for connection that it offers, but also for the (perhaps unresolvable) mystery of its original meanings and functions and the opportunities for projection such a mystery enables.

These dialectical tensions are at the center of my understanding of the role of rock art in the contemporary cultural landscape.

Rock Art in the Contemporary Cultural Landscape

After decades of relative neglect, North American archaeologists and other scholars have been focusing on rock art and its cultural significance, leading to tremendous growth in the published rock art literature. This renewed focus among academics parallels the rising popularity of rock art imagery, metastasizing commercial reproductions, reports of increased site visitation from land managers, and the increased activities of rock art enthusiasts and avocationalists, who not only visit rock art sites but also circulate their photographs and interpretations (and in some cases the specific locations of sites). Additionally, many people not particularly interested in rock art encounter it in the course of visiting a variety of national parks and monuments, state parks, and developed sites managed by the US Forest Service, Bureau of Land Management (BLM), other land management agencies, and private entities, especially in the western United States. Increased visitation to rock art sites is evidenced by rising rates of vandalism as well as unintentional cumulative damage from visitors, an increasing number of guidebooks and websites featuring directions to rock art sites and interpretations of rock art symbolism, and increasing coverage of rock art in newspapers, magazines, and other media.

A visit to many tourist destinations in the western United States, especially in the greater Southwest (roughly encompassing much of Utah, Nevada, Arizona, New Mexico, western Colorado, western Texas, and southeastern California; see Figure 1.1), will result in exposure to a vast amount of rock art–derived imagery, even though most tourists may not visit any rock art sites. The popularity and commercial appropriation of rock art imagery are evident upon entering almost any visitor center, souvenir store, museum, or Native American arts-and-crafts outlet in the Southwest. By far the most common is the image of the hump-backed flute player generally known as Kokopelli. Other rock art motifs, however, are also commonly used, including a variety of other anthropomorphic figures, stylized handprints, geometric designs such as spirals, and images of animals such as bighorn sheep, cougars, and snakes. Such imagery appears on printed materials for national parks and other recreational sites, on informational and commercial signage, and, most inescapably, on a variety of tourist merchandise. In addition to calendars, guide books, picture books, postcards, and posters that specifically represent and discuss rock art, clothing, sculptures, jewelry, mugs, key chains, light-switch covers, potholders, and a variety of other tourist merchandise are composed of or adorned with rock art–derived images. Hotels, campgrounds, restaurants, galleries, gift shops, tour companies, real estate developments, and other commercial establishments also utilize rock art–derived imagery to identify and market their products and services (see Figure 1.2). Such rock art–derived imagery has decentered previously dominant images for marketing the Southwest: the saguaro cactus and howling coyote (Tisdale 1993).

These rock art–derived images contribute to the representations of Native American cultures perpetuated through a variety of other media, such as photographs, books, films, and television. Examination of rock art imagery and the meanings assigned to it serves as another entry point into the dynamics of Western representations of the Indian. In addition to its contribution to shaping the image of the Indian, the possibly "unknowable" and definitely multiple and ambiguous meanings of much ancient rock art imagery enable it to serve as a site for the projection of Western fears, fantasies, and ideologies. I am guided by the assumption that interpretive models and other systems of meaning involved in rock art reveal at least as much if not more about contemporary cultural trends, dynamics, and tensions as they do about the original meanings and uses of rock art by the indigenous cultures that produced it. Such projections and systems of meaning have very real implications for Anglo-American identity, dominant views and evaluations of Native Americans, and the possibilities of Anglo-American/Native American cultural relations.

While many scholars and avocationalists have researched and published extensively on rock art, largely from archaeological and anthropological perspectives, and while many scholars have examined media representations of Native Americans and the appropriation of Native arts, crafts, symbols, and rituals, this book attempts to break new ground through a sustained focus on the role of *ancient* rock art in the *contemporary* cultural landscape, and specifically its deep relationships with media representations and commercial exploitations of Native American peoples and cultures. Rock art provides an important source for imagery used to cue or represent Native Americans in general, especially Native cultures of the Southwest.

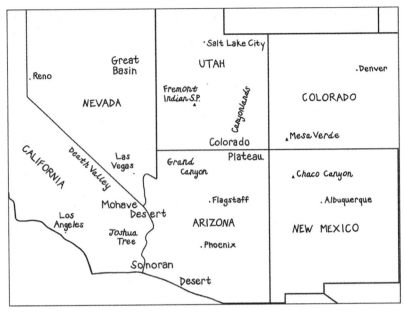

FIGURE 1.1—This map shows select geographic regions, natural features, and archaeological sites in the southwestern United States.

FIGURE 1.2—Rock art–decorated housing development sign, Hieroglyphic Trails, Gold Canyon, Arizona. Many housing developments and other commercial entities in the Southwest use rock art–inspired names and/or imagery to brand their enterprises.

Rock art research is driven primarily by anthropological and archaeological questions concerning cultures of the past—in the case of North America, predominantly precontact, indigenous cultures. Archaeologists and rock art scholars often mention concerns over the projection of present values onto the past and other cultures, and some even make direct, critical claims regarding such projections (e.g., Hays-Gilpin 2004; Schaafsma 1997). Nevertheless, these arguments are often made at a very general level or within the context of correcting such distortions of the past (e.g., Malotki 2000), a distinct and different goal than that of this project. In short, there has been relatively little in-depth, systematic research on the questions raised by the increasing popularity and appropriation of ancient rock art imagery in contemporary cultural contexts (exceptions include the explorations by Dowson 1999; Heyd 2003; Lewis-Williams 1995; Schaafsma 2013; Welsh 1999), let alone the complicity of archaeology and rock art studies in those appropriations (exceptions include Dickey 2012; Quinlan 2007a). Therefore, in this work I focus on the contemporary reproduction, appropriation, interpretation, circulation, management, and appeal of rock art from and in the United States. A direct and sustained analysis of the contemporary projections cast onto rock art offers insights into contemporary cultural dynamics and advances a more nuanced understanding of ancient rock art's contemporary functions.

I concentrate on the rock art of the southwestern United States, primarily the Colorado Plateau and Great Basin, which is the area where I have the most experience visiting sites and the most knowledge of the relevant rock art and archaeological literatures (see Figure 1.1). In contrast to most archaeological, anthropological, and ethnohistorical approaches to rock art, this project is not focused on discovering the meaning and function of rock art in the cultures that produced it. Instead, it is concerned with the meaning, valuation, appeal, and function of rock art at the intersection of multiple cultures and ideologies in the present. Various groups—such as New Age spiritualists, Indian hobbyists, commercial artists, rock art enthusiasts, tourists, archaeologists, and land managers, as well as, of course, living Native peoples—assign varying values and meanings to indigenous rock art. The multiple meanings and values assigned to rock art make it a rich site for studying the dynamics of contemporary Western/indigenous relations.

My central questions include the following: Why are non-Native peoples drawn to indigenous rock art and/or rock art imagery? What is its appeal? In what contexts (environmental, social, political, economic) is rock art imagery reproduced, consumed, and discussed? What structures of meaning inform, mediate, constrain, and enable the interpretation and valuation of rock art? What does this reveal about contemporary cultural dynamics? What are the ethical and ideological issues involved in the appropriation of rock art imagery? What structures of meaning inform the preservation of rock art sites? In all these activities, what/whose interests are being served?

Promises of Connection, Opportunities for Projection

As I mentioned above, my first substantive memory of encountering rock art in situ is of the handprints next to the natural window in Canyonlands National Park. Those handprints and the many others like them that appear across the Colorado Plateau, alone and in collections of hundreds, plain and patterned, positive and negative (stenciled), painted in a variety of colors, are tantalizing in their concreteness—a direct, material imprint of another human being who stood in the same place as visitors do today (see Plate 1). While rock art in general appeals to a desire to connect with the thought worlds of its makers, the concreteness of handprints seems, experientially at least, to bypass the problem of interpretation by enabling a direct, multisensorial connection to the rock art's producers and their environment. Someone was here, where I stand, pressed their hand in paint, and applied it to the wall in front of me, leaving the direct imprint that I am looking at now. In my personal experience and based on observations of others, an encounter with a handprint often leads to the placement of the viewer's hand over or next to the print (hopefully without touching it!). This act seems to involve both a comparison—how does my hand fit with theirs?—and the desire to reach out, to touch where and how the print's maker placed their own hand. I have also similarly marveled at the finger lines left in the mortar binding rocks into ancient walls and the fingerprints left on corrugated pottery fragments. The direct relationship between the image and the thing represented by that image (the person's hand), however, still leaves many questions: Why was the handprint made? Why was it placed here? What might it have meant to those who placed it here?

As with many rock art images, "we"—people living today, or white/Western people living today, or rock art scholars . . . the shifting meanings of "we" are part of the problematic dynamics in play here—do not and in many cases probably cannot know what many of these hand-prints meant (symbolically) to their producers and ancient viewers. But that has not stopped many people from generating hypotheses and presenting them with greater or lesser degrees of qualification and evidence. These kinds of handprints are sometimes interpreted as "signatures," a statement of "I was here" with the distinct sense of indi-viduality the modern, Western "I" implies. One panel of many positive handprints located in Grand Gulch, in southeastern Utah, has been dubbed the "FBI panel." This name reflects, in a sense *imposes*, a whole set of culturally specific assumptions onto these images: assumptions about individuality, uniqueness, "making my mark," the link between our material bodies and our presumably stable and singular identities, as well as of crime, the police, science, surveillance, and the state. Perhaps such "signatures" are part of a rite of passage, a marker along a journey, and/or a social statement of affinity. Regardless, they offer me a sense of concreteness, and hence an illusion of connection. But what seems outside of the bounds of illusion, and perhaps what makes my memory cling to those handprints in the Needles District of Canyonlands, is the brute materiality of a shared place, of being immersed in a locale that, while dynamic, archaeologists and climatologists tell us was not radically different than what it is now (Schwinning et al. 2008). The sharing of such space does not bridge the chasms of time and culture, but it offers a bodily sense of commonality with an absent and, to me, profoundly alien other.

This "otherness" of rock art—its temporal and cultural distance, and its presumed potential for the bridging of such gaps—offers not only the possibility of connection, but also projection. Indigenous rock art images become symbolic sites for circulating Western fantasies about the primitive Other, and specifically Anglo-American fantasies about the indigenous peoples of North America. The relative prevalence and visibility of rock art in the southwestern United States combine with the symbolic role of the Southwest as America's mystical playground and hotspot for spiritual rejuvenation (Dilworth 1996; Hinsley 1996), enabling such projections while simultaneously shaping the specific forms those projections take. In the New Age, with Iron Eyes Cody's single tear and *Dances with Wolves*'s rejection of modern American life clearly visible in our rearview mirrors, it comes as no surprise that much rock art has been interpreted—and such interpretations widely propagated—as the activity of shamans. Resonating with the cultural dynamics that created the stereotype of the Ecological Indian (Salvador and Clark 1999), fueled the popularity of Kevin Costner's *Dances with Wolves* and James Cameron's *Avatar*, and drive the well-intended appropriation of Native American spirituality, rock art has increasingly been interpreted as a record of journeys to the other world, of communication with powerful spirits, undertaken to help cure the sick, bring rain, ensure a good hunt, or promote fertility (e.g., Whitley 1996, 2000a).

Different, but not entirely unaffiliated, frames were projected onto rock art in one of the earliest Anglo-American attempts at an in-depth study of the subject, Garrick Mallery's (1894) *Picture-Writing of the American Indians*, published by the Bureau of Ethnology under the direction of John Wesley Powell. In discussing the rock art of Utah, Mallery recounts a rather blatant case of projection, in which early Mormon leaders translated a petroglyph panel near Manti, Utah, consistent with the LDS Church's doctrinal belief in the migration of Israelites to North America, with some becoming what we know as Native Americans: "I, Mahanti, the second King of the Lamanites, in five valleys of the mountains, make this record in the twelve hundredth year since we came out of Jerusalem. And I have three sons gone to the south country to live by hunting antelope and deer" (originally reported by Lt. J. W. Gunnison in 1853; as quoted in Mallery 1894:118). Examining the drawing of the petroglyph panel used by Mallery (see Figure 1.3), I can imagine how someone could come up with "five valleys of the mountains" and perhaps antelope and deer, but the rest seems conjured out of nothing but the fabric of LDS theology. Mallery's (1894:118) source for the report, Charles Rau, appears to hold the same basic sentiment, noting that the Mormon leaders' translation "made this aboriginal inscription subservient to their religion."

Mallery proceeds, however, to subject rock art to his culture's secular version of human history and the place of Native Americans in that history. Specifically, he positions rock art as a form of "picture-writing" that eventually led, in evolutionary fashion, toward the alphabet:

> The importance of the study of picture-writing depends partly upon the result of its examination as a phase in the evolution of human culture. As the invention of alphabetic writing is admitted to be the great step in marking the change from barbarism to civilization, the history of its earlier development must be valuable. (Mallery 1894:26)

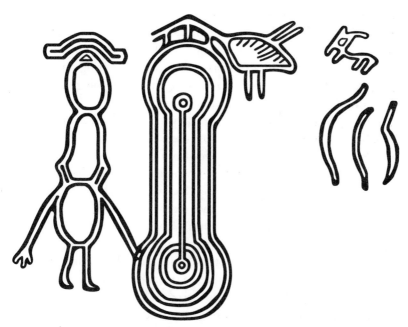

FIGURE 1.3—Manti, Utah, petroglyphs. Mallery (1894:118) presented a drawing of the petroglyphs referenced in an 1853 report from Lieutenant Gunnison about a Mormon translation of the images, but cites Bancroft (1875) as the source of the image used in his book. These representations of the petroglyphs are therefore drawn after Bancroft (1875:717). Bancroft's and Mallery's images are very similar, but in Mallery's the anthropomorph's hand does not connect to the central geometric element, as it does in Bancroft's. The degree of fidelity between either of these drawings and the actual petroglyphs discussed by Mallery, Bancroft, and Gunnison is unknown.

While the contemporary view of rock art as traces of shamanic practices and Mallery's evolutionary frame interpret rock art differently, they nevertheless share a common perspective, projecting not dissimilar Western ideas about the "primitive" onto rock art. Mallery saw it as an inferior form of writing that was eventually superseded by a superior form, while today's New Age–influenced tourists may see it as an expression of a superior way of life in which an authentic spirituality and a deep connection with nature were still possible. Both see rock art as a part of "our" (human) past, as an earlier stage of human culture; they disagree on the relative desirability of that past and their present.

Multiple and apparently contradictory ideas of the past are projected onto rock art imagery, but strong commonalities among them are evident. Twenty years after encountering the Needles handprints as a rock art neophyte, I stood in a university classroom, offering an "expert" presentation on rock art with a colleague from anthropology to a group of community members. At one point, I displayed the "Holy Ghost" from the Great Gallery in Horseshoe Canyon, an island unit of Canyonlands National Park (see Plate 3). Given the widespread reproduction and deployment of this and other images from the Great Gallery, I anticipated that some audience members would be familiar with it—that was part of my purpose in displaying this image. What I did not know was that it had been highlighted in a recent episode of the Discovery Channel's series *Ancient Aliens*. Within a few seconds of the appearance of the image on the screen, a hand popped up and a middle-aged white woman (a demographically typical audience member) commented that surely this image makes clear that at least some rock art records the visitation of ancient humans by extraterrestrials.

Both I and my colleague were well aware of the UFO school of thought in rock art interpretation, and as "serious" rock art scholars we knew we should hold such interpretations at arm's length, positioning them as the "lunatic fringe." However, our presentation highlighted the limitations of interpretations of ancient imagery, the unknowable nature of the meaning and function of much rock art, and, most importantly, the ubiquitous, unconscious projection of our own cultural assumptions, fears, and fantasies onto the imagery. The images at the Great Gallery, due to their greater antiquity and more tenuous connections with the living peoples and cultures of the Colorado Plateau (Schaafsma 2013), are prime examples of the kinds of interpretive barriers and projective possibilities we were discussing. I was not prepared, in other words, to tell this person that her interpretation was wrong; nor was I comfortable with licensing her interpretation through my supposed authority on the subject. In addition to the recent episode of *Ancient Aliens*, the image called the Holy Ghost (the name itself involving some serious projections!) does have rather apparent similarities to the images of aliens circulated in Anglo-American culture for much of the twentieth century, such as large "bug" eyes and a large, oval-shaped head. Verbal, visual, and cinematic representations of extraterrestrials, like those of Native Americans, become symbolic sites for working through contemporary Western issues, such as a longing for connection (e.g., *Contact, E.T.,* and *Close Encounters of the Third Kind*). The issue becomes not which interpretation is plausible, but the conditions of possibility behind these projections and the work such projections do.

Chasms and Contexts

Fremont Indian State Park was one of countless places that I frequently drove by, noting that I needed to visit the rock art there someday. After years of passing by, I finally set this as one of my destinations on a lengthy rock art tour through Arizona, Utah, Nevada, and southeastern California. The park, located in Clear Creek Canyon, east of the intersection of Interstates 15 and 70 in central Utah, was created after the construction of I-70 in the 1980s, which uncovered a large Fremont village on Five Finger Ridge, right in the path of the planned highway. The village was excavated and recorded (i.e., "salvaged") prior to its destruction, and the state park was created in 1987 to showcase the remaining traces of the Fremont in the area, including a large amount of rock art. "Fremont" is an archaeological category for the material remains of the precontact inhabitants of much of what is now called

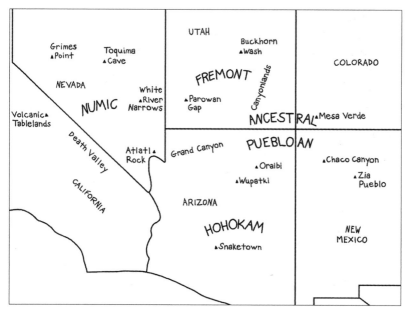

FIGURE 1.4—This map shows select precontact archaeological cultures, archaeological sites, and natural features in the Southwest.

Utah from about 600 to 1400 CE, existing north of but in many ways mirroring the ancestral Puebloans ("Anasazi") of the Four Corners region (Schaafsma 1980; Simms and Gohier 2010; see Figure 1.4 for the archaeological cultures referenced here and elsewhere in the book).

Fremont Indian State Park is a rather bizarre place, I discovered. While its nominal purpose is to preserve the archaeological remnants of the Fremont culture and to educate the public about the Fremont, its campground and road system function as the base for a network of off-road vehicle (ORV) trails, which seems to be the primary recreational activity in and around the park. Additionally, the park, located in a mountain canyon, is bisected by I-70, on which trucks, buses, and cars zip through at high speeds, all day, every day. As I briefly recounted above, at one point I found myself at a viewing station composed of a short metal pipe mounted in a fixed position, through which I viewed a large red rectangular pictograph composed of geometric designs, painted high on the canyon wall opposite the viewing station (see Plate 2). In between the viewing station and the painting runs I-70, complete with widely separated double lanes, wide shoulders, and fences, not to mention the roar of the almost-constant traffic. An interpretive sign at the viewing station describes the painting as an "Indian blanket pictograph," and recounts the legend of a Paiute mother who painted the blanket to keep her deceased infant, buried nearby, warm in the winter (see Figure 1.5). (A park brochure acknowledges the source of this "legend" to be local, non-Native residents.)

Maybe the image is indeed of a blanket. The geometric designs can be identified as similar to those found in textiles, both contemporary and, more importantly, those uncovered in archaeological digs in the region. Similar patterns are also found on decorated pottery, which is how Julian Steward (1937:Plate 6) described this same pictograph, but the pottery designs can also be understood as replicas of textile patterns. I have seen other "blanket" images, both pictographs (painted) and petroglyphs (pecked), and they indeed seem to be blankets based on the designs as well as their rectangular shape. However, in all these cases, the image had already been labeled as a blanket prior to my exposure to it. I already had the idea, via the verbal label, that those specific images—and now, others like them—are representations of blankets, so I do not think that the "literal" referents of these images are as self-evident as they seem. This "gaze and guess" conundrum holds true at almost any rock art site (Lewis-Williams 2006; Loendorf et al.

FIGURE 1.5—"Indian blanket" viewing station, Fremont Indian State Park, Utah. See Plate 2 for the view through the pipe.

2005). Even when the direct referents of the images seem obvious—e.g., that image represents a person holding a bow and arrow, or that is a painting of a blanket—such unreflective inferences are not very productive to the systematic study of rock art, especially in relation to precontact cultures about which little or no substantive ethnographic information is available.

Even if we can correctly identify the material referent of an image, that does not mean that we have any idea of what the image meant to its viewers—that is, the mental concepts and associations it triggered, its possible metaphoric meanings, and the purposes it served. Even if we are correct that an image on rock represents a human holding a bow and arrow in shooting position, that does not mean we are seeing images of warfare or hunting (as is commonly assumed from such imagery). Indeed, we may not be seeing a literal representation of anything, but a visual metaphor or reference to something more abstract, possibly narrative in nature, even ideographic (Chippindale 2001; Whitley 1998a, 2011). That is, in their originating cultures such images may have triggered associations as deep and complex as those triggered today by Edward Curtis's sepia-toned photograph of an Indian chief wearing an eagle-feather headdress mounted on a horse amidst an ocean of grass on the Great Plains. So maybe it's a blanket, maybe it's not—even if so, who knows what that image *meant* to its producers and what *functions* it served.

More deeply, however, the metaphor offered by my viewing of the "Indian blanket" pictograph seemed almost too obvious to consider for inclusion in this book. I sat on one side of the canyon, looking at a very large pictograph through a "simple" (mass-manufactured) metal pipe, an alien shape and texture in the environment of Clear Creek Canyon. My viewing experience was framed in a narrow, fixed manner by both distance and the method of locating and viewing the image. In between the image and me were not only the viewing pipe and several hundred yards of space, including a stream and a steep canyon wall, but a major interstate highway facilitating industrialized commerce, travel, and tourism by means of petroleum-powered, internal combustion engines. I'm over here, the pictograph is over there, and in between lay the materialization of industrialization, automobilization, capitalism, and cold war national defense. Over there, the material traces of a (likely) precontact Native American culture on a three-dimensional, natural cliff face; over here, a square, smooth, silver metal sign providing me with information about the image's size, the origin of the minerals used to make the paint, and, most prominently, "The Legend of the Indian Blanket."

But the contexts are even larger. I am viewing this pictograph in a state park whose primary function appears to be to facilitate ORV recreation, with people zooming around on individualized vehicles designed to traverse less-developed ground. The highway that facilitated the creation of the park plowed through many remnants of the "Fremont culture," an archaeological abstraction, not to mention the remains of many ancient *people*, which is about as concrete as it gets. The "discovery" of the archaeological "resources" did not alter the planned highway, but instigated the required salvage operation: excavating, recording, and collecting the remnants, then curating (and in a small minority of cases, displaying) the recovered artifacts at the park museum and other institutions. And I now sit in the park, viewing the red geometric image across the interstate highway through a round metal tube, my viewing experience already shaped not only by the tube and the alphabetic message inscribed into a metal plate, but by the interstate, the traffic, the fences and concrete, by my own approach to the park via private vehicle on I-70, by the white-on-brown recreational sign marking the space as "Fremont Indian State Park," by the park brochure and map that directed me to "point of interest #12" on the "driving tour," the roads and parking lots I used to get there, and of course the museum, which had already told me much about what "we" know about the Fremont.

And the contexts get larger. Any time I encounter the material traces of Native American cultures, be they in museums, on driving tours, along signed trails, or just existing, unmarked on the landscape, I do so amidst a deep web of meanings about "the Indian." This web includes not only the view of Indians as "primitive"—an earlier stage of cultural and technological development, with its attendant connotations of being backward, less developed, less sophisticated, barbaric, and even "savage"—but also of the "noble savage," in which the "primitive" state becomes a basis for positive evaluations and deeply felt yearnings: harmonious, authentic, intensely communal, deeply spiritual, skilled in survival, and connected to nature.

At Fremont Indian State Park, the pictograph was there, beckoning, highlighted by the park, but was also inaccessible, visible only through a small metal pipe, dictating where and how I could view it and *experientially* enabling a structure of feeling that the pictograph (and the culture that produced it) could only be viewed from a distance. The seeming concreteness of the identification of the pictograph as a blanket and the emotion-laden story of the Indian mother's loss offered possibilities for connection, but my contextual experience of the pictograph worked against any such possibilities.

As this discussion of Fremont Indian State Park and the Indian blanket pictograph makes clear, this book approaches the subject of Native American rock art not primarily from an archaeological perspective on the past, but from a critical perspective on contemporary cultural dynamics, although archaeological discourses and knowledge play essential and substantial roles throughout the book. My goal is less to discover what rock art meant in the past than to understand how it comes to be seen, interpreted, and used in the present and, critically, what and whose interests that serves. Therefore, some rock art scholars and enthusiasts may find my approach rather odd (if not irrelevant). I therefore turn to a brief discussion of the audiences for this book and an in-depth explanation of how I approach this topic from both communication and critical/cultural perspectives.

Audiences

The intended audiences for this book are multiple. My academic training and appointment is in the field of communication studies, specifically in rhetoric and intercultural communication. Perhaps most important for understanding my orientation, I primarily associate myself with the interdisciplinary arena known as critical/cultural studies, which draws from media studies, literary theory, feminist theory, queer theory, political economy, critical race theory, postcolonial theory, European social theory, philosophy, and many related areas. One important audience for this book is scholars in critical/cultural studies, especially those interested in representations and appropriations of Native American and other indigenous cultures, or in critical approaches to archaeology or cultural resource management, but also to those with broader interests related to representation, appropriation, and other cultural dynamics involving gender, race/ethnicity, and neocolonialism.

My second, and in some ways more important, audience is those involved, as producers or consumers, in rock art research. Primarily composed of archaeologists and anthropologists, this field of research also includes art historians, literary critics, semioticians, and others from a variety of academic disciplines and professions. This audience also includes rock art avocationalists and enthusiasts, those with no or less relevant academic training and professional experience who are highly invested in not only visiting, photographing, and otherwise "collecting" rock art (in the form of commercial photographs, coffee-table books, high art reproductions, etc.), but also in learning about rock art through books, videos, lectures, museum exhibits, and other media, and in some cases actively engaging in rock art interpretation, preservation, and research. For this second audience, I have worked to shape my use of the concepts and jargon from critical/cultural studies in a way that is understandable to an educated nonspecialist and that enhances our understandings of the role of indigenous rock art in the contemporary cultural landscape.

Constitutive and Critical Perspectives on Communication

I approach the topic of the role of rock art in the contemporary cultural landscape from two standpoints: as a rock art enthusiast and avocationalist, and as a scholar trained in communication studies generally and critical/cultural studies specifically. My avocational interests draw me to rock art as a research subject. My academic training and specializations shape how I approach the subject, providing theoretical perspectives, concepts, and analytic tools for advancing claims and making arguments about the role of rock art in the contemporary cultural landscape. To clarify how I approach the subject of rock art in contemporary culture, in this section I explain how I understand communication and what a critical/cultural studies perspective adds to that understanding.

Communication as Constitutive

Along with many scholars of communication, I hold an understanding of communication that conflicts with the dominant, "common sense," Anglo-American view of communication as a delivery system. That is, common conceptions of communication (at least in the West) see communication as a tool by which a sender transmits a message through one or more channels (or media), with the desired outcome being the delivery of information, meanings, and motivations (Fiske 1990). Sometimes referred to as the "transmissional," "post office," or "dump truck" model, symbols and the messages of which they are a part are carriers of meaning, transporting meanings (ideas, emotions, and material referents) from the mind of a sender to the mind of one or more receivers. Communication can be judged as successful when the resulting meanings in the mind of the receiver and/or the responses of the receiver match those intended by the sender (i.e., meaning is shared), and as unsuccessful when the sender's intent and the outcome in the receiver differ to greater or lesser degrees.

In addition, in the transmissional model, the individual symbols that make up a message are predominantly understood in terms of their *referents*—the actual things (including ideas and emotions) to which they refer (Burke 1966). In this view, messages are often judged in terms of accuracy: the degree to which they present an undistorted reflection of the "real world." Messages and acts of communication can therefore be evaluated in two ways: by the degree to which they achieve the sender's intentions and by the degree to which they accurately describe the world around them. Both of these judgments are based on a view of communication as secondary, as a mere tool—the sender's intentions and objective reality are each understood as primary in the sense that they precede the act of communication and insofar as they are the basis for determining what constitutes a "good" message or a "successful" act of communication.

In contrast to the transmissional view of communication, I hold to what is variously termed the constitutive view, the ritual view, the epistemic view, the dramatistic view, or the social construction of reality (see, e.g., Berger and Luckman 1966; Burke 1966; Carey 1988; Fiske 1990; Pearce 1989; Rogers 1998). In this perspective, communication becomes primary while thought and "reality" become secondary. We do not merely *express* our thoughts, feelings, and perceptions through communication, but communication *shapes* those very thoughts, feelings, and perceptions. We think in language and other symbolic systems, and our perceptions of the world around us are guided by our symbolic systems. Our perceptions are guided in at least two ways. First, any system of symbols as well as any particular message is necessarily selective, naming or otherwise representing parts of actual objects, events, settings, et cetera; any language, argot, discursive system, or message necessarily directs our attention to what it represents, thereby obscuring those aspects, dimensions, or perspectives it does not label or otherwise represent. In this sense, "even if any given terminology is a *reflection* of reality, by its very nature as a terminology it must be a *selection* of reality; and to this extent it must function also as a *deflection* of reality" (Burke 1966:45). Such selections and deflections are inevitable, but the particular selections and deflections that any particular symbolic system enacts are a result of deeply embedded systems of value.

Second, language and other symbolic systems also shape our thoughts and perceptions in terms of the meanings (the mental images, ideas, and evaluations) we attach to things as a result of the symbols we assign to various referents (Burke 1966; Charon 1998). That is, language not only influences what we pay attention to, but how we interpret and evaluate what we pay attention to. Crucially, we do not respond to the labeled things themselves (the referents), but to the meanings assigned to those things through symbolic interaction. For example, if I am served a dish, eat it, am then told it was dog meat, and I vomit, I am not responding to the dog meat itself, but to the *idea* of eating dog, and my seemingly involuntary act of throwing up is a manifestation of the *symbolic reality* created through the intertwining of culture and communication. In addition, throwing up is itself a symbolic act that (re)constitutes my culture's culinary norms and my identity as a member of that culture. Symbolic systems and acts of communication therefore fabricate our thoughts and our perceptions of the empirical realities in which we live. Thought, feeling, perception, and experience are all mediated by symbolic systems. There is no "pure" thought and no unmediated perception of the world around us. Communication has a primary role in constructing how we perceive and therefore act toward the world, others, and ourselves (Burke 1966; Charon 1998).

In addition, in the constitutive view, communication is understood as the production of meaning (Fiske 1990), whether or not that meaning conforms to the sender's intentions or to objective reality; therefore, there is no "failure" to communicate as long as meaning is produced. If receivers interpret messages in ways contrary to the sender's intentions, this perspective does not judge the communication a failure, but proceeds to explore how and why such differences in interpretation and meaning came to be (Fiske 1990). The constitutive view, therefore, has particular value and relevance when studying intercultural communication, wherein messages produced in one cultural context are interpreted in the framework of another culture.

In the constitutive view, communication is defined as the symbolic process whereby social reality is constructed, maintained, repaired, and transformed (Carey 1988). Given that communication shapes social reality—our definitions of self, others, relationships, institutions, culture, and both empirical and nonempirical realities—in the constitutive view the primary question shifts from "how do we communicate successfully?" to "what kind of a world are we creating by communicating in these ways?" (Pearce 1989). Culture not only guides communication, but communication constitutes culture, with culture and communication existing in a reflexive, mutually constitutive, and dynamic process.

The interpretation of ancient, indigenous rock art by contemporary Westerners provides a clear case to demonstrate the contrast. From a transmissional view, the meaning of much rock art is lost due to the lack of a shared cultural context for assigning meaning to the symbols. Possibilities for communication failure loom large; without contextual (cultural) information, we are left, at best, with guesses as to the literal referents of some images and almost entirely acontextual (outsider) efforts to "crack the code" of the meaning of the images. From a constitutive perspective, however, meaning is nevertheless produced in the encounter between modern Westerners and the marks on rock left by ancient others. The focus becomes the conditions of possibility that produced those meanings and what those meanings constitute: identities, values, narratives, stereotypes, and ideologies that are both reflective and constitutive of the interpreting (receiving) culture. The interaction with rock art may in many cases do little to truly understand the intentions of their ancient creators, but that does not mean those contemporary meanings should be dismissed as insignificant—instead, they offer insights into the interpreting culture and their relationship with cultural others, be they ancient or living. The question becomes not "are these interpretations correct (the same as the originating culture)?" but instead "how did these interpretations come to be (what are their conditions of possibility)?" and "what kinds of identities, relationships, and social systems are being created through these interpretations?"

Critical/Cultural Studies

Within the interdisciplinary field of critical/cultural studies, which includes scholars not only in communication but from across the social sciences and humanities, the dynamics of power, inequality, oppression, domination, and resistance are of central concern. Given that communication and culture shape who we are, how we relate to others, and how we perceive the world around us, a focus on power immediately raises questions of whose interests are served by the meanings, identities, perceptions, relationships, ideologies, and definitions of reality that are produced through communication. In simplistic terms, a critical/cultural studies perspective is what results when you mix the implications of the constitutive view of communication with a recognition of the existence of deeply rooted, asymmetrical systems of power, be those in terms of gender, sexuality, class, ability, race, ethnicity, nation, or the Global North–South.

A fundamental issue driving older, top-down, deterministic versions of critical/cultural studies scholarship is how a social system gains people's consent to a social system that does not serve their interests. As the French Marxist theorist Louis Althusser (1971) framed it, social control cannot be effectively maintained over the long run solely on the basis of coercion—through, in Althusser's terms, repressive state apparatuses (RSAs) such as the police, military, courts, and prisons. Social control in structurally asymmetrical societies occurs primarily through ideological state apparatuses (ISAs) such as the family, church, school, and media. From the perspective of an individual, the ideologies disbursed by ISAs are the "always already" of social existence, shaping consciousness, perceptions, identities, and relationships from the very beginning. In other words, there is no time when we exist outside of ideology, outside of socially constructed, power-laden systems of sense-making. As a result, in an update of the traditional Marxist take on ideology, all classes of people are subject to the influences of ideology, not just subordinate classes, and the characterization of ideology as false consciousness is untenable (Hall 1985). Given the assumption that systems of sense-making are controlled by the dominant groups/classes via the ISAs, and are backed up by the RSAs in case ideology fails, Althusser's top-down perspective makes the possibilities of resistance seem slim (Fiske 1990).

A key development in critical/cultural studies involved the incorporation of the work of another Marxist theorist, the Italian Antonio Gramsci (1971). Gramsci's conceptualization of hegemony revises the top-down view of domination through ideological imposition and control. In critical/cultural studies, hegemony does not simply refer to the domination of one group over another (the dictionary definition), but to a process by which the "consent" of all classes to dominant social systems is obtained through ideology (Fiske 1990; Good 1989; Williams 1977). Hegemony operates through ideology and, hence, systems and structures of communication. Hegemony does not achieve people's consent by giving them unconstrained choices from a full range of options. Instead, hegemony is achieved through ideology by limiting conceivable definitions of reality, constraining what people can imagine or can at least conceive of as "practical" or "legitimate." The key force operating here is "common sense": the inculcation of unconscious assumptions that the world works in certain ways and not others (Hall 1985; Williams 1977). When people find out I am a vegetarian, many either become defensive or somewhat curious. The curiosity often takes the form of a statement or question such as "I'd like to consider going vegetarian, but I just can't imagine being full after eating a meal without meat." The belief that one needs a meat-based meal to feel complete and full, and the resulting "consent" not only to (excessive) meat eating but to systems of factory farming, is a result of the operation of an ideologically and communicatively constructed "common sense," perpetuated through family conversations and traditions, nutritional curricula in schools, advertising, and everyday metaphors.

A key factor in the successful attainment of hegemony through "common sense" is its operation at the level of the taken-for-granted, outside of conscious awareness. In the United States, dietary "common sense" is both manifested in and perpetuated through a variety of taken-for-granted phrases: "beef—it's what's for dinner," "where's the beef?," and "let's get to the meat of the matter." Further, the ideological operation of the "common sense" of meat is linked to other social systems; in Western cultures in general and in Anglo-America in particular, meat is linked to notions of masculinity. Not only is he a "meat-and-potatoes kind of guy," but he also "brings home the bacon." When "hippies" began to "tune in, turn on, and drop out" of capitalism, materialism, and carnivorous diets, such countercultural populations were ideologically "feminized" through the characterization of their diet from the "common sense" perspective of meat in Anglo-America. "Hippies" and "peaceniks" were ideologically located in California, the Bay Area in particular, which also articulated with the perception of San Francisco as a locus of homosexuality. All this manifested itself in the phrase "California: the land of fruits and nuts"—that is, not only a land of agricultural bounty, but much more importantly the land of both gays and hippies, of both sexual deviants and crazy people, both of whom are positioned as the antithesis of "real men," who eat meat, not fruits and nuts, and certainly not tofu (Rogers 2008). Meat eating is articulated with not only homophobia but the marginalization of a range of alternative lifestyles. The masculinizing of meat eating serves to naturalize contemporary notions of masculinity by creating a symbolic illusion that meat eating, understood as part of the fixed, biological "essence" of manliness, anchors masculinity in something "real." (The gendered symbolism of meat will be an important topic in relation to hunting magic, discussed in chapter 4.) Ideologies are symbolic constructs that work to deny their very nature as constructions; ideologies therefore often work to achieve hegemony by naturalizing arbitrary social systems, giving them an aura of a fixed, objective reality that we have no power or authority to alter. Essentialist claims— the attribution of fixed and universal traits to a group of people—are therefore also red flags for the operation of ideology and hegemony, as they work similarly to divert attention from the human authorship of oppressive social systems.

A third and more recent shift in critical/cultural studies is an increasing focus not only on ideological domination and hegemony, but also counterhegemonic ideologies and practices. For a variety of possible reasons, ideology and hegemony do not perfectly reproduce the systems they are created to support. Resistance may be constantly co-opted through the hegemonic strategy of incorporation, but it continues to occur and has real effects. Different standpoints—that is, social positions such as those of gender, sexuality, race, and class—contribute to constituting different definitions of reality, experiences, perceptions, and knowledges (Harding 1991; Wood 1992). These standpoints manifest different symbolic systems, often utilizing different media for communication, in spite of (or even because of) top-down efforts at control.

In a critical view of communication, any sign becomes polysemic, or open to multiple interpretations (Ceccarelli 1998; Fiske 1986, 1991a; Vološinov 1973 [1929]). If the meaning of symbols is largely determined by context, then a highly homogenous society, one with relatively little stratification or specialization, should be characterized by a high degree of consensus regarding their symbols—single, stable, shared meanings. Such a culture probably never existed, though preindustrial and especially non-Western cultures have often been framed in this way (Fiske 1991a). Regardless of how preindustrial cultures operate(d), if we understand contemporary societies like the United States to be highly stratified (e.g., by class), highly specialized (e.g., by occupation), composed of multiple cultural/religious/ethnic groups, and characterized by conflict between groups with antagonistic interests, then we would expect that such a social context will lead to symbols having multiple, conflicting, and antagonistic meanings (Fiske 1991a). To the degree that one of these meanings "wins" (becomes widely accepted, seemingly by consensus), then hegemony is operating successfully (Good 1989). But multiple meanings cannot be erased. Hierarchical societies with conflicting interests are characterized by distinct, if overlapping and mutually constituting, standpoints that are embodied in the multiple meanings circulating around symbols. Each time a symbol is employed, the person articulating it does so from some perspective, investing the symbol with their particular ideological accent(s), slanting it toward one or more perspectives, often in a way that either builds from or counters previous uses and interpretations of the symbol (Vološinov 1973 [1929]). In a critical perspective, communication is less about the creation of shared meanings (the traditional view) than it is about the struggle over meanings in a context characterized by unequal power and antagonistic interests (Fiske 1991a).

Ancestral Puebloan, Anasazi, or Hisatsinom

A clear illustration of the operation of multiple meanings and conflicting ideological accents that is of relevance to this book is the conflict over what to name the precontact culture(s) inhabiting the Four Corners area of the Southwest, the culture(s) associated with well-known sites such as Mesa Verde and Chaco Canyon. Early in the history of the Anglo-Southwest, this group was often referred to as the "Cliff Dwellers," a name propelled by the prominence of Mesa Verde's dramatic cliff dwellings in the national consciousness in the late nineteenth and early twentieth centuries. Over the course of the twentieth century, however, "Anasazi" became the predominant term after being proposed by Alfred Kidder in 1936 (Roberts 1996). Following its archaeological adoption, it eventually made its way into public discourse via interpretative materials at parks, monuments, and museums across the Four Corners area, as well as into popular culture, such as in *The X-Files*. Since my arrival in the Southwest almost thirty years ago, however, Anasazi has been increasingly replaced with "ancestral Puebloan," at least in the archaeological literature and in the discourse of the National Park Service and many other agencies and institutions. Anasazi, however, remains in wide use in commercial, tourism, literary, and other contexts.

The criticism of the term Anasazi apparently began among Pueblo groups such as the Hopi, groups who see the culture named by the label as their ancestors. Not insignificantly, the Pueblos are also seen by most archaeologists as the descendants of the same precontact Four Corners culture. Pueblo opposition to the term is rooted in its origins and associated implications. Anasazi is the Anglicized version of the *Diné* (Navajo) word *'Anaasází*, which can mean "ancient ones" or "ancient enemies," depending on context and usage (Walters and Rogers 2001). Pueblo concern over Anasazi is therefore twofold. First, it is not a Pueblo name for their Puebloan ancestors, it is a Navajo name for Puebloan ancestors. To complicate this further, the Navajo are understood by most archaeologists to be relative latecomers to the Southwest, arriving after the florescence of the precontact culture in the Four Corners area, perhaps only a few centuries before the Spanish arrived (Childs 2006; Kloor 2009; Saner 1998; Warburton and Begay 2005). There are also a variety of recent and contemporary tensions between the Navajo and the Hopi in particular (Kloor 2009). In this highly charged context, Pueblo and archaeological views of the Navajo converge, denying the Navajo deep roots in the Southwest—and hence affiliations with the "Anasazi"—despite some Navajo views to the contrary (Kloor 2009; Warburton and Begay 2005). Second, and more explicitly, critics of the term highlight the negative connotations of "Anasazi" as not just ancient ones, but ancient *enemy*, a connotation not consistent with the Pueblos' view of their ancestors (Childs 2006; Saner 1998; Walters and Rogers 2001). The result has been that, while many still cling to tradition and use Anasazi, many archaeologists and institutions have gradually replaced it with the seemingly more neutral ancestral Puebloan (Walters and Rogers 2001).

Many non-Natives remain deeply attached to the term Anasazi, an Anglo-American construct that embodies the ideological "essence" of the Southwest. While archaeologists and land managers, who operate under a series of specific disciplinary, institutional, legal, and political constraints, have largely acceded to Pueblo views by avoiding the term, many others, such as those in the tourist industry and writers of popular Southwest literature, continue to use the term and in some cases defend or justify their choice, primarily by criticizing the alternatives.

One alternative is *Hisatsinom*, the Hopi term for their ancestors. This option is typically dismissed because there are other Pueblo groups who also have legitimate claim to this precontact culture as their ancestors, and they have different names for this group (Childs 2006; Roberts 1996; Saner 1998; Walters and Rogers 2001). Why should the Hopi name prevail over those of other Pueblo groups such as the Zuni or Acoma? The other alternative, and the one that has been widely adopted in archaeological circles and many land management agencies, is ancestral Puebloan. Defenders of Anasazi often point out that, first, ancestral Puebloan is still from an outsider's point of view, being composed of an English and a Spanish word. Second, the Spanish did not exactly treat the Pueblos well, and therefore it is an insult to use the Spanish name (*pueblo*) for these cultures as the basis for the English name for their ancestors (Roberts 1996; Saner 1998).

Defenders of the term Anasazi not only criticize the inadequacies of the alternatives, but also defend the term itself. David Roberts (1996) argues that it is a well-defined term that has been in wide use for over half a century. While it may be problematic in some ways, other terms like "Indian" and "Pueblo" are still in use, even by indigenous peoples themselves, despite their "egregious" history and implications (Roberts 1996). Reg Saner (1998:202) goes further, arguing that "overwhelmingly, in actual usage throughout the Southwest, 'Anasazi' is so much a praise word as to honor Pueblos by association." Although this sounds disturbingly like the defenses of Native American mascots for sports teams, and even the downright racist NFL team name "Redskins," as "honoring" Native Americans, Saner does have a point: The meanings of Anasazi for Anglos and other non-Natives are not really rooted in the meanings of the Navajo word, but far more in those articulated by Southwest archaeologists, writers, and marketers.

The "truth" of the situation, for me, is not primarily about resolving who this group was, to whom they are (pre)historically related, and which name is the most accurate, although those are all important issues. The "truth" in a pragmatic sense is that there are different views of who this precontact culture was, to whom they are related, what and whose interests should prevail in terms of how they should be named, and what the implications of such naming are. For me, the clear truth is that these differences are deeply structured in complex relations of power.

For some *Diné*, the *Anaasází* may indeed be "ancient ones," or "ancient others" (i.e., non-Navajo), or even, depending on context, usage, and perspective, "ancient enemies" (Walters and Rogers 2001). For some Hopis, the *Hisatsinom* may be their ancestors, representing their cultural heritage and a variety of other meanings related to identity, cosmology, oral history, and cultural values. For many archaeologists, Anasazi or ancestral Puebloans may refer to a cultural group who occupied the Four Corners area for hundreds of years, left behind characteristic types of material culture, and eventually migrated to become the Pueblo peoples of Arizona and New Mexico. For many aficionados and tourists of the Southwest, the archaeological term Anasazi has grown into something far less technical, rooted not in typologies of black-on-white pottery, tree-ring dates, and architectural forms, but in the "mystery" of their "disappearance" and amazement at their accomplishments, from the monumental structures of Chaco Canyon to the cliff dwellings of Mesa Verde. We do not even know that all of the ancient people clumped under any of these labels saw themselves as a single group, encompassed under a single umbrella term, or that they spoke the same language. Indeed, Pueblo ethnography would indicate that they were not a single people, as they constituted the various clans that eventually came together at places like Hopi, where the clan system and clan identity are still central (Bernardini 2005; Mills 2004). Given this range of meanings and investments, perhaps the most reasonable conclusion I have read on this topic is that of Craig Childs (2006:266): "I see why we cannot agree on a single term. There probably never was one."

There is no neutral term, no empirically accurate term. All representations, however descriptive they may be, come from some perspective, and are therefore partial, biased, and interested. What this precontact culture should be called and what referents and meanings are attached to that symbol are deeply contested. Not only each term, but each particular deployment of each of the terms, articulates one or more ideological "accents," and indeed any use of any of these terms can evoke, be it in a benevolent or malevolent spirit, the other terms and their accents.

A critical perspective, however, is not simply a relativist one: "Oh well, they all have different meanings, so they are all fine!" The task becomes an examination of the ideological accents; their interests, biases, and investments; their hegemonic implications; and the work they do in the world in terms of constructing, maintaining, repairing, transforming, and contesting identities, relationships, and systems of power and authority. Ultimately, I choose to follow the current archaeological and institutional usage of ancestral Puebloan. This is in part because I too operate in certain professional, disciplinary, and institutional contexts, including, albeit in a rather marginal way, archaeology and cultural resource management. I choose ancestral Puebloan, in part, because it seems to be a more neutral, less loaded, and less contested label, as long as the stress on the *relative* nature of these judgments (more than or less than) is kept at the forefront. Perhaps even more central, however, is that, like the label "rock art," it seems to be the best option we have from a range of problematic alternatives (see chapter 2).

I choose not to actively perpetuate "Anasazi" not only out of deference to today's Pueblo peoples and their issues with the use of the original *Diné* word, but also because I see the Anglo term Anasazi as deeply implicated in the primitivist fantasies of Westerners, appropriating the heritage of other cultures in order to assuage the fears and anxieties created by industrialization and modernization (see chapter 3). I certainly do not feel authorized to make judgments about conflicting opinions and interests between the Navajo and Hopi, or between different Pueblo groups. As an Anglo-American who inhabits the Southwest, and as such an inheritor of the privilege resulting from the appropriation of the lands and cultures of the indigenous peoples of the Southwest, I cannot pretend to be sufficiently divorced from my culture's colonialist past and present to be able to exercise some kind of detached judgment on the matter. As a result of feeling neither sufficiently informed nor capable of neutrality, I default to the thoroughly Western term "ancestral Puebloan."

Native American Views of Rock Art

This discussion about what to call the people who inhabited the Colorado Plateau for centuries before the arrival of Europeans is related to a critical issue in rock art studies and in this book: the role of living Native peoples in the interpretation, valuation, and management of rock art. In many ways this book continues a troubling pattern in much rock art research: the relative absence of indigenous peoples as researchers or even consultants. As with Anasazi vs. *Hisatsinom* vs. ancestral Puebloan, this issue presents a challenging set of tensions with no easy resolution. On the one hand, there is a need to counteract the overall absence of Native American voices and the predominance of non-Native perspectives in discussions of Native American rock art. On the other hand is a need to respect the desire of many Native American individuals and communities to keep some information within their culture, be that for internal cultural reasons (e.g., to maintain the compartmentalization of ritual knowledge) or external factors (e.g., previous experience with ethnographers, journalists, documentarians, and the like who publicized or mischaracterized sensitive cultural information). For the purpose of this book at least, I lean more in the direction of respecting the desire to keep some information out of the public sphere. In addition, while I think that more Native voices are needed in discussions of rock art, the politics of representation lead me to believe that Native voices should speak in terms, styles, and contexts of their own choosing, including in collaborations with non-Natives, but not as staged, cropped, retouched, and framed within the largely non-Native disciplinary and professional contexts in which this book operates. Form, content, and politics are all intimately intertwined, and the form, content, and politics of this book are undeniably Western.

While my intent is not to perpetuate the relative absence of indigenous voices in the rock art literature, I nevertheless follow that pattern, so I want to be clear about the focus and purpose of this project. This book is not primarily about how Native Americans, past or present, view rock art. That is an extremely important area for research and, thankfully, a recent anthology containing case studies from a multitude of countries and regions focuses on the role of rock art in contemporary contexts, particularly in contemporary indigenous cultures. Liam Brady and Paul Taçon's (2016) *Relating to Rock Art in the Contemporary World* forms a conceptual complement to this book, which is about how others (non-Natives) have appropriated (reproduced, represented, interpreted) the rock art of indigenous peoples.

In this sense, this book is more about whiteness than about Native American cultures per se. It is parallel to Philip Deloria's (1998) *Playing Indian*, an exploration of Indian play among Euro-Americans, from the Boston Tea Party to the New Age. Deloria acknowledges Native American views of Indian play and is acutely aware of the implications of such performances and their underlying ideologies for contemporary Native American peoples and cultures, but his focus is on how non-Natives have used Indian play to construct Euro-American identities. One of my primary goals is to illustrate that much of what motivates the interpretation and appropriation of rock art is not a genuine desire to engage others, living or dead, but is about compensating for and addressing contemporary cultural dynamics in non-Native cultures. The neocolonialist foundations and implications of the interpretation and appropriation of rock art by Westerners call for attention to the structures that make rock art visible and attractive, and that shape its interpretation and use, as well as the ways that such structures perpetuate the exclusion of indigenous voices. The non-Native desire to know rock art, a desire driven and shaped by neocolonial structures and ideologies, does not in itself constitute a prima facie case for the solicitation and dissemination of Native understandings of rock art.

The Binds and Benefits of Being Marginal

I am a rock art enthusiast, rock art avocationalist, and rock art scholar. As a rock art fan(atic), I visit rock art sites—the more remote, harder to find, and less visited, the better. I obsessively photograph the sites. I read about rock art, view others' photographs of rock art, take friends to rock art sites, attend rock art conferences, and participate in field trips devoted to rock art. And for the last several years, as an academic who studies and teaches intercultural communication, I have been a rock art researcher (albeit an atypical one), and, as a result, I have taught an undergraduate course on the archaeology of rock art for the Department of Anthropology at my home institution, Northern Arizona University.

I am also an avocational archaeologist of sorts. I definitely would not go so far as to call myself an archaeologist without the avocational qualifier out of respect for those with far greater academic training and professional experience. I am acutely aware of at least some of the limitations on my knowledge and authority that result from my lack of archaeological disciplining and certification, while I am also cognizant that not being a formally trained and certified archaeologist frees me in at least two ways. First, I am not constrained by the professional commitments and investments that attend such a status; while I of course desire archaeologists to find my work valuable, my faculty position and disciplinary status are not dependent on an archaeological stamp of approval. Second, while I am limited by my relative lack of systematic, in-depth, broad-based knowledge of archaeological theory, method, data, and research findings (especially outside of the Southwest), I am also not specifically constrained by the perspectives that accompany such knowledge. I am, of course, constrained by my own training and investments, but those are somewhat different constraints than those within academic and professional archaeology.

On the other hand, I also feel compelled to establish my authority, however limited, on the specific subject of rock art as well as related archaeological topics. I read widely about southwestern archaeology, not only rock art. I strive to understand something about archaeological theory and method, and am particularly intrigued by the various debates in Southwest archaeology. I visit archaeological sites as a tourist or enthusiast, but I visit many more in the course of serving as a volunteer for the US Forest Service. In addition to monitoring archaeological sites to prevent or at least identify looting or other forms of vandalism, I also engage in conventional archaeological endeavors such as site relocation, surveys, and site recording. Most of this work does not involve rock art, but artifact scatters and the remains of agricultural features, field houses, pit houses, and pueblos. At least in the Flagstaff region, I have acquired knowledge and abilities related to recognizing, and in some cases identifying, different types of archaeological sites and artifacts, which include materials from at least six archaeological cultures. I have been able to connect my work in the field with my reading of the archaeological literature, aided by the opportunities to engage directly with academic and professional archaeologists that my academic and avocational work provide.

In terms of rock art specifically, in addition to my activities as a rock art enthusiast and reading widely in the rock art literature, I have attended regional and national rock art conferences. I am a member of both the Utah and American Rock Art Research Associations and follow their publications. I not only seek out rock art sites, but also, and just as importantly for my work, I seek out and collect interpretive materials (brochures, pamphlets, and photographs of interpretive signs and museum displays). Beyond museums and cultural centers, I enter gift shops that I probably otherwise would not in order to survey not only any information provided about rock art, but the range of rock art commodities. While I take a mildly principled stand against purchasing rock art kitsch—I make exceptions by opportunistically invoking the label "art" to create a false opposition to crass commercial crap—I collect books and other publications about rock art. I take tours of rock art sites, not only to see the rock art, but to hear what rangers or docents have to say and how the public responds. I intentionally hang out at publicized, well-visited sites to eavesdrop on, and perhaps even contribute to, the conversations that people have about what they see.

Perhaps one of the most important outcomes of my combined roles as site steward, rock art enthusiast, avocational archaeologist, and critical/cultural studies communication scholar is a particular attention to cultural resource management (CRM), as it has come to be known in the United States. CRM issues with rock art include questions about the relative degree of secrecy versus publicity of rock art sites, the kinds of interpretive materials provided at rock art sites, the role of consultations with Native Americans about interpretation and site management, addressing problems of graffiti and vandalism, how and whether sites should be developed, and more.

Preview

Chapter 2 provides a brief, general introduction to rock art and an overview of rock art studies, and will be especially useful for those unfamiliar with rock art and/or rock art studies. However, the discussions of terminological issues, the history of rock art research, the issues involved in interpreting rock art, and the role of the "lunatic fringe" may still be of interest to rock art researchers and avocationalists, especially insofar as these discussions also serve to identify my perspective on rock art and rock art research.

Chapter 3, "Representations and Appropriations of Native American Cultures," provides the primary critical and theoretical foundations for the remainder of the book. These include a review of scholarship on media representations of Native Americans, primitivism, authenticity, and the Southwest imaginary, thereby establishing the broader representational and ideological contexts within which rock art is valued and interpreted. I also establish the cultural and political implications of contemporary appropriations of rock art imagery by outlining the implications of the mass reproduction of images, understandings of the nature of postmodernity, and conceptualizations of cultural appropriation and commodification. The chapter ends with an overview of the appropriation of rock art imagery and a review of the literature on the commodification of rock art. This chapter will be of particular value to those with an interest in rock art but for whom the terminology of critical/cultural studies, especially as it relates to Western–Native American relations, is unfamiliar.

Chapters 4 and 5 explore the gendered dimensions of the interpretation and appropriation of rock art. The gendering of rock art imagery can provide insight into the gendering of the Euro-American image of Native Americans. While some scholars have focused on gendered representations of Native peoples, identifying stereotypes perpetuated about Native American men versus women, insufficient sustained attention has been paid to the almost exclusively male gendering of the dominant images of Native Americans. This focus on Native American men continues in the interpretation of rock art imagery, furthering the masculine characterization of the Euro-American image of The Indian and functioning to ease Western anxieties over the contemporary status of masculinity.

Chapter 4, "Hunting Magic, Shamanism, and the Contemporary Crisis in Masculinity," examines two prominent models for rock art interpretation as contributing to Euro-American representations of Native Americans. In addition to dismissing women's role in indigenous rock art, these models project Euro-American gender ideologies and tensions over masculinity onto precontact indigenous cultures. Specifically, the figure of the Native American shaman models masculine power as symbolic and spiritual, not physical, yet linked to a virile heterosexuality, rescuing elements of blue-collar masculinity and rearticulating them in white-collar, masculinist terms. I highlight the projections of Western gender dynamics onto precontact indigenous cultures and the work that such projections do, in this case centering a primitive spiritual masculinity that responds to the Euro-American "crisis of masculinity."

Kokopelli, "the hump-backed flute player," has become an icon of the Southwest as well as a metonym for the region's Native American cultures. Chapter 5, "Phalluses and Fantasies: Kokopelli, Caricature, and Commodification," analyzes contemporary Kokopelli imagery and discourses as a projection of Euro-American masculinist fantasies and as a contemporary commodity form. Kokopelli imagery models a virile and promiscuous heterosexual masculinity rooted in primitivism and the Euro-American image of the rock star. It articulates intersections of gender, race, and culture that simultaneously highlight and obscure primitive masculinity and racial difference, enabling the use of Native American culture and spirituality to (re)vitalize Euro-American masculinity and promote neocolonialist appropriations.

Shifting away from gender but continuing with the theme of neocolonialist appropriations, chapter 6, "'Your Guess Is as Good as Any': Indeterminacy, Dialogue, and Dissemination in Interpretations of Rock Art," examines the theme of the unknown meanings of Native American rock art in interpretive materials at rock art sites in order to explore the rhetorical constitution of indeterminacy in neocolonial contexts. This analysis demonstrates that indeterminacy is used to license appropriations and polysemic interpretations of the traces of indigenous cultures by non-Natives, thereby enabling the projection of Western cultural imaginings onto the rock art and discouraging engagement with the culture and psychology of indigenous others.

Moving away from interpretation per se, chapter 7, "Overcoming the Preservation Paradigm: Toward a Dialogic Approach to Rock Art and Culture," critically analyzes how contemporary marks on rock are differentially valued through deployment of the terms *graffiti* and *vandalism*. Vandalism and graffiti are normative categories relying on presuppositions regarding the value (or lack thereof) of marks on rock. Preservation, a concept implicated in the salvage paradigm (Clifford 1987, 1988), essentializes culture and assumes that the authenticity of sites is maintained by freezing them in their precontact condition, thereby discouraging an understanding of rock art sites as spatially grounded, asynchronous dialogues between multiple cultures over long periods of time. If rock art sites are forums for such dialogues, their "essence" becomes not *the* culture or cultures which made the rock art, but the *relationship* between those cultures. While not an argument for licensing the contemporary addition of marks to rock art sites, this analysis points to the ways in which the ideology and practice of preservation shapes our understanding of culture and therefore the ways in which rock art can (and cannot) be interpreted.

Chapter 8, "Searching for Flute Players, Finding Kokopelli: Reflections on Authenticity, Appropriation, and Absent Authorities," uses a variety of narratives and personal experiences in order to turn the book's critical gaze more toward myself, generating self-reflective and self-implicative ruminations on key elements in the rock art community, such as secrecy, collecting, authenticity, the lunatic fringe, and the role of living Native Americans. By weaving together several of the main themes found throughout the book, this chapter works to conclude the overall project by clarifying some of the central challenges and ideological investments involved in the contemporary research and appreciation of rock art.

CHAPTER 2

ROCK ART AND ROCK ART STUDIES

Rock Art: A Primer

Rock art is a generally accepted and widely used umbrella term to describe various kinds of marks placed on rocks. The two primary forms of rock art are petroglyphs and pictographs. Petroglyphs are pecked, incised, or scratched into rock, often removing a darker "patina" on the rock surface to reveal the lighter material underneath (see Figure 2.1), although there are exceptions (see Plate 4). As a general rule, petroglyphs are more durable than pictographs, which are images painted onto rock (see Figure 2.2). The categories can get fuzzy, however, as some rock art was produced with both petroglyphic and pictographic methods (see Plate 3). Identifying the defining characteristics of rock art becomes more challenging with the inclusion of earth figures, large designs created on the ground surface such as the famous Nazca Lines in Peru (Whitley 2011). The definition of rock art as "painted or engraved images placed on natural rock *landscapes*" attempts to encompass these three basic types (Whitley 2001a:7; emphasis added). However, my focus in this book, as with the vast majority of rock art research, will be on petroglyphs and pictographs, images painted on or pecked/etched into rock surfaces.

The primary characteristic of rock art is its placement on natural rock surfaces (Whitley 2011; Quinlan 2007b). These surfaces may be on boulders, cliff walls, and rock outcroppings, as well as inside caves. As a result, rock art is essentially fixed in place (Loendorf et al. 2005), with exceptions involving the movement of rock surfaces due to natural processes, the brute removal of parts of rock art panels with powered saws or chisels (see chapter 7), and the relocation of boulders containing rock art (for the latter, see Figure 2.3 as well as Beauchamp

FIGURE 2.1—Petroglyphs on basalt, Coconino County, Arizona. These petroglyphs, associated with the Sinagua or other ancestral Puebloans, demonstrate the effect of removing a patina to reveal the lighter rock underneath.

FIGURE 2.2—Head of Sinbad pictographs, San Rafael Swell, Emery County, Utah. While pictographs are more susceptible than petroglyphs to weathering and other factors, some pictographs, including Barrier Canyon Style panels such as this, may be thousands of years old.

[2013], Gronemann [2014], and Marcom [2006]). Given its placement on natural rock surfaces and its place-bound nature, rock art can be understood as a form of landscape art (Hays-Gilpin 2004; Whitley 2011). In addition, rock art is relatively enduring in time, especially in comparison to other types of material culture such as textiles. Significantly, unlike many other forms of material culture that have been the traditional focus of archaeology, accessing rock art generally does not require excavation, making it available to researchers—as well as the general public—without many of the complications of traditional dirt archaeology.

Rock art is found throughout the world and throughout North America. Due to a variety of factors, however, rock art in the Southwest has been the most visible in the Anglo-American cultural landscape. The geography, geology, climate, and biological environments of areas such as

FIGURE 2.3—Relocated petroglyph boulder, Churchill County Museum, Fallon, Nevada. Boulders containing rock art have been relocated for a variety of reasons. Here, a boulder from the Grimes Point rock art site is on display outside the nearby Churchill County Museum. Smaller relocated petroglyph boulders can also be seen outside of the Furnace Creek Visitor Center in Death Valley National Park and the Pueblo Grande Museum in Phoenix, Arizona.

the Colorado Plateau, the Mojave Desert, the Sonoran Desert, and the Great Basin further enhance rock art's enduring nature, as factors such as available rock surfaces, the weather, and the relative scarcity of plant life result in much slower degradation processes and enhanced visibility. In addition, the special role of the Southwest in both Anglo-American archaeology and tourism (Dilworth 1996; Hinsley 1996; Lekson 2008) has brought significant attention to the rock art of the region.

While the definition of rock art as in situ marks made on natural rock surfaces would seem to include contemporary and historic marks made by non-Native populations (see Figure 2.4), the term is generally used in the context of Anglo-American rock art studies and interpretive materials to refer to "prehistoric" (precontact) and "historic" (postcontact) rock art made by indigenous peoples. Rock art produced by non-Natives and by indigenous peoples in contemporary times occupies a marginal space in rock art studies, usually portrayed as "graffiti," not rock art (see chapter 7).

The appeal of rock art is intimately linked to both its association with ancient indigenous peoples and the presumed nature of rock art imagery itself in contrast to other kinds of archaeological materials. As Loendorf, Chippindale, and Whitley (2005:3) state in *Discovering North American Rock Art*, "no other kind of archaeological material is more direct and thrilling on first encounter than rock art, the actual images made by prehistoric people." This is because "rock art is full of meaning in a direct way unmatched by stone or pottery fragments"; the pictures are "direct statements by ancient people of how they saw and knew their worlds" (Loendorf et al. 2005:4–5). In *The Archaeology of Rock Art*, Paul Taçon and Christopher Chippindale (1998:2) similarly argue that the "special merit" of rock art in the context of archaeology is "its directness": "These are images from ancient worlds as ancient human minds envisioned them. . . . They are all direct material expressions of human concepts, of human thought." As Polly Schaafsma puts it in *Images in Stone*, "rock art is an artifact of ideas" (Muench and Schaafsma 1995:16). When combined with the qualities of being fixed in place and enduring in time, rock art therefore holds the potential for a relatively direct connection to ancient peoples and their thought worlds, as contemporary peoples can occupy the same spaces, view the rock art in the same basic physical context, and thereby presumably come closer to "how *they* saw and knew *their* worlds."

FIGURE 2.4—Contemporary rock art, Emery County, Utah. Contemporary rock art is rarely included in rock art studies outside of the context of complaints about graffiti and vandalism.

The appeal of rock art, therefore, is very much about a contemporary Self attempting to make contact with *them*, an ancient Other. This appeal is structured by two dialectical poles: on the one hand, the promise of bridging enormous cultural and historical chasms, of connecting with the Other; on the other hand, paradoxically, the possibly unsolvable mystery of its meanings due to the highly contextual nature of symbolic systems and the frequent lack of direct ethnohistorical or ethnographic evidence about a particular corpus of rock art sites and imagery.

Rock "Art"?

The ongoing desire to determine what rock art is about—to identify what it meant, how it functioned, and what it reveals about the thought worlds of ancient peoples—is reflected in debates over the appropriateness of the term *rock art*. While *pictograph* and *petroglyph* are widely used in Anglo-American contexts without significant discussion or debate, *rock art* is contested and, even when used, is often acknowledged as inadequate but, in the end, "the best we have" (e.g., Bernardini 2005; Christensen et al. 2013; Murray 2011; Taçon and

Chippindale 1998; Young 1988). Debates center not around *rock*, but around *art*. The primary concern is that the use of the term *art* imposes relatively modern, Western ideas about what art is onto these traces of non-Western cultures (Malotki 2007; Murray 2011; Schaafsma 2013; Taçon and Chippindale 1998). Certainly, it is reasonable to question the applicability of the romantic notion of art as an intense form of personal expression, or the similar twentieth-century idea that art is anything that an artist calls art, to the aesthetic/symbolic creations of indigenous cultures both past and present. Both of these views empha-size the essence of art as the free creation of the individual artist, a notion based on liberal individualism, a very Western and relatively recent idea (Chippindale 2001). Rock art, in other words, was not nec-essarily produced by and for the individual, or purely for the purpose of pleasing the senses (i.e., as "aesthetic" in the narrow sense). Much of what anthropologists and others know about these indigenous cultures, what we sometimes even know about the specific role of rock art in those cultures, and what contemporary Native Americans have to say on the subject further support the inappropriateness of modern, Western notions of art for understanding indigenous rock art.

In addition to the risk of imposing Western notions of art onto material traces that may have been understood in radically different ways by the cultures that produced them, the Western idea of art can also affect how rock art is viewed, interpreted, and studied. As Julie Francis (2005) argues, labeling petroglyphs and pictographs as *art* leads us to treat the images as we treat other art: as aesthetic objects, detached from social and physical contexts. The tendency to photograph, paint, and reproduce rock art imagery, and then frame it and hang it on a wall, or place it in a coffee-table book, evidences the efficacy—the rhe-torical operation—of the label *art*. This view of rock art encourages—persuades—viewers and researchers to focus on the image itself and its formal qualities, which is perfectly consistent with the ongoing project of identifying distinctive rock art styles absent contextual infor-mation (Francis 2005). Not only are the specific styles that researchers identify categories that are imposed on the art from the outside, but the very focus on formal qualities of the imagery—as opposed to, say, their placement on the landscape—may itself have little to do with the psychology and culture of those who made the images. As Michel Foucault (1970:xix) has written in his history of the human sciences, *The Order of Things*, "There is no similitude and no distinction, even for the wholly untrained perception, that is not the result of a precise operation and of the application of a preliminary criterion. . . . Order is that which has no existence except in the grid created by a glance, an examination, a language." In other words, not only the specific categories or styles of rock art, but the very notion of "style" itself is a culturally specific frame for making sense of imagery and is grounded in dominant Western views of art.

The treatment of rock art by archaeologists, whose traditional focus was on artifacts related to subsistence (e.g., stone tools), has often been one of definition and marginalization by emphasizing what it is not. As Angus Quinlan (2007b:2) states, "Rock art can be minimally defined as non-utilitarian intentional human-made markings on rock surfaces." The negative condition of being "non-utilitarian" presumably refers to rock art's positive nature as a symbolic system, one often assumed to be linked to ritual, cosmology, and religion (Quinlan 2007a; Whitley 2011). This points to rock art's potential for understanding ritual and cosmology, but also the frequently presumed irrelevance of rock art to archaeology's traditional focus on subsistence and adaptation to the environment. Assuming that rock art is expression for expression's sake, or art for art's sake, raises concerns over ethnocentrism and the attendant implications for our ability to understand the images made on rocks by ancient cultures (Hays-Gilpin 2004). Indeed, although clearly not his intent, Quinlan's (2007b) definition of rock art as "non-utilitarian" could be seen as perpetuating the Western idea of art as mere embellishment and relatively superfluous (Malotki 2007).

However, the Western notion of art has been relativized due to intracultural debates in the West over what constitutes art, and scholars in fields such as art history, anthropology, religious studies, cultural studies, and media studies regularly grapple with much broader, fluid, culturally variable, and contested ideas of both what art is and how it functions socially. David Whitley (2011) and Polly Schaafsma (2013) argue that to deny the use of the term *art* for the products of non-Western, traditional cultures perpetuates the idea that "we" (Westerners) make art, while other cultures produce something else, something lesser. As a result of the broader notions of art that circulate in both mainstream and academic circles, the already widespread usage and general acceptance of *rock art*, and the lack of appealing alternatives, most scholars continue with the use of *rock art* or, in some cases (following Chippindale 2001), *rock-art*. I, too, follow this uneasy consensus.

For myself, as a critical/cultural studies scholar attuned to the power of symbols in constructing our views of and relations with other cultures, other taken-for-granted terms used in the literature are more problematic than *art*. The US rock art literature, following its predominantly Euro-American and archaeological contexts, distinguishes between "prehistoric" and "historic" periods in indigenous North American cultures, reflecting major cultural changes resulting from contact with Europeans and the processes of genocide and colonization, as well as marking the types of records and data—written versus solely archaeological—available for reconstructing the past. While I readily acknowledge that contact with Europeans represents the beginning of radical destructions, disruptions, and changes for the indigenous peoples of North America, I avoid this usage when possible insofar as the distinction is ethnocentric, graphocentric, and complicit in both colonialism and the discourse of the primitive. "Historic" refers to the existence of written records, reflecting the dominant Western epistemological privileging of written evidence. In addition, as I discuss in chapter 3, the conceptualization of the nature of the profound break between precontact and postcontact Native America is deeply implicated in the ideology of primitivism, a view that denies indigenous cultures the same kinds of agency, dynamism, and inventiveness that are presumed to operate in "civilized" cultures. In the case of my own expressions, I therefore commonly substitute "precontact" for "prehistoric" and "postcontact" for "historic," and at other times may conflate these periods into "(pre)historic" (i.e., precontact and postcontact but not the modern period) except when I need to follow the dominant temporal categorization for analytic purposes.

Rock Art Studies

A comprehensive survey, synthesis, or analysis of the rock art literature is beyond the scope of this book. Rock art studies includes a wide range of topics, research questions, approaches, methods, institutional contexts, and academic traditions. Some major types of research include detailed site descriptions, recording methods, stylistic identification and analysis, dating techniques and applications, spatial analyses using Geographic Information Systems (GIS), image analyses using digital imaging technologies, ethnographic and ethnohistorical research, cultural landscape studies, structuralist and semiotic analyses, phenomenological accounts, reconstructing ancient religious and social systems, development and criticism of a variety of interpretive models, approaches to conservation and restoration (cultural resource management), and many other topics and approaches.

Both researchers and members of the larger rock art community are increasingly concerned about the preservation of indigenous rock art sites. Increased visitation, intentional efforts at defacement and theft, urban sprawl, and resource extraction have accelerated the degradation of rock art sites throughout the western United States. In response, a variety of land management agencies, state offices of historic preservation, and rock art organizations have enacted educational campaigns, land-use restrictions, volunteer site steward programs, and more vigorous legal prosecution of vandals. A quick review of rock art publications, conferences, and websites makes evident the strong and increasing concern over the protection and preservation of indigenous rock art. In addition, an increasing amount of the professional practices surrounding rock art involves not research in the traditional sense, but cultural resource management: site development, management, conservation, restoration, consultation or even collaboration with affiliated tribes, and related activities (Whitley 2001a, 2011).

Rock art researchers are a diverse lot, ranging from academics (in archaeology and anthropology, but also art history, astronomy, geology, linguistics, studio art, and others) to land managers and professional archaeologists to avocational researchers and amateur enthusiasts with wide-ranging interests, talents, and backgrounds. The heterogeneity of this group is identifiable, for example, by flipping through almost any volume of *American Indian Rock Art*, the proceedings of the annual conference of the American Rock Art Research Association (ARARA), published since 1975 (see Hays-Gilpin 2005). In addition to ARARA, a variety of other state-level rock art organizations, which in my perception are predominantly composed of avocationalists, offer annual conferences and print or online publications for the dissemination of rock art research. Much of the published rock art literature, however, is in academic outlets in archaeology and anthropology, including monographs, anthologies, and journals such as *American Antiquity* and *Current Anthropology*. In addition to the diversity of the researchers, the variety of outlets for rock art research—ranging from refereed academic journals to online newsletters from largely avocational rock art organizations to self-published books and blogs—offers a partial explanation for the wide range of paradigms, methods, forms of reasoning, types of claims and evidence, and styles evident in the rock art literature.

The basic methodological division between formal and informed approaches characterizes one of the basic tensions in the study of rock art. Formal approaches rely on analyses of empirical characteristics of the rock art itself, including factors related to the rock art, such as its location vis-à-vis other rock art, other archaeological features, or natural features (Taçon and Chippindale 1998; Whitley 2011). Identifications of rock art styles and their distribution, for example, are based on analyses of the rock art images, such as subject matter, method of manufacture, norms, and conventions, as well as their location on the landscape and their potential relationship with other archaeological features such as habitation sites. Formal methods are *etic* in nature, meaning that the categories and systems of sense-making used to analyze rock art are imposed from the outside: They are shaped by the assumptions, paradigms, purposes, and tools of the researcher, not how the people who produced the images would make sense of them (Whitley 2011). In cases where no living peoples have knowledge of the rock art's production, formal methods are the only ones available, and are more consistent with archaeological approaches to the study of other types of material remains of past cultures.

Informed methods, on the other hand, are based on an *emic*, or insider's, perspective (Whitley 2011). Informed methods rely on ethnohistorical and ethnographic methods and materials to understand rock art's meanings and social functions, based on reports provided to ethnographers by native consultants (Taçon and Chippindale 1998). Ethnographic analogies are also frequently used, involving the extension of ethnographic information about similar cultures (e.g., other hunter-gatherers), though the use of such analogies is controversial and strains the boundaries of "informed" methods. Informed, emic, ethnographic methods are the classic domain of cultural anthropology and, as we shall see in the next section on the history of rock art research, the tension between archaeology and cultural anthropology provides one frame for understanding the development of the field despite the fact that, in practice, formal and informed methods are now frequently used in a complementary fashion to advance the understanding of rock art (e.g., Bernardini 2005; Keyser and Whitley 2006).

A History of US Rock Art Research

Native American rock art has become increasingly visible, not only in general and "tourist" art and literature, but also in academic circles. After a long period of relative neglect, archaeologists and other scholars are increasingly focusing on rock art and its significance for archaeology, anthropology, and related fields. Almost all scholars who discuss the field's history, be it in a paragraph- or a chapter-length treatment, follow this common refrain: Rock art was long ignored as a topic of research in the United States, especially by archaeologists, and is now experiencing a tremendous blossoming, especially within archaeology (Francis 2005; Hays-Gilpin 2004; Loendorf et al. 2005; Quinlan 2007b; Schaafsma 1985; Whitley 2001a, 2008, 2011; Whitley and Clottes 2005; Whitley and Loendorf 1994). This rough scaffolding has been repeated at least since 1980 (Schaafsma 1980). However, the development of the field has been less of a steady progression than a series of struggles and oscillations between a multitude of internal tensions and external forces. What follows is not *the* history of rock art research in the United States, but my history—a combination of previously published histories, my own reading of the literature, and my own interests, standpoints, frames, and assumptions. I do not present this as definitive, but as a framework that informs later chapters and signals to readers my perspectives on rock art and rock art research.

Aside from a variety of mentions of rock art by Spanish explorers, the first documented rock art research in Anglo North America was of Dighton Rock in Massachusetts. The earliest drawing and description of the petroglyphs date to 1680, with additional work by Puritan scholar Cotton Mather as early as 1690 (Delabarre 1928). Mather's account of the panel was published in 1714 by the Royal Society of London (Delabarre 1928; Molyneaux 1998; Pearson 2002). Over the next two centuries, Dighton Rock inspired dozens of in-depth explorations of its meaning, including what are the now all-too-familiar stories of Atlantis and the Phoenicians, Egyptians, and Norse, not to mention Druids from the British Isles (Delabarre 1928).

Setting the stage for almost two centuries of subsequent research into rock art in the United States, Mather's discussion of Dighton Rock "assumed that rock art motifs formed an early kind of writing" (Whitley and Clottes 2005:165). The outright rejection of the view that rock art is a form of proto- or picture-writing is widespread among rock art researchers, who decry it as strongly as the view that much rock art is "mere doodling." This rejection is based on both its inaccuracy and, especially when combined with an evolutionary frame, its racist and colonialist implications (Francis 2005). The last consequential work to consider rock art as a proto-writing system was also the first major synthesis of rock art in the United States (Whitley and Clottes 2005): Garrick Mallery's (1894) *Picture-Writing of the American Indians*. As discussed in chapter 1, Mallery combined the view of rock art as an early stage in the development of writing with an evolutionary view that posits Native Americans as representing an earlier stage of human development; alphabetic writing replaces picture writing as inevitably as . . . well, the implication is pretty clear: as inevitably as (civilized) Euro-Americans replace (barbaric) Indians.

Remnants of the proto-writing view remain, however, as in a Bureau of Land Management (BLM) sign for a rock art site on Potash Road outside of Moab, Utah, that in 2014 was still titled "Indian Writing." Perhaps the most popular name for rock art sites remains "Newspaper Rock." The popularity of LaVan Martineau's 1973 book *The Rocks Begin to Speak* also evidences the appeal of understanding rock art as a kind of written language (Francis 2005). Despite its repeated debunking by "serious" rock art scholars, I found few books on US rock art, including popular guide books, with a higher Amazon sales ranking than Martineau's book, and the age of the book combined with its frequent presence in used book stores probably weights the Amazon rankings against its popularity compared to more recent books on rock art. More subtly, the universally accepted term *pictograph* utilizes the Greek word for writing (graph), perpetuating a culturally pervasive privileging of the written word (Francis 2005). Interpretive signs at some rock art sites emphasize that rock art is not a form of writing; however, such denials point to the ongoing, widespread existence of that view, especially as a tacit assumption of naïve viewers. Ironically, some interpretive signs intended to undo the false perception of rock art as a form of writing end up further perpetuating some of the primary problems with that view, such as ethnocentrism and racism grounded in an evolutionary paradigm. A BLM sign at Sand Island along the San Juan River near Bluff, Utah (and still present on my last visit in 2006), states, "This primitive bulletin board contains the dreams, ambitions and fears of people who had no written language." As with many of the "myths" perpetuated by older rock art research, the view of rock art as a written language remains in the sedimented deposits of the collective rock art knowledge in the United States, still supporting and shaping the landscape of sense-making upon which we stand when viewing rock art.

From Mallery, histories of US rock art research typically move to the early decades of the twentieth century and the development of professional archaeology as well as the wave of salvage ethnography across the western United States. Salvage ethnography was driven by an ideological view of the implications of contact between Western and indigenous peoples, in which "primitive" peoples give way in the face of progress, becoming culturally if not biologically extinct. Salvage ethnography endeavored to preserve these cultures by hastily documenting them before their inevitable disappearance (Clifford 1988; Gruber 1970; Lyman 1982).

While rock art was not the focus of these ethnographic works across the western states, the ethnographic record nevertheless contains relevant information about rock art (Whitley 1994a), and in some cases ethnographic information was collected about specific rock art sites (e.g., Colton and Colton [1931] and Titiev [1937] on the Willow Springs site in northern Arizona). Difficulties arose, however, in applying recent ethnography to what were often precontact rock art sites and styles (Francis 2005). Whitley and Clottes (2005) point out that the salvage ethnography in the western United States was focused on quickly gathering ethnographic data and publishing it in relatively raw form without substantial synthesis or analysis, further contributing to its ineffectiveness in rock art studies. In addition, ethnographic information in the western United States often indicated spirits made the rock art; some researchers inferred that this meant that the cultures living in these areas knew nothing about the rock art and that it must have been made by other cultures that previously inhabited the area (Francis 2005; Whitley 1994a, 2011). Therefore, ethnography and cultural anthropology more broadly reached an apparent dead end in the study and interpretation of rock art by World War II. As a result, informed methods were largely set aside in favor of formal methods.

At the same time, "for the first half of the twentieth century, rock art studies were effectively marginalized by archaeologists" (Whitley and Clottes 2005:165). In the "traditional" period in Anglo-American archaeology, the discipline's purpose was largely descriptive, creating classifications of cultures and developing spatial distributions and chronologies. This "culture history" approach would later coalesce in rock art studies' long-term (and ongoing) emphasis on style. Stylistic classifications were used to establish stylistic areas and chronologies and, therefore, presumably, cultural areas and chronologies (Schaafsma 2013). However, the reliance of rock art research in the early twentieth century on informed, ethnographic methods marginalized it in the context of archaeology, which relied on formal analyses of material remains to reconstruct ancient cultures and identify culture areas and chronologies. The inapplicability of many traditional archaeological techniques to the study of rock art, the heavy reliance on ethnography in rock art research, and the view that rock art was an ethnological, not an archaeological, topic all contributed to archaeologists largely ignoring rock art as a topic of research (Whitley and Clottes 2005).

In this period, Julian Steward's 1929 *Petroglyphs of California and Adjoining States* appeared. This major synthesis of western North American rock art shaped the understandings of anthropology's role (or lack thereof) in rock art studies and initiated an era in which the interpretation of rock art was avoided. Ironically, Steward, an anthropologist who made significant ethnographic contributions in the far western United States, played a key role in the rejection of ethnology's relevance for rock art studies (Whitley and Clottes 2005). Steward made much of the Native denial of knowledge about rock art, its meaning, and its makers, despite the fact that such denials were made about other subjects as well and, in general, ethnographic participants are known to exhibit reticence to talk about various topics—denial not necessarily equating to an absence of knowledge (Whitley and Clottes 2005). In attempting to explain how Steward could claim that rock art was essentially unknowable due to the lack of indigenous knowledge at the start of the same chapter in which he presented ethnographic data on rock art's meanings and makers, Whitley and Clottes (2005) turn to his evolutionary view of Numic culture, the anthropological category encompassing the peoples who lived amidst the Great Basin hunter-gatherer rock art that was a primary focus of his work. Steward understood Numic culture as "gastric" in nature, not advanced enough to exhibit ritual, symbolism, or any social organization beyond the family (Whitley 2001a). Their denial of knowledge about the rock art's makers was easy for Steward to accept given that his overall perspective of the culture was inconsistent with the production of interesting and complex rock art (Whitley and Clottes 2005).

Following Steward (1929), and consistent with the culture history approach of the archaeology of the time, stylistic classification became the primary research agenda in rock art studies for fifty years (Whitley 2001a; Whitley and Loendorf 1994). Indeed, in 1985 Schaafsma could legitimately claim that rock art studies up to that point were largely in a "descriptive phase" (Schaafsma 1985:189), reflecting this stylistic focus. After World War II the primary focus of rock art research was on classification and typology via the concept of style (Francis 2005). Archaeologists could more easily adopt the focus on style, a purely formal, taxonomical approach that allowed for distributional analysis, contributing to culture history while avoiding issues of symbolism and meaning (Whitley and Clottes 2005). Much archaeological research presumed that rock art was uninterpretable without relevant ethnographic information (information that anthropologists such as Steward denied even existed), leaving rock art studies to the tasks of data gathering and data classification—"empiricism in its most unvarnished form" (Whitley 2001a:13). This focus on style, beginning in the 1930s, marked a transition away from ethnography (informed methods) and set the stage for a formal approach to rock art that could be made consistent with the "new" or "processual" archaeology that was on the horizon.

Beginning around 1960, but with earlier roots, the rise of "new" or "processual" archaeology marked a move away from the largely descriptive culture history approach and toward a fully developed *science* in the Anglo-American, positivist sense: one grounded in a rigid empiricism and focused on uncovering the universal laws governing human cultures (Pearson 2002; Whitley 1998b). This was driven in part by an attempt to bring archaeology back into anthropology, with processualism allowing archaeologists to go beyond reconstructing the past of a particular culture at a particular time and move toward uncovering the laws that govern the development of all cultures, thereby contributing to the larger questions of anthropology as a whole (Francis 2005; Pearson 2002). Specifically, this paradigm led archaeology toward various forms of cultural materialism, in which external material conditions such as environment and climate are not only drivers, but the determinants of cultural change (Pearson 2002). Archaeology becomes the study of cultural adaptation to environmental change. This "new" archaeology understood human behavior through "ecological and biological models, notably optimal foraging theory" (Francis 2005:187).

Beyond understanding human behavior and culture as fundamentally responses to external conditions, processualism led to an emphasis on subsistence, and hence on those material remains understood to be related to subsistence, such as stone tools. Rock art, clearly a symbolic system, and therefore necessarily tied to cognition and ideation, and perhaps related to ritual and cosmology, was seen as largely irrelevant to the questions pursued by archaeology. In addition, the interpretation of rock art is hardly amenable to the rigid empiricism of post–World War II US science, which required objective, measurable, verifiable data in order to advance a valid claim. Relying on etic approaches, processualists were not going to talk to the Natives to obtain emic accounts of rock art (Francis 2005)—even if they believed, contrary to the received wisdom of Steward, that doing so was potentially fruitful.

At the beginning of the processualist era, the next major synthesis of rock art in the western United States after Steward appeared. Robert Heizer and Martin Baumhoff's (1962) *Prehistoric Rock Art of Nevada and Eastern California* became, arguably, the most influential US rock art publication to date (Whitley and Clottes 2005). Heizer and Baumhoff's project was consistent with the already dominant approach focusing on identifying styles and their distributions, and in many ways with the rising processualist paradigm as well. They presented a stylistic chronology and ignored relevant ethnography (Whitley and Clottes 2005). They relied on etic but not emic approaches, formal but not informed methods.

However, contrary to both the stylistic, culture history approach and the rise of processualism, Heizer and Baumhoff (1962) made a strong argument about the purpose, if not the precise meaning, of the petroglyphs of the Great Basin, though without reference to ethnographic (emic) data. They advanced the hunting magic hypothesis for much Great Basin rock art, a framework guided by similar interpretations of Paleolithic art in Europe. As a form of sympathetic magic, based on like creating like, rock art images of game animals were interpreted as intended to ensure a bountiful hunt. Consistent with archaeology's use of formal methods, they relied on analyses of the presumed content of the imagery (e.g., large game animals) and the placement of the images on the landscape (e.g., near game trails) to support their hypothesis. Heizer and Baumhoff pushed the boundaries by including interpretation, but the hunting magic hypothesis did "fit the bias of American archaeology at that time," emphasizing "adaptation and cultural ecology" (Whitley and Clottes 2005:173). To be a legitimate subject, rock art had to be tied to the quest for food, reduced to "an aspect of diet" (Whitley and Clottes 2005:173), as is clear in Heizer and Baumhoff's concluding remarks:

We feel that for the first time we have demonstrated that petroglyphs in Nevada and eastern California are evidence of the purposeful and rational action of historic peoples. They are not aimless "doodling," nor are they deliberate and planned expressions of the artistic impulse. We think that we have proved that the petroglyphs in the area we have studied are to be understood as a part of *the economic pursuit of hunting large game*. (Heizer and Baumhoff 1962:239; emphasis added)

Hunting magic served as the dominant model for interpreting rock art in the far western United States for at least two decades (Whitley and Clottes 2005), and is still found frequently repeated on interpretive signs and in informational pamphlets across the West. If Steward's 1929 synthesis broadcast the idea that living Indians don't know anything about rock art, then Heizer and Baumhoff broadcast the idea, not only among archaeologists but into the public consciousness as well, that rock art was about hunting magic.

Despite the impact of the hunting magic hypothesis on both research and public understandings of rock art, in the processual era, running from roughly the 1960s to the 1980s, the dominant archaeological view was that rock art was outside of what archaeology could deal with and that it could not contribute to the larger questions archaeology should pursue. Etic approaches remained dominant, and both nonutilitarian material remains and ethnography remained largely irrelevant (Francis 2005). By the late 1960s, "professional archaeologists had largely moved out of rock art research. . . . By about 1970, it was essentially a dead archaeological topic" (Whitley 2001a:16–17). During the 1960s and 1970s, large regional surveys of archaeological sites often ignored the existence of rock art (Whitley 2001a).

Beginning in the mid- to late 1980s and well in place by the 1990s, a "revolution" (Whitley 2011) occurred in rock art research, as indicated by a growing interest in and acceptance of rock art research within archaeology, a return to interpretation and ethnography, the rise of the shamanic hypothesis, improved methods and dating techniques, increasing popularity of rock art and site visitation, and an increasing focus on cultural resource management, including consultations with Native Americans (Whitley 2008). These trends mostly paralleled the rise of postprocessual archaeology.

Mirroring shifts in other disciplines in the humanities and social sciences, the 1980s saw the beginnings of postprocessual archaeology (Whitley 1998b). This term encompasses a variety of different yet related movements and emergent paradigms, including postpositivist, interpretive, and "postmodern" perspectives, as well as qualifications or rejections of the positivism undergirding processual archaeology. The skepticism toward positivism, a rigid view of science focused on discovering universal laws that negate any role for human agency, is perhaps the more properly "post" aspect of postprocessualism. Consistent with developments in other disciplines in the humanities and social sciences in the United States, it also includes various critical approaches, those attuned to the operation of power and the social dynamics of privilege and domination/subordination, including feminist, queer, antiracist, and postcolonial perspectives. Postprocessualism also includes cognitive archaeology, attempts to reconstruct the psychological and ideational processes of precontact peoples, or at least granting human cognition an active role in human development, and as a result researchers began "to engage religious beliefs, ethnicity, gender, and a variety of other subjective states that most processualists considered taboo or dismissed as wholly epiphenomenal and therefore uninteresting" (Pearson 2002:14). As Whitley (2011:15) argues, "One of the (rare) beneficial effects of postmodernism" is "a revived archaeological interest in art, symbolism, and belief."

More broadly, and central to what is often pejoratively labeled "postmodern" (as in "postmodern claptrap," i.e., antiscience), postprocessual archaeology reflects broader disciplinary shifts in the US academy towards perspectives that reject deterministic models, are suspicious of naïve empiricism (especially positivism), and highlight the processes by which social, cultural, and especially symbolic systems constitute human social realities, institutions, identities, perspectives, and experiences (Pearson 2002; Whitley 1998b). Taken to an extreme (as in the "straw man" set up by critics who reject postmodernism outright), this results in a perspective that dismisses the role of material (environmental and economic) forces and rejects any meaningful knowledge of empirical, "objective" reality in favor of a self-enclosed set of symbolic and media systems that feed back on themselves to create a self-enclosed symbolic reality. That is, of course, an oversimplified characterization of a set of epistemological shifts in the Anglo-American academy based on a small, and early, subset of what has been referred to as the social construction of reality, the interpretive turn, the discursive turn, poststructuralism, and postmodernism: a perspective that acknowledges the profound influence of symbols, discourses, communication, media, social institutions, and cultural systems on how human societies have come to be as they are. Some of these perspectives highlight the role of human agency, as opposed to a deterministic materialism, in shaping social realities (Whitley 1998b). These perspectives relativize academic knowledge as socially and discursively constructed as well as deeply ideological, driven by systems of meaning that privilege some groups at the expense of others. This is in sharp contrast to the processual view that human societies develop in a fashion determined by external (environmental) changes as governed by universal laws, and that such laws are discoverable through objective measures of empirical reality and a scientific process presumed to be acultural—not relative but absolute, resulting in objective (impartial and unpositioned) knowledge.

The rise of postprocessual approaches opened up new possibilities for rock art studies within archaeology in terms of both taking rock art seriously and the possible paradigms and methods that could be employed in studying rock art (Francis 2005). Increasing archaeological attention given to the material traces of "nonutilitarian" behavior, such as those related to symbolism, cognition, ritual, and religion, provided a legitimate place for the study of rock art. In terms of research goals and paradigms, interpretation of rock art was seen as less of a fringe activity. Paralleling the renewed focus on interpretation, the return of ethnographic approaches, particularly rereadings of the salvage-era ethnography that had been declared a dead-end by the likes of Steward (1929), opened up new avenues for rock art research and questioned previous assumptions regarding who produced the rock art, when, and with what purposes (Francis 2005; Whitley and Clottes 2005). Ethnography allowed for the advancement of new models of interpretation, further reducing the marginalization of ethnography and interpretation in archaeological studies of rock art (Whitley and Clottes 2005).

A key development of the 1980s, and continuing through today, is the advancement of the shamanic hypothesis for much of the rock art of the Great Basin and other areas in the far western United States (Francis 2005; Whitley and Clottes 2005). Shamanism was successful in largely displacing the hunting magic hypothesis and has become one of the most widely discussed topics in rock art research and beyond due to its dissemination through popular books and interpretive materials such as educational signs and pamphlets. This approach, in its rough form, holds that some rock art records the experience of altered states of consciousness (ASCs), primarily that of ritual specialists (shamans), but also of others who undergo ASCs during, for example, rites of passage or vision quests. David Whitley (1994b, 1996, 1998a, 1998c, 2000a) has been the primary proponent of the shamanic hypothesis for far western North American rock art, a perspective that was facilitated by the increasing legitimacy of religion, cosmology, and consciousness as archaeological topics. Central to Whitley's arguments are rereadings of previously dismissed salvage ethnographies (Whitley, 1994b, 2001a) and reliance on the neuropsychological (N-P) model developed by David Lewis-Williams and Thomas Dowson (1988, 1990) in the context of both Paleolithic cave art of western Europe and San rock art in southern Africa. While both Whitley's work with Great Basin rock art and Lewis-Williams and Dowson's work with San rock art utilize ethnography, the N-P model is ultimately based on an understanding of human neuropsychological universals related to the experience of ASCs, involving a limited set of images and combinations thereof, and identifiable stages in hallucinatory experiences. In addition to leveraging the possibilities opened up by postprocessualism, Francis (2005) argues that the N-P model specifically is important because it is a radical departure from the stylistic approach still very dominant in rock art research and it is not based on the Western idea of art.

The rise of postprocessualism has not meant, however, that the power of empiricism and the commitment to archaeology as a true ("hard") science has gone away or has not affected the direction of rock art research. The embodied nature of the experience of rock art, an experience inseparable from the natural contexts in which rock art occurs, seems to beg for phenomenological investigations. Phenomenological approaches center on sensual, affective, and cognitive experience, focusing on the systematic analysis of consciousness, and stand in stark contrast to the traditional methods of empiricism (e.g., Abram 1996). Significantly, phenomenological studies of rock art are mostly produced in European academic contexts as well as in the Anglo diaspora (e.g., Firnhaber 2007; Smith and Blundell 2004), but rarely in the US academy, nor are such studies commonly cited in US academic rock art literature. Whitley (2011:179) assesses phenomenological approaches to the study of rock art in scientific terms: "The interpretations that result are more akin to an art critique (exploring the emotional and aesthetic qualities of the site) than to empirical research per se, and there seems to be no way to judge the result." Similarly, there has been increased attention to the role of animism in understanding rock art, although such research continues to struggle with the tensions between animist world views and the epistemological expectations of Western scholarly discourse (Poor and Bell 2012; Robinson 2013). As with phenomenological studies, animist research seems to be concentrated outside of the US academy, even though such research does sometimes focus on rock art in the United States.

The presence of postprocessualism has by no means replaced more processual orientations, especially by archaeologists outside of the academy. The debates over the possibility of interpretation (discussed below) clearly signal the ongoing presence of broadly processualist views in rock art studies. In addition, beyond the larger trends of postprocessualism, other factors have also affected the perceived validity, utility, and importance of rock art and rock art research within archaeology, three of which I will discuss here: advancements in dating, an increasing focus on cultural resource management (CRM), and the longstanding presence of the "lunatic fringe."

Dating Rock Art

Improvements in the dating of rock art via new chronometric techniques are a commonly mentioned cause for the increasing acceptance of rock art studies in archaeology (Whitley 2008, 2011; Hyder and Loendorf 2005). In Francis's (2005) view, the focus on this "hard science" aspect of rock art research probably has more to do with rock art's perceived legitimacy within archaeology than postprocessualist trends discussed above, pointing to the ongoing power of processualism. Understanding the significance of these advances requires a brief discussion of traditional dating techniques and their limitations. As Francis (2005:189) writes, "Until recently, we have been severely hampered by the lack of numerical dating techniques and an empirical basis by which to construct cultural-historical sequences."

The time periods assigned to various rock art motifs, panels, sites, or styles are often based on relative dating methods, such as the consistent superpositioning of certain images or styles over others, leading to a clear sequence but not anchored by any specific dates. Another sequential approach involves the relative repatination of the rock surface. Petroglyphs are often produced by pecking away the "desert varnish" or "patina" that forms on rock surfaces, revealing the lighter material underneath. Over time, the patina reforms. On some panels and at some sites, some motifs are more repatinated than others, leading to inferences about relative age. However, the rate of formation of the patina can be affected by a variety of factors, even on different places on the same panel. Judgments about repatination are not always made using replicable methods but are instead based on subjective and relatively unsystematic perceptions of repatination. Regardless, these methods provide, at best, only relative, not absolute, dates, prohibiting the temporal correlation of rock art with other types of material remains, culture histories, and environmental factors.

Other images can be said to have been made after a certain time due to their subject matter, such as bows and arrows, corn, horses, or trains. Comparisons of the imagery and style to those present in directly or indirectly datable artifacts (e.g., painted designs on pottery) can also help establish a rough time period for the art, although inferences large or small are always involved. Recent research reported in the *Journal of Archaeological Science* (Benson et al. 2013) dated petroglyphs near Reno, Nevada, from between 10,500 and 14,800 years old based on the presence of datable carbonate crust left by an ancient lake. The images, in other words, are presumed to have been produced only during those times when the rock surfaces were above the water level. Such an approach, however, would only apply to a very small subset of rock art.

The overall lack of "absolute," or even of good relative dating techniques poses a particular problem for the study of rock art, as traditional archaeology has been largely defined by the methods of stratigraphy and, later, radio-carbon and other chronometric dating techniques (Hyder and Loendorf 2005). As Christensen, Dickey, and Freers (2013:39) state, "The Holy Grail for rock art studies would be the ability to obtain calendar dates from selected pictographs, and even more whimsically, petroglyphs" and that the achievement thereof would force "even the more conservative archaeologists" to see rock art "on a par with traditionally coveted artifacts." Absent such advancements, however, the view that rock art's value for archaeology is extremely limited if not nonexistent due to the lack of chronometric dating remains strong among many.

At least two views of the potential of dating rock art exist: (1) that the technical problems with the absolute dating of rock art have not been overcome and are unlikely to be any time soon due to their "monumental" nature (Christensen et al. 2013:26); and (2) that significant advances have been made with the promise of more to come (Whitley

2011). While their validity and utility may be debated, some possible techniques for chronometric dating have been developed (see Rowe [2005] and Whitley [2011] for more complete and technical summaries of the methods and results). While organic materials present in pictographs offer the potential for radio-carbon dating, methodological difficulties, especially those related to potential contamination of samples, present substantial hurdles. The dating of petroglyphs via analysis of "desert varnish" and related techniques is even more difficult and controversial (Whitley 2011). Despite advances in chronometric techniques, even the optimists acknowledge that the absolute dating of rock art images remains elusive (Whitley 2011).

Dowson (2001) approaches the dating of rock art from a different perspective. Whereas the above debate centers on whether or not rock art is becoming datable, and by implication whether rock art has a role in archaeology, Dowson questions the value of dating in two ways. First, he criticizes the fetishizing of absolute dating from a feminist perspective, naming "chronocentrism" as "the phallocentrism of archaeology" (Dowson 2001:316). Archaeology claims to have the ability of absolute dating—the symbol of power, or phallus, of archaeology— and thereby marginalizes (feminizes) rock art studies due to its lack of absolute dating. However, archaeology's claim to having a firm grasp on dating is itself questionable, as all chronometric methods involve probabilities and some degree of inference as well—not uncommonly, substantial inferences. Therefore, the rejection of rock art by archaeology can be understood as maintaining the illusion of the archaeological phallus by opposition: ignoring the problems in archaeological dating by emphasizing rock art's lack of reliable dating techniques. In dating, Dowson sees a return to empiricism in rock art studies as an attempt to meet the standards of traditional, masculinist, scientific archaeology. Second, Dowson questions what dating has done for rock art studies. He sees the recent advances in rock art research as having little to do with chronometric techniques, but instead with ethnography and the neuropsychological model. For Dowson, the focus on dating is more about securing rock art's status in archaeology as opposed to achieving greater understanding of its meanings and functions.

Cultural Resource Management

A second trend in rock art studies and its relationship to archaeology— one whose larger cultural and political significance is far greater than absolute dating—is an increasing focus on cultural resource management (Whitley 2001a). This reflects a shift within archaeology generally, away from dirt archaeology and excavation, away from the identification of covering laws and the development of deterministic theories of cultural change, and instead toward the management of cultural resources (or the less objectifying "cultural heritage," as it is often known outside the United States). In addition to this trend in Anglo-American archaeology generally (Nicholas and Wylie 2012), the increasing focus on CRM within rock art studies can also be linked to the increasing popularity of rock art and site visitation (and hence site degradation) as well as, more importantly, legal developments that are profoundly affecting the relationship between archaeologists, land managers, and Native Americans (Whitley 2008).

With the rejection of ethnography that dominated rock art studies from the 1930s until the 1980s, combined with the end of the early twentieth-century project of salvage ethnography, living Native peoples were largely ignored by rock art studies. For much of the twentieth century, Native peoples were also largely irrelevant to the management of rock art and other archaeological sites ("cultural resources"). Consistent with the most commonly used language on site etiquette signs placed at rock art and other archaeological locales by land management agencies, these sites are part of "our" past. While the "our" operating here could mean everyone, the clear implication of the discursive positions from which the signs "speak" is an archaeological, CRM, land management, and legal perspective, one ideologically and physically occupied by non-Natives, specifically Anglo-Americans and other Westerners. Academic archaeology has had "a long-standing but implied claim to exclusive control of the archaeological past" (Whitley 2001a:20; see also Nicholas and Wylie 2012; Welsh 1999). As Matt Schmader (2008:7) puts it, "There is an inherent audacity to the idea that cultural treasures made centuries ago and which are still tied to traditional communities can be 'managed' by a non-participant dominant culture."

However, the 1990s saw important legal developments with the passage of the Native American Graves Protection and Repatriation Act (NAGPRA), amendments to the National Historic Preservation Act, and executive orders requiring that land managers consult with affiliated Native American tribes and manage sites that are sacred to Native Americans as traditional cultural properties. As Francis (2005:188) puts it, these laws and orders have "forced many archaeologists, some kicking and screaming, to interact with Native peoples." While there has been resistance to the restrictions on archaeological practice resulting from NAGPRA and related legislation and regulation, the required involvement of affiliated tribes holds the potential not only to assist in less ethnocentric and colonialist approaches to site management, but also to increase the possibilities of interpretation through consultation with Native peoples (Nicholas and Wylie 2012). Put another way, NAGPRA and related laws and orders not only force archaeologists to interact with Native peoples, but they also force them, to some degree, into postprocessualism (Francis 2005): the relativization of scientific and archaeological knowledge, the decentering of archaeological authority, and the use of ethnohistory and ethnography (e.g., Kloor 2009). Archaeological "resources" are to some degree reframed as "traditional cultural properties," implying potentially more substantial claims to both ownership and authority by one group (indigenous peoples) over others (Anglo-American institutions and professions).

Amateurs, Crackpots, and the Lunatic Fringe

A third factor in rock art's relationship to archaeology is not so much a trend as an ever-present burr or, in my view, a sometimes-questionable opposition used to shore up the academic, professional, and archaeological validity of rock art studies. As with other academic disciplines, particularly those whose status and legitimacy are questioned by well-established disciplines, rock art studies polices its boundaries, establishing its legitimacy through the identification and marginalization of quacks. These policing activities are more visible in rock art studies because of the prominent role of avocationalists. All discussions of the field as a whole include some reference to avocationalists, amateurs, and enthusiasts. Often these are what I interpret as expressions of polite deference to the largest audience for rock art publications and conferences, not to mention a large part of the membership of groups such as ARARA. Former ARARA presidents William Hyder and Lawrence Loendorf (2005), for example, in their discussion of the role of avocational archaeologists in rock art research, point out that many important figures were avocationalists, including Garrick Mallery (1894), the army officer who compiled the first synthesis of US rock art, and Campbell Grant, a commercial artist who produced significant books in the 1960s and 1970s on US rock art as a whole (Grant 1967), of the Coso Range in southeastern California (Grant 1968), and of Canyon de Chelly in northeastern Arizona (Grant 1978). Many other examples abound, such as Kenneth Castleton (1984, 1987), a retired professor of medicine, who published a two-volume survey of Utah rock art. However, few avocationalists receive praise or even recognition from "serious" rock art scholars.

Other discussions contain outright judgments of the poor methodologies of untrained experts: "Casual and unsophisticated rock art theories . . . cloud the perspectives of people who are genuinely interested in learning" (Christensen et al. 2013:199). Although he acknowledges significant exceptions among avocational researchers, Whitley (2001a:16) states that "most of these works were deficient on a number of counts, including basic data collection techniques. Nor were they subjected to the kinds of rigorous review processes that professional publications enjoy." The work most commonly singled out for dismissal is Martineau's (1973) *The Rocks Begin to Speak*, which claimed that rock art was a kind of written language used universally amongst American Indians (e.g., Christensen et al. 2013; Francis 2005; Schaafsma 1980). Other comments more subtly marginalize avocationalists, as in Whitley's (2011:137) identification of one of the three factors contributing to the revolution in rock art research as "a heightened *professional* archaeological interest in rock art" (emphasis added). The central role and presence of avocational researchers, along with their substandard methodologies, is also often cited as a reason why archaeologists have avoided the study of rock art (Hays-Gilpin 2004; Meighan 1982; Whitley 2001a). Ironically, the abandonment of rock art as a topic of serious archaeological research in the mid-twentieth century created a vacuum that was filled by amateurs and avocationalists; in turn, the less-than-academic approach of these avocationalists became further justification for archaeologists to avoid rock art (Whitley 2001a).

Policing rock art studies is made both easier and more important due to the presence of not just avocationalists, but outright "crackpots and crazies" (Hyder and Loendorf 2005:228). "There is a feeling that rock art reports have been often superficial and impressionistic, if not downright loonie, and that this is an area the cautious scientist would do well to stay clear of" (Meighan 1982:225). As Kelley Hays-Gilpin (2004:3) puts it in her gendered history of the field, archaeologists avoided rock art studies because it was perceived as "the purview of a 'lunatic fringe' prone to uncritical identification of alien invaders, lost alphabets, treasure maps, and complicated astronomical formulas in rock art imagery." In discussing the role of avocationalists in rock art research, Hyder and Loendorf (2005) quote at length from Julian Steward's 1937 diatribe against the ever-present amateur, who

> stoutly resists the threats of science. . . . Popular fancy musters petroglyphs in support of theories abandoned by science half a century ago. It offers them as proof that Egyptians, Scythians, Chinese, and a host of other Old World peoples, including the Ten Lost Tribes of Israel . . . invaded America in ancient days. It claims them to be markers of buried treasures, signs of ancient astrology, records of vanished races, symbols of diabolical cults, works of the hand of God, and a hundred other things conceived by feverish brains. (Steward 1937:405)

Hyder and Loendorf (2005:228) follow the lengthy quote with the statement, "We would need to add only aliens from outer space for Steward's assessment to remain true." As a result, they argue, "through the years self-respecting archaeologists have shied away from the study of rock art lest they be associated with the crackpots and the crazies."

Most of the "craziness" when it comes to rock art relates to its interpretation. From a positivist perspective, meaning is awfully hard to grapple with, making interpretation something that is, almost by definition, "soft," "subjective," "intuitive," and a host of other feminine-coded descriptors. This combination of positivist skepticism and ongoing intrusions from the lunatic fringe feeds the energy around the question: Can rock art be interpreted?

Interpreting Rock Art?

Much of the rock art research in the United States over the last eighty years has focused on stylistic classification and the distributions of styles and motifs. Reflecting the reign of positivism and the marginalization of ethnography in mainstream archaeology, the interpretation of rock art—the attribution of intent, meaning, function, or social context to rock art—was generally avoided. Bemoaning the lack of scientific investigations of rock art, Steward (1937:409) wrote that "petroglyphs are so variable and generally so crude in form that it is all too easy for a person bent on proving a thesis to read into them whatever he desires and to find any shapes he seeks." Since the 1960s, however, a number of models for interpreting the meaning and function of rock art have been proposed, including representations of mythic and historic narratives, clan identification, boundary/territorial markers, route markers, astronomical observation, maps, hunting magic, fertility rituals, rites of passage, vision quests, and shamanism.

Beyond the debates over one interpretive model versus another, a deeper issue in rock art studies, especially in relation to the rock art of those precontact cultures lacking (or presumed to lack) meaningful continuity with living peoples, is whether or not it is possible to interpret rock art. Most obviously, this issue manifests the processual/postprocessual debate, as well as questions over the role of ethnography in archaeology.

Rock art researchers who are processual archaeologists or, more generally, possess a deep faith in the mid-twentieth century view of science as acultural, objective, and efficacious in generating empirically valid hypotheses, tend to express strong skepticism about any form of interpretation. As William Mulloy stated in 1958 in the context of Great Plains rock art, "Their pictographic significance must remain obscure . . . for such symbolism is a highly individualized thing, capable of decipherment only by the original artist and his community. . . . [A]rchaeologically we cannot cope with petroglyphic meanings" (as quoted in Francis 2005:185; see also Molyneaux 1998). "Interpretation," Rick Bury (1999:154) states, "can be no more than an adjunct to the hard science of documenting and preserving rock art. It is fraught with tendencies to cross the line into the realm of opinion and belief." A 2010 report prepared by professional archaeologists for a project partnering the Deer Valley Rock Art Center, Arizona State University, and the BLM states, "The meaning of prehistoric rock-art is something that we today will never know because of the specific cultural connotations involved in its creation" (Huang 2010:36). Christensen, Dickey, and Freers's recent *Rock Art of the Grand Canyon Region* demonstrates that processualism and its implications are alive and well in rock art research: "Much of the function and meaning behind these images remains hopelessly unknowable" (2013:xx) and "the interpretation of most rock art is at best a subjective exercise" (197). They express skepticism toward almost all efforts at interpretation, except those (seemingly quite rare) cases where valid ethnography or Native consultants are available. Without that insider view, "serious investigators have tended to restrict their studies towards more descriptive analysis and informed conjecture" (Christensen et al. 2013:xxi).

The dominant view of the mid-twentieth century—that rock art could not be interpreted because the only way to do that would be through ethnography, and there were no living informants or those alive denied knowledge of its meaning (Whitley 2001a)—is alive and well. However, there is a growing body of research reviving the use of ethnography in advancing interpretive models (Whitley and Clottes 2005). Ethnography remains one way forward from the interpretive morass posited by positivism and processualism, but a contested and necessarily limited one. While many researchers decry efforts at interpretation, they are also often still rock art researchers. The research report quoted above as saying that rock art's meaning is unknowable follows that statement with, "but it is still possible to know the systematic relationships between the peoples who created the rock-art and their socio-physical environment" (Huang 2010:36). Symbolic systems are ordered and that order is discoverable. Even if those discoveries cannot answer the question "what does it mean?" they can still provide insight, especially in combination with other archaeological materials and relevant ethnographic accounts (Loendorf et al. 2005). Whitley (2011:102), a strong proponent of the use of both ethnography and various formal methods, goes so far as to say that "we can no longer argue that an interpretive understanding of all rock art is beyond our reach."

Despite disagreements about the desirability and validity of interpretive studies of rock art, there is widespread agreement that an inherent difficulty that must be guarded against in interpreting rock art is the influence of cultural conditioning and biases. Students, enthusiasts, avocationalists, and researchers are warned of the dangerous appeal of the "gaze and guess" method. Chippindale (2001) demonstrates how even the simple identification of apparently realistic figures is fraught with difficulty, let alone inferences such as an apparently horizontal human indicating a sleeping or dead person (Loendorf et al. 2005). In addition to mentions of general cultural conditioning (e.g., Christensen et al. 2013), Francis (2005:189) points to the particular effect of Western rationalism, arguing that it is this "simple fact that lies at the root of our inability to 'explain' rock art"; prior to the 1980s, she continues, "we all innocently imposed notions and organizational concepts of art in Western culture on something that is distinctly non-Western in origin." On an even more specific level, Schaafsma (1997) examines how Western notions of secular and sacred affect contemporary understandings of rock art, such as a presumption that sacred imagery would be found inside structures while secular or heretical images are found outside, in nature. As Hays-Gilpin (2004:63) sums up the state of affairs, "The myths in the rock art literature so far are mainly ours, not those of prehistoric people."

The Stakes in Interpretation

The effects of cultural conditioning, social positions, ideologies, identities, epistemologies, power structures, and a host of other factors are not only worth discussing because of the potential distortions they introduce into the interpretation of indigenous rock art. These are not simply "biases": they are interests that shape and investments that motivate the production, circulation, and deployment of meanings, social relations, pleasures, identities, and cultural, social, political, and economic capital. These factors are not passive players but active participants, not only shaping how we view rock art but directing our attention to rock art in the first place. The interest in rock art is not solely (or even primarily) about the imagery itself or about the cultural context of its original production. Powerful ideologies and discourses assign value to rock art, driving and shaping the motivation to find, view, use, and interpret it. Rock art, relatively long-lived and widespread, is inescapably present on the landscape, but contemporary ideologies and cultural trends are necessary to explain its visibility and perceived worth in contemporary culture.

The polysemic quality of rock art imagery, its openness to multiple interpretations, facilitates the projection of Western ideologies, struggles, and contradictions onto precontact rock art imagery via the development of interpretive models designed to explain the meaning and function of rock art in the non-Western cultures that produced it. These projections and the ideologies that shape them not only "distort" Western understandings of indigenous cultures, but may also (unintentionally) perpetuate structures of power. Past complicities between North American archaeology and hegemonic systems of sense-making highlight the importance of reflexive political analysis in the human sciences (Deloria 1995, 2003; Kehoe 1999; Smith 2004). In particular, the interpretations of anthropologists, archaeologists, and others can feed back into contemporary Native American cultures, becoming "part of the fabric of evolving native identity" (Bury 1999:150), thereby not only perpetuating Western stereotypes but threatening the integrity of traditional cultural knowledge.

As documented by Jane Young (1988) at Zuni, one line of rock art research, archaeoastronomy, entered the feedback loop and altered contemporary Zuni understandings of their rock art heritage. In 1979, one of Young's Zuni colleagues offered an interpretation of a petroglyph panel that was "almost identical" to an interpretation of the same panel offered by Zunis in 1930, raising the possibility of either strong cultural continuity, the influence of the published account from the 1930s on contemporary Zunis, or both (Young 1988:220). Featuring the moon, a star, a long zig-zag, and an owl, this panel was interpreted in 1979 (and 1930) as showing the owl's flight during the night to spy on enemies and then return to report on their size and location. A year later, however, the same Zuni colleague reported that the panel showed a supernova explosion from long ago, an interpretation also offered by the tribal historian in 1981. Young reports that visitors to the pueblo had shared with the Zuni the hypothesis that this panel and others like it in the Southwest (showing a star paired with a crescent moon) depicted the supernova explosion in 1054 CE that created the Crab Nebula. The evidence clearly indicated that this interpretation did not originate with the Zunis, but was adopted from the ideas of Western archaeoastronomers. In another parallel instance, the widely publicized interaction between "daggers of light" and a spiral petroglyph at Fajada Butte in Chaco Canyon, marking events such as the winter solstice, also changed some Zunis' view of the meaning of spirals. These interpretations also changed in the course of a few years, from depictions of the journeys of ancestors to the idea that spirals interact with light and shadow to function as calendars, although the new interpretation was not taken as excluding the earlier one (Young 1988).

Recent research by Krupp, Billo, and Mark (2010) questions the widespread identification of rock art compositions featuring a paired crescent moon and star as depictions of the 1054 Crab supernova. The idea originated in the 1950s with William Miller, a photographer for the Palomar Observatory, based on two rock art sites in northern Arizona. The astronomical community in particular embraced this interpretation, and in the 1970s John Brandt and his colleagues identified additional examples, with the Peñasco Blanco pictograph panel in Chaco Canyon becoming the "poster child for supposed Crab supernova rock art" (Krupp et al. 2010:36). Krupp and his colleagues eventually relocated and reexamined Miller's original two sites and identified a variety of problems with the Crab supernova hypothesis, including the likely dates of some of the images being later than 1054, incorrect orientation of the crescent moon at one of the sites, a lack of visibility of the supernova from one of the sites, alternative interpretations of the imagery identifiable by rock art experts and others familiar with Southwest iconography (which Miller presumably was not), and failure to take into account surrounding imagery. Krupp et al. (2010:42) conclude that "features that appear to be at odds with the supernova interpretation strongly suggest that the supernova interpretation of other rock art sites can only be considered after a careful study of the sites and their local and regional context." The implication is that many rock art sites claimed to represent the Crab supernova have been identified primarily based on the proximity of a crescent image and a star image, a pairing that can be easily misidentified and which in itself is a questionable identifier of a supernova depiction. Young (1988:227) hypothesizes that some Zunis accept these astronomical interpretations due to their implications for traditional Zuni knowledge and sophistication, "emphasizing that science is not the sole propriety of the Euro-American." Ironically, Krupp and colleagues' (2010) rigorous scientific approach demonstrated a potential lack of scientific rigor in the views of archaeoastronomers—not to mention the hordes of rock art enthusiasts who see the Crab supernova in many rock art sites—that directly affected Zuni interpretations of their traditional imagery.

The stakes in the interpretation of rock art are substantial. Interpretations of rock art's original meanings and functions, especially when passed on to the public through guide books, museum displays, and interpretive materials at rock art sites, have the potential to shape perceptions of Native Americans, challenging or reinforcing dominant perceptions of indigenous cultures and histories (Whitley 2001a). Non-Native interpretations can also feed back into contemporary Native cultures, shifting the social locations from which authoritative statements about Native cultures can be made, delegitimizing Native authority over Native culture and history, and potentially introducing distortions into Native self-understandings (Bury 1999; Young 1988). Beyond issues of accuracy, the interpretation of the material remains of precontact cultures articulates structures and discourses of power, including cultural authority and identity claims (Smith 2004). The rhetorical constitution of the relationship between material culture (rock art), its originating culture (the rock art's producers), and the interpreting culture (contemporary Westerners) shapes what kinds of claims can be made, by whom, and with what authority, thereby contributing to the contemporary status of indigenous cultures and enabling (or constraining) ongoing neocolonial relations. The depth and implications of the ideological processes of stereotyping, appropriation, projection, and displacement, and their articulation with colonial and neocolonial systems of domination, will be further explored in chapter 3.

Impressions

As Francis (2005:188) sums up much of the recent history of rock art research, "For at least fifty years, archaeologists have believed that we have had no way of learning about rock art." The absence of reliable methods of absolute dating resigned rock art to the archaeological dust bin (Francis 2005; Meighan 1982; Schaafsma 1980). There is generally no dirt to dig, requiring different methods than the all-too-familiar reliance on stratigraphy (Meighan 1982; Schaafsma 1980). And worst of all, maybe our insights are inherently limited unless we talk to the Natives. Echoing Dowson's (2001) arguments about dating (above), Hays-Gilpin (2004:3) puts a feminist twist on the familiar narrative: Rock art doesn't fit well with the archaeologists' view of themselves as the "cowboys of science," engaging in dirt archaeology, backed by "hard" empirical methods. Rock art is "girlie stuff": nonutilitarian, less amenable to scientific methods, requiring subjective interpretation and hence listening to Native peoples (Hays-Gilpin 2004:3). Rock art research, in short, has been posited as "soft" (feminine) while dirt archaeology and "hard" science are more appropriately masculine. "What we are seeing here is the gendering of subject matter and activities based on a hierarchy that values . . . 'hard' science . . . over the art historical, psychological and aesthetic approaches" (Hays-Gilpin 2004:3). To make matters worse, however, such "hard" approaches seemed unable to, well, *penetrate* rock art, to uncover its secrets, to reveal its meanings and other mysteries (cf. Dowson 2001).

In looking over my reading of the broad history of Anglo-American rock art research, I am intrigued by the parallels between what has and is happening in rock art studies, not only to archaeological, anthropological, and broader academic trends, but to even broader social, economic, and cultural changes. For example, as I have signaled above, whether we study rock art, how we study it, the questions we ask, and the answers we accept are all tremendously influenced by largely

unacknowledged, tacit assumptions about gender—not just biological
sex, but the ways in which academic disciplines, methods, types of
knowledge, symbolic systems, and professional identities are structured, interpreted, and evaluated according to dualistic and hierarchical
ideologies of gender: masculinity as hard, rational, and scientific; femininity as soft, sensual, and impressionistic. For example, as I argue in
chapter 4, I do not think that hunting magic declined and shamanism
arose as a popular explanation for Great Basin rock art simply because
of comparatively better forms of empirical evidence, nor do I think that
it is solely the result of the rise of postprocessualism and the attendant
return to ethnography. Anglo-Americans and other Westerners were
"primed" for the shamanic hypothesis by the increasing focus since the
1970s on the spiritually in-tune Indian in various New Age discourses
and Hollywood portrayals (Bury 1999; Schaafsma 2013). I suspect that
the hunting magic and shamanic hypotheses were competing not only
on and for archaeological ground, but on and for the shifting cultural
terrain surrounding Anglo-American masculinity.

I also think that the shifts and changes in rock art studies over the
last one hundred years are not simply due to tensions over the relationship between archaeology and anthropology, empirical versus
ethnographic methods, and etic versus emic perspectives, but to the
broader relationships between Anglo-America and Native America. The
hardline processualist position that truly understanding the past—that
is, developing models and covering laws that explain the growth and
development of all human cultures, as determined by external forces
such as environmental factors—is *extrinsic* to the peoples and cultures
who made the artifacts studied is not simply a methodological and
epistemological preference or paradigm, but a political stance about
who holds the authority over the past, and hence over the present as
well (Smith 2004). In *Playing Indian*, Philip Deloria (1998) discusses
the cultural logic of the cold war era, in which what he terms "object
hobbyists"—white, middle-class peoples highly invested in the acquisition of authentic Native artifacts and/or the painstakingly authentic
reconstruction thereof ("artifakery")—constructed the "authenticity" of
the Indian Other (upon which their own identity was built) via objects.
That is, in contrast to the "people hobbyists" who visited reservations,
participated in powwows, and defined "authenticity" as involving
contact with real, living Indians, for object hobbyists "authenticity" was
antithetical to living Native peoples.

In part, locating authenticity in objects justified the avoidance of the potential discomforts involved in direct interaction between whites and Indians, but perhaps more importantly, living Indians were seen as inauthentic by definition: living on reservations, contaminated by Western culture and technology, and far too separated from the presumed authenticity of their existence prior to European contact (Deloria 1998). In short, living Native peoples are "degraded," no longer really Native (Lacroix 2011; Miller and Ross 2004). They are still racially less than, and now culturally less than—not because of the inferiority of their traditional culture but because of their tenuous connections to it.

The avoidance of Native Americans in rock art research for much of the post–World War II period is an extension of larger cultural patterns involving the appropriation of Other cultures for the purposes of shoring up white American identities and maintaining the artifice of "authenticity" so central to twentieth-century whiteness. Etic rock art researchers, in other words, were not only similar to Deloria's (1998) "object hobbyists" in their marginalization of living Native peoples, but also not radically unlike the hordes of whites engaging in the widespread appropriation of African-American dance and musical forms such as jazz, R&B, rap, and hip-hop. Both the 1950s' hipster and the 1990s' suburban rap fan were intensely invested in these "authentic" forms of expression but were often profoundly uncomfortable with the idea of interacting with the actual peoples and social conditions that produced the objects of their affection, the imagined antidotes to their psychological and cultural dis-ease. Rock art, too, is valued by middle-class Anglo-Americans for its "authenticity," and living Native peoples often have little to do with establishing or defining that authenticity.

CHAPTER 3

REPRESENTATIONS AND APPROPRIATIONS OF NATIVE AMERICAN CULTURES

While my first unmediated experiences of rock art were of Newspaper Rock and the handprints in Canyonlands, my first exposure to rock art imagery may well have been Godfrey Reggio's 1983 film *Koyaanisqatsi*. *Koyaanisqatsi* is an environmental documentary presented in an unconventional format—without dialogue, narration, or characters—composed of a series of moving images set to a sometimes dizzying score by modernist composer Philip Glass. The film's title is taken from a Hopi word that can be translated as "life out of balance" or "a way of life that calls for another way of being."

The film's environmentalist message is delivered in two primary parts. The first, largely composed of beautiful cinematography of the southwestern sky and landscape, provides a clear sense of a harmonious natural order characterized by fluidity and the cyclical rhythms of nature. This is most decidedly not *koyaanisqatsi*, as life appears eminently in balance: calm, peaceful, flowing, and whole. There are no humans or clear evidence of human impact in this part of the film. What is represented is "nature," which, following standard conventions of modern preservationist messages, is idealized through the erasure of evidence of human presence (DeLuca and Demo 2000).

In the second part of the film, viewers are jarringly immersed in *koyaanisqatsi* through images of modern, industrial lifeways in North America. Glass's score turns frantic and frenetic. The images range from high-speed shots of city traffic to aerial views of city layouts that look shockingly like the computer chips against which they are visually juxtaposed, from atomic explosions to the Black Mesa coal slurry pipeline violating the nonlinearity of the natural landscape of the Colorado Plateau. Visual juxtapositions that identify similarities between seemingly disparate structures are central to the film, such as images of hot dogs moving through an assembly line placed against images of subway riders exiting to the street via escalators, the people visually positioned as equivalent to hot dogs. The overall message of the film is clear: Modern, industrial lifeways are fundamentally out of balance, destructive, and dehumanizing, as the juxtaposition to natural rhythms makes quite evident.

Koyaanisqatsi does not depict Native American people. It does, however, evoke Native American cultures in two ways. The first is through the title of the film, as well as other Hopi words used in chants in the score. At the end of the film we are given the only other verbal message present in the film (outside of the title and credits), which provides English translations of *koyaanisqatsi* and the chants, symbolically anchoring the film's message in Hopi culture.

The second evocation of Native American culture occurs in the opening and closing scenes. These scenes frame the film's overall message by providing a condensed juxtaposition of the "natural" harmony of the first half of the film with the "life out of balance" presented in the second. This juxtaposition is established, and in a sense resolved, via images of rock art from the well-known Great Gallery in Horseshoe Canyon, an island unit of Canyonlands National Park in Utah. The long and essentially static opening shot of the film focuses on the "Holy Ghost" panel of the Great Gallery (see Plate 3), its large, vaguely anthropomorphic, limbless red figures floating on the sandstone wall as we hear slow chants of "*koyaanisqatsi*." This image dissolves, replaced by an exploding ball of fire, which we are eventually able to see is from a rocket taking off from a launch pad. The film opens with an ancient, static image of Native American culture being visually destroyed by the epitome of modernization, industrialization, militarization, and science: the ability and desire to escape the constraints of gravity as well as, more broadly, "mother earth" (Garb 1990). Leaving the bonds of earth demonstrates human mastery over nature and perpetuates the ideology that (modern) humans operate above nature's laws, a key element in the exploitation and destruction of the natural world (Abram 1996; Plumwood 1993; Rogers 1998).

The closing scenes of the film return to both the Great Gallery and the rocket. Viewers see the rocket complete its fiery take-off, slowly achieving its escape from the earth's gravity and then speeding high into the sky, only to explode. The camera follows a piece of the rocket as it falls, spiraling, back toward the earth, as "*koyaanisqatsi*" is chanted over and over again, with the scene lasting nearly five minutes. This shot then dissolves, replaced with another panel of pictographs from the Great Gallery. After a fade to black, the film ends with the translations of *koyaanisqatsi* and other Hopi chants used in the film.

In *Koyaanisqatsi*, ancient pictographs are used to symbolize an ideal of "life in balance," highlighting several themes of central relevance to this chapter and this book as a whole. First, indigenous rock art is used metonymically to stand in for indigenous cultures. Second, the film only represents a precontact Native American culture. While contemporary Americans of diverse ethnicities are portrayed in the film, no Native Americans are identifiable. Instead, the material traces of an ancient hunter-gatherer culture are used to stand in for a whole way of life, presumably one shared by all ancient, indigenous peoples. Third, these ancient cultures are idealized as living in "balance": meaningfully, sustainably, and in harmony with the natural world. Fourth, when the use of the Great Gallery pictographs is placed in the context of the film as a whole, it is clear that these ancient and idealized Native American cultures are symbolically collapsed into nature, rhetorically constituted as a part of it. If *koyaanisqatsi* is embodied in rockets, cities, assembly lines, atomic explosions, mines, and dams, then its opposite—the ideal of a life in balance—is embodied in two ways: in the southwestern landscape (sans humans) and in the pictographs. Visually, narratively, and ideologically, "natives" and "nature" are equated. Finally, the film points to the central role of the Southwest and southwestern Native peoples in Anglo-American culture, with the Southwest landscape, Hopi culture, and what is perhaps the most visible rock art site in the Southwest representing not only the antithesis of modern American life, but the antidote for its ills.

This brief reading of *Koyaanisqatsi* introduces the central topics of this chapter and illustrates their relevance to understanding the role of rock art in the contemporary cultural landscape. To further illustrate their relevance to the study of rock art and to establish a foundation for the chapters that follow, in the remainder of this chapter I discuss representations of Native American cultures, with particular emphasis on the role of primitivism and the construction of "authenticity," followed by the primitivist construction of the Southwest as a locus of "authenticity." I then discuss the implications involved in the reproduction, appropriation, and commodification of elements of non-Western cultures, provide an overview of some of the more visible representations and appropriations of rock art imagery, and conclude with a review and critique of the literature on the appropriation and commodification of indigenous rock art.

For readers with a background and/or interest in rock art studies, archaeology, and related areas, my extensive discussions in this and later chapters of images of Indians in popular culture may seem somewhat out of place or off track. These in-depth reviews and discussions form a core foundation for my arguments about the ways that the interpretation, appropriation, visitation, collection, research, management, and preservation of rock art are deeply embedded in a multifaceted cultural matrix. The webs of significance that we ourselves have spun (Geertz 1973) about rock art are small parts of a web that includes not only archaeology and anthropology but sculpture, film, novels, photography, television, tourism, collecting, journalism, education, and more. These elements intertwine and, crucially, are woven into larger strands representing constructs of gender, sexuality, race, class, and nation. Not only are the various parts of this web similarly patterned and mutually influential, but are mutually constitutive, with changes in one area affecting other areas as well as the fundamental structures by which they are all connected. Not only are there deep parallels between popular culture and rock art studies, but rock art studies both respond to and participate in the larger cultural web.

Representations of Native Americans

Scholars have examined the development of the dominant image of Native Americans in Anglo-American culture through a variety of media representations. Edward Curtis's photographs (1907–1930) depicted noble but "vanishing" American Indians (Gidley 1998; Lyman 1982) and James Fraser's 1915 sculpture "The End of the Trail" cemented the idea that Native Americans were at the end of their cultural journey (van Lent 1996). Contemporary romance novels continue to play upon deeply embedded stereotypes of Native American men as both sexual threats and objects of desire (Bird 2001; van Lent 1996). Native American mascots, such as the University of Illinois's Chief Illiniwek (no longer an official mascot, but still present in the university community's culture), also draw upon romanticized imagery as well as stereotypes highlighting the savage nature of American Indians (Black 2002; King 1998). Films and television programs from the Cowboy-and-Indian genre popular through the 1960s typically portrayed Indians as uncivilized savages while films such as 1990's *Dances with Wolves* highlighted a shift toward more positive, if still stereotypical, Western representations of the Indian Other (Bird 2001; Torgovnick 1996). With the rise of the counterculture and environmental movements in the 1960s and 1970s, Native Americans became strongly associated in the popular consciousness with environmental stewardship through a speech attributed to Chief Seattle and the Keep America Beautiful campaign featuring Iron Eyes Cody shedding a tear as he surveyed a polluted and littered landscape (Salvador and Clark 1999), an association further developed in films such as Kevin Costner's 1990 *Dances with Wolves* (Torgovnick 1996), Disney's 1995 *Pocahontas* (Buescher and Ono 1996), and James Cameron's 2009 *Avatar* (the highest grossing film of all time). New Age commodities and rhetoric extend this image, constituting Native spirituality as a cure for the ills of Western civilization (Huhndorf 2001; Torgovnick 1996). New Age practitioners, clothing companies, music festival attendees, and professional sports teams, schools, and universities have appropriated Native American myths, symbols, spiritualities, and costumes, continuing a long Anglo-American tradition of "playing Indian" (Black 2002; Churchill 1994; Deloria 1998; Huhndorf 2001; King 1998).

These representations do not stand in for specific individuals or Native cultures, even when they appear to do so (e.g., Chief Seattle and Pocahontas). Elements from specific cultures are appropriated, altered, and combined into images and meanings that obscure and distort the existence of distinct Native tribes, identities, and cultures (Churchill 1994; Kadish 2004; Stuckey and Morris 1999; Whitt 1995). Anglo-American representations of Native Americans cue as well as contribute to an *abstraction* called "Native American" or "Indian," embodying notions of barbarism, nobility, stoicism, inevitable disappearance, harmonious spirituality, environmental stewardship, and other shifting and contradictory themes (Berkhofer 1978; Bird 1999, 2001; Buescher and Ono 1996; Deloria 1998; Torgovnick 1996; van Lent 1996).

In his classic work *The White Man's Indian*, Robert Berkhofer (1978:xv) states, "The essence of the White image of the Indian has been the definition of Native Americans in fact and fancy as a separate and single other." Images and stereotypes of the Indian are at their root dualistic, based on a self/other, us/them, civilized/primitive dichotomy. The primitive Other has long served as a site for projecting Western fears and fantasies, for working through anxieties and conflicts while maintaining an illusion of the integrity and superiority of Western cultures and identities (Gilman 1985; Torgovnick 1996). Therefore, "to understand the White image of the Indian is to understand White societies and intellectual premises over time more than the diversity of Native Americans" (Berkhofer 1978:xvi).

Representations of the Indian are bifurcated into the ignoble and noble savage (Berkhofer 1978; Salvador and Clark 1999; van Lent 1996). On one hand are the longstanding representations of Indians as barbaric, violent, and immoral due to their intrinsic nature or lack of a civilizing influence. This negative view of Native Americans justified their extermination and/or assimilation, as well as the expropriation of their lands and children. This view also provided support for Anglo-Americans' perceptions of themselves as "civilized," constituting an American identity by opposition to the uncivilized savage (Deloria 1998). On the other hand is the noble savage, who, by living "close to nature and the natural state of things," retains "a moral purity lost to" Westerners, who are "corrupted by civilization" (van Lent 1996:211).

With the noble savage, the uncivilized state of Indians is a cause for their idealization, not their vilification. They are still the Other, opposed to Anglo-American and other Western colonizers, but the valuations of "primitive" and "civilized" have flipped. This bifurcation parallels Marianna Torgovnick's (1996) explication of the trope of the primitive. In the context of critical/cultural studies, a trope refers to a stock set of metaphors, character types, narrative patterns, and other cultural codes. "Trope" goes beyond the narrower and more static concept of "stereotype," often pointing to the operations of underlying ideologies. Following Torgovnick (1996), through the trope of the primitive, primitive Others alternately or simultaneously serve as models of the desirable and undesirable based on a shifting set of binary oppositions: barbaric/civilized, nature/culture, pure/contaminated, innocent/corrupt, emotion/reason, body/mind, communal/individualist, violent/peaceful, and virile/impotent. The primitive Other symbolizes what is desired yet forbidden, attractive yet repulsive, lost but yearned for (Gilman 1985). The trope of the primitive is deeply sexualized, projecting and displacing Western sexual ideologies, desires, and conflicts while justifying colonialism (Gilman 1985; Torgovnick 1996). The trope of the primitive shapes dominant images of Native Americans not as fixed sets of ideas but as dynamic forces articulated to power, consciousness, and social structure.

Primitivism

The more positive characterization of the noble savage and the trope of the primitive articulate with an ideology that is central to understanding the role of ancient rock art in the contemporary cultural landscape: primitivism. Primitivism is the ideology that primitive peoples live in a highly desirable state of purity and harmony, and possess a cure for the ills of Western civilization (Bousé 1996; Dilworth 1996; Hays-Gilpin 2004; Kadish 2004; Torgovnick 1996). From Edward Curtis's early twentieth-century photographs to Iron Eyes Cody's tear in the 1970s Keep America Beautiful campaign, from 1990's *Dances with Wolves* to 2009's *Avatar*, Native Americans (or their stand-ins) are frequently represented through the lens of primitivism.

Primitivism assigns various characteristics to primitives, each operating dualistically with a corresponding characteristic in modern, industrial societies. While industrialized capitalism, epitomized by the assembly line, feeds a sense of alienation from the products of one's labor through fragmentation of production and deskilling of the workforce, primitivist Indians are skilled in survival and subsistence, such as hunting and tracking, and produce hand-crafted works of great utility and beauty. While urbanization disrupts traditional communal ties, and, later, automobilization and suburbanization further isolate individuals from their communities, primitivist Indians are integrated in stable, close-knit, cooperative, and interdependent communities. While urban life is frenetic and stressful, filled with sensory overload and artifice, primitivist Indians live in natural settings, often pastoral, sublime, or serene. While commodity capitalism's possessive individualism strains any authentic sense of self and spirituality, primitivist Indians make what they need and gain fulfillment and peace through a deeply spiritual life. While mechanistic science and capitalism enact a profound desacralization of the natural world, turning it into a lifeless object, devoid of spirit and suited for exploitation, primitivist Indians are deeply connected to nature, materially and spiritually, and engage in mutual, sustainable relationships with elements of the natural world.

In short, in a primitivist view, primitive cultures are psychologically, relationally, communally, spiritually, economically, artistically, and environmentally "authentic," whereas modern cultures are artificial, "spurious" (Sapir 1924; see also Kadish 2004). Primitivism does not merely proclaim the superiority of simpler ways of life—it ideologically and rhetorically constitutes the greater authenticity of primitive lifeways through reference to what is presumed to be an earlier time, representing something more primary, more natural, perhaps even essential—both necessary and intrinsic—to human life (Dilworth 1996).

Primitivism critiques modern/Western lifeways and produces positively coded representations of indigenous peoples, but primitivism's ideological operations support contemporary neocolonial relationships more than they resist or undermine Western hegemony. Primitivism is an outcome of modernization, expressing a profound dissatisfaction with modern, industrialized, "civilized" existence (Dilworth 1996). Through the idealization of "simpler" ways of life, primitivism says less about the traditional lifeways of Native Americans and other indigenous peoples than it does about the alienations experienced in the modern, civilized world. While appearing in the guise of idealized representations of peoples living outside of Western progress and modernity, primitivist representations are objectifying, constituting primitive peoples as resources for Westerners seeking an outside position to critique their own culture (cf. Deloria 1998), managing their dissonance through compensatory identifications with the Other, and thereby deflecting possibilities for genuine resistance to the cultural and material systems that are the source of their alienation. Primitivism is, ultimately, more therapeutic than countercultural, more hegemonic than radical.

Primitivism is rooted in nostalgia, but of the forms that Arjun Appadurai (1990) terms "nostalgia without memory" and Renato Rosaldo (1989) calls "imperialist nostalgia": a nostalgia created by and for the colonizers, manifesting a longing for the very forms of life they intentionally altered or destroyed. Primitivism is ultimately not about addressing the current state of colonized peoples, but the anxieties and alienations of the colonizer. It is not about critically revisiting history, but creating fantasies that treat indigenous cultures as resources, fetishes, commodities. While primitivism expresses genuine social-historical issues in its critique of modernity, its overall function is to channel Western dis-ease deeper into the very (post)modernity that

defines the contemporary West. Primitivism may express a more positive view of Native Americans; however, it continues to constitute them
as objects, not subjects. Primitivism relies on a stereotype, a generalization about a whole group of people based on some presumed common
essence. Yet this is not their essence, if they (or anyone) have one, but
the "essence" rhetorically constituted by Western discourses and ideologies, ultimately serving Western interests. As such, in primitivism relatively little attention is paid to variations within the group (e.g., tribal
differences), as they are categorized as a single, fixed Other against and
from which Westerners constitute and manage their identities.

The Primitive, the Ethnographic Present, and Authenticity

The primitive, as a category, is conceptually temporal in nature: it represents an earlier stage of human development, despite the temporal
coexistence of both "civilized" and "primitive" cultures (Fabian 1983).
The primitive is not only one side of a binary opposition, but it is also
an evolutionary stage, be it biological or cultural. "They," therefore,
represent "our" past, as in Garrick Mallery's (1894) nineteenth-century
evolutionary view of rock art as an early form of proto-writing (see
chapter 1). Given this logic, contact between "civilized" (more evolved)
and "primitive" (less evolved) has an inevitable outcome: "The primitive" will be wiped out, biologically (through extermination) and/or
culturally (through assimilation). The primitive cannot survive contact
with the civilized, and especially modern, world. In the case of Native
Americans, dominant discourses constitute the "vanishing race" that
has reached "the end of the trail." The closer "they" came to "vanishing,"
the greater the drive to "know"—that is, objectify—them (Gruber
1970; Lyman 1982). The late nineteenth and early twentieth centuries
in particular manifested a variety of efforts to document, record, and
preserve the remaining indigenous cultures in western North America before they disappeared, paralleling the rise of the new science of
anthropology (Clifford 1987, 1988; Smith 2005).

These attempts to document and preserve what were believed to
be vanishing cultures in the western United States are exemplified by
Edward Curtis's monumental photographic project, *The North American
Indian* (1907–1930), and the larger movement within which his project
was carried out, the "salvage ethnography" that began in the nineteenth
century (Gruber 1970). The logic underlying these projects is directly
linked to a key aspect of the civilized/primitive binary: While Western

culture is dynamic, inventive, and progressive, primitive cultures are extremely conservative and slow to change, essentially static (Fabian 1983). However, upon contact with whites, Indians begin to change quite rapidly. This has two implications. First, this change is presumed to be a result of their contact with Westerners, proving white/Western superiority. Second, because these cultures are changing, and because the very notion of change has presumably been introduced to them, they are not simply different than before, but qualitatively different, no longer Indian or primitive (Lyman 1982).

This posed a problem for Curtis and the salvage ethnographers. By the above logic, their very presence (and that of those Westerners who came before them) meant that their subjects were already contaminated by civilization, and hence quickly losing their remaining Indianness. This logic not only created the felt need to document and study these cultures quickly, but also posed an epistemological paradox, which was resolved through the creation of the "ethnographic present" (Clifford 1988; Francis 2005; Gruber 1970; Lyman 1982). In this frame, living indigenous peoples were studied and documented by Westerners in "the context of the time when their ethnicity was thought to have last existed in a 'pure' form. . . . Researchers attempted to study Indian cultures in terms of what they were—actually what they were imagined to have been—prior to contact with Whites" (Lyman 1982:51).

How the ethnographic present is constructed is demonstrated through Curtis's photographic techniques (Lyman 1982). Curtis paid and posed his subjects. As museums often do with artifacts, Curtis often decontextualized his subjects, photographing them in front of a cloth backdrop or intentionally using a narrow depth of field in order to obscure the background, which might contain evidence of Western culture. In some cases, Curtis cropped his prints and retouched his negatives, erasing modern objects such as clocks that would disrupt the illusion that his subjects were "pure." Curtis carried props and clothing with him, as his subjects would sometimes be wearing Western clothing (Lyman 1982). This kind of artifice, with members of different tribes wearing the same clothing, makes clear that it was not cultural authenticity or purity that was represented in the photographs, but the illusion thereof: the ethnographic present.

While in the long run Curtis's work did much to shape the twentieth-century image of the Indian, his work was already actively shaped by the stereotypes, assumptions, anxieties, and fantasies of his cultural milieu (Lyman 1982). Given the ideological frameworks of his time, Curtis likely understood the manipulations described above as justifiable in search of the truth about the soon-to-vanish Indian. The essentialist nature of the construct "Indian" meant that tribal variations were of secondary concern; the manipulations were carried out to capture the perceived essence of the Indian. A commercial dynamic was in operation as well: Curtis knew he would have a hard time finding audiences interested in images of "contaminated" and hence "inauthentic" Indians. Yet again, this is based on his and his audiences' perceptions of authenticity: horses, sheep, rifles, and other materials clearly of Western origin were not cropped or erased because they were already woven into the popular image of the Indian (Lyman 1982).

While the salvage ethnography of the same era used different techniques to establish the ethnographic present in their largely verbal accounts of cultures, the basic intent and structure of such moves paralleled Curtis's (Clifford 1988; Fabian 1983; Gruber 1970). This does not mean that there is no ethnographic value in Curtis's photographs or the salvage ethnography of the time, but it does mean that such documents should be approached as constructions of a particular culture, at a particular time, for particular purposes, and operating under powerful conventions and ideologies. This becomes an important factor, for example, in assessing the use of salvage ethnography to inform understandings of rock art in the western United States.

Intertwined with both primitivism and the preservation/salvage project described above is a potent interest in a particular definition of authenticity, which has profound effects on the valuation of indigenous arts and crafts, rock art, and living Native cultures and peoples (Clifford 1988; Torgovnick 1996). Under the intertwined logics of primitivism and the salvage paradigm, primitive cultures are only authentic when they are pure—without substantive contact with civilization. The authenticity of ethnographic data as well as of cultural objects is intimately linked to their origin in precontact times, or at least their origin in peoples with substantial remaining memory of and continuity with their precontact culture (i.e., the ethnographic present). In effect, authenticity is attributed to peoples and objects by taking them *out of time* (Clifford 1987)—people by the temporal sleight of hand involved in the ethnographic present, objects by documenting them or removing them to museums where they can be "preserved." This system of meaning places value on precontact and much historic rock art, but denies positive value to rock art from contemporary Native peoples (see chapter 7). This view of authenticity is based on two factors: the belief in the essentially static nature of primitive cultures and the belief in the superiority or "contaminating" nature of Western culture. The result is the denial of indigenous agency and inventiveness, disallowing their positive existence in modernity: if they change and adapt to circumstances (largely imposed upon them), then they are no longer real Indians; if they resist acculturation, they are doomed to extinction. This places contemporary Native Americans in a double-bind, as they are valued for their authenticity but such an authenticity is defined so as to be impossible to attain for indigenous people living amidst Western culture. This bind is particularly evident in the overall absence in Anglo-American culture of representations of contemporary Native Americans, and the "degraded" (inauthentic) status they are typically assigned when they are represented.

Representations of Contemporary Native Americans

Consistent with the vanishing race theme, as well as the logic underlying both primitivism and salvage ethnography, dominant images of Native Americans remain rooted in the past, with few prominent representations of contemporary Indians. In film, contemporary Native Americans, especially as central characters, are few and far between, with a few significant efforts to represent contemporary Native Americans in mainstream media with some degree of an indigenous perspective, such as 1989's *Powwow Highway* and 1995's *Smoke Signals*, although cinematic Native self-representations are increasing (Raheja 2010). Television also offers very few contemporary Native American characters, with recent exceptions including periodic characters in Fox's *King of the Hill* (1997–2010): John Redcorn, New Age healer and masseur; NBC's *Parks & Rec* (2009–2015): Ken Hotate, tribal leader and casino operator; HBO's *Big Love* (2006–2011): Jerry Flute, tribal representative in a joint casino venture, and his son Tommy; and Netflix's *House of Cards* (2013–): Daniel Lanagin, tribal casino operator and corrupt political donor. As reflected in the recurring but not regular Native American characters on *Parks & Rec*, *Big Love*, and *House of Cards*, the last three decades have seen an increasing focus on contemporary Native Americans in the context of tribal casinos, with one-time skits or storylines also appearing on shows such as *South Park*, *Family Guy*, *Chapelle's Show*, *The Simpsons*, and *Saturday Night Live* (Lacroix 2011).

The overall absence of contemporary Native Americans in popular culture can be understood as a way to enhance the collective amnesia regarding the contemporary state of Native America, with alarmingly high rates of poverty, unemployment, disease, and violence, while also celebrating the primitivist idealization of the noble savage, enabling an avoidance of the dissonance created by setting the two side-by-side. However, the logic of primitivism actually *requires* that contemporary indigenous peoples be degraded: physically, economically, socially, culturally, and psychologically. The degraded Indian functions to confirm the authenticity of the primitivist noble savage. In examinations of both popular culture (Lacroix 2011) and news accounts (Miller and Ross 2004), the "degraded Indian" emerges as a predominant stereotype for framing dominant understandings of living Native peoples.

The degraded Indian takes different forms, but at its core the stereotype understands the pathetic state of contemporary Indians to be the result of either their own internal flaws (e.g., lazy and undisciplined) or embracing the vices of Western civilization instead of its virtues. A longstanding form of the degraded Indian stereotype is the drunken Indian, but the casino Indian puts a different spin on degradation. Casino Indians are upwardly mobile, wealthy, and self-sufficient, but their success in a capitalist economy makes their authenticity incoherent, in and of itself making them degraded. As James Clifford (1988) puts it, given the longstanding image of postcontact Indians as pathetic, impotent, static, and vanishing, Native efforts to reestablish their sovereignty by actively and strategically using modern legal, political, and economic systems are scandalous, disallowing their status as authentic Indians, which is the very status that allows them to reclaim land and operate casinos (see also Torgovnick 1996).

Of particular importance is the way that casino Indians are understood to relate to and use their traditional culture in the context of capitalism, be it in casinos, the production and sale of arts and crafts, or commodifications of Native spirituality for non-Native, New Age audiences. Following the logic of the stereotype, casino Indians do not care about their traditional culture in and of itself, but only in terms of its potential for exploitation (Lacroix 2011), as a means to make money from naïve whites lured by either "authentic" or, more often, degraded (stereotypical, Disneyesque) symbols of Indianness. The implication is that they lack genuine cultural continuity due to either a lack of traditional cultural knowledge (degraded as in lost or at least distorted and/

or incomplete) or a willingness if not active desire to exploit their traditional culture for profit (degraded as in immoral, amoral, or capitalist).

The degraded Indian relates directly to how the salvage ethnography from the pre–Word War II era, post–World War II ethnographic research, and the contemporary participation of Native Americans in research is understood and assessed. Some versions of the degraded Indian stereotype can be used to question the validity of even early postcontact ethnography, not to mention early twentieth-century salvage work in the western United States (as I do in chapter 4), but avoiding ethnography becomes almost obligatory once those with living memories of life prior to complete colonization are no longer available as sources of information. The underlying logic is fundamentally the same as the pop culture stereotype, though couched differently in academic discourses. As Polly Schaafsma (2013:74) summarizes one view on this issue, "In general, the idea that oral histories will amplify an understanding of rock art and other archaeological data should be approached with extreme wariness"; not only do "time and change distance contemporary groups from ancient rock art in their environments to varying degrees," but so does "loss of traditional knowledge and degree of acculturation." All reasonable statements, of course, but nevertheless mutually reinforcing with the degraded Indian stereotype, furthering the predominance of non-Native views on rock art. At the same time, however, this rejection of living peoples as sources of valid knowledge increases the perceived value of the rock art itself, as rock art, often portrayed as "containing" the thoughts and perceptions of its makers, promises us moderns a means to access pure precontact— "authentic," "genuine," "primitive"—cultures.

The Southwest Imaginary

Much of the rock art granted visibility in Anglo-American culture is located in the Southwest, traditionally understood as Arizona and New Mexico plus parts of adjoining states, but also linked to the broader southwestern region that ranges from western Texas to southern California and as far north as Nevada, Utah, and Colorado (see Figure 1.1). The Southwest, however, is not simply a place, or a self-evident region, but a social, cultural, and political construct. Its name reveals the perspective from which it was constructed: the eastern United States (Colwell-Chanthaphonh 2010). The name goes beyond labeling a direction or a fixed region from a particular perspective; it brings with it an accretion of meanings, the collective representations of explorers, writers, scholars, artists, tourists, and collectors of both ancient artifacts and contemporary arts and crafts. Before ever setting foot in the Southwest, they were (and we are) already primed by culture, social positions, ideologies, and histories to experience and understand the region in some ways as opposed to others. The Anglo-Southwest is and has been a particularly powerful symbol of primitivism, strongly linked to Native American cultures, anthropology, archaeology, tourism, Native arts, and, more recently, New Age commodities and practices. As Leah Dilworth (1996:2) writes in *Imagining Indians in the Southwest*, "It is a region of imagination . . . on which Americans have long focused their fantasies of renewal and authenticity" (see also Bsumek 2008). Representing Southwest Native Americans as primitives "was part of the rhetoric of empire building and colonialism" (Dilworth 1996:6), with the Southwest functioning as a kind of "American Orient."

Descriptions of the Southwest abound with primitivist themes, sometimes linked to Native peoples (Dilworth 1996) and sometimes with a focus on the landscape (Neumann 1999). In the terms of New Mexico's official state slogan, it is the "Land of Enchantment," an appealing alternative to the desacralization of the world in the age of science and industry. In Charles Lummis's words from the late nineteenth century, it is a land of "poco tiempo" (as quoted in Dilworth 1996:1), a clear contrast to the hustle and bustle of northeastern urban existence. As Curtis Hinsley (1996:203) explains in *The Southwest in the American Imagination*, "the early shapers of the southwest imaginary" were looking to recover a preindustrial aesthetic of time: "a denial of historical change, an emphasis on temporal stasis, an appeal to natural rhythms." This focus on cyclical time and peaceful communalists living harmoniously with the land and its natural rhythms constitutes the Southwest as unchanging, outside of "progress." In the post–Civil War period, living amidst exploding industrialization and urbanization, Anglo-Americans

> sought a different epistemology: the poetic knowledge that the Southwest . . . appeared to promise. It would serve as an antidote to prosaic industrial daylight, to the militant time-clock world their fathers had made. It would serve as a way to reclaim the land through experiential connection . . . and to blur the

painfully sharp grids and boundaries of the world from which they came. (Hinsley 1996:204)

In the Southwest imaginary, Indians and nature are merged. The qualities assigned to the Southwest as a region and landscape blur with the qualities assigned to the indigenous peoples of the Southwest. Native peoples were (and are) seen as part of the nature of the Southwest: the natural landscape is presented as eternal and unchanging, as are its peoples, essentialized and fixed in a primitivist mold. The harshness and beauty of the landscape attests to its reality, its authenticity, and such authenticity accrues to Southwest peoples as well.

As Philip Deloria (1998) has documented, "the Indian" has long served a central role in efforts to establish and maintain an Anglo-American identity, by both opposition (the ignoble savage) and identification (the noble savage and primitivism). Both Deloria (1998) and Berkhofer (1978) demonstrate that the particular versions of the Indian invoked at particular times shift and change in response to Anglo-American cultural dynamics. Hinsley (1996) argues that in the late nineteenth century, with the opening of the Southwest via the railroads, the development of the tourist industry, and the "discovery" of the remains of an ancient civilization in places like Mesa Verde and Chaco Canyon, there was a strong national focus on the ancient inhabitants of the Southwest and the Colorado Plateau in particular: the Cliff Dwellers, later to become the Anasazi and, most recently, ancestral Puebloans. While the Pueblos, those with the clearest ties to this "vanished" civilization, were not the only Native groups to be highlighted, they have and continue to play a central role in the particular primitivist twists and turns that shape the Southwest in the popular imagination. The Pueblos were framed in terms of their harmonious, egalitarian, and communal nature, as manifested in labor, ritual, and social structure (Dilworth 1996; Hinsley 1996; Lekson 2008; Schaafsma 2013). For many Southwest writers, the Southwest imaginary provided the possibility of an American future based in its "prehistoric" past: "a human world premised on cooperation rather than destructive competition, mutual tolerance and interdependence rather than divisive greed, peaceful commonwealth rather than warlike imperium" (Hinsley 1996:206). This primitivist frame for understanding the Southwest was further perpetuated by elements of the counterculture, environmental, and New Age movements, as in this 1972 statement in a San Francisco–based environmental magazine:

For those early people, who are still reflected in the traditional
Indians of today, the Southwest was the spiritual center of the
land mass we know as the North American continent. Life in
this sacred place required a synthesis of intuitive awareness of
the flow of nature and a basic minimum technology born of
common sense. To grow crops of corn, beans and squash in
Hopi country, one must plant, pray—and haul water. (as quoted
in Geertz 1994:267)

In contrast to advancing industrialization, the Southwest offered an
image of genuine labor—not only communal, but also undeniably
"real," both authentic and exceptional due to the harsh environment.
A focus on Native artisans and Native arts and crafts has been central
to Southwest tourism, from the late nineteenth century to the present
(Dilworth 1996). Seen as seamless, integrated, and harmonious instead
of specialized, fragmented, and alienated, the cultures of the Southwest
produced pottery, weavings, jewelry, and more that came to embody
these same traits, making them not only art in a purely aesthetic
sense, but concrete manifestations of spiritual, cultural, and regional
authenticity—fetishes that embodied "the logic of the Indian artist as a
therapeutic Other for a machine-driven civilization" (Hinsley 1996:182).
    The primitivism associated with the Southwest landscape and the
indigenous peoples who inhabited it is clearly manifested in Reggio's
(1983) film *Koyaanisqatsi*. The static, ancient rock art of the Colorado
Plateau and the peaceful natural rhythms of the region are contrasted to
the hectic, destructive, hierarchical, and alienating qualities of modern,
industrial life. With the increasing modernization and contamination
of the living indigenous peoples of the Southwest, the primitivist slant
of the film is incompatible with representations of those peoples. As a
result, the pictographs of the Great Gallery stand in for the ethnographic
present, enabling the primitivist idealization of pure, precontact cultures.
In *Koyaanisqatsi*, these cultures blur with nature: the pictographs, a Hopi
word, and the natural landscape merge to represent the favored alternative to the film's depiction of modern, industrialized lifeways.
    The use of rock art imagery to promote tourism and constitute the
indigenous cultures of the Southwest as resources for the symbolic rejuvenation of Westerners has become pervasive throughout the greater
Southwest in the last three decades. Indigenous rock art has become an
important source of imagery used to represent Native American culture

in general, but especially Native cultures of the Southwest. Many Southwest tourist destinations expose visitors to a large amount of rock art–derived imagery and, in some instances, direct tourists to specific rock art sites. The relationship between rock art and the Southwest is mutually reinforcing: rock art images serve as symbols of the Southwest while the Southwest has been key in the visibility of rock art in the national consciousness, not only due to the rock art–friendly climate and geography of the region, but the defining role of tourism in the history of the Anglo-Southwest and the central role of the region in Anglo-American anthropology and archaeology.

Postmodernity, Appropriation, and Commodification

While a central dimension of rock art in the contemporary cultural landscape is its role in representing Native American cultures, an equally central and closely related dimension is the appropriation of rock art imagery. Rock art imagery is reproduced, and hence appropriated, in a variety of ways: more or less "realistic" two-dimensional reproductions of individual motifs or whole panels through media such as photography, video, painting, drawing, and engraving; the use of more abstracted rock art symbols in graphic design such as logo marks and book ornaments; and three-dimensional representations of rock art images through media such as papier-mâché, plaster, clay, or metal (as in sculptures and jewelry). Insights into the dynamics of these appropriations can be gleaned from at least three perspectives: understandings of the dynamics of art in an age of mass reproduction, critical conceptualizations of cultural appropriation, and commodification.

Mass Reproduction and Postmodernity

Walter Benjamin's (1989 [1936]) classic essay "The Work of Art in the Age of Mechanical Reproduction" explores what happens to works of art when they enter a system of mass reproduction. Benjamin posits that prior to mass reproduction technologies, a work of art possessed an "aura" due to its uniqueness and its meaning was bound to a particular physical context, such as a church or a wealthy merchant's home. This physical context cued certain social and ideological contexts, which in turn limited the possible meanings and social functions of the art. When art is reproduced, it becomes decontextualized, not only spatially but also socially, enabling rearticulations of the art with different ideologies and sociopolitical interests. The political dynamics of art are profoundly changed in an age of mechanical reproduction. The mass reproduction of images enables decontextualization and recontextualization—that is, appropriation—and this makes art political in the sense that its meanings are no longer fixed but become sites of ideological, social, and cultural struggle.

Rock art provides a clear example of Benjamin's (1989 [1936]) argument, though in a radically different context than the European tradition of art of which he wrote. While visitation at rock art sites has increased in recent decades, I think it is safe to say that many more people encounter representations of rock art than encounter rock art unmediated: in its fixed place, its original physical, geographic, and environmental context. While the original rock art images and their locales serve as the referential anchor for the "authenticity" of such reproductions, reproductions of rock art function precisely and directly to sever the tie to that anchor. Photographs, drawings, paintings, and other reproductions of rock art images directly facilitate the resignification of rock art imagery not only within the larger contexts of Anglo-American and Western cultures, but within specific contexts such as tourism, the arts market, evolutionary theory, archaeology, ufology, primitivism, and New Age spiritualities.

To return to *Koyaanisqatsi*, the Barrier Canyon Style images from the Great Gallery in Horseshoe Canyon, images produced by the hunter-gatherers who occupied what is now southern Utah, have been decontextualized—removed from their geographic and cultural settings—and recontextualized within a film designed to critique Western lifeways and idealize non-Western, preindustrial cultures. In the film, these images represent a primitivist abstraction, not the specific culture(s) that produced the images. The images are deployed to advance a particular kind of modern, Western environmentalist argument, something that is almost certainly alien to the belief systems, ideologies, and cosmologies within which the images were originally deployed. The connections between these images and the living indigenous cultures in the Southwest are tenuous, reducing the potential negative implications of particular groups having their cultural heritage decontextualized and recontextualized outside of their control. However, the implications of mass reproduction extend to rock art that is more directly tied to living cultures, such as the decontextualized reproduction of flute player images labeled as "Kokopelli" that are connected not only to Puebloans as a whole but to specific groups with particular ties to such imagery, such as the Hopi Flute clan (see chapter 5).

Benjamin (1989 [1936]) wrote at a time of great advancements in the mechanical reproduction of images. Subsequently, we have moved into an electronic/digital era, further enabling the reproduction, mass dissemination, and widespread resignification of rock art imagery in diverse contexts. No longer is it necessary to obtain a copy of an expensive coffee-table book or attend an exhibit of photographs to peruse rock art from a distance; the internet not only makes viewing reproductions of rock art much easier, facilitating exposure to a much larger number of more diverse images, it also enables individuals with a digital camera, a computer, and an internet connection to disseminate reproductions without the constraints and costs of producing, marketing, distributing, and selling a book or creating a museum-grade collection of images. Individuals with no knowledge or even awareness of rock art can discover images online that they can reproduce in artistic and commercial works, further distancing the reproduction and reception of rock art imagery from its originating contexts (cf. Nicholas and Wylie 2012).

Benjamin's (1989 [1936]) work, despite its mechanical as opposed to digital frame, presaged a key condition of postmodernity: the endless circulation and recirculation of images that obscures any sense of "reality," "authenticity," or the "original" (see, e.g., Baudrillard 1983). Images multiply and fragment, and so do meanings, identities, and cultures. Indeed, images themselves are hybridized, created through the sometimes bizarre juxtaposition of multiple styles or cultures, or through pastiche, the cannibalization of styles for no particular end other than their endless reproduction and the erasure of genuine cultural and historical content (Jameson 1991). While some embrace the liberatory potentials of the free play of meanings and identities, celebrating the loss of a fixed anchor, others bemoan the loss of fixed foundations as the cause of civilization's decline and individuals' experiences of anomie and alienation (Kaplan 1988). Regardless, in the age of the mass spectacle, with many people interacting mainly with human fabrications and representations, representations come to be the de facto "reality" that grounds our social and psychological experiences and perceptions (Debord 1983).

The authenticity of living Native Americans, for example, may be judged by comparison to Hollywood films and Edward Curtis's

photographs of Indians. As Donald Trump said in testimony before
the US Congress in 1993, opposing the development of the Foxwoods
Casino by the Mashantucket Pequots under the Indian Gaming Regulatory Act, "They don't look like Indians to me, and they don't look like
Indians to Indians" (Cockburn 1993). This statement is an apparently
unreflective invocation of the contents of white (Hollywood, Curtis)
stereotypes of Indians as legitimate standards for determining the
authenticity of identity claims by living Native peoples, as well as of
the primitivist/salvage definition of authenticity: "Real" Indians must
look, act, and think like the "prehistoric" Indians of the Western imagination, and any degree of assimilation or intermixing with non-Native
groups signals the inauthenticity of their cultures and identity claims.
This is despite the irony that the very standards of authenticity being
deployed are themselves little more than pastiche: multiple, contradictory, abstract, ahistorical constructions, not of, by, or about the culture
being represented, but of a postmodern aesthetic, a culture of endless
images and the commodities marked by such images.

Amidst the dizzying array of representations and the felt normless-
ness that characterizes (post)modernity, primitivism becomes central,
as the very systems of representations that feed a sense of unreality
produce images embodying what is presumed to have been lost: sin-
gularity, stability, identity, purity, authenticity, and reality. Both the
Southwest and Indians are antidotes to (post)modernity, even though
these are also representations created by the very system that feeds a
sense of dis-ease. Following Benjamin (1989 [1936]), and consistent
with some of the more interesting conceptualizations of the nature
of postmodernity, mechanical and digital reproduction does two key
things: destroys the conditions of possibility for "authenticity"—pure,
singular, stable—while simultaneously creating the very conditions—
multiplicity, hybridity, unanchored, and contradictory—under which
"authenticity" becomes appealing.

Cultural Appropriation

Cultural appropriation, defined broadly as the use of one culture's
symbols, artifacts, genres, styles, rituals, or technologies by members
of another culture, is inescapable when cultures come into contact,
including virtual/representational contact (Rogers 2006). Cultural
appropriation is also inescapably intertwined with cultural politics.
Critical scholars in a variety of disciplines have explored its involvement

in the assimilation and exploitation of marginalized and colonized cultures, as well as in the survival of subordinated cultures and resistance to dominant cultures (e.g., Brunk and Young 2012; Churchill 1994; Deloria 1998; Goodwin and Gore 1990; Huhndorf 2001; Kadish 2004; Nicholas and Wylie 2012; Ono and Buescher 2001; Rogers 2006; Shugart 1997; Torgovnick 1996; Wallis and Malm 1984; Walsh and Lopes 2012; Whitt 1995; Ziff and Rao 1997).

Merriam-Webster offers two definitions of the verb "appropriate" relevant to the use of the term by critical scholars: "to take exclusive possession of" and "to take or make use of without authority or right." "Appropriation" is derived from the Latin *appropriare*, meaning "to make one's own," from the Latin root *proprius*, meaning "own," also the root of "property." These meanings parallel the use of the term in legal contexts, strengthening the connotation of an unfair or unauthorized taking (theft). For example, in response to controversies over the use of elements of First Nations cultures by non-Natives, the Writer's Union of Canada defined cultural appropriation as "the taking—from a culture that is not one's own—of intellectual property, cultural expressions or artifacts, history and ways of knowledge" (as cited in Ziff and Rao 1997:1; see also Young and Brunk 2012). As Helene Shugart (1997:210–211) states in the context of rhetorical acts of appropriation,

Appropriation refers to any instance in which means commonly associated with and/or perceived as belonging to another are used to further one's own ends. Any instance in which a group borrows or imitates the strategies of another—even when the tactic is not intended to deconstruct or distort the other's meanings and experiences—thus would constitute appropriation.

I use a broad sense of appropriation as the use of elements of one culture by members of another culture—regardless of intent, ethics, function, or outcome. I do not limit cultural appropriation to instances where those engaged in appropriation do so "to further [their] own ends" or in a way that necessarily serves their own interests. Cultural appropriation, however, is an *active* process and in this sense retains the meaning of a "taking." Mere exposure, for example, to the music or film of another culture does not constitute cultural appropriation. The active "making one's own" of another culture's elements occurs, however, in various ways, under a variety of conditions, and with varying functions and outcomes. The degree and scope of voluntariness (individually or culturally), the symmetry or asymmetry of power relations, the appropriation's role in domination and/or resistance, the nature of the cultural boundaries involved, and other factors differentiate acts of cultural appropriation (see, e.g., Walsh and Lopes 2012).

Acts of appropriation and their implications are not determined by the intent or awareness of those engaged in such acts but are instead shaped by, and in turn shape, the historical, social, economic, and political contexts in which they occur. In John Fiske's (1991a) terms, all acts of communication are socially positioned: Communicative relations are always social relations, and hence political relations. Acts of communication, including cultural appropriation, both reflect and constitute the identities of the individuals and groups involved as well as their sociopolitical positions. Socially positioned subjects engage in acts of appropriation for a variety of reasons and with a variety of understandings concerning the implications and ethics of such acts. These intentions, motivations, and interpretations are part of the system in which such acts occur, and can serve to reinforce, modify, cope with, or actively resist that larger system.

In the context of rock art studies, the particular form of cultural appropriation that is of greatest concern is what I term cultural exploitation (Rogers 2006), the form of appropriation that is seen as an illegitimate taking, a type of theft (Young and Brunk 2012). Cultural exploitation involves the use of elements of a subordinated culture by a dominant culture without substantive reciprocity, compensation, permission, or concern for the interests of the appropriated culture. Cultural exploitation focuses on the commodification and incorporation of elements of subordinated cultures in ways that further the interests of the dominant by perpetuating the objectification and redefinition of the subordinate culture.

Cultural exploitation commonly involves the appropriation of elements of a subordinated culture by a dominant culture in which the subordinated culture is treated as a resource to be "mined" and "shipped home" for consumption, as in the use of indigenous folk music by Western musicians and companies without financial compensation (Wallis and Malm 1984; Goodwin and Gore 1990). Cultural exploitation includes appropriative acts that appear to indicate acceptance or positive evaluation of a colonized culture by a colonizing culture, but which nevertheless function to establish and reinforce the dominance of the colonizing culture, especially in the context of neocolonialism (Buescher and Ono 1996). Whereas colonialism can be understood in terms of the exploitation of natural resources and the necessary acts of genocide, removal, or assimilation that accompany such exploitations, neocolonialism can be understood in part by the treatment of colonized *cultures* as resources in and of themselves. These instances often carry the connotation of stealing or in some way using the culture of a subordinated group against them. Studies of appropriations of Native American cultures are especially prominent in this regard, due in large part to the enormously disproportionate presence of appropriations of Native American cultures in Anglo-America, such as "Indian" mascots for sports teams, New Age appropriations of Native spirituality, the use of Native American symbolism by the Boy Scouts and other groups, the widespread use of Native American symbols in advertising and marketing, archaeological appropriations, and non-Natives claiming Native American identity and/or ancestry (e.g., Black 2002; Brunk and Young 2012; Buescher and Ono 1996; Churchill 1994; Deloria 1998; Huhndorf 2001; Kadish 2004; Nicholas and Wylie 2012; Ono and Buescher 2001; Torgovnick 1996; Whitt 1995).

Bruce Ziff and Pratima Rao (1997) identify four concerns expressed about acts of cultural exploitation (which they call appropriation), concerns mirrored by many other authors on the subject (e.g., Churchill 1994; Brunk and Young 2012). The first is cultural degradation. Exploitative appropriations "can have corrosive effects on the integrity of an exploited culture because the appropriative conduct can erroneously depict the heritage from which it is drawn"; insofar as the depiction of the exploited culture is distorted, "tears can appear in the fabric of a group's cultural identity" (Ziff and Rao 1997:9). In the case of the appropriation of Native American culture by the New Age commodity machine, for example, one concern is that non-Natives (some of whom claim to be "real Indians") claim authority to define what Native Americans really are, distorting not only non-Native but also Native understandings of Native American cultures (Churchill 1994; Whitt 1995). Appropriations are not one-way, especially in colonial and neocolonial contexts, where the dominant culture's appropriative distortions of subordinate cultures can feed back into the originating culture, distorting those culture's own perceptions of their culture and history, assisting with the colonization of the consciousness of subordinated groups by the symbolic constructs of the dominant.

The second concern identified by Ziff and Rao (1997) is the preservation of cultural elements. Arguments against cultural exploitation on the grounds of cultural preservation claim that cultural objects, symbols, and practices are best understood in their native contexts and that the priority should be preservation of the integrity of marginalized cultures. This raises concerns over not only the physical removal of cultural objects (e.g., to museums), but debilitating effects on the culture being appropriated, such as the disrespect for and inevitable distortion of Native spiritual traditions enacted by (perhaps unknowing) New Age producers and consumers and, more broadly, a "cultural smorgasbord" approach to other cultures fostered by possessive individualism and commodification (Churchill 1994).

A third concern about cultural exploitation is deprivation of material advantage. Cultural products, either of past or living cultures, are "wrongfully exploited for financial gain" (Ziff and Rao 1997:14). Here we enter a set of legal issues both nationally and internationally, in which intellectual property, a Western concept, mediates competing claims of ownership. Copyright laws favor individual ownership over collective ownership (Hampson 2013) such that "traditional" cultural forms are placed in the public domain (Wallis and Malm 1984; Whitt 1995). For example, Kokopelli imagery, based on variations of flute player imagery from indigenous petroglyphs and other visual media of the precontact Southwest, is widely used by non-Natives without compensation to living groups due to its presumed legal status as part of the public domain. While the Indian Arts and Crafts Act (IACA) of 1990 prohibits falsely suggesting an item is Indian produced, an Indian product, or the product of a particular Indian, Indian tribe, or Indian arts and crafts organization (Indian Arts and Crafts Board 2015), it does not prevent the wholesale appropriation of Native American cultural elements, including rock art imagery. Its stated goal is consumer protection through guaranteeing truth in advertising, which seems to indicate an intent to protect the largely non-Native consumers of such items, although it also expands "the protection of Native American arts and crafts by encouraging tribes to register their trademarks [e.g., tribal names] and by assisting Native American artists to market their works" (Guest 1995/1996:115). While NAGPRA offers some control over the traditional cultural property of tribes, the IACA is limited to items produced after 1935 (Indian Arts and Crafts Board 2015) and is grounded in intellectual property rights, which "are driven by the economics of free enterprise and profit" and are understood in secular, individualist terms (Guest 1995/1996:115).

Intellectual property laws have nonetheless enabled specific legal actions by some Native American tribes. Zia Pueblo has demanded compensation from the state of New Mexico for the use of its Zia sun symbol on the state's flag (Brown 1998; Nicholas and Wylie 2012). Some companies that use the Zia sun symbol, such as Southwest Airlines, have donated to a fund for tribal members pursuing a college education as compensation for their use of the symbol (Upton 2005), and the New Mexico Senate requested a report from the Department of Cultural Affairs on the rights and restrictions associated with the symbol's use (*Santa Fe New Mexican* 2014). In Canada, the Snuneymuxw First Nation has trademarked ten petroglyphs, making them off-limits for reproduction by outsiders (Associated Press 2000). While these recent events are significant, currently few Native American/First Nations cultural elements enjoy substantial legal protections (Nicholas and Wylie 2012). Indeed, in the case of the Zia sun symbol, the New Mexico Department of Cultural Affairs' (2014:3) report unequivocally concluded that, in purely legal terms, "no person, business, government, or tribe is prohibited from using the symbol" and that no person or entity (including the Zia) can trademark the symbol due to its use in the official state flag. The report suggests that "non-legal mechanisms such as education, political lobbying, and informal negotiation" may help to limit the commercial use of the symbol (New Mexico Department of Cultural Affairs 2014:6).

Closely related to issues of material compensation and intellectual property rights is the fourth concern over cultural exploitation identified by Ziff and Rao (1997): the failure to recognize sovereign claims. While Western legal systems and concepts of ownership support the widespread appropriation of elements of traditional cultures without remuneration, they also often prevent traditional cultures from blocking what they perceive as inappropriate uses or adaptations. In the case of Kokopelli imagery, the cultures affiliated with these images have no formal authority over their use and adaptation. Bruce Springsteen may have had the economic resources, cultural capital, and legal standing to impede the Republican Party's appropriation of "Born in the USA," but the indigenous cultures of the Southwest that claim affiliations with flute player imagery do not have comparable control over the use of their cultural heritage due to imbalanced access to resources and the appropriating culture's establishment of the rules. Indeed, economic survival, the dynamics of tourism, and the market for Native American arts and crafts may push Native peoples to participate in the alteration and commodification of that very heritage, either their own or that of other tribes, as is the case with kachina dolls (Guest 1995/1996) and the images labeled Kokopelli (see chapter 5).

The concerns expressed by Ziff and Rao (1997) are centered, appropriately, on the direct effects on the indigenous cultures whose elements are being appropriated. Laurie Ann Whitt (1995), however, also focuses on the ideological effects on those who engage in well-intentioned appropriations of indigenous cultures, specifically the diversionary function of such acts. Such acts not only trivialize and distort elements of importance to colonized cultures, they also advance hegemony, in this case by enabling the consent of well-intended people immersed in the ideology of primitivism (Whitt 1995). The superficial appreciation of Native cultures, akin to what Stanley Fish (1998) describes as "boutique multiculturalism," obscures people's comprehension of their own participation in the ongoing subordination and exploitation of indigenous peoples by treating them as a resource. This is a key function of imperialist nostalgia (Rosaldo 1989); as David Lewis-Williams puts it in the context of the reproduction of South African rock art imagery on t-shirts and coffee mugs, "Genocide is masked by a gloss of fun" (Lewis-Williams 1995:321). Indeed, such a gloss is a core outcome of the process of commodifying cultural elements such as rock art.

Commodification

Commodification (or commoditization) is often used in nonscholarly (and some scholarly) accounts as if it is limited to the transformation of an object, person, or idea into something to be bought, owned, and sold. This view limits the implications of commodification to issues of sacrilege (e.g., the commodification of sacred rituals, images, and objects) and appropriate permission and compensation, missing many cultural implications of commodification. In the conditions of capitalism, any object that enters the exchange system is inescapably commodified. Commodification abstracts the value of an object (or form, idea, person, culture, etc.) so it can enter systems of exchange. In this process, the use-value and the specificity of the labor and social relations invested in the original object are lost; it becomes equivalent to all other commodities (Marx 1986). To create the appearance of difference (and hence value) amidst this equivalence, additional meanings are attached to the commodity, such as through product design, packaging, marketing, and advertising.

Building from the anthropological concept of a fetish as an inanimate object believed to be imbued with great power (e.g., spirits or deities), when a thing becomes a commodity it becomes a fetish. Imbued with presumably life-transforming powers, commodities function to represent meanings, values, and identities with no intrinsic relation to the object's use-value, production, and circulation (and the social relations involved therein). These meanings are the (illusory) ends to which the commodity itself becomes the means of attainment. These meanings are reifications; their artificiality must be obscured, forgotten, collapsed into the object. This both enhances the illusion of the commodity's seemingly intrinsic (fetishized) value and serves to obscure the social relations involved in its production and consumption. By concealing the product's real origins behind its commodified meanings, consumers are not faced with an awareness of their participation in the exploitation of others' labor, homeland, culture, and identity (Ono and Buescher 2001; Whitt 1995). In the context of cultural exploitation, cultural elements are radically decontextualized, with their commodified meanings functioning to obfuscate their real origins and implications even while framing their commodified and fetishized meanings as "authentic." Commodification is accelerated and centralized in the conditions of postmodernity (late or commodity capitalism), in which, in a fundamental cultural sense, images replace material realities while the search for authenticity is furthered by the ubiquity of representations, replicas, and spectacles grounded in pastiche.

Commodification articulates powerfully with neocolonialism. In colonialism, the labor and homelands of colonized peoples provided the material foundation for the production and circulation of commodities, primarily for consumption by the colonizers. In neocolonialism, the culture of the colonized becomes a focus of commodification. These neocolonialist appropriations are based on the belief that they positively value the culture of the colonized. The commodified meanings attached to the cultural forms of the colonized provide those who consume these commodities with an affirmation of their appreciation and respect for the "formerly" colonized cultures. This affirmation functions hegemonically by cultivating the consent of the "former" colonizers, as their consumption of the commodified Other obscures their consent to, even active participation in, ongoing colonialist relationships as well as awareness of the ongoing effects of historic systems of colonization.

The commodification of rock art and the exercise of pastiche is represented on a t-shirt I purchased in my home town, Flagstaff, Arizona (see Figure 3.1). Sold in a tourist gift shop, the shirt features a colored rendition of five anthropomorphs with internal decoration, headdresses, and other elaborations. Below the composite image is the word "Flagstaff." I immediately recognized the petroglyphs that directly provided the anthropomorphic images, sans color: They are very well-known (at least in rock art circles) "shamans" from the Coso Range in southeastern California, associated with the cultural Great Basin. These images have been widely reproduced in coffee-table books, postcards, and the like. Geographically, regionally, culturally, and stylistically these images have, at most, tenuous connections with the Flagstaff area. Not only are they over three hundred miles from Flagstaff, their more likely cultural affiliations are with the Great Basin, not the Colorado Plateau, and with Numic peoples, not ancestral Puebloans. The rock art in the immediate vicinity of Flagstaff has not been particularly visible in the Southwest imaginary or the tourist consciousness, with its precontact culture, called the Sinagua by archaeologists, occupying a mere footnote (if that) in most discussions of precontact Southwest cultures, overshadowed by the "Anasazi" and even the relatively obscure (in the public consciousness) Mogollon and Hohokam. These images from the Coso Range have been pulled from their geographic and cultural homes and inserted into the tourist culture of the Southwest, specifically Flagstaff. Their abstracted meanings—of Indianness, of the Southwest, of a primitivist aesthetic, of indigenous imagery, ritual, and cosmology—provide a fetishized value to the commodity known as "Flagstaff," a souvenir of a visit, a token to take home. In so doing, they obscure both the pre- and postcontact cultural heritage, both of what we now call Flagstaff, and of the rock art of the Coso Range and its affiliated cultures.

Commodification, by abstracting the value of a cultural element, necessarily removes that element from its originating context, changing its meaning and function, and raising concerns about cultural degradation. Commodification also plays a key role in perpetuating unequal systems and relations of power, such as neocolonialism. In fetishizing and reifying "artificial" (alien and colonizing) meanings onto the

FIGURE 3.1—This souvenir t-shirt features petroglyph images not from north-central Arizona, but from the Coso Range in southeastern California, over three hundred miles from Flagstaff. T-shirt graphic copyright Dreamcatchers.

elements of living cultures, the social relations and history involved in that act of commodification are obscured and neocolonial relations are justified. Ultimately, many acts of appropriation, even when carried out under the banner of "honorable motives" such as cultural preservation, expression of admiration, and cross-cultural understanding, function to undermine the cultures being appropriated and serve the interests of the dominant. Commodification is therefore a key element in the hegemonic strategy of incorporation, in which an alternative or oppositional practice is redefined by the dominant culture in order to remove any genuinely oppositional meaning or function (Fiske 1989, 1990). Those appropriating Native American cultural elements may believe they are opposing the very system they are supporting through their consumption and circulation of commodities, potentially degrading the very culture they intend to honor and protect (Churchill 1994). This is directly supported by the infusion of meanings of "authenticity" onto these elements, based less on the originating culture than on the ideology of primitivism that plays a large role in shaping these acts of commodification. The commodification of cultures, in other words, necessitates that the potential for subject-subject relationships be replaced with a structure predicated upon subject-object relationships, in which the appropriated culture is a resource that serves the interests of the appropriators. The definition of authenticity embedded in primitivism effectively shrouds this objectifying relationship in the guise of honoring, respecting, and wanting to learn from the cultures being commodified.

Appropriation generally and commodification specifically involve the abstraction of the meaning and value of an object, as in commodities such as dream catchers, Chief Seattle bumper stickers, and faux eagle-feather headdresses that have come to stand for an abstract concept "Indianness," erasing their specific cultural origins and meanings. The implications of those appropriations for the appropriated cultures are obscured by the object's abstracted meanings, which often take a primitivist slant such as deeply spiritual, naturally environmentalist, and harmonious. Little if anything about the originating culture is learned, and awareness of the effects of such appropriations on those cultures is derailed by the abstraction. The commodity's image displaces its attendant material realities, social relations, and histories.

Appropriations of Rock Art Imagery

The appropriation of rock art imagery is readily evident in tourist and other venues in the greater Southwest and beyond. Rock art symbols are used on signage and as "art" in a variety of media (see Figure 3.2). They serve as official or unofficial logos for regions, municipalities, cultural institutions such as museums and monuments, and a wide range of commercial entities. Photographs, paintings, drawings, and other two-dimensional representations of rock art are reproduced as fine art; in coffee-table books and calendars; and on pottery, postcards, greeting cards, posters, bumper stickers, bandanas, and t-shirts. Rock art images are also reproduced in the form of jewelry, textiles, ironworks, statuary, and stuffed toys, and incorporated into furniture and other household fixtures. Large reproductions of rock art images on freeway structures such as overpasses can be found across the urban Southwest (see Figure 3.3). While images of the hump-backed flute player misnamed "Kokopelli" account for many of these images, they are by no means alone, with various other rock art–inspired anthropomorphs, zoomorphs, and geometric shapes also widely used. From tourist kitsch shops to high-end Native arts galleries, from national parks to small-town museums,

FIGURE 3.2—Rock art images on bathroom door, Puerco Pueblo, Petrified Forest National Park, Arizona.

FIGURE 3.3—Rock art images on freeway support pillars, Las Vegas, Nevada. Across the Southwest, overpasses, interchanges, and other public works are increasingly adorned with rock art imagery.

from private tour companies to tribal casinos, reproductions of rock art imagery are inescapable. Their ubiquity reflects their appeal yet also enforces a sense of banality as they become part of the visual noise that is filtered out once the imagery becomes familiar and predictable.

In Kanab, Utah, the exterior of the Kane County Visitors Center was painted with regional rock art images, as was a gift shop in Castle Dale, Utah (see Plate 5). These images may be targeted at tourists, but they expose many others to these images as well. While rock art imagery is particularly visible in tourist contexts, by no means is it limited to tourist settings. In addition to commercial establishments visible to both tourists and nontourists alike, in west Albuquerque, one can buy a home in Petroglyph Estates and just outside of Phoenix in Gold Canyon, Arizona, one can do the same in Hieroglyphic Trails (see Figure 1.2). For the most part, these appropriations do not involve any consultation, permission, or compensation with affiliated tribes and communities, although key exceptions do exist. The Museum of Northern Arizona (2013), for example, engaged in an active consultation process with regional tribes as part of the design of their new Easton Collection Center, which resulted in a variety of alterations to the design. The exterior of the building includes reproductions of Barrier Canyon Style images, chosen at least in part because of the relative lack of clear affiliations between such imagery and contemporary tribes on the Colorado Plateau.

While many Southwest tourist destinations expose visitors and residents to a large amount of rock art–derived imagery, there is also substantial evidence of people actively seeking out rock art and rock art imagery. In addition to signs of increased visitation at rock art sites (Dean 1998a, 1998b; Gonzalez 1997; Whitley 2011), a variety of regional guidebooks to rock art sites are available (e.g., Barnes 1989; Bicknell 2001, 2009; Farnsworth 2006; Sanders 2005; Slifer 2000a; Welsh and Welsh 2000; Whitley 1996). Another kind of guidebook offers interpretations of common rock art symbols (e.g., Harris 1995; Patterson 1992; Stokes and Stokes 1980; Welsh 1995). Rock art organizations, archaeological societies, and site steward programs are also popular with rock art enthusiasts, at least in part because of the possibilities they offer for visiting sites on field trips and obtaining information about sites so they can visit them on their own (Dickey 2012). While these organizations engage in education and advocacy, and are actively involved in preservation and recording projects, their appeal and function for many, in my view, has much to do with gaining access to rock art sites. Rock art organizations in the United States include the American Rock Art Research Association, the Utah Rock Art Research Association, the Nevada Rock Art Foundation, the Colorado Rock Art Association, the Rock Art Foundation (Texas), and the Bay Area Rock Art Research Association.

An active interest in rock art also manifests itself in the consumer market. Rock art lends itself to certain media formats, such as coffee-table books (oversized books in which images and aesthetics are the primary focus, although substantial and substantive text may be included). In terms of the broader Southwest, these include *Rock Art of the Grand Canyon Region* (Christensen et al. 2013), *Sacred Images: A Vision of Native American Rock Art* (Kelen and Sucec 1996), *The Forgotten Artist: Indians of Anza-Borrego and Their Rock Art* (Knaak 1988), *Tapamveni: The Rock Art Galleries of Petrified Forest and Beyond* (McCreery and Malotki 1994), *The Rock Art of Arizona: Art for Life's Sake* (Malotki 2007), *Stone Chisel and Yucca Brush: Colorado Plateau Rock Art* (Malotki and Weaver 2002), *On the Edge of Magic: Petroglyphs and Rock Paintings of the Ancient Southwest* (Mancini 1996), *Images in Stone* (Muench and Schaafsma 1995), *Traces of Fremont: Society and Rock Art in Ancient Utah* (Simms and Gohier 2010), and *The Art of the Shaman: Rock Art of California* (Whitley 2000a).

While coffee-table books are highly visible in the cultural landscape and may be actively sought out by enthusiasts, other uses of rock art imagery call less attention to themselves, operating as taken-for-granted elements in the symbolic landscape, especially vis-à-vis the Southwest. The University of Utah Press, for example, which publishes books on rock art among other anthropological topics, uses a petroglyph image as the press's colophon: "The Defiance House Man colophon is a registered trademark of the University of Utah Press. It is based upon a four-foot-tall, Ancient Puebloan pictograph (late PIII) near Glen Canyon, Utah" (Simms and Gohier 2010:iv). In addition to presses, individual books that never mention rock art use rock art imagery as part of the books' graphic design. *Testimony*, a collection of statements supporting Utah wilderness preservation compiled by Stephen Trimble and Terry Tempest Williams (1996), utilizes a different rock art image for the first page of each chapter as well as a petroglyph spiral for the book's cover. In this case, rock art imagery cues both the Southwest imaginary and the conflation of precontact indigenous cultures with the Southwest landscape, without any linguistic reference to the rock art images.

Many books that involve the appropriation of rock art imagery are very much about rock art. General readers as well as rock art enthusiasts have ready access to a wide variety of publications. These include LaVan Martineau's (1973) often-derided but still popular *The Rocks Begin to Speak* as well as various regional surveys of rock art (Castleton 1984, 1987; Cole 1990; Grant 1967; Hurst and Pachak 1989; Keyser and Klassen 2001; Moore 1998; Schaafsma 1971, 1980; Slifer 2000b; Stokes and Stokes 1980), surveys of the rock art of particular places (Bostwick and Krocek 2002; Grant 1968, 1978; Zoll 2008a), books on flute players and Kokopelli (Cheeks 2004; Glover 1995; Malotki 2000; Slifer 2007; Slifer and Duffield 1994; Walker 1998; Young 1990), and self-published avocational research (e.g., Norman 2007; Petry 2013; Zoll 2008b). Several novels, some self-published, also incorporate rock art into their storylines (Coel 2007; Ensenbach 2012; Jarrard 2012; Munro 2010; Sublette 2013).

Importantly, along with the above works, all of the more technical, specialized, or narrowly academic publications about rock art (including this book) are themselves acts of appropriation, de- and recontextualizing rock art imagery in diverse ways. Credentialed and institutionally based researchers necessarily and unavoidably engage in the appropriation of rock art imagery—not only through photographs, drawings, and verbal descriptions (Welsh 1999), but also in terms of the subjugation of the imagery and its indigenous meanings, functions, and cultural affiliations to whatever the research agenda may be: advancing or critiquing interpretive hypotheses, assessing conservation methods, defining rock art styles, or examining rock art as part of cultural landscapes. In addition, the activities of many rock art organizations—organizations whose missions are centered on the protection of rock art—are directly involved in the appropriation of rock art; enhance the appropriative possibilities available to others, be they researchers, artists, or enthusiasts; and, by circulating site information, increase the risks of site degradation, vandalism, and theft (Dickey 2012; Quinlan 2007a; Schaafsma 2013).

Quinlan (2007a) makes an uncommon argument about rock art researchers' role in enabling as well as enacting the commodification of rock art, though he does so in the context of criticizing others, specifically those who promote shamanism and other religious explanations.

His thesis is that "academic study of rock art helps create the conditions necessary for the commodification (or wider circulation) of rock art imagery by giving it a social and cultural resonance for Western publics who are culturally unrelated to it" (Quinlan 2007a:140). Quinlan argues that both research in general and the bias toward religious interpretations are culpable in the commodification of rock art. Rock art research in general not only makes rock art imagery more accessible for commercial exploitation, as well as more vulnerable to degradation and vandalism, but commodifies rock art by using it to enhance researchers' academic capital. In addition, magico-religious explanations such as shamanism work specifically to enhance rock art's appeal via primitivism and feed concerns about commodification, because if rock art is sacred then it is even more inappropriate to commodify it.

When examining the visibility of rock art in the contemporary cultural landscape as well as the appropriation of rock art imagery, the Internet is central. With the advent of affordable, portable digital cameras and the explosion of the World Wide Web, individuals and organizations began electronically publishing large collections of rock art images, available to anyone with an Internet connection and a computer, tablet, or smart phone. Such websites are too numerous to view, let alone catalog or list. Examples of such online galleries from individuals include those of Don Austin (2013), Carl Bjork (2013), Bob Forsyth (2015), and Doak Heyser (2015). Commercial entities such as archaeological contract firms and not-for-profit rock art organizations displaying rock art galleries include Greer Services (2015), the Nevada Rock Art Foundation (2014), Rupestrian CyberServices (2015a), and Western Rock Art Research (2010). Advances in digital imagery have enabled incredibly complex and detailed documentation, aesthetic presentation, and interpretation of rock art sites, as with Rupestrian CyberServices's (2015b) panoramas and mosaics and, to depart from my focus on the United States, the French Ministry of Culture's online tour of Lascaux Cave (Aujoulot 2014). Social media sites, such as Facebook and flickr, offer additional venues for distributing rock art images, further enabling their appropriation. YouTube has opened the possibilities of sharing audio-visual representations of rock art, such as the numerous videos offering "translations" of the "Prophecy Rock" petroglyph panel by individuals portrayed as Hopi elders, edited and framed to support a variety of often questionable interpretations of the panel and Hopi worldviews (see Geertz [1994] and Schaafsma [2013] for extended discussions of Prophecy Rock). My point is not that the openness of the web is inherently bad, but among the many things the web enables is appropriation of imagery, including rock art.

Collecting

The widespread presence of photographic galleries of rock art on the internet points to something fundamental to understanding the appropriation of rock art imagery as well as the culture of rock art enthusiasts: collecting. Rock art enthusiasts "collect" rock art sites by visiting them and, perhaps even more importantly, photographing them (Schaafsma 2013). Conference field trips and other organized visits to rock art sites often include obsessive, and sometimes rude or intrusive, efforts to photograph the sites (Dickey 2012).

Personally, I have had to work hard to untrain myself of the habit of entering a rock art site with my camera at the ready, photographing before really taking in the site, not only visually, but through all the senses. I still, however, thoroughly photograph the site, and will sometimes return later when the light or other conditions impedes my efforts at both documentation and aesthetic reproduction. Later, I download the photographs to my computer and catalog them into a digital asset management system. The resulting database of over ten thousand images is organized by locale and searchable via verbal descriptions of the sites and imagery. Collected over fifteen or so years (since I have had high-quality digital cameras), I imagine my collection of rock art images is actually modest compared to many.

Photography becomes a means of collecting something that cannot be literally taken home, of documenting visits to sites, of sharing them with others, and of constituting the identity of rock art enthusiast. Enthusiasts read guidebooks, scour the internet and research reports for clues as to the locations of new rock art sites, and often exhibit a high level of selectivity in sharing site locations with others. When site locations are shared, the information functions as a kind of currency, constituting either trade or a trusted relationship with another insider. Having visited sites and knowing site locations are central forms of cultural capital in the rock art world, and photographing, videoing, and GPSing sites are the physical manifestations of that capital (Schaafsma 2013). Not surprisingly, therefore, guidebooks and websites offering directions to rock art sites have been frequently criticized for publicizing site locales (Gonzalez 1997; Marymor 1999–2000). While such criticisms and policing are justified by the legitimate goal of protecting rock art sites from degradation and vandalism, such actions are also the product of the rock art economy, in which site locations are the most valued form of capital.

The ideological dynamics of collecting are complex and multifaceted, especially in the contexts of commodity capitalism, postmodernity, and neocolonialism (Belk 1995; Clifford 1988; Stewart 1984). Collecting often manifests a longing, a nostalgia for times past (Stewart 1984), consistent with the ideology of primitivism (Clifford 1988). The collected objects—in this case, rock art sites and images—become fetishes, commodities that manifest the longings of their collectors, fantasies and desires that are products of their material conditions, ideological orientations, and attendant structures of desire (Stewart 1984). Collecting not only becomes a form of cultural capital, evidencing the accrual of value and status, but a compensatory act. Collecting is a communicative and appropriative act through which identities are constituted and fundamental contradictions are managed. A white, female, middle-class engineer visits rock art sites, photographs them, and offers reproductions on her living room wall. In so doing, she may be manifesting her affinity with indigenous peoples and their presumed cosmologies, or marveling at their ingenuity and artistry, thereby compensating for felt lacks in her own life, be it through imagining the brute materiality of their relationship with nature, their spirituality, or their alien imaginations. The collection becomes a means to manifest, for oneself and/or for others, one's desired identity and values. At a cultural level, collecting as a constitutive act works to manage ultimately unresolvable ideological/material contradictions, temporarily smoothing over profound tensions between rural and urban, tradition and progress, individualism and community, spirituality and secularism.

Grappling with the Commodification of Rock Art

Although the commodification of rock art is frequently condemned in the literature, there have been relatively few efforts to systematically engage the issues involved in the appropriation and specifically the commodification of rock art. While many rock art publications devote a few sentences or paragraphs to bemoaning (or, in some cases, defending) commercial appropriations, in this section I review those works that engage the subject in greater depth (Dowson 1999; Heyd 2003; Lewis-Williams 1995; Quinlan 2007a; Schaafsma 2013; Welsh 1999). I include two essays on appropriations of rock art in southern African contexts (Dowson 1999; Lewis-Williams 1995), both because of the similar issues involved between the United States and southern Africa, and because those essays, along with many of the others discussed below, form the canon of rock art commodification literature that US rock art researchers in particular cite when discussing the issue. Of course, the issues addressed in this literature are by no means distinct to only the United States, as they are particularly potent in contexts where both the colonizing and colonized cultures exist in overlapping physical, social, economic, and political regions (e.g., Australia, Canada, and South Africa; see Hampson [2013] and Smith [2016]).

Lewis-Williams (1995), writing from the context of South Africa, situates the commercial and artistic appropriation of rock art imagery amidst its visuality, enhancing the illusion that it offers a "window into the past." Articulated with and by primitivism, this past often becomes an idyllic, Edenic one, a contrast to and compensation for the industrialized present. Lewis-Williams (1995:319) defines appropriation broadly, however, and without the automatic implication of theft or exploitation: "the ways in which designers, advertisers, business people, artists and the media use rock art motifs in their work, thus recontextualizing and redefining them." Outlining his approach to appropriation, he clarifies that "the social and economic status of the community whose products are appropriated is all-important" (Lewis-Williams 1995:319). In other words, and consistent with the approach to cultural appropriation outlined above, power relations are central to understanding the dynamics of appropriation. Lewis-Williams also divides acts of appropriation into two categories, commercial and artistic, indicating that the context, including who is doing the appropriating, in what ways, and for what purposes, also affects the positive or negative assessment of appropriations.

Lewis-Williams (1995) articulates the fairly conventional view that commercial appropriations of rock art, such as mugs and t-shirts with rock art images, trivialize and devalue the art, reducing it to a source of fun and amusement, and thereby diverting attention away from the past and present realities of the peoples whose cultural heritage the rock art was and is. Such appropriations secularize the sacred. Contemporary artists, however, especially indigenous artists or those advocating for indigenous peoples, can gain inspiration from rock art and use the imagery to empower indigenous peoples by reinterpreting the past into their present realities (Lewis-Williams 1995). Overall, Lewis-Williams's concerns about commercial appropriations of rock art mirror those advanced in the context of other exploitative appropriations, especially of colonized cultures (e.g., Churchill 1994; Whitt 1995).

Thomas Dowson (1999) also writes from a southern African context, and focuses on the "decorative purposes" to which rock art imagery is put. Dowson's (1999:4) concerns about reproductions of rock art are clearly focused: "The most striking and obvious issue concerning this contemporary use of rock art is . . . the accuracy of the reproduced image." He outlines three concerns about the accuracy of reproductions of rock art. First, the visual reproduction of images should be accurate representations of those images. However, many commercial appropriations are not direct reproductions of specific, actual rock art images. In addition, Dowson highlights that there is always some loss in any reproduction: A meticulous, highly accurate line drawing of a pictograph, for example, still involves a loss of color and the rock's texture, not to mention the landscape setting. The standard becomes, therefore, the sensitivity and faithfulness with which the image is reproduced. Second, Dowson addresses the ways in which the selection of images for reproduction can create distorted perceptions and feed stereotypes of "primitive" peoples, such as an overemphasis on hunting scenes from an entire corpus of rock art. Third, the placement and use of commercial reproductions often separates the rock art images from "real" (Western) art, their very ubiquity and banality devaluing them in comparison to works hung in galleries and museums. Following Lewis-Williams (1995), Dowson is also concerned with the ways in which contemporary artists and others can use reproductions of rock art to challenge stereotypes and hierarchies. He concludes that rock art imagery in art can "have a power to transform and re-negotiate popular perceptions, not only about so-called 'primitive art,' but also the past—which itself is constituted in the present" (Dowson 1999:13).

Both Lewis-Williams (1995) and Dowson (1999) work to identify the negative outcomes of appropriations, especially commercial ones, and use the problematic commercial/art distinction to identify the ways in which contemporary reproductions can operate in negative and positive ways vis-à-vis contemporary indigenous peoples. Ultimately, their position is that appropriations and reproductions of rock art imagery can be put to positive or negative purposes. Crucially, however, the evaluation of acts of appropriation is not made on the basis of the intention of producers and consumers of rock art imagery, but contextually, with attention to the power dynamics involved and the implications for indigenous peoples.

Shifting to the US context, Peter Welsh (1999:31) explores rock art's commodification, "the encompassing term usually used to describe the inappropriate economic use of sites and images." Welsh approaches commodities not as objects with inherent value; their value is constructed through social relations. Rock art is a form of cultural property; while some indigenous groups may see a body of rock art as their cultural property, implying some level of exclusivity, archaeologists and other outsiders may see it as universal cultural property, belonging to all of humanity. This claim to rock art's universal status functions as a basis for researchers to obtain exclusive control over sites (Welsh 1999). Crucially, adopting a broader view of commodification leads Welsh to see both commercial appropriations and the use of rock art in research as forms of commodification, in which the value of something is constituted through social relations, not originating from inherent properties.

Rock art's status as cultural property, whether as something significant to specific, affiliated cultures or as something that belongs to all of humanity (and hence under the control of archaeologists), makes its status as a commodity especially problematic. While the conventional use of commodification refers to the assigning of economic value and its role in economic exchange, Welsh (1999:34) argues that cultural property has a particular commodity status, "one that resists the potential to acquire economic value." Both indigenous cultures whose heritage is commodified and archaeologists and other researchers often decry the commercialization of rock art imagery; even though each may define rock art's status as cultural property differently (as affiliated or universal), both see the placement of rock art in systems of economic exchange as a form of degradation. Either way, the decontextualization of sacred designs and their commercial recontextualization is a clear ethical violation.

For Welsh (1999), however, following his broader understanding of commodification, the issue is not limited to economics. The use of rock art imagery in commercial contexts is unfortunately inevitable. The question shifts to the social relations that constitute things as commodities: "who is in control of, and who will benefit from, activities that involve rock art images and sites" (Welsh 1999:36). Rock art is cultural property, but whose cultural property, who determines that, and who is in control of the rock art as a result? In Welsh's view, the issues around the appropriation of rock art are far broader than those involved with cheap commercial kitsch, and extend to rock art researchers, land managers, artists, and indigenous communities.

In a US context, Angus Quinlan (2007a) applies Dowson's (1999) concerns about the accuracy of reproduced images, both the accuracy of specific reproductions and the ideological biases involved in the selection of images to be reproduced. Following common usage, Quinlan (2007a:145) characterizes commodification as the broad distribution and "economic valuation" of rock art images, but reserves his strongest critique for rock art researchers. Researchers, while decrying commercial appropriations, turn rock art into a form of academic capital. They directly promote commercial appropriations by making reproductions available and by interpreting rock art in magico-religious terms, feeding into the primitivist biases of Westerners in general and the New Age movement in particular. Holding that there is no a priori reason to assume that all rock art is religious in nature, Quinlan points out the paradox that such interpretations feed commercial appropriations, while at the same time their characterization of rock art as sacred is a primary reason for being disturbed by its commercial use.

Ultimately, Quinlan (2007a:149) dismisses the relative significance of commodification of rock art: "Complaining about the public uses of rock art imagery seems a trivial activity when sites are being destroyed through looting, unsupervised public access, and professional poor practice." This perspective, however, seems problematic when placed in the light of Welsh's (1999) arguments about the role of rock art as a form of cultural property affiliated with specific groups, for whom it forms an essential part of their cultural heritage and identity. That is, for these groups, the appropriation and commodification of rock art imagery—its decontextualization and recontextualization by the dominant culture—could pose as much of a threat to cultural continuity, identity, and sovereignty as the destruction of sites themselves. Quinlan's emphasis on preserving sites, while framed in terms of the interests of both archaeologists and traditional peoples, seems more focused on the material resource itself, the container of information about the past, rather than the rock art and its meanings in the context of living cultures—which involves not only the material resource but also its ideational, symbolic, and relational dimensions, including the ways in which rock art has been reproduced, circulated, and interpreted by the dominant culture. In Quinlan's framework, rock art continues to be a fetishized object, a thing, not a relationship, be it positive or negative.

As a philosopher focused on aesthetics and ethics, Thomas Heyd (2003) focuses on the aesthetic appreciation of rock art and how such a view of rock art entails appropriation. Heyd (2003:37) uses the sense of appropriation as "an illegitimate borrowing or taking of a valued item," explaining that such acts are "perceived as not legitimate, not fair, or, in general, not attentive to the rights and needs of those with prior claims to the items appropriated." Three moral problems are entailed in such acts, which unsurprisingly parallel those reviewed above about cultural exploitation, as that is the definition of "commodification" that Heyd relies on. First, appropriation constitutes a taking—in effect, theft. Second, appropriation changes the things appropriated, leading to a degradation of authenticity, and hence altered understandings of the originating culture by both insiders and outsiders. Third, appropriation threatens the identity of members of the originating culture, and hence their sovereignty and survival, by creating distortions in the culture, fundamentally altering the meaning of what is appropriated and subverting indigenous authority over their own culture. As with both Lewis-Williams (1995) and Dowson (1999), Heyd ultimately concludes that not all acts of appropriation are inherently negative, specifically defending the aesthetic appreciation of rock art against a priori negative moral evaluations. Aesthetic appreciation of rock art is not morally illegitimate as long as it is taken within its context, undistorted by problematic racist ideologies, and not directly exploited for profit. If one strives for accuracy (that is, proper contextualization within the originating culture) and uses "standards of intercultural etiquette and respect" (Heyd 2003:42), then everything is good. Appropriation, it seems, as with Lewis-Williams and Dowson, is a tool that can be put to morally negative or positive uses.

In 2013, Polly Schaafsma published a book-length monograph on rock art and ethics titled *Images and Power*. Having found Schaafsma's (1997) work valuable in relation to the unconscious imposition of cultural ideologies in the interpretation of rock art, I approached the work with positive anticipation. The book begins, however, by seeming to set aside in-depth explorations of the ethics of appropriation: "While 'rock art ethics' are relatively straightforward when 'hard' issues are at stake, such as image appropriation toward commercial ends, there are many more additional concerns" (Schaafsma 2013:1).

Schaafsma (2013) does rehearse common concerns over the commercial appropriation of rock art imagery: Such appropriations decontextualize the imagery from its landscape and cultural contexts, secularize and trivialize the imagery, are demeaning if not imperialistic, and enable profit-making by outsiders with no compensation to affiliated communities. While Schaafsma pulls few punches when it comes to commercial and particularly New Age appropriations of Native American cultures, she develops three arguments that function to diminish concerns over appropriations of rock art imagery.

First, Schaafsma (2013) explores the appropriation of rock art imagery, but with a focus on indigenous groups appropriating ancient imagery to their own contemporary ends. However valued those ends may be, such as the reconstruction—or in Schaafsma's italicized term, *reinvention*—of their past, it is still not just appropriation but, in Schaafsma's (2013:56) terms, "cultural thievery." In her view, such appropriations are no more innocent than archaeological appropriations. For example, Schaafsma cites a Tiwa group's appropriation of a rock art image for use in its casino, despite archaeological indications that the image is affiliated with the Apache, not the Tiwa. While not made entirely explicit, the implication of this focus on indigenous appropriations of indigenous imagery for commercial ends seems to be "if they do it, so can everyone else." This position seems to ignore the Western notion of property, based on exclusive use, in which the Tiwa have been forced to operate. Schaafsma deploys the Tiwa's willingness to use a symbol that they (falsely, in her view) see as an important Tiwa religious symbol to promote their casino as evidence that Native peoples are willing to put their own sacred symbols to commercial ends.

Schaafsma (2013) also cites statements by a member of the Cochiti Pueblo criticizing the use of rock art images by non-Natives to make money. She takes the statements that outsiders profit from the rock art while affiliated groups get nothing, as well as a reference to "compensation," as further proof that indigenous peoples are willing to put a price tag on their sacred cultural heritage, again ignoring their involuntary entrance into a capitalist commodity system. The clear implication is that non-Native commercial appropriations of indigenous imagery are less illegitimate due to the practices of some indigenous individuals and tribes, in which they commercialize their own cultural heritage and in some cases steal from other indigenous groups to enhance their own profits—a view with the potential to both reinforce and draw energy from the broader cultural stereotype of the degraded, casino Indian.

In making reference to indigenous groups turning to intellectual property law to protect cultural symbols from commercial exploitation by others, Schaafsma's (2013) implication seems to be that Native peoples cannot legitimately complain about the commercialization of their sacred symbols while willingly commodifying those symbols by making legal claims to their ownership of them. However, the invocation of intellectual property rights is the only option granted by the dominant culture for indigenous groups wishing to protect their traditional imagery. In effect, Schaafsma seems to ignore the critical factors of power relations and social positioning in the examination of acts of appropriation.

Schaafsma's (2013) second argument is that rather than theft or appropriation, the widespread use of rock art imagery can be seen as a form of dynamic participation in a society in which cultural boundaries are permeable and unclear. This argument combines the classic liberal belief in the positive effects of intercultural contact (integration) with a superficial dose of the contemporary postmodernist, antiessentialist view of culture as lacking any clear boundaries (a view examined in chapter 7). While I have sympathy with both of these perspectives, I am also aware of the ways in which they are used rhetorically to justify the commodification, objectification, exploitation, and domination of others, be it through boutique multiculturalism (Fish 1998) or the position that rock art constitutes humanity's cultural heritage, legitimating the subjugation of Native sovereignty to the disciplinary and professional practices of archaeology and land management (Welsh 1999). While Schaafsma admits that engagement with rock art is unlikely to lead to any genuine ideological change, she sees it as a possible entry point, which, when combined with education and the willingness of Native peoples to share information about their culture, can facilitate genuine cross-cultural understanding.

Citing heavily from Brown's (2003) work *Who Owns Native Culture?*, Schaafsma ultimately falls back on a neoliberal view of culture, economics, and appropriation, in which any form of external, institutional constraint on individuals' access to knowledge, symbols, and means of expression is inherently negative, even if the lack of such constraints has "threatened" rock art's meanings and "the cultural integrity of rock art's origins" (Schaafsma 2013:69), threats which she seems to take quite seriously.

What is overlooked by Schaafsma and many others in discussing cultural appropriation is that the lack of clear boundaries between cultures does not mean that issues such as theft, exploitation, assimilation, and asymmetrical power are magically made irrelevant (Rogers 2006).

Third, Schaafsma (2013) echoes others on the inevitability of the commercial appropriation of rock art. Rock art will be reconfigured, its meanings changed, because that is the reality of an age of mass reproduction. Yes, commodification is bad, but it is here, it is not going away, so let's make a genuine effort to bridge cultural differences through full and open sharing of images and ideas instead of allowing the Natives to keep it all secret. A seemingly noble goal, but one dovetailing with my previous point: the ideologically driven, pragmatic effect of the claim that cultural boundaries aren't clear and impermeable is that appropriations (including what Schaafsma herself sees as exploitations) are ultimately fair game.

Schaafsma's (2013) primary criticisms are reserved for Native communities who wish to keep rock art imagery and/or insider information about rock art out of the public sphere, as well as for archaeologists who participate in the suppression of archaeological information out of deference to the wishes of affiliated tribes. That is, instead of focusing on the distortions, alienations, and exploitations that are necessarily involved in the commodification of rock art imagery, she shifts her focus to efforts by Native communities to keep rock art images and/ or cultural information about rock art secret, such as at Petroglyph National Monument (examined in detail in chapter 6). These Native communities and the archaeologists who accede to their demands are barriers to cross-cultural tolerance and understanding, as the refusal to fully share imagery and information leaves cultural outsiders with little to understand the rock art beyond their own cultural biases and projections. In addition, those who support secrecy by refusing to share or suppressing what has been shared are alienating humanity at large from the cultural heritage of humanity at large by protecting the sovereignty of particular cultures over their particular cultural heritage. What is not highlighted in this formulation is that the "humanity" that is being alienated from its "universal heritage" can be argued to be a very narrow subset of humankind—Westerners generally and archaeologists specifically. In addition, the history of Western-indigenous relations shows that the effort to know indigenous cultures has often been motivated by ethnocentric efforts to position indigenous peoples lower on the evolutionary ladder, colonialist efforts to control indigenous populations, and neocolonialist efforts to appropriate indigenous cultures to serve the interests of the dominant.

The ethical bottom line in Schaafsma's (2013) book is that archaeologists who give in to Native demands and political pressures by withholding information from the archaeological record are violating their ethical commitments as professional archaeologists. When nonarchaeological ethical systems and frameworks call for a different action—such as suppressing sensitive information about rock art and other archaeological sites—then those ethical demands must be overridden by those of archaeology. This ethical position, following the nature of Western ethical systems, is based on universal principles that diminish the role of the specific histories, power dynamics, and social relations involved.

Representation, Appropriation, and Neocolonialism

In this chapter, I have not only reviewed material that will be of use in understanding the more focused chapters that follow, but have hopefully begun to make a case for the relevance of these issues to understanding the role of rock art in the contemporary cultural landscape. The contemporary reproduction, appropriation, and interpretation of rock art are usefully understood not only by assessing them with archaeological knowledge to determine their accuracy and criticize their distortions. They can also be understood and assessed in the context of the matrix of media representations and anthropological/archaeological investigations of Native Americans, the power dynamics of appropriation and commodification, and the neocolonial relationship between Anglo-America and Native America. By paying attention not only to accuracy, but to representation, stereotyping, compensatory projections, appropriation, and commodification, we can gain substantial insight into contemporary cultural dynamics and assess their implications not only for understandings of rock art, but for the role of Native peoples, past and present, in the Anglo-American cultural consciousness.

CHAPTER 4

HUNTING MAGIC, SHAMANISM, AND THE CONTEMPORARY CRISIS IN MASCULINITY

Probably nothing in the entire field of archeology has produced greater excesses of misinformation than the significance and authorship of petroglyphs. Unintelligible, mysterious, and supposedly occult, they have stimulated a veritable orgy of mad speculation. Surely their primitive makers would have hesitated had they been able to foresee the furor their efforts were to cause.

Steward's (1937:407) diatribe against the crackpots and crazies presents a kind of contradiction: criticizing unscientific efforts to interpret rock art in a decidedly unscientific tone. Steward's statement exemplifies the level of energy and emotion that unfounded hypotheses generated (and continue to generate) among those who see themselves as serious scholars and scientists. Also of note in this particular statement are the negative invocations of sexual excess (orgy), irrationality (madness), and imagination (speculation), implying the author's (and the intended readers') possession of the opposing traits: restrained, rational, and empirically grounded. Such statements manifest the mid-twentieth-century view of the scientist: implicitly male, implicitly white, disciplined, and rational. Yet as with many versions of white/Western masculinity, the presumed superiority of the traits possessed by the scientist encouraged, almost demanded, that Steward engage in the very traits that he derides: emotional, excessive, and overtly value-laden. These highly rational scientists seem to be deeply troubled by such irrationalities, inciting them to notable levels of passion and hyperbole. As Kelley Hays-Gilpin (2004) has noted, the contrast between the scientist and the "crackpots and crazies" is a deeply gendered one. Nevertheless, the gendered codes operating in Steward's statement and others like it go largely unnoticed and unnoted, as there is little there that is troubling in terms of the dominant (and largely unconscious) ideologies of gender, masculinity, and science in the United States.

Gender can be a troubling thing (Butler 1990). Gender can be troubled—challenged, complicated, resisted, destabilized—by non-normative performances and representations of gender (Butler 1990), such as Laverne Cox's rise to prominence on Netflix's *Orange Is the New Black* in 2014 and Caitlyn (formerly Bruce) Jenner's coming out as a transgender female in 2015. Gender can also be deeply troubling—disturbing, unsettling—particularly when faced with nonnormative gender performances. Such performances can activate and upset, as reflected in a recurring *Saturday Night Live* skit from the early 1990s featuring Pat, an androgynous person who confounded people's ability to automatically assign a gender to everyone they meet. In Western contexts, gender is particularly troubled and troubling when it violates the gender binary: the belief that there are only two genders, everyone is assumed to be one or the other, and gender is based on if not entirely equivalent to one's biological sex (as determined by genitalia and/or chromosomes). And gender is troubled and troubling when the stereotypical attributes assigned to each sex/gender are violated, as in the presumption that effeminate males and masculine females must be homosexual ("inverts"). And of course gender is troubled and troubling when the hierarchy of the binary pair is challenged, such as with the perceived privilege granted to women due to legal efforts such as Title IX and affirmative action.

A few key definitions are necessary to explore the gendering of rock art. First is the distinction between *sex* and *gender*. For scholars in a variety of disciplines, sex is predominantly understood as a biological category, with gender referring to the meanings, roles, and expectations that are layered on top of biological sex (Dowson 2001; Hays-Gilpin 2004; Wood 1992). Sex is biological, and hence presumably innate and relatively immutable, while gender is cultural: learned, variable, and relatively arbitrary. Sex is referenced as male/female, whereas gender refers more to socially constructed notions of masculinity and femininity. While gender is placed on top of and ideologically collapsed into sex in order to make arbitrary notions of gender appear innate and immutable, there is no necessary relationship between the biological categories and the cultural constructs placed on them. Biology does not determine or even substantially limit cultural gender constructs (Jandt and Hundley 2007).

A case in point is hegemonic masculinity, which refers to forms of masculinity that are based on the domination of others. Hegemonic masculinity is manifested in contemporary Anglo-American culture as work in the paid labor force, subordination of women, heterosexism, virile and even uncontrollable sexuality, autonomy, control, and aggressiveness (Connell 1995; Prokos and Padavic 2002; Trujillo 1991). While these traits are ideologically framed as intrinsic, as the essential and unchanging characteristics of "normal" masculinity, research demonstrates their historic and cultural variability, as well as the interdependent, intersectional construction of gender, sexuality, race, ethnicity, nation, class, and other lines of difference (Dowson 2001; Rogers 1993; Sloop 2005).

There is little troubling, either of or by gender, in the rock art literature (exceptions include Dowson 2001; Hays-Gilpin 2004). The overall presumption that almost all rock art is by, about, and for men calls for attention not only to the erasure of women, but to the image of masculinity presented and the work such erasures and images perform. While there are signs of an increasing sensitivity to gender in rock art studies, androcentrism in rock art research is deeply embedded and is alive and well despite the appearance of feminist-informed rock art research. The often-implicit, largely unproblematized presentations of gender in rock art studies need to be troubled, not only to call attention to the distortions they potentially introduce into our understandings of the past, but also to highlight the work they do in the present.

Interrogating Masculinity

From the 1970s through much of the 1990s, most feminist and other gender-based research in the humanities and social sciences focused on women and femininity, in part as a reaction against the androcentrism of most research in these disciplines. So, for example, a compilation of the great speeches in US history might have between 90 and 100 percent of its content from male speakers despite being labeled as the greatest speeches, not the greatest speeches from men. Therefore, a feminist rhetorical scholar might focus on great speeches by women or on more "feminine" forms of discourse not addressed in the discipline as a whole. In other words, given two factors—the presumption that "male" is an unnecessary qualifier to history or philosophy or rhetoric, and the resulting absence of women in the research of those and other disciplines—most feminist research focused specifically on women and femininity, often with the starting point of women's absence and the associated goal of increased inclusion and visibility.

By the late 1980s and early 1990s, however, feminist scholars began to recognize that while we were studying women and the academic mainstream was studying men (under the guise of studying all people), very few scholars were applying feminist methods, theories, and perspectives to the study of men and masculinity. In this sense, feminist scholarship was participating in the presumption of male as the norm, as the unmarked dominant, and many feminist scholars began to focus explicitly on masculinity (e.g., Connell 1995; Kimmel 1987). This included a focus on representations of masculinity in the media as well as, for example, the ways in which homosocial interactions among men are just as much about gender as interactions between men and women are.

During this same time, critical scholars focusing on race and intercultural communication began to make a similar shift, calling for research on whiteness, not just nonwhite races and non-European ethnicities (e.g., Nakayama and Krizek 1995; Wander et al. 1999). Whiteness itself needs to be understood as a cultural construct, not a taken-for-granted backdrop, an unnamed, hegemonic norm. This move redefines discussions of "race" as not only about nonwhite races or relationships between whites and nonwhites: a film with all white characters is as inevitably and substantially about race as a film with all Native American characters. The end of the twentieth century and the beginning of the twenty-first, therefore, has seen a vast increase in research on both masculinity and whiteness, as critical scholars analyze the construction of these dominant social categories, refusing to take them for granted and enacting a different kind of resistance through the marking and interrogation of the unmarked dominant.

Much of the literature on masculinity focuses on the "crisis of masculinity," particularly white masculinity. Historian Gail Bederman (1995), for example, analyzes the crisis of middle-class Anglo-American masculinity circa 1900, identifying its sources in shifting patterns of work, threats from Others (women, working class, and racial minorities), and tensions over masculinity as based in physical strength versus self-mastery. Whatever the origins and regardless of the "reality" of the crisis, "working class and immigrant men . . . seemed to possess a virility and vitality which decadent white middle-class men had lost" (Bederman 1995:14). Similarly, many analyses of the contemporary crisis in Euro-American masculinity point to shifts in work and economics: "Foreign investment, corporate flight, downsizing, and automation have suddenly left members of the working class without a steady family wage," leaving "many white working-class men feeling emasculated and angry" (Fine et al. 1997:53). Journalist and feminist Susan Faludi (1999:85–86) focuses on the loss of "utilitarian masculinity," which "required that a man wrest something out of the raw materials of the physical world" and that his work be "critical to society." Not only blue-collar but also white-collar masculinity is experienced as being under siege by the corporate feminization of (male) professionals. "Whereas corporations have long supplied an institutional anchor for white, middle-class masculinity" (Ashcraft and Flores 2000:23), "contemporary discourse casts suspicion on the white collar, as well as the notion that a man is defined by his professional achievements and material possessions" (22).

Rock Art and the Crisis of Masculinity

Key themes in the discussions of the crisis in masculinity—tensions between physical strength and mental/moral capacity as the basis for masculinity, anxiety over the loss of virility due to changes in work, fear of the incapacity to fulfill the role of breadwinner—are manifested in a seemingly strange discursive terrain: archaeological interpretations of the meaning and function of precontact Native American rock art. These parallels are especially apparent in an article focusing on gender, subsistence, and rock art in the Coso Range of southeastern California. Originally published in *World Archaeology* in 1994, David Whitley's (1998a) "By the Hunter, for the Gatherer: Art, Social Relations and Subsistence Change in the Prehistoric Great Basin" presents a complete narrative of a crisis of masculinity and its resolution, a narrative strikingly similar to that of the contemporary crisis of masculinity.

Whitley (1998a:262) explains that during a period in which big-game hunting, a male activity, became less important and gathering, a female activity, became more important to the subsistence of the Numic cultures of the Cosos, "the seed-eating Numic produced a massive corpus of art that, taken literally at least, emphasized hunting, an activity of reduced importance to them."

> With the transition to a less mobile, seed-oriented gathering economy at *c.* AD 1200, it must be inferred that the then-existing social relations were, at least, threatened: the increasing emphasis on foods supplied by women and diminished importance of game hunted by men had the potential to change gender relations. In particular, this change made women effectively independent economically. And since male independence (from other males) was predicated on marriage and the resulting control of a woman's gathered foodstuffs, this increased the men's dependence on women and marriage. (Whitley 1998a:269)

Whitley sets out "to explain why people who principally ate seeds and nuts made art that emphasized mountain sheep and bows and arrows" (Whitley 1998a:258). "While there could have been a series of solutions to avert the potential social disruption that might have resulted by this changing subsistence pattern, the archaeological evidence suggests that a response in the Cosos involved a dramatic increase in the production of rock engravings" (Whitley 1998a:269).

Whitley (1998a) interprets these rock engravings as products of male shamans, a social and spiritual role that allowed men to maintain their powerful position vis-à-vis women. Changes in subsistence practices decentered men's role as providers, threatening their social status and their culture's gender arrangements. In response, men used a role predicated on supernatural power and esoteric knowledge that manifested itself in rock art. Whitley's essay provides one narrative of how men respond to a felt crisis of masculinity—a narrative that may say as much about the contemporary crisis of masculinity as the precontact Numic culture in the Cosos.

Following the rhetoric of inquiry (Simons 1990), the rhetoric of the human sciences (Nelson et al. 1987), feminist standpoint theory (Harding 1991), and feminist work in archaeology generally (Gilchrist 1999; Hollimon 2001; Kent 1999; Nelson 1997, 2006; Trocolli 1999) and rock art studies specifically (Bass 1994; Cannon and Woody 2007; Hays-Gilpin 2004), I contend that contemporary archaeological knowledge, specifically that concerning ancient rock art in western North America, is reflective of and an active participant in contemporary gender ideologies and struggles, including the crisis of masculinity. Using Barry Brummett's (2004) concept of discursive homology, I argue that the figure of the shaman in the literature on Native American rock art not only mirrors the perceived causes, tensions, and contradictions involved in the contemporary Anglo-American crisis of masculinity, but engages the crisis and offers a potential resolution. Following Kenneth Burke's (1973:109) definition of rhetoric, the shamanic interpretation of rock art offers "a strategy for encompassing a situation," articulating narratives, ideologies, and motives of contemporary Anglo-American masculinity in the form of archaeological interpretations of the traces of precontact indigenous cultures. If communication is the symbolic process whereby social reality is constructed, maintained, repaired, transformed, and struggled over (Carey 1988; see chapter 1), then explaining rock art through shamanism can be understood as one means to repair, to shore up, hegemonic masculinity in the face of perceived threats to its dominance and stability. Indeed, the strong resonances between shamanic explanations of rock art and the contemporary crisis in masculinity offers one explanation for the tremendous impact of the shamanic hypothesis in the interpretation of US rock art.

To establish that shamanic interpretations of Numic cultures and rock art of eight hundred years ago do not merely parallel but actively reflect and engage the contemporary crisis of masculinity, I review existing research on gendered images of Native Americans and the crisis of masculinity. With this foundation, I analyze two perspectives on rock art—hunting magic and shamanism—for their participation in the ongoing construction of the image of Native Americans and its involvement with contemporary forms and crises of masculinity. Identification of discursive homologies between contemporary Anglo-American masculinity and archaeological interpretations of precontact indigenous cultures offers a powerful approach for identifying unconscious ideologies and motives, as well as rhetorically appealing projections and displacements, operating in and between apparently unrelated discourses. Finally, I discuss the implications of the shaman as a model of Native American masculinity for the felt crisis in Anglo-American masculinity, suggesting that this figure represents a new strategy to "revive" hegemonic masculinity by straddling the physical/mental binary of masculine performance via a spiritual role grounded in virile male heterosexuality.

Gendered Representations of Native Americans

Although a variety of scholars have examined Western and specifically Anglo-American representations of Native Americans (see chapter 3), they have generally done so without sustained attention to gender (exceptions include Bird 1999, 2001; Buescher and Ono 1996; Marubbio 2006; Ono and Buescher 2001; van Lent 1996). Specifically, little attention has been paid to the almost exclusively male image of Native Americans: Iron Eyes Cody crying in response to a trashed landscape, the Hollywood brave on his horse defiantly raising his feathered spear, Chief Seattle's words and image on a bumper sticker, Geronimo gripping his rifle, and various "Indian" mascots. Elizabeth Bird points out that while historically images of Native women were central to colonialism, "Indian men, more than women, were the focus of the wave of fascination with things Indian that first crested in the 1960s and 1970s when the counter-culture embraced Indians as purveyors of ancient wisdom and spiritual knowledge" (Bird 2001:75; see also Bird, 1999; van Lent 1996). Even with the rise in films and a few television shows in the 1990s focusing on Native Americans, American Indian women were still largely absent, appearing in supporting roles such as wives or pretty maidens. The one significant exception to this pattern is Disney's 1995 animated *Pocahontas*, the first mainstream movie to have as its leading character a Native American woman (although the other main character is, of course, a white man). In addition to noting this imbalance, Bird (1999, 2001) and Peter van Lent (1996) have focused specifically on differences in media representations of Native American men and women. To provide a baseline for my analysis of gender dynamics in rock art interpretation as well as to demonstrate certain continuities between popular representations and models for rock art interpretation, I review their discussions of popular representations of Native American women and men.

Through analyses of films, television series, and romance novels, Bird (2001) identifies two predominant images of Native American men and two predominant images of Native American women. The first image of Indian men is the Doomed Warrior. This character has a strong sexual dimension reflecting both positive and negative images of Native Americans, articulating Indians as (sexually) dangerous savages while the figure's bravery and physicality also create sexual appeal. The fear of male Indian sexuality is manifested in the longstanding captivity narrative in which a Native man abducts a white woman. Van Lent

(1996) notes a decline in the captivity/rape narrative, with more recent images still focusing on the sexuality of the Native male but with a positive valence. The Indian Brave/Warrior of films and novels is not merely sexy due to his physical strength but due to his greater sensitivity to women, a trait often highlighted by comparisons to insensitive white men. According to Bird (2001), however, the recurrent narrative pattern paints the Doomed Warrior as physically strong but structurally impotent, a figure whose place in history will inevitably be eclipsed, a set of meanings powerfully articulated in Fraser's 1915 sculpture "The End of the Trail," featuring "an exhausted, beaten warrior slumped over his equally weary horse. No longer is the feathered spear raised in defiance. Instead, it hangs down from war-weary arms and points to the ground" (van Lent 1996:214). The bifurcation of the male image of the Doomed Warrior—desirable but repulsive, virile but savage, strong but doomed—parallels the bifurcation of Native Americans as the noble and the ignoble savage.

The second image of Native American men identified by Bird (2001) is the Wise Elder, who, in contrast to the Doomed Warrior, is not a subject or object of sexual desire but is defined by an emphasis on wisdom and spirituality. The Wise Elder may anticipate and bemoan the loss of Native life-ways in the face of white colonization; however, he offers not resistance (as the Doomed Warrior does, futilely) but his ancient wisdom to both Natives and whites alike, furthering the character's receptivity to New Age commodification and appropriation by environmental movements, as with Chief Seattle and Iron Eyes Cody.

Bird (2001) argues that Native women have become largely invisible in mainstream media representations with the exception of Pocahontas. Nevertheless, by examining representations from colonial times to the 1990s, Bird (2001:89) identifies two types of Native women, which also parallel the bifurcated image of Native Americans in general: "sexy exotic Princesses or Maidens" or "faceless, rather sexless Squaws in minor roles." Paralleling the Western virgin/whore dichotomy (Bird 1999), both of these images are sexualized, though in different ways and with different evaluations.

The Princess/Maiden is sexualized as an object of desire for Western men and, as in the examples of Pocahontas and the Indian maiden of Land-o-Lakes butter, is often used to represent the virgin landscape and her/its desire to be colonized by Europeans (Bird 2001; see also Buescher and Ono 1996; Marubbio 2006). The Indian Princess is above all virginal, as well as attractive by Western standards, attracted to white men, and willing to both teach white men Indian ways and learn white ways. She is diminutive, relatively passive, and unthreatening. As Elise Marubbio (2006) details in her study of Hollywood's version, the Princess/Maiden trope involves her interest in white culture, falling in love with a white man, and her inevitable death, as exemplified in films such as *Broken Arrow* (1950). Beginning in the 1970s, a primitivist variant of the narrative involves the Princess offering the white hero an alternative to his corrupt civilization, mediating his psychic conflicts (Marubbio 2006).

The Princess is opposed to the Squaw, but not in the same way that the Wise Elder contrasts to the Doomed Warrior; there is no female equivalent to the Wise Elder in the dominant imagery of Native Americans (Bird 2001). An Indian woman becomes a Squaw when she has sex with a man (Bird 1999). Squaws lack individual identities, are at the beck and call of their white or Indian husbands, and live lives of drudgery (Bird 1999). They lack sexual appeal, but their status is defined by having sex, especially indiscriminate sex. Squaws are the whore in contrast to the virgin figure of the Maiden/Princess.

This review of gendered representations of Native Americans offers guidance for analyzing interpretations of rock art, serving as a baseline of the imagery and stereotypes operating in other media and broader social contexts, representations with the potential to affect the interpretation of indigenous rock art. It enables an understanding of how interpretations and uses of rock art imagery take place (1) within a diachronic (historical) context and (2) with synchronic relations to other dynamics within contemporary culture (e.g., environmentalism and gender discourses). Returning to Berkhofer (1978), dominant images of Native Americans—in all their continuities, changes, and contradictions—are responsive to dynamics within Anglo-American culture. In order to highlight contemporary gender dynamics in relation to representations of Native Americans, specifically homologies between contemporary narratives of masculinity and those in the rock art literature, I turn to the "crisis of masculinity."

Crisis of Masculinity

The crisis of masculinity, both historically and in the post-1960s United States, has been the subject of several analyses. Central to the crisis is a series of tensions or contradictions characterizing Western masculinities: physical strength versus intellectual and moral capacity, virile sexuality versus emasculation/impotence/restraint, and blue- versus white-collar work (Ashcraft and Flores 2000; Bederman 1995; Robinson 2000; Rotundo 1993). In her examination of the crisis of Anglo-American masculinity circa 1900, Bederman (1995) focuses on the tension between civilized and primitive masculinities. In racial and national terms, the superiority of Anglo-American masculinity was predicated on the deployment of a civilized masculinity (based on self-mastery and intellectual capacity) over and against the primitive masculinity (based on bodily strength, sexual virility, and a lack of moral control) of racialized, subordinated, and colonized Others. Civilized masculinity, however, was also seen as a sign of the feminization of middle-class Anglo-American men, threatening traditional signs of male superiority such as physical strength and sexual virility, and questioning the inferiority of racial and working-class Others. This created a desire on the part of bourgeois men for what "primitive" males were presumed to possess: strength and virility (see also Bordo 1999; Robinson 2000; Rotundo 1993; Stecopoulos 1997). Hence, Bederman (1995) notes a decline in the Victorian model of civilized manliness and a rise in the discourse and appeal of primitive masculinity circa 1900, although both models of masculinity remained in circulation throughout the twentieth century and remain alive and well in the twenty-first (Rogers 2008). Discourses and performances of both primitive and civilized masculinity were deployed in support of the hegemony of men over women, the bourgeois over the working class, and whites over immigrants and colonized peoples.

Ashcraft and Flores (2000) argue that the basic tension identified by Bederman is in play one hundred years later in the contemporary crisis of white-collar masculinity, manifested in popular culture phenomena such as *Fight Club*. Focusing on discourse that "mourns the imminent collapse of the corporate man, over-civilized and emasculated by allied obligations to work and to women" (Ashcraft and Flores 2000:2), they identify a "civilized/primitive" masculinity that demands both civilized and primitive masculine performances. The underlying tensions between these models of masculinity are not resolved, functioning to maintain an unstable, elastic, and historically mobile hegemonic masculinity.

A summary of the basic narrative structure often used to explain the current crisis establishes a basis for identifying parallels between the discourse of the crisis and interpretations of indigenous rock art. The narrative is grounded in a period of (mythical) gender stability most commonly represented as "the 1950s," in which gender roles were clearly defined, with man as breadwinner and woman as homemaker, and produced stable identities and social harmony. Economically, (white) men occupied productive roles, either as blue-collar workers involved in industrial manufacturing or as white-collar "corporate men" who were offered meaningful employment and job security in return for loyalty to the corporation.

According to this dominant narrative, beginning in the 1960s and continuing today, several factors eroded the stability, clarity, and harmony of the established gender configuration and specifically threatened the identity, social role, and prestige of (white) men. Feminism and the women's movement challenged the desirability and validity of traditional gender roles and promoted women's entry into previously male-only realms. More broadly, a range of related social movements (civil rights, gay rights, antiwar) challenged the validity of white male privilege. At the same time, economic changes eroded the basis for (white) male identity. The guarantee of a good income and job security was weakened as a result of globalization and corporate strategies such as downsizing, outsourcing, and automation. Industrial production also gave way to an increasingly information- and service-based economy. The loss of blue-collar work, the rise of feminized (pink-collar) work, and the perceived feminization of white-collar work parallel a perceived loss of status at home. The overall result is a sense of emasculation and feminization, feelings of disempowerment and anger. Various versions of the narrative offer different implied or expressed resolutions to the crisis, including the scapegoating of women, minorities and/or "soft men" and, importantly, a return to primitive masculinities via means such as extreme physicality, predatory sexuality, homosocial relations, and preindustrial spiritualities (Ashcraft and Flores 2000; Churchill 1994; Faludi 1999).

This basic narrative demonstrates that masculinity is not an intrinsic and unchanging male essence, but is culturally relative, continually (re) constituted, and a site of struggle, reflecting and responding to social, economic, and political changes. Given the conflictual and contradictory character of social, economic, and political systems, masculinity reflects, utilizes, and obscures such conflicts and contradictions. A focus on the dynamics of these tensions and contradictions is important for avoiding oversimplified diagnoses of the crisis of masculinity as simply a loss of what was once stable. Shifts in and struggles over masculinity are diagnostic of social structure and consciousness, and reveal masculinity, not as essence, but as multiple, complex, and contradictory—as "a historical, ideological process" (Bederman 1995:7). As Robinson (2000:4) states in her discussion of the post-1960s crisis of masculinity, "Rather than seeing that struggle as a singular, pitched battle between the white man and his various others, it is much more accurate—and fruitful, as well—to think about how normativity, constantly under revision, shifts in response to the changing social, political and cultural terrain."

Hegemonic masculinity utilizes and obscures the conflictual and contradictory character of dominant systems and ideologies, operating through intersections with race, class, and other axes of difference. Such intersections are central to the tensions and contradictions as well as the instabilities and dominations embedded in, for example, primitive masculinities (Ashcraft and Flores 2000; Bederman 1995; Robinson 2000; Stecopoulos 1997). Specifically, a long Anglo-American history of turning to Native American cultures for a way out of the trap of modern (feminized) masculinity, a trend which appeared again in the late 1980s and early 1990s in the guise of the mythopoetic men's movement, points to ongoing links between Euro-American masculinity and dominant perceptions of Native Americans (Bederman 1995; Robinson 2000; Rotundo 1993). Representations of Native Americans and of men are not only reflective of the internal conflicts in Anglo-American culture but are rhetorical forces, shaping consciousness, social relations, and power. Within this framework, the interpretation of Native American rock art is not only a site for the circulation of the image of Native Americans in Anglo-American culture, but articulates gender and sexuality in an engagement of the crisis of masculinity.

Analyzing Interpretations of Great Basin Rock Art

This analysis focuses on two models for interpreting rock art in the western United States: hunting magic and shamanism. More specifically, I focus on interpretations of the rock art of the precontact hunter-gatherer cultures of the Great Basin. The Great Basin as a geological, specifically hydrological, area encompasses most of the state of Nevada, about half of Utah, and smaller portions of California, Oregon, and Idaho. In archaeological and ethnographic terms, the cultural Great Basin includes areas in southeastern California around what today is Death Valley National Park, including the Coso Range (see Figure 1.1).

This geographical, cultural, and temporal choice is driven by the quantity and diversity of research done in this area and the role of rock art studies of the Great Basin in developing or expanding potentially generalizable models for rock art interpretation. The bulk of this research appears in the context of academic anthropology and archaeology, and rock art studies specifically. While all types of rock art research reflect and enact gendered and cultural biases (Bass 1994; Cannon and Woody 2007; Whitley 2011), interpretive models are especially rich and relatively explicit sources for identifying cultural projections. The widespread presumption (correct or not) of the ultimate indeterminacy of rock art's "real" meanings facilitates projection of Western ideologies, struggles, and contradictions onto such imagery, as does the (often unconscious) dependence on existing (etic) structures of meaning in the development of models to explain the meaning and function of rock art in the cultures that produced it. As discussed in chapter 2, models for the interpretation of rock art are likely to reveal as much if not more about contemporary ideologies and dynamics in the cultures that produce them as they are about the cultures that produced the rock art (Hays-Gilpin 2004; Schaafsma 1997).

More important than the particular geographic focus on the Great Basin, two factors guided my choice to focus on hunting magic and shamanism instead of other interpretive models and other kinds of rock art research (e.g., stylistic classification). First, hunting magic and shamanism have both been applied to many bodies of rock art across the world, from Paleolithic European cave art to precolonial rock art in southern Africa. In the US context each has occupied the position of a dominant model for the interpretation of Great Basin rock art in particular, a dominance which extended each model's application to a multitude of regions and rock art styles beyond the Great Basin and facilitated both models' dissemination beyond the academy. These two models have influenced the presentation of rock art to the general public in the form of coffee-table books, guide books, videos, websites, museum displays, pamphlets, interpretive signs, and information provided by tour guides. These models frame the general public's understanding of rock art's nature and significance as well as contribute to the public's understanding of Native American cultures, histories, and (often implicitly) gender constructs. Identification and critique of cultural projections can reveal ideologies operating in the human sciences and passed on to various nonacademic audiences.

Second, these two models are sequential, an important factor in tracking their relationship with the contemporary crisis of masculinity. Hunting magic was firmly in place by the 1960s, began to decline in the late 1970s, and was largely dismissed by the 1990s (Whitley and Clottes 2005). Shamanism appeared as a major explanatory framework in the 1970s (Hedges 1985) and achieved a position of dominance, replacing hunting magic, by the 1990s (Keyser and Whitley 2006; Quinlan 2000). Due to their prominence in the literature, their impact on the presentation of rock art to the general public, and the movement away from hunting magic and toward the shamanic hypothesis over the last four decades, these two models are well suited for tracking changes in rock art interpretation and the implications of those changes for the image of Native Americans and the dynamics of Anglo-American masculinities.

Based on explorations of the rhetoric of inquiry and the rhetoric of the human sciences (Nelson et al. 1987; Simons 1990), as well as feminist critiques of science (Harding 1991; Martin 1991), it follows that models for rock art interpretation are not solely or even predominantly determined by archaeological, ethnohistorical, and ethnographic evidence, and are thereby potentially symptomatic of the (unconscious) projection of Western ideologies, including gender ideologies. Models for rock art interpretation are not simply hypotheses formed from available evidence by hermetically sealed epistemologies, but can serve to project Western ideologies, tensions, anxieties, and fantasies onto Native American cultures through a dependence on existing frames of reference, structures of meaning, and narrative patterns.

The relationships between rock art interpretation and the contemporary crisis in masculinity can be identified through the concept of discursive homologies. Brummett (2004:1) defines homology as "a pattern found to be ordering significant particulars of different and disparate experiences." Such a pattern "is most interesting when it is observed as a linkage among *disparate* orders of experience" (Brummett 2004:2). Part of what makes a text—a speech, song, film, advertisement, or an interpretive sign at a rock art site—appealing or rhetorically effective is the use of implied, often unconscious parallels to other texts or lived experiences. As with metaphors and analogies, such parallels are neither givens nor self-evident; they are rhetorical constructions that affect how a situation is understood and evaluated. The use of formal patterns to link different particulars leads Brummett (2004:41) to the principle of vulnerability: "One experience may have rhetorical effects on how people perceive and order another experience or group of experiences if they are formally linked"—even (or especially) if the parallels between the two situations and/or the underlying homology itself is outside of conscious awareness. "Attunement to rhetorical homology . . . allows one to track lines of rhetorical influence that might otherwise be obscured" (Brummett 2004:3).

In an extension of the basic tenets of the rhetoric of inquiry and standpoint theory, I hold that academic knowledge and literature not only embody and perpetuate particular cultural and ideological biases, but also function, as with both scientific and popular discourses (Gilman 1985; Torgovnick 1996), to project and work through contemporary cultural tensions. Through discursive homologies and the principle of vulnerability, contemporary discourses can influence archaeological interpretations of the past, while archaeological interpretations can in turn influence or at least respond to other contemporary dynamics, such as the crisis of masculinity. I do not mean to deny that archaeological knowledge is disciplined, that is, it is presumably (as with other academic research) more systematic and self-reflective than many other genres of discourse. It would be naïve, however, to presume that such discourses are not equally "worldly" (Said 1983), both reflective of and actively engaged in their cultural milieu on both conscious and unconscious levels.

The vulnerability of archaeological knowledge to influence by contemporary values, narratives, and ideologies has been demonstrated by a variety of gender-based and feminist critiques of North American archaeology (Galloway 1998; Gilchrist 1999; Nelson 1997; Trocolli 1999; Watson and Kennedy 1998). In terms of rock art specifically, Bass (1994), Cannon and Woody (2007), and Hays-Gilpin (2004) have also demonstrated how implicit gender ideologies shape whether and how rock art sites are recorded, whether and how other associated archaeological resources are identified as potentially related to the rock art, how rock art motifs are identified, and how rock art is interpreted. The most obvious gendered pattern in rock art studies is an almost complete absence of women in rock art production and use (Hays-Gilpin 2004), a pattern that parallels contemporary media representations of Native Americans (Bird 1999, 2001). A focus on Native men and the marginalization of Native women continues in the interpretation of rock art, furthering the androcentrism of the Anglo-American image of the

Indian and enabling it as a site for working through the contemporary crisis of masculinity.

In this analysis I draw from gendered critiques of archaeology and, when available, rock art studies in particular—not to demonstrate which interpretations are right and which are wrong, and not primarily to correct for distortions in rock art interpretation, but to establish such interpretations as neither self-evident nor produced in isolation from the standpoints and ideologies of researchers, thereby identifying potential projections of contemporary ideologies and tensions onto indigenous rock art. While I draw from literature that engages or otherwise adds to debates over the empirical, ethnohistorical, and/or ethnographic accuracy of rock art interpretation, my primary focus is on the ideologies and gender dynamics that are potentially projected onto indigenous cultures by the interpretive models. To support the case that the homologies I identify between these two discourses are not merely a set of coincidental parallels or the manifestation of cross-cultural patterns of gender or patriarchy, I first engage in rather conventional gender critiques of the two models for rock art interpretation. This is a necessary step in demonstrating that the discourses of rock art and the crisis of masculinity are homologous and potentially mutually influential. This conventional critique helps identify both overt and subtle parallels between the two disparate discourses under examination here, parallels that suggest possible vulnerabilities between the discourses. Building on these critiques, I then analyze the models in relation to the crisis of masculinity with particular focus on the implications of the decline of hunting magic and the rise of shamanism.

Rock Art as Hunting Magic

In the context of precontact hunter-gatherer societies in the Great Basin, many researchers interpreted rock art as hunting magic (e.g., Bettinger and Baumhoff 1982; Grant 1968; Heizer and Baumhoff 1962). Images of game animals and weapons, hunting scenes, and depictions of game animals with protruding arrows or darts, as well as the placement of rock art sites near hunting areas, were taken to indicate that the production of rock art was intended to insure a good hunt, a form of sympathetic magic in which like is used to produce like. Well established in the 1960s, this was the dominant interpretive model for Great Basin petroglyphs in particular into the 1980s. Over the last three decades, however, this model's dominance has diminished due in part to a lack of corroborating ethnohistorical evidence, ethnohistorical evidence directly denying hunting magic as a function of rock art, rock art sites often not being correlated with hunting areas, the relatively low frequency of many game animals among rock art motifs, and the rise of shamanic interpretations (Cannon and Woody 2007; Keyser and Whitley 2006; Ricks 1999; Whitley 1998a, 2001a, 2011; Whitley and Clottes 2005). I argue that changes in the conditions of Anglo-American masculinity played a role in the decline of the hunting magic model—it lost favor due to not only its inability to account for relevant evidence, but its inadequacy for articulating certain images of Native peoples and forms of masculinity. That is, hunting magic no longer resonated with contemporary discourses of masculinity to the degree it did before; it no longer was rhetorically effective as a "strategy for encompassing a situation" (Burke 1973:109). To set the basis for this argument, I analyze the gendering of the hunting magic model and the structure of meaning that frames it, the Western view of hunter-gatherers.

Feminist critiques of anthropology and archaeology have identified a rather homogenized view of hunter-gatherer societies with regard to gender and subsistence: Women gather, men hunt (Nelson 1997). Women's role in this process is essentially passive, involving in its simplest incarnation women trading sex for the meat obtained by men (Gilchrist 1999). The assumptions were that hunting is the more important of the two means of subsistence (Kent 1999), and men are the hunters due to their greater physical strength and lack of constraints from child-bearing and rearing (Watson and Kennedy 1998). According to Roberta Gilchrist (1999), this view of men being hunters and hunting being more important (in terms of actual subsistence and/or social values) was fueled by male archaeologists focusing on what they perceived as valuable activities: large game hunting and the related use and production of hunting tools (see also Sundstrom 2008). Susan Kent (1999) argues that anthropologists and archaeologists have perceived hunting as more important because of its association with Western notions of masculinity. As Sarah Nelson (1997) puts it, the stereotype is that what men do is heroic and exciting (e.g., hunting), while women's activities are by definition dull and repetitive (e.g., gathering and processing plant foods). As Linea Sundstrom (2008:168) summarizes the situation, women's role in hunter-gatherer cultures is largely invisible in traditional Anglo-American archaeology because "scrapers are just not considered as sexy as spear points."

This model has several problems. First, cross-cultural evidence questions the empirical validity of such generalizations. In many instances, men engage in gathering and preparing plants, and women engage in activities that could be called hunting (Gilchrist 1999; Kent 1999; Nelson 1997; Sundstrom 2008). However, as Kent (1999) points out, when women do hunt (such as participating in drives to capture small game animals), these activities have been defined in the anthropological literature as gathering, enabling the perpetuation of the illusion of a strict gendered division of labor, and by implication binary models of gender. Second, the man-as-hunter/woman-as-gatherer model projects Western ideas about what constitutes valuable activities onto non-Western peoples, who may well consider these contributions to subsistence to be different but equally valuable (Kent 1999). The value attached to these activities by archaeologists is also empirically questionable insofar as several studies have demonstrated that women, primarily through gathering, provide the bulk of the nutrition in hunter-gatherer societies (Nelson 1997). Finally, this model functions to essentialize a particular view of men and women. By insisting on a strict, gendered division of labor, and therefore a strict, gendered division of the associated skills and attributes, Western gender roles are reified through their identification in other (and, in the Western evolutionary frame, developmentally earlier) cultures. These ideas guide what archaeologists look for in their excavations and analyses of artifacts, creating a system of circular reinforcement whereby the observations made and questions asked shape research findings.

Cannon and Woody (2007; see also Pendegraft 2007) examine gender and rock art in the northern Great Basin. They state that despite advances in addressing androcentrism in archaeology generally, in rock art studies in the Great Basin "male bias seems as strong as ever" (Cannon and Woody 2007:37). Specifically, they argue that much Great Basin rock art (at least at the northern Great Basin sites they analyze) occurs near ground stone (e.g., mortars and metates), traditionally taken as evidence of women's food-processing activities, and domestic features (e.g., house rings). As a result, they reject the presumption in Great Basin rock art research that women did not produce or utilize rock art and that women's activities are not reflected in the rock art. This potentially domestic and/or feminine dimension of Great Basin rock art sites has been overlooked, both because rock art recording projects often avoid recording related archaeological features and

because the androcentric bias in archaeology resulted in many archaeological sites being recorded without careful attention to ground stone.
"Previously, researchers who recorded archaeological sites evidenced a
tendency to record projectile points (traditionally interpreted as male
hunting implements) in great detail, while artifacts traditionally interpreted as indicating female behaviors—especially ground stone—were
overlooked or casually recorded" (Cannon and Woody 2007:44). Both
of the dominant models for interpreting Great Basin rock art (hunting
magic and shamanism, the latter to be discussed below) presume that
rock art would be located away from habitation or processing sites, near
game trails or at isolated sites where shamans engage in vision quests.
Indeed, the association of rock art sites with game trails, hunting blinds,
and related features was one of a list of empirical claims provided in
support of the hunting magic model (Grant 1968; Heizer and Baumhoff 1962). The gender ideologies in play in Great Basin archaeological
practice shaped the record, as well as the interpretation of that record,
consistent with a binary system of gender that is also hierarchical—
ground stone was not just associated with women, but devalued as a
result of androcentrism generally and the gender duality built into the
understanding of hunter-gatherers specifically.

This dualistic conceptualization of gender in hunter-gatherer societies relates directly to the application of the hunting magic model in
developing larger archaeological explanations. If only men hunt, then
rock art depicting hunting scenes, weapons, and large game animals
(some with weapons protruding from them) was presumably made by
men, in support of male activities. This chain of reasoning is clear in
Robert Bettinger and Martin Baumhoff's (1982) discussion of Great
Basin rock art in the context of the replacement of pre-Numic hunter-
gatherers by Numic (Paiute, Shoshone, and Ute) hunter-gatherers
between 1000 CE and the "historic" (postcontact) period (see Figure
1.4). In this 1982 monograph from *American Antiquity*, Bettinger and
Baumhoff use optimal foraging theory to propose that different hunter-
gatherer strategies characterized these groups, with the pre-Numic
populations being "travellers," a strategy reliant on large-game hunting
and procurement of high-quality plant resources (which require less
processing). Groups adopting such a strategy "are required to maximize the procurement of large game . . . and to gather information
about the density and distribution of high-ranked plant resources
over a fairly large area" (Bettinger and Baumhoff 1982:492). Because

large-game hunting and long-distance traveling "generally fall to males and because processing tasks, which generally fall to females, are minimized, it follows that travellers should adopt practices that produce high male/female ratios, i.e., a male-rich society" (Bettinger and Baumhoff 1982:492). In contrast, Numic groups used a "processor" strategy involving lower-quality plant resources, less travel time, and greater extraction and processing time. "In processing societies, therefore, the sex ratio should strike a more even balance between males and females or produce female-rich societies" (Bettinger and Baumhoff 1982:492).

While this traveler/processor model has numerous implications, my focus is on the role of rock art in Bettinger and Baumhoff's (1982) application of the model to the displacement of pre-Numic by Numic populations. They assume that the apparent lack of knowledge about Great Basin rock art among postcontact Great Basin populations reflected in the ethnography of the area means that little of this rock art was produced by those populations (an assumption that has been contested; see Whitley [1994a] as well as the discussion of Julian Steward's work in chapter 2). Therefore, they argue that almost all Great Basin rock art was produced by the pre-Numic travelers. That is, the rock art of the region was made by hunters at a time when hunting was a larger part of the adaptive strategy, and the relative absence of Numic (processor) rock art is due to the relative lack of importance of hunting in their adaptive strategy. The attribution of most Great Basin rock art to pre-Numic populations supports their contention that the processors displaced the travelers.

The linkage of the traveler/processor model to the interpretation of rock art as hunting magic clarifies the gendering of the rock art: Numic processors "were insufficiently reliant on large game to account for such a practice" and "incapable of maintaining male groups of sufficient size in sufficiently continuous association to sustain hunting cults of the sort likely to have been responsible for Great Basin rock art" (Bettinger and Baumhoff 1982:494). While other resolutions of this incongruity are possible (e.g., the rock art had purposes other than hunting magic), they are not considered, I would argue, due to the rigid stereotyping associated with a presumably rigid division of labor. Feminized societies, it follows, produce little rock art or rock art of inferior quality compared to that of "male rich" societies heavily reliant on hunting.

This image of rock art makers is based in more than a strict division of labor. The interpretation of rock art as hunting magic attributes agency to men through the use of symbols and rituals to enhance control over the environment and other entities that inhabit it (cf. Hays-Gilpin 2004; Watson and Kennedy 1998). There is more at stake in the man-as-hunter/woman-as-gatherer model than the heroic image of men as hunters: A key element in this binary system is (male) activity versus (female) passivity. Native men are active and adventurous; skilled in survival, travel, tracking, hunting, and the production of tools; and in possession of ritual and imagery designed to enhance their power. Women's activities such as gathering and processing are defined as passive because they are women's activities, not because of their lack of importance or a low level of knowledge and skill required to do them. Implicit in the hunting magic model is the stereotypical Squaw of popular culture (Bird 1999): Native American women engaged in lives of drudgery, awaiting the return of men with the meat needed for survival while tediously gathering and processing plant foods. Most important for my focus here, however, is the image of masculinity the hunting magic model presents: physically strong, skilled in the ways of nature, provider of sustenance, and possessing power derived from ritual activity. In the pre-Numic Great Basin, men's social role was secure, their contribution (meat) was important, and their material traces (e.g., rock art and projectile points) are valued by later cultures. But when their social structure was compromised by changes in subsistence practices, the men and the rock art literally declined and were supplanted by a less interesting, "female rich" society that did not produce rock art or at least not rock art that is valued.

Rock Art as Shamanic Practice

Many alternative interpretive models have been advanced for the rock art of various regions and traditions: mythic and historic narratives, clan identification, territorial and route markers, astronomical observation and time-keeping, fertility rituals, and rites of passage (Hays-Gilpin 2004; Whitley 1996). However, while these interpretive models have been used to analyze specific rock art sites and symbols, arguments concerning the relative merits of the shamanic hypothesis dominated interpretive rock art studies for much of the 1990s and 2000s. While shamanism has been a factor in the interpretation of rock art in the western United States since the 1970s (Hedges 1985), the debates of the 1990s and 2000s focused around the flurry of shamanic interpretations that were fueled by not only a general shamanic hypothesis, but specifically the neuropsychological (N-P) model introduced by David Lewis-Williams and Thomas Dowson (1988, 1990) in the contexts of Paleolithic Europe and precolonial southern Africa. In addition, these new shamanic interpretations were linked to a rise in the use of ethnographic data in rock art studies in the western United States (Whitley and Clottes 2005; see also Francis 2005). As Hays-Gilpin (2004:13) notes, "'Shamanism' emerges as one of the most important and controversial concepts in rock art interpretation all over the world." Bury (1999) and Schaafsma (2013) add that shamanism is an attractive explanation to the public, especially one immersed in New Age spiritualities and images of the spiritually in-tune Indian. Most importantly for this analysis, by the 1990s shamanism had clearly replaced hunting magic as the dominant model for rock art interpretation in the Great Basin and other regions in the western states.

The shamanic/N-P model was developed by Lewis-Williams and Dowson (1988, 1990) through their work with San rock art in southern Africa and Paleolithic cave paintings in Europe (see also Lewis-Williams 2002). The model has also been applied to rock art across western North America (Turpin 1994), including the Great Plains (Keyser and Klassen 2001), the Sonoran Desert (Bostwick and Krocek 2002), the Colorado Plateau (Schaafsma 1994; Stoffle et al. 2000; Malotki 2003), California (Whitley 2000a, 2000b), and the Great Basin (Lewis-Williams 2002; Whitley 1994b, 1998a, 1998c). In the United States, David Whitley has been the primary developer and proponent of the shamanic hypothesis, especially for Great Basin rock art, as well as the primary target for opponents of the hypothesis. My analysis focuses on Whitley's formulations due to his numerous publications, their prominence in the literature, and their clear influence on rock art interpretation in a variety of contexts. My intent is not to criticize Whitley for personal projections and gender biases. Indeed, whether I agree with his arguments or not, I greatly respect the energy, focus, and expertise he has brought to rock art interpretation in the western United States. What I analyze below is a body of discourse centered around the author known as "David S. Whitley," which is a symbolic construct, not the individual, flesh and blood person (whom I do not know). I interpret the patterns and issues I identify in the published works of David S. Whitley as manifestations of the larger cultural and disciplinary contexts and discourses in which these works operate. As Burke (1966:6) once posed the issue, "Do we simply use words, or do they not also use us?" Despite dominant

ideologies of individualism, be it in their romantic, possessive, rugged, or other forms, the production of knowledge not only flows *from*
individual consciousness but in large part flows *through* it. In turn, the
rhetorical expression of such knowledge may or may not resonate with
various audiences; the influence of David S. Whitley's work on rock
art scholars, cultural resource managers, enthusiasts, and the general
public points to powerful resonances with the cultural contexts that
shape those audiences' responsiveness, much as Heizer and Baumhoff's
(1962) hunting-magic model resonated with their audiences.

The shamanic/N-P model represents one of the, if not *the*, most
complex and multifaceted attempts to explain a large portion of rock
art in the western United States. While proponents point out that
shamanism does not explain all rock art in the western states, Lewis-
Williams's (2001:347) claim that "without a doubt, the evidence now
points unequivocally to shamanism as one of the principal, probably *the* principal, context in which rock art was made on [the North
American] continent" is representative of the explanatory power
its proponents believe the model offers (see also Schaafsma 2013).
Whitley (2011:137) names "a dramatic advance in interpretations of
shamanistic rock art" as one of three main factors responsible for a
"revolution in rock art research" in the 1990s and 2000s. Such statements offer one explanation for strong resistance to the shamanic
model (e.g., Bury 1999; Hedges 2001; Kehoe 2002; Kitchell 2010;
Monteleone 1998; Quinlan 2000, 2007a; Quinlan and Woody 2003;
Ross 2001; see Lewis-Williams [2003] and Whitley [2000b, 2003]
for responses to some of these criticisms). Despite both empirical
and ideological criticisms of the shamanic hypothesis, especially of
its primitivist inclinations, little sustained attention has been given
to its gendered implications. However, the primitivism of the shamanic model—including not only the scholarly discourse advancing
it, but also the ways in which others appropriate and deploy that
discourse—is most decidedly gendered in nature, demonstrating the
inescapable intersectionality of constructions of race, culture, and
gender. Before discussing the gendering of rock art in this model,
however, an overview is necessary.

Literal interpretations of Great Basin (and much other) rock art
imagery face several hurdles (Whitley 2011). While many anthropomorphic figures can be interpreted as humans, various distortions to
the human form, such as anthropomorphs with the heads and/or feet

of birds, challenge literal readings. In addition, various images, such as those of bighorn sheep, are often rotated or inverted in ways that literal readings strain to explain. Finally, much Great Basin rock art includes abstract geometric forms such as zig-zags and dots in grid patterns as well as meandering lines. In some cases, these geometric and curvilinear elements are attached to or otherwise associated with anthropomorphs or other seemingly representational or naturalistic figures. The shamanic/N-P model, however, is able to explain the literal, the fantastic, and the abstract/geometric elements of many Great Basin rock art sites (not to mention many other regional/cultural styles). The N-P model is grounded in the assumption that much rock art is a record of altered states of consciousness (ASCs). ASCs may be involved in shamanic journeys, vision quests, or initiation rites, and may be induced by drugs, sensory deprivation, fasting, chanting, and/or drumming (Lewis-Williams 2001). The stages experienced in ASCs explain both abstract geometric forms as well as distortions of representational elements via patterns of hallucination grounded in human neurological structures (Lewis-Williams 2001).

Central to an understanding of the N-P/shamanic model is that it is actually two models that are potentially linked. The N-P model itself is based in an understanding of the panhuman nature of the imagery experienced during ASCs, and can be applied to rock art in a purely formal manner—that is, based on an analysis of the rock art imagery itself. The shamanic model, on the other hand, is an informed approach, based largely in relevant ethnography demonstrating both the existence of shamanic practices in the culture in question as well as evidence linking shamanic practices (or other practices involving ASCs by nonshamans, referred to as shamanistic) to the culture's rock art (Taçon and Chippindale 1998; Whitley 2011). The N-P/shamanic model has been applied in a formal manner to imagery where ethnographic data is absent (e.g., the Paleolithic cave paintings in Europe and the Barrier Canyon Style of the Colorado Plateau) as well as to rock art produced by cultures where relevant ethnography is available (e.g., San rock art in southern Africa and Great Basin rock art in the United States). Criticisms of the model are focused on the validity of the N-P model itself, the limitations of purely formal analyses using the N-P model, the primitivist nature of shamanic explanations, and the relevance, validity, and interpretation of the available ethnographic data.

In terms of the N-P model itself, the link between ASCs and rock art is entoptic ("in the eye") patterns (Lewis-Williams 2001; Lewis-Williams and Dowson 1988). The model holds that a limited number of recurring entoptic patterns are experienced during ASCs: grids, dots, circles, parallel lines, zigzags, meandering lines, and nested curves. These entoptic forms are rooted in universal human neurological structures and can be recognized in rock art motifs. The N-P model also identifies seven principles of perception that can explain variations on the basic entoptic forms, variations also identifiable in rock art imagery: replication, fragmentation, integration, superpositioning, juxtapositioning, reduplication, and rotation.

According to the N-P model, those experiencing an ASC go through three stages: (1) the perception of entoptic patterns; (2) their elaboration into iconic forms recognizable by the person experiencing an ASC; and (3) full-blown hallucinations, in which the iconic objects in stage 2 take fuller form and participate in elaborate visual hallucinations (Lewis-Williams 2001; Lewis-Williams and Dowson 1988). While stage 1 entoptics are rooted in human universals, the construal of those entoptics into recognizable forms (stage 2) and their development into full-blown hallucinations (stage 3) are substantially mediated by the cultural context in which the ASC occurs, as is the identification of which images are significant and what they mean. Stage 3 also involves the person becoming an active participant in the hallucinations; sometimes those in an ASC change into animals or experience other somatic hallucinations such as flight, drowning, elongated limbs, or extra limbs or digits. Stage 3 phenomena are also identifiable in rock art imagery (e.g., anthropomorphs with elongated limbs, bird heads, etc.). In a purely formal analysis of rock art imagery using the N-P model, the six entoptic forms, the seven principles of perception, and the three stages of ASCs are used to assess the probability that the imagery originated from ASCs. However, not all cultures equally represent all three stages in their rock art (Whitley 2011). Significantly, the N-P model itself does not posit interpretations of the imagery—what it symbolized to its producers and viewers—but instead explains the origin of the imagery (Whitley 2011). Meaning comes from the cultural context, specifically the shamanic practices leading to the imagery's production and the larger cultural cosmology in which shamanic practices occur and rock art is viewed.

A key aspect of the shamanic hypothesis for rock art is connecting ASC-induced imagery (the N-P model) to the shamanic beliefs and practices of specific cultures—that is, the use of informed approaches alongside the formal analysis of the rock art imagery itself via the N-P model. According to Whitley's (1998a, 1998c) reading of the relevant ethnography, in the precontact Great Basin shamans were understood as having special powers enabling them to travel to another world where they interacted with spirits, obtained spirit helpers, and accessed knowledge to help them in various activities in the mundane world, such as curing (or causing) ailments, controlling game animals, and bringing rain. Shamans entered this supernatural world through ASCs and subsequently recorded their visions on rock (Whitley 1994b). Such recordings may have helped them remember their visions, reconnect with the supernatural, or re-enter an ASC at a later time (Whitley 1994b).

This model not only allows Whitley to make sense of bizarre anthropomorphic figures and abstract curvilinear and geometric designs in Great Basin rock art; it also enables metaphoric readings of the imagery. For example, certain motifs at rock art sites, such as birds and frogs, are seen as significant because these animals cross boundaries (land/sky, land/water) much as shamans travel between worlds. By extension, anthropomorphs with birdlike attributes indicate a shaman. Images of apparently dead animals (e.g., upside-down or impaled bighorn sheep) or of humans killing animals are taken as metaphors for entry into the other world: "death" equals "entry into the supernatural." Flight, drowning, fighting, bodily transformation, and sexual arousal/intercourse/release are other metaphors for supernatural travel (or trance) identified by Whitley (1994b, 2011).

Gender and Shamanic Interpretations of Great Basin Rock Art

While much Anglo-American shamanic rock art research sidesteps the issue of gender, Whitley (1998a, 1998b, 1998c) addresses the gendered dimensions of shamanism in great detail and complexity. However, as with many areas within archaeology (Nelson 2006), the most obvious gender issue in the shamanic model for the Great Basin is the absence of women, as both subject matter and producers/users of rock art. In his discussion of Coso Range rock art, Whitley (1998a:270) claims that "completely absent in the Coso engravings are representations of women's crafts and utensils (e.g., basketry), or, for that matter, their product: the plants they gathered," therefore "all of the symbols of the shaman [i.e., the rock art imagery] are masculine." The only objects considered female are those that fit the woman-as-gatherer model, and the absence of overt evidence of women's involvement means that the rock art must have been made by and about men. One manifestation of this gender binary is pointed out by Quinlan and Woody (2003) in their discussion of Great Basin rock art: underreporting or ignoring the domestic context of much rock art in the Great Basin (a context contrary to both the hunting magic and shamanic models) and the frequent presence of nearby groundstone (e.g., bedrock mortars), stereotypically associated with women's processing activities. As Monteleone and Woody (1999:59) hypothesize about Coso rock art, "Could it be that women, too, produced rock art as a part of their ritual activity associated with harvesting and processing plants?"

Similarly, the gender identification of anthropomorphic figures in Great Basin rock art appears to be guided by a set of self-reinforcing assumptions: Rock art was made by shamans, most anthropomorphic rock art figures are therefore representations of shamans, and shamans were almost universally men, so images of shamans must be images of men. As Nelson (1997:136) explains in her discussion of male bias in archaeological interpretation, "If women are posited as shamans, strong proof is demanded, while if any activity is gendered male, not even a bridging argument is required."

Whitley (1994a, 1996, 2000a) denies that women produced (shamanic) rock art because women were not shamans in most far western indigenous cultures. His language varies from characterizing a shamanic initiate as "usually a male" (Whitley 1996:8) to his statement, citing ethnographic sources, that in the Great Basin "the art was produced by male shamans" (Whitley 1994a:83). When acknowledging that there were female shamans in the far western United States, he characterizes them as "exceptions" (Whitley 2000a:24). These rare female shamans were necessarily understood as malevolent sorceresses (Whitley 1996).

However, "female shamans were also frequent in many, but not all, Native American groups of the western United States" (Hays-Gilpin 2004:89). Kroeber's (1925:853) *Handbook of the Indians of California* indicates the existence of female shamans in many California tribes, including some groups in which "the shaman was almost invariably a woman." To the north of the Great Basin, "there is abundant ethnographic evidence across the Columbia Plateau that women can and did become shamans" (Taylor et al. 2008:145). Mairi Ross (2001) points out that in many cultures women were thought better suited to the altered states of consciousness required for shamanic practice.

While Whitley appropriately counters these generalities by citing ethnographic evidence specific to the Great Basin and particular cultural groups he discusses, such as the southern Paiutes, Ross (2001) also argues that female shamans were demonized as a result of European contact, questioning the validity of ethnographic evidence on this matter. In California and the Southwest in particular, Spanish colonization, accompanied by Catholicism, followed by Anglo-Protestant rule, and in some areas the presence of Mormons, increased the pressures on cultural continuity and integrity, particularly around topics such as shamanism and gender roles (Quinlan 2000). Admittedly, however, such dynamics did not affect all indigenous groups equally, and concerns about the contamination of ethnographic data due to already existing assimilationist effects on the cultures being studied may or may not apply as strongly to the Paiutes and related groups that are Whitley's primary focus as they do to other groups.

However, an additional factor is that the use of early ethnography must take into account that the ethnographic record was often constructed by white men (and sometimes women) based on conversations with indigenous men, but not necessarily women (Sundstrom 2008), potentially obscuring key aspects of women's participation in shamanic or other cultural practices. For example, Willard Park (1934) reports that among the northern Paiute (Paviotso), both men and women could become shamans and that shamanic power was sought in caves. Park (1934:102) then states, "Only men usually seek power in the caves according to the male informants, but Rosie Plummer insisted than women could also become shamans in the same way." The men could have been either unaware of women's use of the caves or ideologically invested in the narrative of male exclusivity, among other possible explanations, but Park's inclusion of Rosie Plummer's statement provides a glimpse into the effects of standpoint (in this case, gender) on ethnographic data. Indeed, outside of the context of shamanism, Whitley (2011) acknowledges the androcentric nature of many early ethnographies in particular, although he also makes arguments in support of strong cultural continuity across the contact boundary, thereby defending the validity of the ethnographic present (see chapter 3).

In a specific critique of Whitley's use of the ethnography of the Great Basin and California, Quinlan (2000:95) argues that "the role of women in doctoring practices is underplayed since, with the exception of the Kawaiisu, shamanism was open to both sexes in the Great Basin,

although in southern California it was predominantly a male pursuit."
Based on a review of available ethnographies, shamanism was practiced
by both sexes among the Chemehuevi and other Paiute groups in the
cultural Great Basin (Quinlan 2000:102). Isabel Kelly (1936) makes
multiple references to female shamans among the Chemehuevi, with
additional mentions in the context of the Las Vegas Paiutes (Kelly
2016). Kelly's (1939) review of southern Paiute shamanism indicates
that, overall, women were equally skilled and as benevolent as male
shamans. Some variability between the groups (or perhaps just individual consultants) was reported: among some groups women were never
rattlesnake shamans while in other groups they were, among some
groups women shamans did not cure when menstruating while among
other groups they did. However, southern Paiute consultants consistently indicated the existence of both male and female shamans (Kelly
1939:166). "Women shamans were considered almost without exception
malevolent" only among the Las Vegas group, although Kelly (1939:161)
names two Las Vegas women shamans who were acknowledged as powerful healers. This contradiction can be explained by understanding
that ethnographic queries sometimes evoke answers based on ideology
more than actual practice.

Whitley does put forth extensive explanations as to the general
absence of female shamans in the cultures whose rock art he studies—
that is, it is not simply an unnamed presumption, but an interpretation
grounded in reasoning and evidence. Perhaps most centrally, Whitley
(1998c) explains the lack of female shamans by emphasizing that shamanism in far western North America, and specifically in the Numic
Great Basin, was deeply gendered and relied on inversions of gender
symbolism. Rock art sites were gendered feminine, linked linguistically
to female dogs, baskets (made and used by women), and the color
red (symbolizing menstrual blood) (Whitley 1998c). These sites were
portals through which shamans entered the supernatural. Specifically,
rock art sites were "symbolic vaginas" and a shaman's ritual journey was
understood through a metaphor of heterosexual intercourse (Whitley
1994b, 1998c).

By defining shamanic journeys as intercourse with female sites/
spirits, Whitley (1998c) explains the dearth of female shamans through
symbolic inversions. The metaphoric link of heterosexual intercourse
with shamanic journeys is based on hallucinations involving sexual
relations with spirits; some hallucinogens used by shamans resulted in

priapism, which, along with nocturnal emissions, was understood as shamans having intercourse with supernatural entities (Whitley 1998c). Shamans, by opening the "earth's vagina" (e.g., a crack in the rock at a rock art site), "restore[d] life and fecundity to the world" (Whitley 1998c:19). On the literal side of the intercourse metaphor, shamans were known for their "unusual virility" and "extreme sexual appetites" (Whitley 1994b:21); "they were thought sexually predatory, and young girls were cautioned to keep away from them" (Whitley 1998c:19). Whitley (1998c) cites one 1936 ethnographic report indicating that shamanism was so heterosexualized that homosexuals could not be shamans. This report (Toffelmier and Luomala 2006 [1936]), however, is specific to the Kumeyaay of southwestern California and came after over 150 years of Catholic, Spanish, Mexican, and Anglo influence.

According to Gilchrist (1999), "third genders" (or gender variants) such as the "two spirit" were associated with the role of shaman or healer in some of the 150 Native American cultures in which such practices were documented, questioning Whitley's reliance on gender binaries and associated conceptions of heterosexuality. A small portion of males in nearly every traditional Native American society took on a feminine gender identity (Hays-Gilpin 2004), and cross-dressing occurred among some shamans (Ross 2001). "Shamans in many parts of the world do not conform to the same gender norms as nonshamans. . . . Some probably become shamans because they have ambiguous gender identities to begin with, and some cross-dress or blend indicators of more than one gender for spiritual reasons" (Hays-Gilpin 2004:89). In most of these cultures shamans "are expected to combine, confound or transcend sex and gender categories" (Hays-Gilpin 2004:61–62). Similarly, Sandra Hollimon (2001:125) highlights the association of gender "difference" (genders that exceed the binary) with supernatural power in much of precontact North America: "Not all shamans were of 'alternative' gender, nor were all alternative gender persons shamans; nevertheless, spiritual sanction was required to be a shaman, an alternative gender person, or both, in nearly all these societies."

The rigidity of the binary gender arrangement Whitley describes is potentially explained by the impact of Christian missionaries and other Europeans on indigenous cultures and ethnographic accounts (Hollimon 2001), although not all cultural groups were equally acculturated. Critically, ethnographic evidence of gender dualisms, patriarchy, and heteronormativity among precontact Native American cultures should not be taken as automatic indications of distortions of the ethnographic record; the presumption of egalitarian, nonbinary, and harmonious gender relations among indigenous peoples is a common manifestation of contemporary New Age primitivism. At the same time, however, indications of gender fluidity and/or the existence of third genders should be attended to, precisely because of the overriding (and often unconscious) influence of binary systems of gender among Western cultures. Kelly (1936:130) discusses a young Chemehuevi female who was acquiring shamanic power and had previously been thought to be becoming a bedarche, a problematic anthropological term of the time for what we might now reference as a two spirit or third gender. While it was determined that she was not becoming a third gender, my point is that the idea of a third gender was not alien to the Chemehuevi, or to the southern Paiutes more generally (Kelly 1939:161; 2016:147).

The existence of third genders and/or gender fluidity problematizes the sex/gender identifications of anthropomorphic figures and other rock art elements, identifications that are a key piece of support for the claim that only men were shamans in Great Basin cultures. In relation to the rock art of the Coso Range, Whitley, apparently relying upon Grant's (1968) earlier tabulations, states that of the four hundred "patterned body anthropomorphs" (which he identifies as shamans), "only about a half dozen are female" (Whitley 1996:121). Discussing what he labels a very rare portrayal of a female shaman, Whitley (1996:121) explains, "Based on general conventions of rock art representation across the West, female figures are typically represented by the depiction of a pendant labia and/or a characteristic bottle-shaped body, as opposed to straight up and down."

Three problems with these claims can be identified. First, my review of the tabulations he references and photographs of examples he discusses lead me to believe that in the absence of overt "female" markers, figures are assumed to be male even if no male-specific markers (e.g., a penis) are present. Second, the existence of third genders questions the use of culturally based gender codes to identify biological sex, such as Whitley's (1996) identification of the convention of "bottle-shaped" versus "straight up and down" bodies in rock art imagery in the western United States. Third, in his discussion of the use of historical ethnography in rock art interpretation—which is crucial both to his ascription of shamanism to far western rock art and to the arguments of some of his critics (e.g., Hedges 2001)—Whitley (1994a) emphasizes that many informants spoke in metaphorical terms and hence many of their statements must be interpreted figuratively, not literally. However, he does not suggest that either ethnographic statements about the sex/gender of shamans or visual markers in rock art (e.g., apparent penises or pendant labia) could themselves be metaphorical, or at least nonliteral, which would be consistent with the above discussions of gender fluidity and third genders, especially among shamans. Whitley appears to operate from a binary system of gender closely mapped onto biological sex, two assumptions that may be projections of Western ideologies (Hollimon 2001), although one should also not presume that these gender ideologies did not exist among indigenous groups.

Whitley's (1998c:21) most repeated explanation for why there were no (or few) female shamans is that "menstrual blood was thought so inimical to supernatural potency that women, during menstruation, were prohibited from participating in rituals, and effectively excluded from becoming shamans." While postmenopausal women could be shamans, they were "an oddity" and "necessarily believed to be sorceresses, or evil shamans" (Whitley 1996:123), for "while male sexuality was equated with intelligence and controlled supernatural potency, female sexuality was unbridled, dangerous and generally malevolent" (Whitley 1998c:21).

Whitley (possibly based on the language in ethnographic reports) consistently describes menstruation's relationship to shamanic power as "inimical": "having the disposition of an enemy," characterized by "hostility or malevolence" (per Merriam-Webster). Though he does not explicitly use the pollution metaphor often used in Western/Judeo-Christian cultures to name the effect of menstruation on the sacred, the effect is similar. Patricia Galloway (1998) argues that these views of menstruation are often transferred to other cultures' menstrual taboos and distort the ethnographic record by forcing the Western "male=sacred/female=polluting" structure onto cultures that may not operate from such a hierarchy. Ruth Trocolli (1999:52) argues that menstrual separation "can be viewed as a power issue" because "women bleed and do not die—a process heavily imbued with metaphors of power." If menstruation was seen as powerful, as opposed to "polluting" or "inimical," this can explain Kelly's (1936:134) Chemehuevi consultant's statement that "a woman had stronger power than a man" and "not all women doctors [shamans] were bad; some cured." Kelly's (1939) report on southern Paiutes indicates that among some groups women shamans did not practice when menstruating while among others they did, questioning a generalized ascription of meaning to the relationship between menstruation and shamanic power.

Whitley's characterization (based on ethnographic reports) of the indigenous view of female sexuality is strikingly homologous with Western/Judeo-Christian sexual ideologies (see Schott 1988): Female rock art symbols, such as the vulva-forms found in the Great Basin, "most likely represent examples of shamans' activities as sorcerers: in this case, harnessing the malevolent powers of the supernatural to steal another's soul, or otherwise cause them harm"; "female sexuality generally and the vagina specifically were associated with bewitching" and only male shamans "could control the power contained in" such rock art sites (Whitley 1998c:21). While Whitley acknowledges that shamanic power was viewed as ambivalent, able to be used for good or evil, and that a shaman's sexual potency was a sign of both his power and his dangerousness, he nevertheless reproduces the dualistic view (i.e., manifests a homology) that menstruation and female sexuality are unambiguously evil.

Relevant ethnographic evidence does support Whitley's arguments, such as Kelly's (1936:134) report that most Chemehuevi consultants "agreed that women shamans . . . invariably were sorcerers." However, potentially intervening factors include the cultural effects of contact with Westerners, the distance of the salvage ethnography from pre-contact times, and the social positions and interests of ethnographic consultants. Significantly, despite the views about female shamans expressed by most of her consultants, Kelly (1936:134) notes that "my chief Chemehuevi informant, however, declared that women were not always malignant," adding, "this may perhaps be attributed to a delicate consideration of my interpreter, whose mother is a shaman."

One area where Whitley (1994a, 1998c) acknowledges the female production and use of rock art in the far western United States is in association with puberty rites in southwestern California where ethnographic works directly identified such practices among the Luiseño and Serrano. These puberty rites ended with a race to a rock on which diamond-chain patterns and zig-zags, representing rattlesnakes, were painted with red paint, symbolizing menstrual blood, as well as hand-prints. "In an inversion of gender symbols, phallic rattlesnake was considered the ideal spirit helper for these young girls; hence, this girls' art is dominated by schematicised rattlesnake paintings" (Whitley

1998c:15). Whitley (1994b:5) characterizes sites used for female initiation rites as "dominated by these geometric motifs" (diamond chains and zig-zags), whereas shamans' sites "are characterized by a diversity of geometric and iconic forms" representing shamans, their spirit helpers, and the experiences of multiple ASCs over long periods of time. Whitley's discussion of rock art associated with female puberty rites continues common patterns. Women are only granted visibility when explicit and unambiguous evidence is available. Men engaged in "heroic" activities more than women since (male) shamans produced rock art and engaged in visions throughout their lives while women did so less frequently, perhaps only once. As Whitley (1998a:262) states, "These [vision quests/ASCs] were considered perilous and usually began with a supernatural test of worthiness and inner strength." Based on these verbal descriptions of (male) shaman's rock art versus that produced in female puberty rites, male rock art is more varied and complex, and hence by implication more interesting, and represents the successful performance of hegemonic masculinity.

The point of this lengthy recital of potential inaccuracies and projections in Whitley's arguments supporting a shamanic interpretation for much far western rock art is not to claim that his hypothesis is necessarily wrong, or that the model is equally flawed in relation to each and every specific case/region/culture he discusses. One point is, at a minimum, to open up the possibility to question these interpretations, particularly regarding gender—that is, to regard them as not solely determined by the available case-specific evidence. In addition, even if these applications of the shamanic hypothesis to the Great Basin and other areas in the far western United States have yielded empirically accurate explanations, I argue that aside from their empirical validity and explanatory value there are underlying cultural and ideological reasons for the ways in which these ideas have resonated with many researchers and avocationalists. The longstanding rhetorical efficacy of the hunting magic hypothesis cannot be explained by its empirical accuracy, after all—something else was in play. A central argument of this chapter and of this book as a whole is that models for interpreting rock art are, in large part, rhetorically effective due to their resonance with and ability to respond to contemporary cultural dynamics. Even if the shamanic model has substantial validity, its function in contemporary culture is not limited to supporting one way of understanding rock art over others, but certain ways of understanding gender as well.

In terms of gender roles and divisions of labor, shamanism in the Great Basin is not fundamentally different from hunting magic. Men are active parties who take on dangerous tasks: traveling far away, whether in the mundane or supernatural world; tackling dangerous creatures, whether through hunting or encountering spirits in the other world; and making magic to control their environment. I see no more wavering from the line of men as active, heroic, and exciting—and women as passive and dull—than in the hunting magic literature. Just as hunting (the male realm) was seen as more important than gathering (the female realm), in shamanism the hunt has become a symbolic or supernatural one. The centrality of the male figure, his power, and his tools remains. The various forms of power gained by shamans through trances/journeys and the production of rock art enables them to influence the mundane world through their prestigious social role and by their shamanic ability to affect the weather, cure, influence animal activity, or engage in sorcery. Women remain largely absent from rock art, both as subjects and producers. The drudgery of Native women's lives represented in the stereotype of the Squaw (Bird 2001) is manifested here by their minimal relationship to rock art: In this narrative, women only produce rock art once in their lives, as they transition from Maidens to Squaws. Embedded in the shamanic interpretation of Great Basin rock art is an ideology identifiable in other discussions of shamanic rock art: a Western "worldview that stresses masculine activity and female passivity" (Hays-Gilpin 2004:68). In this sense, both the hunting magic and shamanic models appear to perpetuate Western gender ideology. However, the dynamics of the shift from hunting magic to shamanism are especially significant for the parallel to the contemporary crisis of masculinity, specifically the shift from a material (subsistence) to a symbolic (social-spiritual) basis for hegemonic masculinity.

Shamanism and the Crisis in Masculinity

The role of the shamanic interpretation of rock art not only in offering a particular model of hegemonic masculinity, but in articulating the contemporary crisis in masculinity, is particularly evident in Whitley's (1998a) article "By the Hunter, for the Gatherer," which I briefly discussed early in this chapter. Using this article, the homology underlying the shamanic hypothesis and the discourse of the crisis of masculinity can be established through parallels in implied standpoint, diction, and narrative structure.

The narrative begins prior to 1200 CE, when Numic subsistence in the Coso Range "was based on a generalized hunting-gathering strategy" (Whitley 1998a:259). "Men were solely responsible for big game hunting" while women gathered plant foods and captured small game (Whitley 1998a:266). Meat obtained by men was communally shared, while women's contributions were reserved for their immediate families. As a result, women need not marry, but marriage was "necessary for a man to be independent from other men" (Whitley 1998a:266). Using specific regional evidence, which is then sorted and completed with a generalized model of marriage and inequality in classless societies, Whitley posits a stable system of gender inequality linked to this subsistence pattern:

> Although women were not necessarily considered inferior to men, the prescribed Numic means for acquiring and maintaining respect, prestige and ultimately authority essentially excluded them from it. Prestige, for example, was measured by the number of wives a person could obtain and hold, and discourse emphasized masculine traits and accomplishments, to the complete exclusion of feminine activities and undertakings, as hallmarks of success. Since success was defined exclusively in masculine terms, causality was necessarily linked to male activities and attributes, and feminine skills like gathering and child-rearing were devalued. (Whitley 1998a:266)

Around 1200 CE, however, "evidence suggests an increasing importance in plant foods at the expense of hunting and game" (Whitley 1998a:260). Men's loss of their provider role "threatened" to increase their dependence on women and decrease women's dependence on men (Whitley 1998a:266). Paralleling the narrative of the contemporary crisis, subsistence changes turn a previously "utilitarian masculinity" (Faludi 1999) into something economically insignificant and socially devalued.

The standpoint embedded in the repeated use of "threat" to describe the challenge to the existing gender system is revealing. Why this change would be a "threat" is not self-evident unless examined from the point of view of the privileged male role that Whitley claims existed prior to the subsistence change. Whitley indicates this change increased women's economic independence, and no reasoning is provided for why women would perceive this as a threat. While much of Whitley's description is couched in generic terms—e.g., "the threat to established gender relations" (Whitley 1998a:269)—the threat is to a social order that Whitley indicates benefits men. Paralleling the contemporary crisis of masculinity, whether or not changes in gender roles and ideologies constitute a "crisis" and "threat" depends on one's perspective, interests, and investments.

This foray into postprocessual and specifically cognitive archaeology, reconstructing a "system of beliefs and worldview" (Whitley 1998a:272), appears limited to masculine cognition and anxiety over the loss of male status, a perspective enabled by the broader disciplinary and social contexts in which this work is produced and circulated. For example, Whitley (1998a) describes the post–hunting-oriented Numic peoples as "seed eating" (262) and reliant on "seeds and nuts" (258). These terms, serving as a contrast to the earlier period of meat-eating, are perhaps innocently denotative in archaeology but are extremely loaded within contemporary Anglo-American gender ideologies, with "meat" equating to "manliness" and "seeds and nuts" equating to vegetarians, Californians, hippies, tree-huggers, gay men, and other stereotypically feminized groups (Adams 2003; Rogers 2008).

The response to the "threat" of women's independence and men's loss of status was a rise in shamanism, which Whitley (1998a) argues is recorded in the region's rock art. Noting a decrease in archaeological evidence for big-game hunting and an increase in rock art motifs such as male anthropomorphs, weapons, bighorn sheep, and hunting scenes, Whitley (1998a:269–270) constructs this "speculative" hypothesis: "The response to the threat to established gender relations precipitated by the change in subsistence . . . was to emphasize male—specifically, the male shaman's—control over women's plant gathering activities." Specifically, "the changing subsistence system in the western Great Basin appears to have precipitated a dramatic increase in weather control shamanism" (Whitley 1998a:269). Given the ubiquity of bighorn sheep imagery, including hunted or killed sheep, and ethnographic evidence indicating that killing a bighorn (mountain) sheep was a metaphor for bringing rain, Whitley emphasizes the role of rain shamans in responding to the threat to men's status, power, and prestige:

> Male shamans controlled women's plant gathering . . . not because they controlled plants and the ritual symbols of women.

Instead, it was because of their relationship with an important part of the world of men, the supernatural, from which they obtained *poha* [supernatural power], as symbolized metaphorically by hunting mountain sheep; and due to their control of the symbols of men—hunted game and weaponry. . . . The shaman thus demonstrated his importance to women's subsistence activities by metaphorically killing a mountain sheep and by recording this supernatural act in rock art, as well as emphasizing the continuing importance of male hunting, in general, by the selective use of these literal masculine symbols. (Whitley 1998a:270)

In this narrative, a threat to men's power in the mundane world was countered by men's exclusive claim to supernatural power through the role of the shaman and associated rock art. The rock art, therefore, records the successful performance of hegemonic masculinity in the face of a crisis of masculinity: "Given their ownership of esoteric knowledge, shamans were advantaged at a fundamental level: their access to the supernatural enabled them not only to cure (and cause) disease, and thereby exercise some social control through fear, but more generally enabled them to manipulate the workings of the universe to their own benefit" (Whitley 1998a:270–271). Echoing a hegemonic masculinity grounded in heterosexual virility, shamans had more access to females "given their enhanced desirability to women" due to their social and spiritual power (Whitley 1998a:270). For it was "only through the acquisition of shamanistic power that men could truly become political actors, and gain prestige and status in Numic society" (Whitley 1998a:268). Finally, "not only did the Numic shaman control nature through his rain rituals, and thereby directly aid the material reproduction of society, but he also fostered the stability of Numic social relations . . . by maintaining the established gender asymmetry" (Whitley 1998a:270). Shamanic masculinity restored the hunter's utilitarian and hegemonic masculinity and resolved the crisis of masculinity.

This narrative of gender and subsistence change reflects and engages the contemporary crisis of masculinity. Both Whitley's (1998a) narrative and that of the contemporary crisis focus on threats to the male provider role. Changes in subsistence practices (work) threaten that role by destabilizing the basis of hegemonic masculinity and by increasing women's participation and/or effectiveness in the realm of economics/

subsistence. Changes in economics/subsistence alter the performances constituting hegemonic masculinity, replacing physical/bodily activities with mental/symbolic ones. In the contemporary context, this relates to a presumed loss of primitive masculinity and sexual virility by the blue collar due to shifts towards a white- and pink-collar economy, the feminization of the white collar by corporations and bureaucracies, and the increased presence of women in the paid workforce.

Important for this analysis are not only the ways the narrative of the crisis of contemporary masculinity parallels Whitley's (1998a) narrative of the Numic crisis in the Cosos, but also the responses to and solutions for the crisis. In contemporary terms, masculinist responses include a return to primitive physicality, predatory sexuality, homosocial relations, and preindustrial spiritualities as well as the scapegoating of women, especially those who enter into previously male-only realms and roles (Ashcraft and Flores 2000; Bederman 1995; Churchill 1994; Ferber 2004).

One parallel between responses to the contemporary crisis of masculinity and the shamanic interpretation of rock art is the demonization of women. Regarding the exclusion of women from shamanism, Whitley (1998a:266) writes, "Shamanic power, believed the key to all success and authority, was inimical to menstrual blood, thereby effectively excluding women from prestige." The characterization of the relationship between male power and female essence as not only mutually exclusive but hostile points to a homology in the discourse of the contemporary crisis, in which women are often identified and scapegoated as the cause of men's wounding, the loss of their masculinity and of meaningful social and economic roles (Ashcraft and Flores 2000; Faludi 1999; Ferber 2004; Fine et al. 1997; Robinson 2000). In both the Numic crisis and that in contemporary Anglo-America, the mere presence of females in male realms is defined as malevolent. Coso rock art is not only masculine, but is constituted by Whitley's shamanic narrative as the phallus: the symbolic manifestation and material trace of the performance of exclusionary hegemonic power. Whitley (2006) holds that if there were female shamans (a woman in a man's realm), then they must have been evil sorceresses; similarly, female symbols depicted in rock art (a male realm), as in the vulva forms present at many sites in the Great Basin, indicate malevolent sorcery practiced by male shamans. In short, any mixing of male and female, of masculine and feminine, violates the gender binary and the gender hierarchy, and is therefore "evil" or "malevolent."

The androcentrism of the Great Basin shamanic model is high-lighted by Woody and McLane (2000) in their reading of vulva-forms in Great Basin rock art. Whereas Whitley argues that female shamans were considered malevolent sorcerers and that vulva-form sites must have involved male shamans performing malevolent magic, Woody and McLane (2000:35) suggest that female shamans may have been best suited to "negotiate and manipulate the evil power of the vulviform," challenging the claim that only men made rock art. Further, turning Whitley's foray into cognitive archaeology on its head, they employ a female standpoint, suggesting that if Numic society was as patriarchal as Whitley suggests, "it may well be that women participated in the production of these images as a way of ventilating aggression and frustration with the status quo" (Woody and McLane 2000:35).

Another parallel is between Whitley's positing of shamanism as a resolution to the crisis and the oft-noted connection between the crisis of masculinity and the mythopoetic men's movement of the 1980s and 1990s, which relied on the appropriation of various indigenous spiritualities to reconstruct Anglo-American, middle-class manhood (Bederman 1995; Churchill 1984; Ferber 2004). Spiritual roles seem to offer not only a justification for patriarchy that goes beyond economics/subsistence and physical strength/skill, but in some cases such roles license a "primitive" and virile masculinity. The Great Basin shamanic model incorporates heterosexuality, virility, and promiscuity into a role defined by its esoteric, symbolic nature. Shamanism centers symbolic/social/spiritual work amidst a virile hegemonic masculinity, offering a negotiation of the tension over changes in work and masculinity from blue to white collar. This preserves "primitive" sexuality and social prestige, offering one resolution to the apparent contradictions between primitive and civilized masculinities and changing forms of work. Reclaiming the primitive has long been central to Anglo-American masculinity—however, shamanism offers not simply a physical primitivism (e.g., utilitarian masculinity), but a spiritual primitivism that is (re)articulated to sexual potency, promiscuity, and even predation. In an Anglo-American frame, a decline in physical contributions to subsistence symbolically threatens male virility, but shamanism offers the image of a highly virile manipulator of symbols.

Hunting magic emphasizes physical abilities while adding a magical/ritual component. The shamanic model moves further away from physical skills and material acts toward a masculinity defined in terms of symbolic manipulation ("supernatural power" and "esoteric knowledge"), and in so doing positions (hetero)sexuality as central to Native masculinity. Shamanism in the rock art literature resonates with contemporary anxieties over masculine (hetero)sexuality in that it centers sexual virility both literally and metaphorically, and highlights a link between the revival of masculinity and sexual behavior that resists contemporary criticisms of male promiscuity and sexual predation. A return to blue-collar work may not seem a viable solution to the felt feminization/emasculation that characterizes the contemporary crisis, while a revival of male (hetero)sexual prowess may be a way to symbolically counter the perceived "softening" of masculinity within the (limited and fragile) prestige of the white collar.

All symbol use is rhetorical, and rhetoric is "a strategy for encompassing a situation" (Burke 1973:109)—a strategy that often operates far outside of conscious intent, originating in the realm of ideology and the cultural unconscious. The application of the shamanic model for rock art interpretation to the Great Basin posits a male Native figure, the shaman, who blends aspects of Bird's (2001) Doomed Warrior and Wise Elder. The figure manifests the prowess and agency of the Warrior with the spiritual knowledge of the Wise Elder, using the latter as means of engaging in symbolic travel, communion, and combat in order to manifest the hegemonic masculinity of the former. The (hetero)sexuality of the Warrior is highlighted both as a metaphor for the shaman's ritual power and as a literal description of his behavior, with the shaman's sexual potency reframing the spiritual wisdom of the asexual Wise Elder. In relation to the contemporary crisis, this offers a resolution to the tension between a physical, bodily, sexual, and "primitive" masculinity and a "civilized" masculinity of self-control, intellect, and willpower. Insofar as the origin of the contemporary crisis is often located in the changing nature of work, as traditional blue-collar masculinity gives way to a white-collar version, and as the prestige of white-collar work itself is problematized through corporate and bureaucratic feminization of the workforce, the shamanic narrative, through its homology with the narrative of the contemporary crisis, promises social prestige and sexual virility to the legions of emasculated paper pushers and corporate lackeys (including academics and archaeologists) who supposedly embody the white middle-class crisis of masculinity. Once again, Native American cultures are used as a screen for projecting Anglo-American cultural tensions and as a resource to (at least vicariously) resolve such tensions. Racial and cultural differences as well as historical distance enable the displaced expression of middle-class masculinist fantasies and resolutions to the crisis of masculinity while obscuring the underlying discursive homology.

Symbolic Power and Sexual Potency

The shamanic and hunting magic models both rely on binary opposi-tions: male/female, active/passive, sacred/secular. Native men are not only active, but enhance their physical activity through spiritual/mag-ical activity such as rock art. Native women are not only passive, but live lives focused on the material actions of processing gathered foods, birthing, and raising children. Native women's lives are largely unen-hanced by spiritual or symbolic activity, making them faceless Squaws (Bird 1999) with little to offer contemporary Westerners. Native men, in contrast, possess positive physical attributes, skills for survival in the material world (hunting, tracking), and special insight into the spiritual world gained through shamanic journeys and spirit helpers. For West-erners looking to compensate for what is lacking in contemporary exis-tence—physical survival challenges, a close relationship to nature, and a deeply felt spiritual wisdom—the image of Native American men, but not women, in rock art studies offers a rich resource for primitivist appropriations and projections.

In addition, during a period in which gender binaries have been increasingly challenged through the women's movement and feminist theory, the LGBTQ movement and queer theory, and in fashion and mass media imagery, both the hunting magic and shamanic models posit fixed and dualistic gender configurations. Even though the invocation of shamanism offers opportunities to question the stability of gender categories and their close mapping onto biological sex (Hays-Gilpin 2004; Hollimon 2001), the model's application to the Great Basin instead reinforces gender duality and hierarchy:

At any time in history, many contradictory ideas about manhood are available to explain what men are, how they ought to behave, and what sorts of powers and authorities they may claim, as men. Part of the way gender functions is to hide these contradictions and camouflage the fact that gender is dynamic and always changing. Instead, gender is constructed as a fact of nature, and manhood is assumed to be an unchanging, transhistorical essence, consisting of fixed, naturally occurring traits. (Bederman 1995:7)

In the case of both of the interpretive models discussed here, a rigid gender duality, characterizations of men as active and women as passive, and the centrality of fixed gender roles over long periods of time serve to reify historically and culturally specific gender configurations. Following Bederman (1995), however, close analysis of gender discourses can serve to highlight shifts and contradictions that can demystify gender ideologies.

The shift in masculinity from the hunting magic of the 1960s to the shamanism of the 1990s offers insight into changes and tensions in Anglo-American masculinity. While the images of men in both models are consistent with hegemonic masculinity—they hold to a strict gender duality, posit men as active agents, and value men's over women's contributions (Connell 1995; Trujillo 1991)—there are significant differences. First, while both emphasize the supernatural in the form of magic or spirits, there is a shift from hunting magic as supportive of material subsistence to shamanism as a source of social power that compensates, at least in part, for a loss of status due to decreased contributions to subsistence. Such a shift not only follows the move from processual to postprocessual archaeology (see chapter 2), but also parallels economic trends often cited as central to the contemporary crisis of US masculinity: the displacement of men from their role as breadwinners, the move from blue- to white-collar occupations, and attendant shifts in definitions of masculine competence and power. Second, the hunting magic model highlights men as hunters and ritual practitioners, but does not explicitly foreground sexuality. The shamanic model not only makes male heterosexuality a metaphoric trait of shamanic practice, power, and ideology, it posits heterosexual promiscuity/predation as a trait of the shaman himself. To put it bluntly, Viagra and concerns over erectile dysfunction are products of white-collar, middle-class, white masculinity, not the blue-collar masculinity of the 1950s (a topic I return to in relation to Kokopelli in chapter 5). The image of the shaman (re)defines sexual virility as linked to symbolic/spiritual power (white collar), not physical strength and skill (blue collar). Male sexual prowess, be it desirable or dangerous, is recentered as a key element of hegemonic masculinity, as is the ability to effectively use symbols, in direct contrast to utilitarian masculinity.

The shamanic hypothesis for Great Basin rock art, therefore, can not only be understood as paralleling the contemporary crisis in (white) masculinity; shamanism also offers a model for its resolution. This analysis of masculinity in rock art interpretation suggests a third Anglo-American model of Native American masculinity: the Shaman. This image combines aspects of the Doomed Warrior and Wise Elder (Bird 2001), but is not reducible to either. Neither of these existing images alone is sufficient for resolving the crisis of primitive/civilized masculinity (cf. Ashcraft and Flores 2000; Bederman 1995). The Doomed Warrior offers a physical/sexual vitality addressing a felt lack in contemporary white-collar masculinity, but such a physicality is no longer viable, as reflected in the Warrior's status as "doomed"—physically strong but structurally impotent (Bird 2001). No viable space for a purely physical masculinity exists in the modern world for middle-class whites or Indians. The Wise Elder, while offering a positive portrayal of spiritual wisdom, offers no compensation for emasculated idea workers in search of a vigorously sexualized masculinity. The Shaman's mystical power and sexual virility revitalize hegemonic masculinity through the displacement of male power and virility from the physical to the social and spiritual while retaining the centrality of male heterosexual potency. Indigenous spirituality is positioned as a link between the "lost foundation" of masculinity—the primitive, sexualized body—and masculinity's manifestation in symbolic performances. Addressing economic changes may be beyond the power of individual men; a vicarious or behavioral engagement of an unabashed sexual potency may therefore be more gratifying. Importantly, this is not the "sensitive (Indian) man" identified by van Lent (1996), but one who appears to relate to women (in the material world at least) not as subjects but as objects.

Identification of this particular "strategy for encompassing a situation" (Burke 1973:109) contributes to understandings of the contemporary crisis of masculinity, clarifies one possible function of the androcentric representation of Native Americans, and highlights the mutual vulnerability of seemingly unrelated but nevertheless homologous discourses. Homologies can not only enhance the appeal of particular texts and discourses, as well as shape perceptions and evaluations through the principle of vulnerability (Brummett 2004); they can also assist the operation of cultural projections and the "working through" of cultural tensions via tropes such as the primitive. Specifically, academic discourses are not only vulnerable to homological influences, but the dominance or acceptance of particular theories and models may be less a result of empirical evidence and validity than of their homology to contemporary conditions, ideologies, and identities. The rise and fall of different hypotheses about the past may well be linked to their ability to effectively resonate with and respond to contemporary cultural dynamics. Since an individual "text calls attention to the particular individuation of form that it is rather than the form itself" (Brummett 2004:20), the role of discursive homologies can be easily overlooked, obscuring important ideological affiliations and rhetorical operations.

Reflexivity and Change

Since the primary publications advancing Whitley's version of the shamanic hypothesis, which appeared from about 1994 through 1998, there has been increased attention to gender in rock art and some increased sensitivity to the blinders imposed by Western gender ideologies. Most visibly, the publication of Hays-Gilpin's (2004) *Ambiguous Images: Gender and Rock Art* seems to have nudged some rock art researchers into more careful and systematic identifications of the makers and subject matter of rock art. The book is cited often, including in many works not focused on gender or advancing a feminist perspective. While the depth to which Hays-Gilpin's arguments will affect the unconscious operation of androcentric, heterocentric, and dualistic thinking remains uncertain, her work has not stood alone in this regard. A number of shorter works have appeared that focus on depictions of women and women's symbols in rock art, women as producers of rock art, and women engaging in ritual activities at rock art sites, particularly in the context of the Great Basin (e.g., Cannon and Woody 2007; Monteleone and Woody 1999; Pendegraft 2007; Quinlan and Woody 2003), but in other regions as well (e.g., Sundstrom 2002, 2004, 2008; Taylor et al. 2008). Some of these works go beyond paying attention to women's role in rock art, engaging in both original research and the critical examination of previous rock art research (Cannon and Woody 2007; Monteleone and Woody 1999; Pendegraft 2007; Quinlan and Woody 2003). This is in stark contrast to the mid-1990s, in which Bass's (1994) criticisms of gender identifications in west Texas rock art stood alone as a feminist critique of US rock art research, and in even starker contrast to the primitivist, essentialist interpretations of women's relationship to rock art in the 1980s (e.g., Vuncannon 1985).

Words may use us as much as we use them (Burke 1966). Language and ideology may speak through us, but there is always the possibility of increasing levels of reflection that help guard against the undesirable intrusion of unconscious cultural biases, anxieties, and investments. We have a long way to go in uncovering our unconscious assumptions and biases, and even farther to understand how those have shaped both our data and our interpretations thereof, but it is my hope that analyses such as those listed above, as well as those I have provided in this chapter, can continue to move us not only away from such biases, but to explore our investments in such biases—that is, not only to their existence, but to the work they do in contemporary cultural contexts.

Of course, academic, professional, and even avocational research is not the only venue in which rock art and Native American cultures are used to construct the sexuality of Native American men in service of Anglo-American masculinity. A reclamation of the primitive is key to Anglo-American masculinity, and therefore will not be easy to dislodge, especially in the realm of popular culture, the primary focus of the next chapter on Kokopelli.

CHAPTER 5

PHALLUSES AND FANTASIES

Kokopelli, Caricature, and Commodification

I ndigenous rock art and other visual media such as decorated pottery are important sources of imagery used to represent Native American culture in general, especially Native cultures of the southwestern United States. Most common in the Southwest is the image of the "hump-backed flute player" commonly (mis)known as Kokopelli. Overwhelming other rock art images, Kokopelli has become a highly recognizable, named icon of the Southwest and a metonym for the region's Native American cultures. The most common versions of Kokopelli include wavy protrusions extending upward from its head as it hunches over, appearing to dance while playing a flute. In all its manifestations and variations, over the last thirty years Kokopelli has largely displaced—but by no means erased—the howling coyote and saguaro cactus as the dominant symbols of the Southwest (Tisdale 1993).

Kokopelli, Icon of the Southwest

Kokopelli kitsch has metastasized across the Southwest and beyond. Shirts, hats, socks, handkerchiefs, paintings, sculptures, pottery, jewelry, key rings, stuffed toys, candle holders, mugs, cups, shot glasses, water bottles, coasters, placemats, napkin rings, aprons, oven mitts, bottle openers, wine stoppers, cookbooks, clocks, calendars, mouse pads, wind chimes, weather vanes, thermometers, coat racks, night lights, lamps, lamp shades, shower curtains, emery boards, incense, doormats, rugs, towels, tapestries, bowls, vases, purses, refrigerator magnets, ceramic tiles, door knockers, beer, wine, Southwest chili mix and other food products, and an almost unimaginable variety of other tourist merchandise incorporate Kokopelli imagery. Carlos Nakai, the well-known Native American flutist, has one album titled *Kokopelli's Café* and another, titled *Changes*, features petroglyph-style flute player images on the cover. Several books about Kokopelli designed for rock art aficionados, tourists, general readers, and even children are widely available as well, as are at least three novels featuring Kokopelli.

Kokopelli merchandise can be found in most gift and souvenir shops, museum stores, visitor centers, and Native arts-and-crafts outlets in the Southwest, as well as grocery stores, convenience stores, gas stations, and high-end art galleries. In many locations, such as Cameron Trading Post on the Navajo Nation just outside Grand Canyon National Park, one can find Native-themed souvenirs including kitschy Indian Princess dolls, toy bows and arrows, bear fetishes, and dream catchers, as well as high-end silver and turquoise jewelry, pottery, kachina dolls, and hand-woven rugs, not to mention a lot of rock art imagery not depicting flute players. Nevertheless, Kokopelli items are numerically and visually overwhelming by comparison.

The name and image of Kokopelli are inescapable as one travels across the Southwest. Passing through Phoenix's Sky Harbor Airport, airline passengers are greeted by the Kokopelli Café. Pulling off I-40 in Camp Verde, Arizona, on the way to Sedona or the Grand Canyon, the Krazy Kokopelli Trading Post presents the "world's largest Kokopelli" at thirty-two feet tall and five and a half tons (see Plate 6 and Lowe 2001). On Highway 89 south of Sedona, a similar giant Kokopelli is displayed in the front yard of a residential structure. On historic Route 66 in downtown Flagstaff, drivers pass a six-foot-tall metal Kokopelli playing a guitar in front of a local music store (see Figure 5.1). In Moab, Utah, a bar and grill also features a huge guitar-playing Kokopelli statue on top of its street-side sign. Outside of Zion National Park, one can grab some lunch at Kokopelli Deli in Hurricane, Utah. Driving through the Navajo Nation in northeastern Arizona, roadside stand after roadside stand uses Kokopelli imagery to draw in travelers to buy the jewelry, pottery, and other goods offered for sale (see Figure 5.2).

Hotels, campgrounds, restaurants, tour companies, outdoor guides, gift shops, wineries, housing developments, real estate companies, golf clubs, hair salons, spas, music stores, storage facilities, landscapers, and other commercial establishments utilize the name and/or image of Kokopelli to identify and market their products and services. In Bluff,

FIGURE 5.1–Guitar-playing Kokopelli, Arizona Music Pro, Flagstaff, Arizona.

FIGURE 5.2–Roadside stand Kokopelli, Cedar Ridge, Highway 89, Navajo Nation, Arizona.

Utah, the bright red, happily dancing flute player on the motel's sign welcomes travelers to the Kokopelli Inn (see Figure 5.3). The inn provides a quarter-size information sheet about Kokopelli not unlike those offered by many other Kokopelli-themed businesses: Kokopelli, the inn's guests are informed, is a symbol of fertility, possibly a trader from Mexico wearing a backpack, and perceived as something of a threat to young maidens and a boon to couples trying to conceive. In nearby Blanding, travelers can stay at Kokopelli Kabyn, complete with dual Kokopellis on the wall above the headboard, a Kokopelli bathroom rug, and Kokopelli dishware in the kitchen cupboards. Other Kokopelli-named lodging opportunities include the Days Inn Kokopelli in the Village of Oak Creek, Arizona; Kokopelli Lodge and Suites in Moab, Utah; Best Western Kokopelli Lodge in Clayton, New Mexico; Kokopelli Cave Bed and Breakfast in Farmington, New Mexico; and the Kokopelli Inn in Estes Park, Colorado.

In Southwest tourist meccas like the Grand Canyon, Zion, Sedona, and Moab, Kokopelli kitsch is often adapted to the local tourist market by having Kokopelli don sunglasses, hike, ride a mountain bike, drive an off-road vehicle, raft down a river, jet ski, water ski, or downhill ski. For those interested in more than buying a t-shirt depicting outdoor activities, one can mountain bike along the BLM's 140-mile-long

FIGURE 5.3–Kokopelli Inn, Bluff, Utah.

Kokopelli's Trail in eastern Utah and western Colorado, book a river-rafting trip in New Mexico with Kokopelli Rafting Adventures, or enter the Kokopelli Triathlon in Hurricane, Utah. Kokopelli imagery has adapted to other tastes and lifestyles as well, as in a pink t-shirt with an image of an Easter bunny–style chocolate Kokopelli with a chunk bitten off, renamed "Cocoa-Pelli." In Kanab, Utah, a Kokopelli-like figure, sans flute and sweating while running on a treadmill, advertises a local fitness center (see Figure 5.4). Las Vegas offers Kokopelli the gambler in the form of the mascot for a convenience and souvenir store, showing Kokopelli, sans flute, dressed in modern clothing and holding two playing cards in his hand.

Kokopelli is often positioned to serve as a greeter, welcoming visitors to a specific establishment or to the Southwest in general. At the Twin Rocks Trading Post in Bluff, Utah, two mirror-image Kokopellis are carved into the large, double wooden doors that serve as the main entrance. Approaching Walnut Canyon National Monument in Arizona, the entrance sign announcing the monument's operating hours features two flute players pointed toward each other, an image

FIGURE 5.4—Kokopelli on treadmill, Adobe Fitness Center, Kanab, Utah.

FIGURE 5.5—Gifts of the West Kokopelli, Kanab, Utah.

reproduced from a petroglyph found in the bottom of the canyon. Visitors to Kanab, Utah, encounter a large Kokopelli figure on the outside of a souvenir shop, beckoning them to stop in (see Figure 5.5).

In the western United States, I have encountered Kokopelli merchandise and marketing in Jackson Hole, Wyoming; Placerville, California; Death Valley National Park, California; Yosemite National Park, California; Eugene, Oregon, and Seaside, Oregon—all areas far outside of the regions where the kinds of flute player rock art imagery associated with Kokopelli are found. In addition, the name and image of Kokopelli have been used commercially far outside the western United States, from cafés on the East Coast to advertising and graphic design agencies in the Midwest to an interior design firm in Washington, DC. Beyond the United States, the name and image have been used by a graphic design firm in the Netherlands, a tour company and restaurant in Costa Rica, and a tour company in Barcelona, Spain. The World Wide Web offers a plethora of Kokopelli images and interpretations, frequently in the context of the selling of Kokopelli, Native American, and/or Southwest merchandise.

In 1993, Shelby Tisdale explored the then-recent rise of Kokopelli imagery in the Southwest, cataloguing the increasing popularity and ubiquity of the name and imagery through an exploration of books, magazines, mail-order catalogs, art galleries, and gift shops, as well as interviews with both retailers and consumers. Finding Kokopelli almost everywhere associated with the Southwest, she remained curious as to "whether the Kokopelli image had really reached the general population," not just rock art aficionados, Native American arts collectors, Southwest collectors, and scholars (Tisdale 1993:217). She therefore headed to a Wal-Mart in Tucson, Arizona, where she found Southwest merchandise but not Kokopelli, leading her to ask, "As he becomes more commoditized and his popularity increases from California to New York, will he eventually show up in discount stores such as Wal-Mart?" (Tisdale 1993:217). By the early 2000s, he had indeed hit the commercial mainstream, with Kokopelli-themed books, music, jewelry, and entire bathroom sets offered through mega retailers such as Wal-Mart, Target, and Amazon. But was he ready for primetime?

Kokopelli had sporadically appeared on television, his most notable early appearance in a 2002 episode of *Buffy the Vampire Slayer*, where he was characterized as a "fertility god." In 2011, however, he spent a month on prime-time broadcast TV in conjunction with Will Ferrell's four-episode appearance as the interim branch manager on NBC's *The Office*. Deangelo Vickers (played by Ferrell), a self-fashioned Southwest aficionado, redecorated his office (featured, consistent with *The Office* pattern, in the opening credits) in a southwestern theme. Signifiers of the Southwest included a cow skull (presumably a reference to Georgia O'Keefe imagery), a cactus, a painting of a deep red desert sunset featuring Saguaro cacti, two figures that appear to resemble kachina dolls, and a dream catcher (the latter having no known role in traditional Southwest indigenous cultures; originating with the Ojibwe, it has become both a pan-Indian and a New Age symbol). Very prominent, however, are also two large, metallic blue Kokopelli figurines, one on his desk and another in front of the sunset painting. Significantly for this chapter's focus on masculinity, *The Office* generally, and the position of manager in particular, is highly symbolic of the emasculated white-collar man in contemporary US culture. Like Michael Scott (played by Steve Carell), the long-time manager on the show, Vickers is highly representative of anxieties over the possibilities of a competent hegemonic masculinity in the contemporary corporate workplace, and his Southwest accoutrements can be understood as part of his symbolic response to those anxieties.

In their study of flute player rock art, Dennis Slifer and James Duffield (1994:3) describe the image and its appeal: "Kokopelli's flute, humped back, and prominent phallus are his trademarks. These features and the widely held beliefs that Kokopelli was a fertility symbol, roving minstrel or trader, rain priest, hunting magician, trickster, and seducer of maidens, have contributed to his popularity." Tisdale (1993:219) explains, "Kokopelli's fertility role is the most notable carryover into the historic period. . . . To new agers he is a mystical symbol of ancient Native American spirituality; to the average tourist visiting the Southwest, he is a happy musician." Ekkehart Malotki (2000:1) writes, "Probably no other image in the entire body of Southwestern iconography has attracted as much attention as that of the fluteplayer." As Kelley Hays-Gilpin (2004:12) assesses the situation, the "so-called Kokopelli, the phallic flute player of the Southwest, . . . probably has more meaning to contemporary Euroamericans than he ever did to Pueblo ancestors."

Reading Kokopelli

Guided by critical understandings of the ideology of primitivism, this chapter analyzes contemporary Kokopelli imagery and discourse as a projection of Euro-American masculinist fantasies and as a commodification of Native American cultures. Kokopelli imagery and discourse models a virile and promiscuous heterosexual masculinity while avoiding visual representations of its anatomical signs. It articulates intersections of gender, race, and culture that simultaneously highlight and obscure primitive masculinity and racial difference, enabling the use of Native American culture and spirituality to (re)vitalize Euro-American masculinity and promote neocolonial appropriations.

As discussed in chapter 3, examinations of Euro-American representations of Native Americans, such as Kokopelli imagery and its attendant discourses, can not only help identify what Native Americans mean in Euro-American culture, but how those meanings operate in relation to contemporary cultural tensions, especially via the ideology of primitivism. Specifically, Kokopelli imagery provides insight into the gendered dimensions of Native American imagery. As discussed in chapter 4 in relation to hunting magic and shamanism, while a few scholars have focused on gendered representations of Native Americans, insufficient attention has been paid to the almost exclusively male gendering of the dominant images of Native Americans in recent decades, a pattern that continues with Kokopelli. Analysis of Kokopelli imagery offers insights into Euro-American gender dynamics, particularly tensions over (white) masculinity, highlighting the work that such images and meanings perform.

In addition to its roles as site of projection and model of masculinity, Kokopelli is an appropriation and commodification of indigenous imagery. Kokopelli is constituted as a fetish, with the many commodities it brands serving as concrete manifestations of its meanings. In addition to identifying gendered meanings circulating around Kokopelli imagery, therefore, this chapter examines the nature and implications of its commodification, moving beyond what Kokopelli means toward an understanding of how the imagery, verbal descriptions, and their attendant meanings work.

Relying on the foundation established by my earlier discussions of Western representations of Native Americans, the ideology of primitivism, gendered representations of Native Americans, and the contemporary crisis of white masculinity (see chapters 3 and 4), I identify a series of tensions and contradictions in Euro-American masculinity that are played out through the primitive masculinity assigned to Kokopelli. Kokopelli imagery engages discourses of Euro-American masculinity by celebrating a virile and promiscuous male heterosexuality while obscuring both the figure's traditional meanings and the implications of neocolonial appropriations. Specifically, racial difference is both highlighted through the deployment of the trope of the primitive and obscured through the abstracted qualities of Kokopelli imagery. The figure of Kokopelli simultaneously essentializes racial/cultural difference while unhinging race from culture, enabling the use of Native American culture and spirituality to revitalize Euro-American masculinity through neocolonialist appropriations.

Kokopelli imagery contributes to male dominance in Euro-American representations of Native Americans and articulates a model of primitive masculinity highlighting sexual potency. A return to the "primitive" side of the masculine duality is enacted through the image of Kokopelli. Kokopelli is one site for working through contemporary Euro-American tensions over masculinity and sexual behavior specifically, recovering the image of the ignoble savage in terms of a virile and unrestrained sexuality but with an attempt to remove moral judgments concerning such behavior.

To understand the images of masculinity and of Native Americans that are circulated through Kokopelli, I begin by identifying differences between contemporary Kokopelli imagery and the traditional imagery and mythology on which it is loosely based. With this foundation, I analyze commercial Kokopelli imagery and verbal texts circulating around it in order to identify recurring themes, especially in relation to masculinity and sexuality. This focus on commercial Kokopelli images and attendant verbal texts is supplemented by references to literature that identifies differences between traditional flute player imagery, the Hopi *katsina* (kachina) from which Kokopelli's name is derived, and contemporary commercial Kokopelli imagery. Some of this literature is produced in the context of academic anthropology, archaeology, and linguistics (Hays-Gilpin 2004; Malotki 2000), while some straddles the academic/popular distinction (Malotki and Weaver 2002; Slifer 2000b, 2007; Slifer and Duffield 1994). All of it, however, is driven primarily by an interest in understanding traditional flute player imagery, and therefore emphasizes distortions and inaccuracies embedded in popular/commercial Kokopelli imagery and literature. While my emphasis is not on correcting such distortions, but instead on understanding their ideological operation, identification of alterations in traditional flute player imagery and the selective appropriation of stories about the Hopi *katsina* provides insight into the articulation of Kokopelli imagery with contemporary cultural dynamics.

Both Kokopelli imagery and popular verbal texts, such as books and websites directed at tourists and collectors, are the subject of this analysis. While many of the same themes are manifested in scholarly and popular texts, and while some of these texts blur the scholarly/popular distinction, my analysis focuses primarily on popular texts surrounding Kokopelli imagery. While others have explored flute player images in both precontact Native and contemporary Western contexts (Hays-Gilpin 2004; Malotki 2000; Slifer 2000b, 2007; Slifer and Duffield 1994), my purpose here is deriving insights into contemporary cultural dynamics via an exploration of contemporary Kokopelli imagery and discourse. While claims about traditional meanings of flute player imagery will necessarily be present, my purpose is less to establish the truth of such interpretations than to use them to identify operations of contemporary Kokopelli imagery.

I do not wish to leave Hopi and other indigenous voices out of this chapter, but I chose not to solicit and represent indigenous knowledge not already publicly available. One implication of this analysis is precisely how such information can be misappropriated; even if dealt with

responsibly by authors, others can still appropriate those more responsible appropriations in less responsible ways. As stated on the official
Hopi website,

> A great deal of knowledge that may have been shared with guests
> as a courtesy or as privileged information, even in moments of
> undeserved trust, has been published. These published accounts,
> be they accurate or misleading, have been misused to replicate
> Hopi ceremonies and spirituality for profit. In many cases, in-
> formation has been altered in a way that ignores any spiritual
> context and religious significance. (Hopi Staff 2004)

I am interested in the implications of meanings in circulation today.
While questions about the inauthenticity of those meanings are
extremely important, those questions have been well addressed in the
current academic literature. Drawing from that literature, I review
claims about the "true" meanings of both flute player imagery and associated figures from Puebloan mythology.

However, my primary focus is on the contemporary function of
those meanings—the work that they do, be they accurate or not. Therefore, given the purpose and focus of this analysis and the intentional
reticence of some Native people, while I draw from existing published
material on Native American views of flute players and Kokopelli, I do
so cautiously and selectively, in an attempt to avoid enabling additional
exploitation of indigenous spiritual traditions as well as the Hopi belief
that "religion is a private matter and that there is already too much
information available to non-Hopis about Hopi spirituality" (Hopi
Staff 2004). At times, Hopi people speak out publicly in an attempt
to convince outsiders that flute players are not Kokopelli; I see a substantial difference between reproducing those kinds of statements as
opposed to specific information about Hopi culture that the Hopis, by
and large, wish to keep to themselves. Finally, while some published
materials may contain information that some Hopis may not want
to publicize, I am painfully aware of the tension between, on the one
hand, respecting Hopi wishes to not further the distribution of some
information and, on the other, the need to examine the information
that is out there in order to critically examine its ideological operations and the implications for both Native and non-Native peoples
and cultures. Hopefully, I have managed to critically examine the

contemporary appropriations of elements of Hopi and other Native cultures while not engaging in additional problematic appropriations. (For a critique of researchers withholding information out of deference to Native groups, see Schaafsma [2013]; for an in-depth discussion of the issues surrounding the sharing or withholding of indigenous views of rock art, see chapter 6.)

Kokopelli: Neither Flute Player nor Kookopölö

The images popularly identified today as "Kokopelli" are based on traditional flute player images from painted ceramics, rock art, and other media, and are quite varied (see Plate 7 and Figures 5.6 and 5.7). According to various scholars, flute player images in rock art date from ca. 500 to 1600 CE (though a few may be older) and occur across the Colorado Plateau and adjacent areas of the Southwest (Hays-Gilpin 2004; Malotki 2000; Malotki and Weaver 2002; Slifer 2007; Slifer and Duffield 1994). They are most consistently, but not exclusively, associated with ancestral Puebloan cultures and their descendants, such as the Hopi, Zuni, and Rio Grande Pueblos. A "flute player"—the term used by most contemporary rock art researchers instead of "Kokopelli"—can occur with or without a penis (often erect and/or seemingly exaggerated when present, thus arguably constituting a phallus: a symbol of masculinity), with or without a humped back, with or without "antennae," and alone or with other figures (Hays-Gilpin 2004; Malotki and Weaver 2002; Slifer 2007). A posture indicative of dancing is fairly common. Humped-back variations may also represent traders carrying their wares in a backpack (Hays-Gilpin 2004; Slifer 2007). Some figures that are otherwise similar to flute players do not have an apparent flute, and in some cases hold a staff (Tisdale 1993).

In Pueblo cultures, the flute is gendered masculine and is key in courtship, strengthening the graphic parallel between flute and penis, with the flute potentially signifying male fertility (Hays-Gilpin 2004; Slifer 2007). Hopi ethnography suggests the cicada—generator of summer warmth to ripen crops by playing its "flute" (prominent proboscis)—as a natural model for at least some traditional flute player images, furthering its role as a fertility symbol (Malotki 2000). Insect models offer one explanation for the antenna-like appendages sometimes present on the heads of flute players. The humped back may also refer to the shape of these insects or to a backpack, possibly filled with seeds.

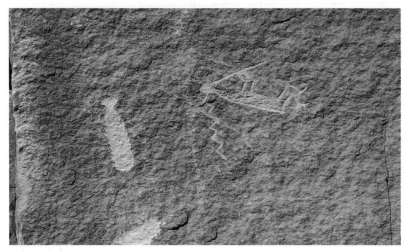

FIGURE 5.6—Reclining flute player petroglyph, Wupatki National Monument, Arizona.

The Hopi *katsina* (spirit being) named *Kookopölö* is also based on an insect model—the robber fly, a persistent copulator—and features a humped back and prominent proboscis (Malotki 2000). Based on late nineteenth-and early twentieth-century ethnographic accounts, *Kookopölö* traditionally wore a prominent gourd "penis" and simulated copulation with bystanders during ceremonial occasions, but did not carry a flute (Fewkes 1903; Hays-Gilpin 2004; Malotki 2000; Titiev 1939). *Kookopölö's* female counterpart, *Kokopölmana*, also demonstrated sexually inappropriate and aggressive behavior, simulating copulation with male observers during dances (Malotki 2000; Titiev 1939). Both verbal accounts and drawings confirm the absence of a flute (see Plate 8 and Turner 1963). Hopi stories about *Kookopölö* (and other Puebloan stories about parallel cultural figures) feature fertility themes and an abnormally large penis, and include the humped back (Malotki 2000).

Fertility is a central theme of both *Kookopölö* and flute player images, be it through the former's association with the robber fly (known for its copulatory tendencies), the latter's association with the cicada (a sign of summer warmth), the latter's flute (associated with the cicada as well as courtship and male sexuality), or the erect penis sometimes associated with both. Linked to the sun and germination as well as courtship and seduction, traditional flute players are sometimes paired with maidens, representing the complementary elements of fertility: female/moisture/

FIGURE 5.7—Grand Gulch flute player petroglyph, San Juan County, Utah.

rain and male/warmth/sun (Hays-Gilpin 2004). Flute players are sometimes depicted next to a copulating couple or participating in copulation (Slifer 2007). Among the Zuni, the hump-backed flute player is associated with fertility and rain (Schaafsma 2010; Young 1988).

Despite some parallels between the two—insect models, humped backs, fertility themes—the *katsina Kookopölö* has been inaccurately conflated with both traditional and contemporary flute player imagery.

The use of the Anglicized name "Kokopelli" (or an earlier Anglicization, "Kokopele") is in the case of most of the imagery discussed here almost certainly in error, but has nevertheless become common usage (Hays-Gilpin 2004; Malotki 2000; Slifer 2007). Among the Hopis, flute player images may be referred to as *maahu* (cicada) or in some cases *lelenhoya* (flute player) or *Lelentiyo* (Flute Boy), but are not referred to as *Kookopölö* (Church 2005; Malotki 2000; Slifer 2007). Flute players are often identified by Hopi consultants as a clan symbol, not the image of a *katsina*, let alone *Kookopölö*. Christy Turner (1963:22) reports that Hopi consultants identified flute player images in rock art in Glen Canyon as a clan symbol and as definitely not *Kookopölö*, as "no one ever speaks of Kokopele being a flute player." According to Malotki (2000), Alph Secakuku was the first Hopi to publicly point out the misidentification of flute players as Kokopelli in his 1995 book *Following the Sun and Moon: Hopi Kachina Tradition*. In 2005, Anasazi State Park in Boulder, Utah, presented a year-long exhibit, created with help from members of the Hopi Flute clan, focused on correcting the misidentification of flute players as Kokopelli (Church 2005). Such efforts seem to have had limited if any effect, however. Tamara McPeak (2004:45) reports an incident in a Flagstaff, Arizona, Native American arts store in which a customer, after being informed that the flute player is not Kokopelli, "was still willing to buy a piece of jewelry with the flute player design, but said that she was going to call the design kokopelli [*sic*], because she liked the sound of the word better than the name flute player." In 2017, Wikipedia's "Kokopelli" entry, as well as many websites providing information about Hopi kachina dolls (e.g., kachina.us and kachina-dolls.com), continue to perpetuate the misidentification of flute players as Kokopelli, as well as of Kokopelli as a flute player, as do many websites providing information about rock art for tourists and tour guides (e.g., zionnational-park.com, desertusa. com, riverguides.org).

The conflation of flute player images with *Kookopölö*, creating a situation where all variations of the former are widely referred to as "Kokopelli," is of concern to many Hopis, especially members of the Flute clan (Church 2005). The possibility remains, however, that some flute player images in rock art could be related to *Kookopölö* (Slifer 2007). Church (2005) also quotes Clay Hamilton of the Hopi Cultural Preservation Office as saying that flute player–like images without a flute but carrying a walking stick or staff may indeed be *Kookopölö*. For my purposes, however, exploring how the conflation called "Kokopelli" is manifested, to some extent regardless of its inaccuracies and blatant cultural confusions, offers insights into the image's appeal and, more importantly, its functions and operations in the semiotic frontier zone between indigenous and Euro-American cultures and in the potent imaginary of the Southwest.

Whereas Hopi concerns center on the inaccurate conflation of flute player images with *Kookopölö*, the most common concern expressed by popular commentators is Kokopelli's supposed castration. Most popular books and many web pages devoted to Kokopelli focus on the frequent presence of a penis on flute players in rock art, with many emphasizing its often erect state and/or its unusual size. They often bemoan its erasure—Kokopelli's "castration"—most commonly explained as a result of Puritan-inspired, Anglo-American prudishness. In his small tourist book *Kokopelli*, Lawrence Cheeks (2004:14) describes contemporary Kokopelli imagery as "neutered and G-rated." In his forward to Slifer's (2007) book *Kokopelli*, Native American flutist Carlos Nakai (2007:x) states, "With the commercialization of this important icon, the perspective of the 'sexy flute guy' is relegated to an emasculated 'sacred scatterer of corn and love.'" Slifer (2007:48) himself states, "He is missing something vitally important. His erect penis, the essential feature of his original role as a god of fertility, is typically lacking. . . . To make the image safe for mass consumption, he has been emasculated and sanitized." The structure of meaning here is clear: Western culture constrains the essence of primitive masculinity, in this case through castration. The emphasis on Kokopelli's penis, its size, its virility, and the emasculation that they believe results from his supposed castration is perhaps most evident on the Zodiac Master website (Peña 1996). This site's readers are instructed to roll their mouse pointer over a conventional commercial Kokopelli image to reveal a photograph of an ancient petroglyph. Upon doing so, Kokopelli is replaced with a traditional flute player with an erect penis. The author then explains, "Maybe that will help illuminate his reputation as the Casanova of the Cliff Dwellers" (Peña 1996).

Kelley Hays-Gilpin (personal communication, 2007) has traced the origins of the contemporary conflation of Kokopelli, *Kookopölö*, and flute player images, and in doing so has shed light on the oft-repeated castration claim. The ur-image for contemporary commercial Kokopelli imagery appears to be a painted ceramic plate and several painted potsherds unearthed at Snaketown, a precontact village in southern Arizona, south of present-day Phoenix and associated with what archaeologists call the Hohokam (see Figure 5.8). Florence Hawley (1937) published an article in *American Anthropologist* arguing that the flute player images from southern Arizona as well as those from northern Arizona, the Four Corners region, and elsewhere in the broader Southwest were all manifestations of Kokopelli, the Hopi (and more broadly, Puebloan) *katsina*. Thus began the misuse of the name Kokopelli for almost all flute player images in the Southwest.

The flute player images from the Snaketown plate and similar Hohokam painted ceramics appear to provide the model for most, though by no means all, contemporary Kokopelli imagery. Drawings and/or photographs of the Snaketown plate were published as early as 1937 in Gladwin, Haury, Sayles, and Gladwin's (1937:Plate CLVIIIi) *Excavations at Snaketown* and Gladwin's (1957:88, 90) *A History of the Ancient Southwest*, along with similar flute player images from Snaketown sherds (see also Haury [1976:240, Figure 12.90] for more Hohokam flute player images from Snaketown ceramics). A likely instigation for the wider public dispersion of the image was its adoption as the logo for the Arizona Archaeological and Historical Society (Kelley Hays-Gilpin, personal communication, 2007). Based on my review of the society's journal, *Kiva*, as well as other printed materials, the society has used a variety of flute player images since at least 1957. From 1962 to 1987, a flute player image similar to the Snaketown plate was used on the cover of *Kiva*. From 1988 to 1999 a second flute player image was added to the standard cover along with the original image. From 2000 to 2008, the flute player from the Snaketown plate began to be used, occupying much of the front and part of the back cover. The use of any flute player image on the cover of *Kiva* ceased in 2009, although the Snaketown plate flute player image continues to appear elsewhere in the journal and in a variety of other places as part of the society's logo.

The linkage of flute player imagery with the name Kokopelli was most likely cemented in the tourist consciousness by the use of the painted design from the Snaketown plate as the cover image for John Young's (1990) *Kokopelli: Casanova of the Cliffdwellers*, a small, inexpensive book still widely available in gift shops at tourist destinations across the Southwest—significantly, the first book published about Kokopelli, appearing right about the time that the image began to metastasize across the Southwest. The book's cover image of the Snaketown plate

FIGURE 5.8—Hohokam decorated ceramic plate, Snaketown, Pinal County, Arizona. These painted figures are quite possibly the ur-image for much if not most contemporary Kokopelli imagery, along with similar images from other Hohokam ceramics. Arizona State Museum, University of Arizona, Helga Teiwes, photographer.

is credited to Gladwin and colleagues' 1957 book. The Hohokam figure from the Snaketown plate plays a flute, has a curved back (though not clearly a humped back per se), wears a kind of kilt, and does not feature a penis or other clear indications of biological sex (Kelley Hays-Gilpin, personal communication, 2007). Its bent legs and curved back, combined with the flute, can easily be interpreted as dancing. As Hays-Gilpin (2004) has pointed out, traditional flute players are often accompanied by a female counterpart, a pattern possibly evident in the Snaketown plate in the form of a "helper" behind each flute player. If anything, in other words, it is the flute player's female counterpart that has been erased in commercial imagery, not his penis (Kelley Hays-Gilpin, personal communication, 2007).

This points to the irony that, in the context of commercial Kokopelli imagery, the most commented upon deviation from traditional

flute players is the consistent removal of the penis and direct indications of sexual activity such as copulation scenes. While the sometimes
present penises on flute players are not present in contemporary Kokopelli imagery, most of that imagery is based on Hohokam flute players,
which did not include penises. Kokopelli's much commented-upon
castration, therefore, is at the least a result of the inaccurate conflation of flute players with *Kookopölö*, and more broadly of Hohokam
with Four Corners–area ancestral Puebloans, but the attention paid to
the nonexistent castration may say much more about contemporary
dis-ease over masculinity and the opportunities offered by Kokopelli
imagery and stories to address those anxieties. Significantly, even
though Malotki (2000), Slifer (2007), and Slifer and Duffield (1994)
all acknowledge Hohokam ceramics as the origin for much commercial
Kokopelli imagery, Malotki (2000:1) maintains his claim to Kokopelli's
commercial castration by arguing that the Hohokam flute player imagery was chosen for use over other flute player images because "it is 'safe,'
for it lacks visible genitals."

To give Malotki credit, it is indeed true that there are very few
instances of commercial Kokopelli imagery that contain a penis (real-
istically depicted) or phallus (in the form of an exaggerated penis). In
many instances, comparison of flute player images in rock art with
their commercial reproductions makes it clear that the penis/phallus
has indeed been left out of the reproductions. In a similar vein, a large
statue of a flute player based on a specific rock art image, complete
with an evident (but not erect) penis, was moved from the front of the
Edge of the Cedars Museum in Blanding, Utah, after concerns over
community values were expressed (Wharton 2008).

I have encountered only a handful of instances where commercial
Kokopelli imagery retained the penis/phallus from the original rock art
images on which they were based (excluding photographs of rock art).
One artist at a street fair in Salt Lake City proudly pointed out to me
that his Kokopelli reproductions were "authentic" due to their retention of the penis, something other artists shy away from. In another
case, after hearing me lecture on Kokopelli, a student entered my office
the next day and proudly presented me with a reproduction of a petroglyph in the form of a refrigerator magnet, which he had found amidst
the tourist merchandise at the gas station convenience store where he
worked. Designed to look vaguely like a petroglyph pecked into a small
piece of sandstone, this Kokopelli figure features a large, club-shaped,

FIGURE 5.9—Ithyphallic Kokopelli souvenir magnet. Unlike many Kokopelli images, this one is directly based on a flute player rock art image, and is rare in its retention of the original image's phallus.

erect penis (see Figure 5.9). I recognized the image, a reproduction of the largest of several phallic flute players at the Sand Island site along the San Juan River near Bluff, Utah.

Given the endless commentary about Kokopelli the flute player's castration, it is significant that concerns over the similar alteration of the traditional Hopi ceremonial form of *Kookopölö* are rarely mentioned. Reportedly, performances of *Kookopölö* at Hopi ritual events were altered as a result of Spanish and then Anglo colonization (Malotki 2000), and *Kookopölö* was possibly "castrated" by removal of the gourd penis. The inattention to this castration is probably because the *image* of this *katsina* performer has not been widely appropriated by Anglos, and just as likely because this case of castration raises direct concerns over the effects of colonization—not a good mix with a happy, fun-loving, Disney-esque character such as Kokopelli. Ironically, despite the absence of the image of the Hopi *katsina* in dominant forms of Southwest tourism and imagery, traditional Hopi stories about *Kookopölö* have been disseminated in abridged form to revitalize the reputedly castrated Kokopelli, as I discuss below.

Whether or not traditional flute player forms have in fact been castrated in reproductions (certainly some have been, though probably a small minority since most are based on Hohokam decorated ceramics), the visual absence of the penis has neither neutered nor desexualized Kokopelli. In verbal interpretations, Puebloan myths about *Kookopölö* are appropriated to revive Kokopelli's virility despite his perceived visual castration. In his book on fertility images in Southwest rock art, for example, Slifer (2000b) writes that in Puebloan cultures Kokopelli served not merely as a fertility symbol but as a mythical figure whose sexual appetites were a concern for young women. Slifer and Duffield (1994) portray Kokopelli as a variant of the trickster: Notorious for his sexuality, according to mythology he cleverly and without her awareness impregnates the most sought-after girl in the village. "Kokopelli carries in his hump seeds, babies, and blankets to offer to maidens that he seduces. . . . As a fertility symbol, he was welcome during corn-planting season and was sought after by barren wives, although avoided by shy maidens" (Slifer and Duffield 1994:7).

The most common Puebloan story about *Kookopölö* recounted by popular authors is used to highlight the enormous size of Kokopelli's missing penis, as well as his virility and moral-sexual ambiguity. (The same story is the one mentioned most often in scholarly works as well, and returns us to issues about scholarly works enabling naïve and commercial appropriations.) Presented in English by Mischa Titiev (1939), and again by Malotki (2000), this Hopi story is repeatedly excerpted, paraphrased, and abstracted, with varying degrees of completeness. The most frequently highlighted part of the story is *Kookopölö's* successful impregnation of a pretty maiden who resisted the advances of the young men in the village. He accomplishes this without her awareness by observing where she relieved herself each day, then digging a long ditch to that spot, lining it with a continuous pipe made of reeds, and refilling the ditch. When the maiden visited her chosen spot each day, *Kookopölö* inserted his long, erect penis through the reed pipe and engaged in intercourse with her. An important factor in this story is not merely *Kookopölö*'s virility and the size of his penis, but the maiden's rejection of all the men's advances, her beauty, and, in the more often quoted Titiev version, her description as "vain." In addition, *Kookopölö* is described by his grandmother as "homely" and, in the Titiev version, hump-backed. These details, whatever they might signify in the context of Hopi culture, fit well into a Euro-American masculinist narrative of female rejection and emasculation followed by the successful performance of virile masculinity. Indeed, another part of the tale depicts how *Kookopölö* eventually proved his paternity of the resulting child and married the beautiful maiden who had been desired by all the young men in the village, despite his relative physical weakness and apparently low social standing.

A major element often left out of retellings of the story involves a group of jealous men who plot to kill *Kookopölö*, but are unsuccessful due to *Kookopölö*'s cleverness, leaving *Kookopölö* and his wife to, in effect, live happily ever after. Significantly, few elements of this story beyond the demonstration of *Kookopölö*'s cleverness, virility, and penile length pertain to (or affect) the overall associations of the contemporary image of Kokopelli. As we shall see, the flute playing commercial Kokopelli is the life of the party, not a socially marginalized figure, in part because of the need to make his virility visible without the benefit of a penis. I present details from Titiev's and Malotki's translations of the story to demonstrate the selective nature of the appropriations made by contemporary writers, raising the issue of why certain parts of the story have been highlighted (e.g., his long penis) and others left out (e.g., jealous men) by contemporary writers, as well as why this story is the most discussed from amongst the Pueblo stories available. What is certainly clear is that "contemporary artists and producers of souvenirs . . . exploit Kokopelli's sexual-musical ambiguity" (Hays-Gilpin 2004:142).

Kokopelli the Native American Rock Star

This exploitation takes place via codes that are less explicit than a large, erect penis, but nevertheless convey Kokopelli's virility and sexualized

masculinity. Commercial Kokopelli images are variable but highly stylized, tending toward an apparently dancing, hunched personage playing a flute with what are described as antennae, feathers, or dreadlocks
on the top of its head; a lifted foot, curved back and wavy "hair" imply
movement (see Plate 6 and Figures 5.2, 5.3, and 5.5)—all generally
consistent with the image from the Snaketown plate, but not with all
flute player images. This pose evokes the image of the (male) rock star,
shown "jamming" intently and, in the mythology of Euro-American
culture, always ready to engage in sexual escapades, a figure coded as
both attractive and dangerous. Commercial artists also portray Kokopelli engaged in various activities, including playing a guitar, riding a
mountain bike, driving an off-road vehicle, snow skiing, scuba diving,
and skateboarding. One souvenir t-shirt for the Grand Canyon, for
example, features four images of a sunglass-wearing Kokopelli engaged
in outdoor activities associated with the Southwest: driving a jeep
through mud, river rafting, golfing, and hiking with a backpack and
walking stick. The connotations of these activities enable them to serve
as displaced expressions of Kokopelli's virility and masculinity—the
flute, symbolizing masculinity and the male component of fertility in
Puebloan cultures, is replaced with contemporary, Euro-American
symbols of (masculine) rugged individuality.

These meanings of Kokopelli, meanings that are key to his role as an
image of contemporary masculinity, can be inferred from visual codes
used in the imagery, but are also articulated verbally in works such as
Slifer and Duffield's (1994) *Kokopelli: Flute Player Images in Rock Art*,
as well as in shorter, more popular books such as the previously mentioned *Kokopelli: Casanova of the Cliff Dwellers* by John Young (1990),
Wayne Glover's (1995) *Kokopelli: Ancient Myth/Modern Icon*, Lawrence
Cheeks's (2004) *Kokopelli*, and Dave Walker's (1998) *Cuckoo for Kokopelli*. Walker's book, though hyperbolic and often tongue-in-cheek,
explicitly articulates the meanings encoded in commercial Kokopelli
imagery as well as those advanced in most scholarly and popular discussions, with the dominant theme being Kokopelli's sexuality. To further substantiate that the themes in Walker's book are representative
of other popular discourses, in 2005 I analyzed ten websites identified
by searching for "Kokopelli" on two common search engines, taking
the top ten unsponsored sites from each, and eliminating sites without substantive information and those not in English (in the analysis
to follow, I quote from five of the ten websites: Bertola [1996], Earth

Studio [2005], Kokopelli Kingdom [2005], Kokopelli.com [2001], and Peña [1996]. I also quote from select websites reviewed in 2013 in order to confirm the perpetuation of the basic themes identified in my original 2005 review, e.g., Twin Rocks Trading Post [2013]). The meanings circulating around Walker's version of Kokopelli, all of which can be found in the other books and on websites, can be placed in three general categories: rock star, trader, and Lothario.

First, commercial Kokopelli imagery taps into the Euro-American image of the musician, specifically the rock star. Walker describes Kokopelli thusly: "Back bent, dreadlocks tossed skyward—that flute-tootin' icon was rocking the kiva" (Walker 1998:ix). Kokopelli is "the one with the horn, the we-be-jammin' posture, and the fashionable dreadlocks tossed ever so jubilantly skyward" (Walker 1998:2). "His posture, his hair (or whatever), his wailing horn, all combine into a unified life-of-the-party image" (Walker 1998:16). "He's our oldest rock star, the pre-Columbian Coolio, the charismatic headliner of Mesoamerican Bandstand. As the patron saint of hospitality in the Four Corners states, he's the guy to call when you want to party like it's 999" (Walker 1998:45). Walker links Kokopelli to Bob Marley, Keith Richards, Jimmy Buffett, Jethro Tull's Ian Anderson, Kenny G, Jim Morrison, and Louis Armstrong. The image is not simply that of a musician, but the male rock star, complete with an emphasis on jamming, partying, and sex. Given the less than hypermasculine associations of the flute in contemporary Euro-American culture, it is no surprise that one of the most common alterations to the Kokopelli figure is to replace the flute with a guitar. In an article featuring interviews with Walker and Malotki, Leo Banks (1999) opens with the statement that "Kokopelli is the ancient Indian version of Elvis." While some descriptions of Kokopelli do not directly reference the rock star or sexual activity, they often present similar traits euphemistically; for example, the Kokopelli Kingdom (2005) website encapsulates the figure's meaning as "Fun Loving Native American Scoundrel," reflecting the moral bifurcation of the male rock star.

Second, Walker (1998) also proposes that the hump-backed flute player of ancient rock art may have represented a trader, a theme reflected in over half of the websites and all of the popular and scholarly literature I reviewed. Walker presents the common hypothesis that "Kokopelli was puchteca—a traveling trader from the Aztec or Mayan cultures of Mesoamerica. . . . The puchteca played a flute and enjoyed the reputation of a sailor or a traveling salesman: a girl in every village, so to speak" (Walker 1998:11). Kokopelli as trader "uses his wares to seduce young girls" (Walker 1998:12). As the website for the Twin Rocks Trading Post (2013) puts it, Kokopelli could be found "playing his flute to seduce his unsuspecting victims or enchant others into trading away their most prized possession." Both the rock star and trader versions of Kokopelli evoke a potent male heterosexuality that is both appealing and threatening.

Third, Walker (1998:4) describes the sexually potent Kokopelli as "a rain-making, traveling-salesman love machine," while mirroring the ambiguity of this potency by emphasizing that "he is not, however, a good mascot for your sixth-grade daughter's softball team." "Various interpretations depict Kokopelli as an unrelenting Lothario and a bit of a cad, a guy who's capable of magically impregnating maidens without their consent", a theme also referenced by half of the websites I reviewed. "He is a potent fertility symbol. Very potent. Kokopelli brings seeds and rain and crops to the fields, and babies to young maidens. . . . Some of the Native lore about Kokopelli's sexual escapades would make Casanova blush" (Walker 1998:5). In addition, all of the books and half of the websites I reviewed mention the traditional inclusion of a penis in flute player imagery with some but not all highlighting its exceptional size. Reflecting the moral ambiguity of sexual potency via links to sexual predation, Max Bertola's (1996) southern Utah tourist information website jokingly warned visitors who camp near a flute player rock art site that "if, during the night, you hear the gentle tones of the flute, you'd better lock up your wives and daughters."

Kokopelli and Masculinity

Kokopelli imagery points to several implications for the contemporary image of Native Americans and its relationship to masculinity. These images continue the trend of diminishing Native American women and placing masculinity at the center of Euro-American representations of Native Americans. Although some discussions do mention Kokopelli's female counterpart in Puebloan mythology, they are only brief asides, especially in popular accounts. In addition, despite the potential for contemporary Kokopelli imagery to be interpreted as androgynous due to a lack of explicit signs of biological sex, all verbal interpretations of Kokopelli imagery identify the figure as male. Kokopelli's supposed visual castration has not emasculated or feminized him.

Despite a range of alterations to traditional flute player imagery, very few commercial Kokopelli images are gendered female through recognizable codes. One of the few examples of female Kokopelli imagery I have encountered was to gender the restrooms in the Rockin' V Café in Kanab, Utah. For the men's room, a conventional Kokopelli image was used. For the women's room, the conventional Kokopelli image was altered to signify "female." Following Western gender iconics, the silhouette of a short, A-shaped skirt was added. More subtly, however, the flute is absent and the figure is instead clapping. This removal is consistent with the code equating flute and penis, but is also significant in that Western codes might then interpret the (male) Kokopelli figure marking the men's restroom as "performer" (active/subject) and the clapping female as "audience" (passive/object). Similarly, in the popular literature's appropriation of Puebloan stories about Kokopelli, women are present primarily as objects of Kokopelli's magical powers, sexual prowess, or tricksterism. Notice, for example, that Bertola's (1996) warning, quoted above, "to lock up your wives and daughters" was clearly written from and to a male subject position, positioning women as passive objects. In these ways, commercial Kokopelli imagery perpetuates the active/passive binary of Western patriarchal gender ideology.

This subject/object relationship between Kokopelli and women is linked to the individualistic presentation of Kokopelli's masculinity. Traditional flute players were often presented with other figures and *Kookopölö* has a female counterpart, *Kokopölmana*. However, in most commercial imagery Kokopelli stands alone or with other (male) Kokopellis, often in a rock band–like grouping. Hays-Gilpin (2004) notes that traditional flute players were sometimes paired with images of maidens, representing the complementary elements needed for fertility. Even the Snaketown plate from which most commercial Kokopelli imagery is derived depicted the flute player paired with a (gender ambiguous) "helper" standing behind (Kelley Hays-Gilpin, personal communication, 2007; see Figure 5.8). Yet in commercial imagery, we see only Kokopelli (or Kokopellis). Whereas Native cosmologies tend to see masculine and feminine as complementary (Hays-Gilpin 2004), the erasure of the feminine half of fertility symbolism perpetuates the concept of fertility as an individualized, not relational, trait, and an exclusively masculine one to boot. In his most recent study of flute players, Slifer (2007:81) perpetuates this decontextualized, androcentric view of fertility, stating that "there is no more obvious or potent symbol of fertility among the world's mythic and supernatural figures." Setting aside the hyperbole, one could easily argue that he should at least insert the qualifier "male" or "masculine" in there somewhere—the Venus figurines from Paleolithic Europe come immediately to mind as a rather "obvious or potent symbol of fertility."

However, Kokopelli's penis was never really erased because it was never there, at least in the case of the Hohokam ceramics that evidently inspired the bulk of the commercial imagery, and a penis is not present in many of the rock art images that also inspire commercial Kokopelli imagery. Instead, what commercial Kokopelli imagery represents is the erasure of the flute player's female partner specifically and the feminine more generally (Hays-Gilpin 2004), such a move being a necessity for his reincarnation as an image of independent, free-standing, self-contained masculinity. Commercial Kokopelli imagery therefore presents a stand-alone image of Native American masculine heterosexuality. While Puebloan myths are often appropriated in verbal accounts to (re)sexualize Kokopelli by portraying his licentious behavior towards Native women, these highly paraphrased (not to mention translated and decontextualized) tales often embody a subject/object, active/passive frame, and hence function less as a complementary gender pairing than as a reiteration of Kokopelli's independent status. In addition, Kokopelli's often-referenced status as a trader or roving minstrel emphasizes freedom from ties and responsibilities. Freedom is enabled by being alone (decontextualized), implicitly referencing the constraints of communal and cultural contexts.

Despite the flute player's supposed castration in commercial imagery, Hays-Gilpin (2004), Slifer (2007), Slifer and Duffield (1994), and Walker (1998) all agree that Kokopelli is a sexually charged image. While Hays-Gilpin (2004:19–21) holds that "most aspects of the Kokopelli myth as it pertains to popular culture are ours, not part of traditional Hopi culture," authors such as Glover (1995), Slifer and Duffield (1994), and Walker (1998) selectively appropriate Puebloan stories and anthropological hypotheses to highlight Kokopelli's sexual potencies and proclivities or, at a minimum, associations with fertility. These alterations of traditional flute player imagery and additions to the image of Native American masculinity can not only be understood as reinforcing patriarchy generally, but specifically as a response to anxieties over Euro-American masculinity. As discussed in depth in chapter 4, for over a century tensions between a "primitive" masculinity of

physical prowess and unrestrained sexuality and a "civilized" masculinity of mental capacity and self-discipline have characterized the
discourses of Euro-American masculinity. Specifically, the shift in
hegemonic masculinity—from being grounded in physical prowess to
being defined by mental and moral capacity—called (and continues
to call) into question the sexual virility of white-collar masculinity
(Bederman 1995). Responses to periodic "crises" of masculinity include
a return to physicality, predatory sexuality, homosocial relations, and
pre-industrial spiritualities (Ashcraft and Flores 2000; Bederman
1995; Churchill 1994; Rotundo 1993). The "primitive" side of this
masculine duality is articulated in Kokopelli, at least partly explaining
its appeal.

Commodification and Neocolonialism

Contemporary Kokopelli imagery is a projection of Western "primitive
masculinity" built on appropriations that commodify and transform
traditional imagery into a fetish with tenuous connections to traditional
images and stories produced by specific Native groups. This section
explores the implications of the commodification of Kokopelli imagery
and mythology in relation to masculinity, race, and neocolonialism.

As discussed in chapter 3, commodification involves far more than
an object or service entering a system of monetary exchange and
being used to make profit. Certainly, and importantly, commodification enables monetary profit via the exploitation of others' labor and
property. To do so, however, commodification abstracts the value of an
object or action so it can enter a system of exchange while simultaneously reproducing the conditions of that very system. In this process,
the specificity of the labor and social relations invested in the commodity are lost and it becomes equivalent to all other commodities (Marx
1986). To create the appearance of difference (and hence value) amidst
this abstract equivalence, meanings are attached to the commodity.
These meanings are the (illusory) ends to which the commodity itself
becomes the means of attainment, transforming it into a fetish. These
meanings are reifications: Their artificiality and social production must
be obscured, collapsed into the object, enhancing the commodity's
value as a fetish and mystifying the relations and exploitations involved
in its production (Whitt 1995).

As the de facto mascot of the Southwest and ubiquitous inhabitant
of tourist spaces, Kokopelli breeds familiarity. The visual and verbal

characterization of him as entertaining and celebratory encourages colonization of the region's landscapes and cultures. As a metonym for southwestern Native American culture, Kokopelli welcomes non-Natives and offers them the wisdom, joy, and freedom of an ancient culture and spirituality. To obscure the historic and contemporary realities of colonization (in which tourists themselves participate), Kokopelli represents an abstracted, precontact Native American culture, functioning out of time, in the imagined purity of the primitive, unburdened by complications of European contact and colonization. Kokopelli's status as a mythic figure and cartoon-like qualities enable the mutation and abstraction of the imagery and its meanings, and their redeployment in support of tourism specifically and neocolonial relations generally.

Kokopelli's timelessness explains the absence of the "vanishing" theme present in many other contemporary images of Native Americans (Bird 2001; Torgovnick 1996; van Lent 1996), as the projections into an imagined past enacted on and through Kokopelli imagery allow for the erasure of issues related to European-Native contact. Kokopelli is positioned as a mythical, not historic, figure; as a spiritual, not actual, personage; and has become a cartoon-like character whose animation (constant re-creation by artists) produces an abstraction, enabling an uprooting from history and a revisioning in the context of neocolonial imaginings of the primitive Other. Because Kokopelli imagery projects fantasies onto an imagined past understood as radically distinct from the present, its explicit meanings need not account for dynamics such as colonization, displacement, genocide, and environmental destruction. These images of a mythic Native American figure are constructed for the subjects, not the objects, of Western neocolonialism; they mask "the *continuing* lived history of people disenfranchised by colonialism by failing to acknowledge colonialism's presence in the U.S. today" (Buescher and Ono 1996:130; emphasis in original).

Kokopelli imagery is a clear case of cultural exploitation and commodification (Rogers 2006). Certain images, stylistic elements, and stories are appropriated from multiple Native cultures without compensation or permission, adapted to the needs of the dominant culture, and used without concern for the interests of the originating cultures. Meanings with little or no relationship to the originating cultures or their symbols are attached, obscuring the real relations that exist between Native and non-Native peoples in the Southwest.

In their analysis of the marketing of Disney's 1995 animated feature *Pocahontas*, Kent Ono and Derek Buescher (2001:24–25) "illustrate the specific nature of U.S. culture's tendency to appropriate, transform, and then (almost obsessively) reproduce figures and forms through the production of commodities." Specifically, in the context of traditional industrial production, "a commodity has value as a product and as a social concept" (Ono and Buescher 2001:26). For example, when I purchase a Patagonia jacket, I am buying a piece of clothing that helps keep me warm, and I am purchasing a symbol imbued with meanings of social responsibility, environmental sustainability, and high quality ("Patagucci"), meanings which have no necessary relationship to the jacket itself. When I purchase a Subaru, I am not simply purchasing a vehicle that gets me where I want to go: As their recent ad campaign tells me, I am buying "love" because "love is what makes a Subaru a Subaru." However, in the conditions of late or commodity capitalism (the dominant form of capitalism in the era of postmodernity), the presence of an object with some actual use-value (warmth, transportation) is not necessary for commodification to occur.

The image of Kokopelli itself has no intrinsic use-value, and many of the objects that he adorns either have no real use-value (e.g., an adornment to add to a key chain) or there is no intention to use them as such (e.g., an oven mitt). Kokopelli, in other words, "is a figure through which various commodities with multiple exchange values are marketed, *and* it is a social concept that circulates like a commodity" (Ono and Buescher 2001:26). Kokopelli is the means by which products are sold, and the selling of products is the means by which Kokopelli's meanings are circulated. Kokopelli is not like a car with an artificial image (meanings) attached to it—the commodity is the image and its meanings. The actual product being purchased (shot glass, oven mitt, t-shirt) recedes in importance. Commercial Kokopelli images and discourses largely displace the images and discourses (Hohokam, ancestral Puebloan, Hopi) from which they are drawn—it is not fidelity to the indigenous cultures of the Southwest that makes Kokopelli "authentic," but its fidelity to other Kokopelli commodities.

Kokopelli's authenticity, while loosely rooted in the presumed authenticity of the Southwest and precontact Native American cultures, is largely self-referential: The authenticity of Kokopelli is determined not by some "original," but by a postmodern, hybridized pastiche that mixes images, words, and stories from multiple cultures to create something with little genuine relationship to those cultures. Kokopelli images refer to Kokopelli images, enabling the possibilities for filling those images with whatever meanings are desired—that is, as motivated by the ideologies and anxieties of the time, and produced from available cultural resources. This accounts for multiple and contradictory meanings in the construction and circulation of contemporary commodities such as Kokopelli. Such multiplicity and indeterminacy can be central to the commodity's function, enabling its deployment in multiple discursive spheres, fluidly highlighting or obscuring various meanings and implications.

"Kokopelli the hump-backed flute player" is constituted by the tourism and culture industries as a hip, mystical, and somewhat shady symbol of fertility, as a metonym for the generic "Indians" of the Southwest and beyond, and as a recognizable icon of the Southwest. A diversity of functions enacted by and through Kokopelli—marketing tool, metonym, icon, mascot, lifestyle, identity, commodity, fetish, art—anchor the free-floating signifier that is its recognizable form but still allow for some bobbing about: fun, carefree, adventurous, independent, clever, magical, powerful, threatening, and virile. Kokopelli imagery and mythology is appropriated by the New Age commodity machine to stand in for Native Spirituality, by the tourism industry to stand in for the Mystical Southwest or Adventurous Individualism, by parks and land management agencies to stand in for Native American Cultural Resources or Our American Heritage, and by Euro-American patriarchal culture to stand in for Heterosexual Masculine Virility.

The form and variants of traditional flute player imagery and the contents of Puebloan myths have been selectively appropriated and adapted by Natives and non-Natives operating in cultural and monetary economies that constitute a bounded diversity of objects recognizable as Kokopelli and to which consumers are drawn by its status as a fetish. This is a structured but not determined creation, produced from at least partially processed, not raw, materials. Flute player imagery and Puebloan myths are symbols and narratives with pre-existing meanings and cultural functions; these meanings and functions are obscured to allow other meanings to circulate and to enable the ongoing processes of neocolonialism in relation to Native Americans. Contemporary Kokopelli imagery is, on the surface, polysemic (open to multiple interpretations), but Kokopelli is not a blank slate, nor are individuals entirely "free" to inscribe onto it whatever they want, however they want, in whatever language they please. While wide, the range of meanings and attributes attached to Kokopelli are limited, and such limits help identify the conditions of possibility for the existence, circulation, identification, appropriation, and modification of this commodified symbol.

The meanings ascribed to Kokopelli images are guided and restricted by Euro-American cultural codes involving stereotypes of Native Americans, images of musicians, the Southwest imaginary, gender discourses, ideologies of colonization, and neocolonial performances of primitivism. While multiple meanings are assigned to Kokopelli, these interpretations are guided by codes operating largely below conscious awareness, at the level of "the natural" and "common sense." In the case of commercial Kokopelli imagery, traditional forms have been selectively appropriated and adjusted in a process guided by Euro-American cultural codes and dynamics. The (at least sometimes intentional) similarity of commercial Kokopelli's antennae to dreadlocks; the powerful cue for the rock star provided by his hunched stance as he plays his flute; the other types of activities he is shown engaged in (e.g., mountain biking, hiking, playing guitar); his nicknames (e.g., Casanova of the Cliff Dwellers); his much-discussed missing male member; his oft-repeated association with fertility and Native American culture, spirituality, and mysticism; the contexts within which he is encountered (national parks, tourist shops, Native arts-and-crafts stores); all serve to limit the types of meanings produced by Kokopelli's producers and consumers. This process is guided by economies that circulate goods, money, bodies, symbols, identities, ideologies, pleasures, and powers (cf. Scholes 1989).

This coding process allows commodities to be a site for the circulation of meanings and, in turn, a means by which the meanings of a commodity are transformed to conceal meaning (Ono and Buescher 2001). Through implicit codes, contemporary meanings ascribed to Kokopelli imagery obscure other meanings and relations, thereby allowing the imagery to do its work on Western ideologies and enactments of masculinity and neocolonialism. In this sense, the sheer repetition and ubiquity of symbols such as Kokopelli are also important. While the history of appropriated symbols may in some minimal sense anchor their meanings and functions, the creation of an almost inescapable, self-reinforcing system of images and products, meanings and commodities, overwhelms any sense of the genuinely historical, even while creating an illusion of genuine historicity as part of commodity fetishism. The "authenticity" of Kokopelli imagery and meanings is determined not by any anchoring original. The commodity system endlessly reproduces the image that comes to function as the de facto original. This is a defining feature of commodity capitalism, which breeds an obsession with authenticity while actively negating the conditions of possibility for genuine authenticity. In the case of Kokopelli, the ongoing distortion of indigenous cultures via commodification is obscured through the presentation of a "pure" (precontact and/or mythical) expression of such (imagined) cultures.

A case of such circular reinforcement in the service of commodification appears in *Cuckoo for Kokopelli*. Walker (1998) mentions the theory that hump-backed flute players are traders and then uses this interpretation of flute player imagery to counter criticisms of its commercialization. In an "interview" with Kokopelli in which Walker asks if the commercial use of his image is bothersome, Walker crafts this response from Kokopelli: "Look, one of my jobs on Earth was a trader. I'm a free-market kind of guy. I'm more than happy to help the small businessman make a buck." Walker's (1998:42) book is often tongue-in-cheek, and this example lays bare the logic of commodification, as a Euro-American author creates an imagined conversation with a figure fabricated by commodity capitalism, which in turn appropriates part of its "own" past life as an important figure in Southwest indigenous cultures to legitimate its creation and exploitation by commodity capitalism.

Masculinity, Primitivism, and Symbolic Virility

In terms of gender, Kokopelli also obscures past meanings to advance a compensatory model for Euro-American hegemonic masculinity. In crafting Kokopelli as an individual bereft of the other figures that have often accompanied flute players (e.g., maidens), this model of "Indian" (i.e., Euro-American) masculinity presents itself as lacking any meaningful interdependence, portraying the Native view of fertility as a solely masculine affair. The complementary gender roles involved in fertility in Puebloan cultures are obscured (Hays-Gilpin 2004) in order to revive a primitive masculinity based on virility, promiscuity, and the denial of women's value and subjectivity (not unlike shamanism; see chapter 4). Kokopelli is one site for working through contemporary Euro-American tensions over masculinity and sexual behavior specifically, recovering the image of the primitive, ignoble savage in terms of a virile and unrestrained sexuality but with an attempt to remove negative moral judgments concerning such behavior.

This pattern is especially clear in *Cuckoo for Kokopelli*. Walker (1998) exhorts us not to apply our own systems of morality to Kokopelli's sexual escapades because "shame" is a European import. After recounting an abbreviated version of the Hopi story in which Kokopelli impregnates a desirable but aloof young maiden by using his lengthy penis to inseminate her, Walker (1998:5) states, "When it comes to this type of legend, the issues of consent versus nonconsent that our shame-enlightened minds beg to be addressed just don't apply." The sexual threat Kokopelli poses is dismissed as a result of the importation of shame-based Western sexual morality, maintaining the image's positive valence in the face of moral ambiguity. This image of masculinity manifests primitivism in its belief that precontact non-Western cultures existed in a natural state, uncontaminated by civilization and its morality, and were thereby sexually free and innocent—despite the fact that Puebloan stories and *Kookopölö* performances clearly serve as moral lessons within the context of those cultures.

Glover (1995) and Walker (1998) both use the primitivism articulated to Kokopelli imagery to call for the suspension of Western sexual morality, obscuring or at least dismissing the implications of Kokopelli's sexuality for contemporary masculinity and gender relations. In an era in which sexual harassment and rape are ongoing topics of discussion and a means for critiquing as well as reinforcing forms of hegemonic masculinity, some of the meanings circulating around Kokopelli imagery imply that not just promiscuity but even sexual predation is acceptable. Indeed, the popular literature often rewrites these behaviors as fun-loving tricksterism and the moral judgments against them as cultural baggage to be tossed aside in the attainment of a free-roving, independent, and virile masculinity. The message, reinforced by Kokopelli's individualized (decontextualized) masculinity, is that (Western) culture constrains the essence of masculinity.

Ironically, the oft-repeated story of *Kookopölö's* use of his long penis to impregnate the desirable young maiden ends with *Kookopölö's* success in heterosexual coupling and reproduction (Malotki 2000; Titiev 1939). That is, in the end the story is not just one of virility and tricksterism, but also of successful domesticity. In contemporary Euro-American culture, however, domesticity is narratively constituted as a dead-end for the fantasy of a "free"—unrestrained, unfeminized, uncultured—masculinity (Rogers 2008), and hence the focus of most popular authors is on the successful impregnation of a vain and aloof young woman, not on *Kookopölö* settling down with his mate and taking responsibility for his children. Kokopelli is at times depicted as driving an off-road vehicle, but never a minivan. The potential moral lessons to be derived from stories about *Kookopölö* are narrowed, in large part by the twin forces of primitivism and contemporary discourses about the crisis in masculinity, with nary a worry about what these stories might mean in the context of Hopi culture.

Kokopelli taps into ambivalent and contradictory attitudes regarding male sexuality by simultaneously idolizing and excusing, as well as minimizing or erasing, male sexual potency. As mentioned earlier, many authors discuss the traditional flute player's penis, its size, and its frozen-in-time erection. A penis is included on some, but by no means all, traditional flute player images, but appears on virtually none of the commercial Kokopelli images I have seen (with the exception of photographs and drawings of some flute player rock art and a few pieces of kitsch, such as the ithyphallic flute player petroglyph refrigerator magnet pictured in Figure 5.9). Some flute player images may have had their literal penises erased, but symbols of Kokopelli's sexual potency have been retained or even highlighted. These symbols include not only the flute, but those surrounding the male rock star. Commercial Kokopelli imagery, by erasing the penis present on some flute players but retaining its symbolic meanings, redefines sexual virility as linked to *symbolic* potency. The absence of the *penis*—the physical, "primitive" site of masculine power—is accompanied by the retention of the *phallus*, defined as any symbol of masculine privilege, power, and potency. The primitive is overtly rejected insofar as the penis is inappropriate for a public, commercial, and widely used image such as Kokopelli while a "primitive" masculinity is retained through less explicit symbolism. Primitive masculinity is thereby detached from its anatomical manifestation and displaced from the physical to the social and the symbolic. Arbitrary symbols of masculinity replace its anatomical sign, while that sign remains the (hidden) anchor for such symbols.

Continuing the pattern I identified in chapter 4 with the shamanic hypothesis, Kokopelli in his diverse manifestations consistently combines aspects of Bird's (2001) Doomed Warrior and Wise Elder, but is not reducible to either. Like the Doomed Warrior, Kokopelli manifests a virile masculinity that is both appealing and threatening. However, unlike the Doomed Warrior Kokopelli does not resist but instead functions to welcome non-Native colonizers/tourists—a role often reserved for Maidens or Wise Elders, both feminized figures. And Kokopelli in no way appears to be "doomed" but is in fact ubiquitous and endlessly multiplying. Like the Wise Elder, Kokopelli offers non-Natives the wisdom, joy, and freedom of an ancient culture and spirituality, but unlike the Wise Elder Kokopelli is strongly sexualized. Kokopelli's virility is certainly constituted in verbal discourses through direct references to his penis, as well as visually through photographs of phallic flute players in rock art. However, in the Kokopelli imagery that everyone in the Southwest and beyond encounters, his masculinity and virility are expressed indirectly, in coded ways, as the rock star and through a variety of masculine-coded outdoor activities.

The absence of the flute player's penis in contemporary Kokopelli imagery obscures the role of such imagery in articulating a primitive Euro-American masculinity through displacement onto symbolic domains such as music, dance, sports, and outdoor recreation. The need, presumably driven by "civilized" cultural standards, to sanitize Kokopelli by erasing signs of sexual potency (the penis) and sexual activity (e.g., copulation scenes) helps to displace and obscure the work the imagery is doing: recovering and revisioning a "primitive" masculinity. In this sense (as well as in economic terms) Kokopelli imagery is constructed for non-Natives, projecting "desirable" but morally ambiguous forms of virile masculinity onto indigenous imagery. Through commercial Kokopelli imagery and popular interpretations thereof, virility and promiscuity are linked to positively coded attributes—freedom, playfulness, and individuality—and male heterosexual prowess is (re)centered as a key element of masculinity. That a populace primed for the marketing of drugs to treat male erectile dysfunction would embrace a figure that traditionally displays a large, erect penis is unsurprising. Advertisements for such drugs parallel Kokopelli imagery, associating a commodified image of virile masculinity with their products via sports metaphors and sexual innuendo while avoiding direct representations of (erect or flaccid) penises. In these ads, masculinity is (re)signified through driving a sports car, using a team of horses to tow a truck and trailer stuck in the mud, and throwing a football through a swinging tire. Hence, as with Kokopelli, symbols of virility replace its anatomical sign, enabling the symbolic reconstruction of Euro-American hegemonic masculinity through a self-reinforcing, unanchored chain of associations. Commercial Kokopelli imagery allows for both the resignification of

Euro-American masculinity and the distortion and colonization of Native culture while appearing to do neither.

Race, Culture, and Caricature

The relevance and evaluation of Kokopelli's masculinity and sexuality for contemporary Euro-Americans raises questions of race; the commodity's operation can be further clarified by examining intersections of gender and sexuality with race, culture, and neocolonialism. Kokopelli is constituted in the model of primitive masculinity via his legendarily large and erect penis as well as proclivities for sexual promiscuity and predation. Kokopelli's sexuality and virility, therefore, are decidedly other-than-Anglo. Even conventional Western references applied to Kokopelli are coded as ethnically Other to the Anglo national identity, specifically as Italian and Spanish, as in Young's (1990) subtitle *Casanova of the Cliff Dwellers* or Robert Wayne Mirabel's description of flute player images as "the hump-backed flute playing Romeo, the Anasazi Don Juan" (Mirabel 2007:xiv). Unsurprisingly, therefore, Kokopelli's masculinity generally parallels Anglo-American images of the black male rapist and especially the Latin lover (Bederman 1995), not to mention the Indian warrior who abducts white women (Bird 2001; van Lent 1996), embodying the sexual ambivalence of many images of the primitive (Gilman 1985). Kokopelli is clearly Native: Whether a puchteca from Mesoamerica or a figure from Puebloan mythology, he is a racialized Other. However, unlike many other ambivalent images of primitive masculinity, Kokopelli does not rape, abduct, or seduce *white* women—confined to a mythical past, in the stories told about him he only interacts with other Native peoples, reducing the figure's role as a sexual threat and enabling its function as a fantasy of potent and promiscuous masculinity. Cultural differences in general and civilized prudishness are utilized to decontextualize Puebloan stories, such that Kokopelli represents an abstract Other to the white/Western Self, appearing to represent a particular precontact region and culture while existing outside of worldly implications and social concerns in a kind of primitive Eden—where, incidentally, public penile exposure was no big deal.

The abstract nature of Kokopelli imagery allows it to be racialized and not racialized at the same time, and this ambivalent racial status is crucial to the imagery's function as regional icon, primitivist fantasy, and fetish. Kokopelli imagery can be understood as a caricature (cf. Stuckey and Morris 1999), not of Native Americans per se but of traditional flute player imagery. Flute player imagery is widely varied, but commercial Kokopelli imagery selects and emphasizes certain features, such as the flute, "antennae," and the hunched/dancing/jamming posture, which necessarily involves the erasure of some of the traditional imagery's other traits, such as the sometimes erect, sometimes present penis and various accompanying figures (e.g., maidens and copulation partners). Such selections and omissions create an image appropriate to its various purposes, creating a friendly, fun, and nonthreatening caricature.

Kokopelli imagery is an abstraction and it refers only to an abstraction. First, unlike the statue "The End of the Trail" or Edward Curtis's photographs, the image does not operate under the guise of realism; its widespread use and popularity may be linked precisely to its cartoonish nature. Following traditional flute player imagery, Kokopelli is most often presented as an outline, a profile lacking significant or "naturalistic" internal detail (see Figures 5.1, 5.2, 5.3, and 5.5). In short, there is an absence of specific, overt racial signifiers in the imagery itself. So while Kokopelli is a "Native American" figure—specifically, a mythical or spiritual personage—the imagery itself is not directly and explicitly racialized. Second, the referent of Kokopelli imagery is not any specific Native American culture or tribe, but an ideal of "Indian" and "Southwest" history, spirituality, and culture, which is necessarily abstract. Kokopelli images do not stand in for Native American/Indian as a racial category (which would include living, colonized Native peoples) so much as they stand in for Native American/Indian as an abstracted and far-removed spiritual/cultural tradition. Kokopelli represents not a group of (especially living) people, but a set of imagined projections about Kokopelli specifically (morally unencumbered, virile, and independent) and Southwest Native Americans or the Southwest generally (pure, spiritual, and mysterious).

However, these projections are linked to a group of people defined in the dominant discourses of Euro-America as a "race": Native Americans. Kokopelli imagery derives its meaning from its linkage to this race because images of the primitive are essentialist: While it may be the (imagined) culture of Native Americans that is appealing, that culture is linked to what is projected as the essence of a people, even if that race/culture configuration is assumed to no longer exist due to genocide, colonization, and/or assimilation. Just as Kokopelli's penis operates through its simultaneous presence and absence (its presence in much of the attendant verbal discourse and in displaced expressions such as sports, its absence in the imagery), Kokopelli's racial associations work by being simultaneously present (through its cultural affiliations) and absent (in terms of overt racial signifiers in the imagery). The specific forms Kokopelli imagery takes (drawings, paintings, carvings, engravings, sculptures) enables its abstraction, and hence the commodification and fetishization of the imagery. Kokopelli's animation (abstraction) is ideal for its commodification as it enables the imagery's dislocation from its historic and contemporary contexts, making it largely self-referential, unanchored by the specific cultural traditions and histories from which it came.

The dynamic combination of the presence/absence of Kokopelli's gender/sexuality and race, and the intersections between gender/sexuality and race/culture, enhances the imagery's role as a commodity as well as its support of neocolonial relations. Kokopelli imagery can stand in for a model of virile and predatory primitive sexuality, and it cannot. Kokopelli imagery can be linked to real Native peoples, and it cannot. Its virile masculinity is linked to cultural traits that are racialized by the essentialism involved in the trope of the primitive, but those racial traits are erased through the process of abstraction, enabling Western identifications with and/or desires for primitive masculinity while ignoring the complications involved in idealizing a racialized Other and its association with living peoples. Kokopelli's racialization is coded into its virility and its association with Puebloan mythology and spirituality, but abstraction allows this to be linked to a projected cultural configuration (the innocence and naturalness of the primitive) without the baggage of both race and history (i.e., colonialism and genocide). For Kokopelli's articulation of primitivism and its role as fetish to operate effectively, culture is essentialized as race. To obscure the contradictions involved in the projection of Western masculinist fantasies onto Kokopelli, race and culture are unhinged and race is erased through the construction of Kokopelli as cartoon caricature.

Beyond Visual Caricature

When Kokopelli imagery shifts from a cartoonish caricature of a mythic figure to a visually realistic portrait of a human male or to a narratively and psychologically in-depth portrayal, the sexualization of the image remains, but the codes predominantly return to the sensitive, brave, doomed warrior (Bird 1999, 2001; van Lent 1996). In Price, Utah, a

FIGURE 5.10—Kokopelli statue, shown here in its original location on Main Street in Price, Utah.

life-sized statue of Kokopelli was installed, first, in 2005 in the middle of an intersection on Main Street, then, in 2014, on the nearby campus of the Utah State University Eastern Prehistoric Museum (Draper 2014; see Figure 5.10). The city-sanctioned presence of the statue relates to Price's tourism economy, which includes its role as the gateway to Nine Mile Canyon, described as "the world's largest outdoor gallery." The bronze statue, created by Gary Prazen, is surrounded by two-dimensional replicas of rock art flute players, grounding its imagined version of Kokopelli in precontact imagery, implicitly supporting the realism of this realistic but totally imagined representation. Visually, the statue is a combination of the young Indian brave of Hollywood films and romance novel covers—wearing only a loincloth and a few feathers, his long hair blowing, his musculature evident on his lean, fit body—and the image of the rock star: dancing, jamming on his flute, positioned on a stage (a dais in this case). There is no homeliness here as there was in the Hopi story of *Kookopölö*, and any indication of a humped back is obscured by his jamming/dancing posture. Absent a penis or phallus, the figure remains deeply sexualized, saturated in primitivist codes of masculine virility.

Kokopelli is certainly a deeply polysemic symbol, but nevertheless one whose meanings are constrained by the stereotypes, imagery, genres, narratives, and ideologies of the cultural contexts and standpoints in which the symbol is deployed. For example, in contrast to trends highlighting the representation of emotionally sensitive Native American men (van Lent 1996), the cartoonish, masculinist version of Kokopelli emphasizing his phallus and/or his licentiousness is most certainly not a "sensitive man," but, as Walker (1998:18) puts it, "a bit of a cad." However, the existence of the character type that van Lent (1996) identifies as the more sensitive, emotional, and often metaphorically wounded Indian Brave enables the deployment of Kokopelli myths consistent with that form of the primitive male, rather than the more predatory take on Kokopelli's mythological manhood. However, even in these (re)deployments, Kokopelli's masculinity remains central and is linked to a sexualized portrayal and independent, unhindered status. Three recent novels demonstrate these more in-depth presentations in which "Kokopelli" by whatever name is a primary character, established for the reader to identify with on an individual, psychological level.

In 2010, Shelley Munro published the M/M (male/male) romance novel *Seeking Kokopelli*, which Munro warns "contains rockin' music, smoky pubs, the mystical legend of Kokopelli and lots of playful, hot manlove." The main character, Adam James, is a Native American musician. Most of the novel involves him traveling with his non-Native rock band, for whom he is the lead singer and saxophone player. Adam's sexuality, deeply linked to the image of the virile young Brave or Latin lover, is central to his character and the storylines of the novel. His band's fortunes are on the rise, mostly due to Adam's capacity to drive his female fans crazy, leading them to throw their panties at him, shout "I love you," and try to sneak into his hotel room after each show. Adam, however, is gay. His family inheritance was his status and power as the next "Kokopelli," a role that magically insures his (unnamed) tribe's agricultural and human fertility. After his sexual orientation was discovered, the tribe revoked his status and the Kokopelli tattoo on his chest disappeared as magically as it had appeared years earlier, though his sexual appeal to both gay men and heterosexual women was apparently undiminished. Adam's morally questionable brother, who had taken over as Kokopelli, performed the role in self-serving ways, eventually leading to Adam's Kokopelli tattoo returning, along with his ability to make flowers blossom and women become pregnant simply by his proximity. In contrast to his brother, Adam/Kokopelli is clearly and unambiguously "good," including interpersonally, as a lover, and as an emotionally sensitive partner.

While *Seeking Kokopelli* (Munro 2010) is classified as an M/M romance, its author, an apparently white, heterosexual woman from New Zealand, is also probably reflective of the novel's primary audience as well, a suspicion confirmed by the readers who reviewed it online, who appeared to be overwhelmingly female (most M/M fiction in general is written and read by women). Nevertheless, even if constructed for and/or consumed by a heterosexual female audience, the character of Adam as both Kokopelli and a rock star is entirely consistent with the characterizations otherwise in circulation about Kokopelli. He lacks social ties (due to being ostracized for being gay), has a potent sexuality, and plays the saxophone, a woodwind instrument that is more strongly coded as masculine in contemporary Euro-American culture than the flute. While presumably not constructed for an audience anxious about its own masculinity, this novel clearly utilizes the basic resources of the Kokopelli myth, stereotypes of Native American men, the image of the rock star, and related discourses to articulate a highly desirable but unthreatening form of masculinity that is presented as decidedly not white.

Perhaps at the other end of the spectrum in terms of its audience and attendant forms of masculinity is G. M. Jarrard's (2012) self-published paranormal mystery novel *Petroglyph*, featuring murder, cattle mutilations, time travel, skinwalkers, Area 51, and conspiracy theories. One of the two main characters is Jack Wilson Redd, a resident of rural central Utah and a veteran with experience fighting the post-9/11 "war on terror," enabling his performance of hegemonic masculinity: "At 6'2", 215 lbs. and physically honed to perfection from four years in the Army National Guard Special Forces, Jack Redd was not a person to be trifled with" (Jarrard 2012:11). Jack also has Native ancestry, both Paiute and Navajo, as well as some early training in Native culture and language from his grandfather, a Paiute shaman, knowledge that will also enhance Jack's ability to act effectively and accomplish his goals, further demonstrating his ability to not be victimized by the world around him. The novel's events are centered in and around Five Finger Ridge, the area known today as Fremont Indian State Park.

A bizarre accident in a human-initiated magic event during a solar eclipse transports Jack back to the thirteenth century of the Fremont, along with his backpack full of supplies, military equipment, and, yes, you guessed it, his flute. His special forces experience, training in Paiute ways, intimate familiarity with the landscape, and modern equipment combine to make him the ultimate survivalist. He befriends the Fremont, who call him Kokopelli after hearing him play his flute. In two successful performances of hegemonic masculinity, Jack helps the Fremont defend themselves from marauding bands of Navajos and, of course, falls in love with, marries, and impregnates a young Fremont woman, whom Jack addresses as "my lovely Indian maiden, my Pocahontas, my Sacagawea" (Jarrard 2012:226). By carving a petroglyph he is able to communicate with his brother and ex-fiancé in the present day; this message, combined with his skills as a warrior and the esoteric knowledge learned from his Paiute shaman grandfather, eventually enables him and his Fremont wife to return to the present during the next solar eclipse.

The character of Jack/Kokopelli aligns with many elements of the presentation of commercial Kokopelli's masculinity despite some unique twists, such as Jack/Kokopelli being a warrior. Certainly, many aspects of the story conform to contemporary narratives of masculinity, but not specifically to contemporary Kokopelli discourses. These disjunctions, however, serve to demonstrate the problematic status of contemporary masculinity, while using imagined ideas of the past and of Native American cultures past and present to diagnose and/or compensate for tensions in and over masculinity. At the beginning of the book, Jack is in emotional turmoil over the demise of his engagement. While he clearly has a birth family, which helps with his eventual rescue, the book opens with his status as an involuntary bachelor, lacking the stable social ties of his own family and children. In terms of hegemonic masculinity, Jack has failed to demonstrate his success in heterosexual romance and coupling.

Jack, however, also struggles due to changes in the definition of masculine success. Jack is blue collar and rural. His engagement ended in part because of his unwillingness to go to college and become white collar. His fiancé's family are "big fish in a little pond" (Jarrard 2012:11) who live in a "'plantation,' the biggest, most ostentatious place in southern Sevier County" (10). His physical performance of hegemonic masculinity is outdated, even in his rural community. At the start of the novel, Jack is struggling not with the physique and physical capacity required of hegemonic masculinity, but instead with the emotional and relational ramifications of its redefinition in terms of occupation, income, and class. In short, "he was an emotional wreck" (Jarrard 2012:11), a wounded man.

After being transported to the thirteenth century, however, Jack is more in line with contemporary Kokopelli imagery and discourse. Beyond the obvious flute, seemingly present only to narratively justify having the Fremont call him "Kokopelli," he is a free-roving, independent man without any social ties, much like the trader version of Kokopelli. Also paralleling the image of Kokopelli the trader (especially Walker's [1998] tongue-in-cheek version), Jack uses his knowledge of capitalism to help the Fremont village grow in size, importance, and material abundance by mining, using, storing, and trading salt. He also employs the traditional cultural, linguistic, and magico-religious knowledge he gained from his shaman grandfather to make friends with the Fremont, manipulate the Navajo, and eventually return to the present. Indeed, we find out that Jack's great-great-grandfather and namesake was Wovoka, aka Jack Wilson, a real historic Paiute spiritual leader and founder of the Ghost Dance movement. Jack's modern equipment also comes across as a form of magic to the Fremont. And, of course, he successfully woos the prettiest maiden in the village, whom Jack calls Gazelle.

However, Jack also, and more broadly, models a successful form of primitive masculinity that aligns with his blue-collar masculinity. His physical capacities, practical skills, and tools become central to his success not only in surviving, but in earning the trust and friendship of the Fremont. They could care less about his income, degrees, or class status, but instead about what he can do, highlighting his successful performance of utilitarian masculinity. Perhaps most centrally, in the imaged world of the primitive, Jack has no difficulty in finding an attractive mate, providing for both her and the tribe, and biologically manifesting hegemonic masculinity by fathering not just a child, but a son. His masculinity is firmly anchored in his physical body, his practical skills and knowledge, his tools, and his virility/fertility. Unlike the stories told about Kokopelli in contemporary discourses, Jack is anything but a "cad," a morally questionable Lothario (Walker 1998), or someone you wouldn't want to leave alone with your "wives and daughters" (Bertola 1996). Unlike some, though not all, Native peoples he encounters in the thirteenth century, he is neither a marauder, thief, or murderer; nor, like some versions of the hypervirile Kokopelli, is he a womanizer or rapist. He is a moral, noble man of great heritage, in stark contrast to the Navajo and some of the Fremont, who represent the ignoble savage.

The book ends with Jack, Gazelle, their newborn son, and Jack's Fremont teenage sidekick, whom he calls Friday, returning to twenty-first-century Utah to live happily ever after. This ending raises issues of central concern not only to Jack's masculinity, but to his racial/ ethnic identity and the role of primitive/civilized masculinity in the story. On the one hand, the domestic ending of the story resolves the tension established at the beginning with the failure of Jack's engagement, cementing his hegemonic masculinity. On the other hand, the ending is contrary to the dominant discourse about Kokopelli—while *Kookopölö* may have settled down, married, and had children in the Hopi story discussed earlier, Kokopelli lives in a timeless state of bachelorhood, forever free-roving, independent, and licentious. While Kokopelli represents a resource for compensating for tensions in contemporary masculinity, he is a compensatory resource, not a resolution per se. Primitivist identifications with primitive peoples may compensate for perceived limitations in contemporary masculinity, but they do not necessarily function as role models of the long-term solution to a crisis in masculinity. As with *Fight Club*, the end result is the incorporation of a primitive masculinity within the confines of civilization, creating a kind of civilized/primitive masculinity (Ashcraft and Flores 2000) that tries to combine the nobility of each, temporarily easing the ideological contradictions structured into dominant definitions of masculinity while still furthering patriarchal and colonialist hegemony.

As Jack and his companions stand in front of the portal that will return them to the present, Jack hesitates, and a classic Wise Elder called the "traveler" (or Tvibo, the name of a historic figure central to the development of the Ghost Dance movement) asks him about his ambivalence over staying versus returning to the modern world. Jack explains:

> I'm returning to a world that has lost its way, where kids spend their childhood staring at screens and living imaginary lives while seeking the next big high. But, I'm taking my son away from a place where slaughter and ignorance and disease hunt men day after day, where slavery and cannibalism are still in style. . . . I'm doing this for him. . . . But I want him to do real things, like help deliver a calf when his own heifer gives birth, learn to hunt and survive with his own skills like his [Fremont]

ancestors and know for himself what it takes to grow your own
food, build things that last and make your own way. (Jarrard
2012:302–303)

Ultimately, Jack chooses civilization over barbarism, but with an
explicit desire to retain the nobility and utility of a primitivist masculinity, selectively combining elements of civilization and elements
of the primitive into a moral and utilitarian, a restrained and potent,
masculinity. Clearly a primitivist tale, Jarrard's *Petroglyph* replicates
common compensations for internal tensions within white masculinity,
which involve selective appropriations of both primitive and blue-collar
masculinities, all within a highly individualist framework: "to know for
himself what it takes to . . . make your own way" (Jarrard 2012:303).

A clear deviation from similar narratives (e.g., Disney's *Pocahontas*) is
the presumably permanent, marital, reproductive relationship between
the white outsider and Indian Maiden. Typically understood in terms
of the fear of miscegenation, in Hollywood and other dominant narratives Indian Maidens usually die as a result of their relationship with a
white man (Marubbio 2006) or the relationship is otherwise blocked
or terminated (Buescher and Ono 1996). However, Jack is not only
part Native, but specifically part Paiute, identified in the book as the
descendants of the Fremont, easing issues of (at least further) miscegenation. Jack's Native ancestry, however, is deployed strategically,
as with the miscegenation issue, or when it is needed to further the
novel's overall narrative. That is, like the cartoonish Kokopelli imagery discussed above, Jack can be coded as white, as Native, or as both
as narrative needs demand. The presentation of Jack, outwardly and
psychologically, is predominantly white. One indication of his overall
identification with whiteness is his naming of his young Fremont sidekick as "Friday," an explicit reference to *Robinson Crusoe* that clearly
positions Jack as the white colonizer and Falling Down Laughing (aka
Friday) as the colonized indigene. Although they do not explicitly
relate as colonizer-colonized, Friday is clearly subordinate in the relationship, and Jack does agree to take Falling Down Laughing back to
the present, which, given the explanation for returning to the modern
world quoted above, can easily be seen as the white man rescuing him
from barbarity. Significantly, while Gazelle and Friday happily accept
the English names Jack gives them in place of their traditional, given
names, Jack does not internalize the Kokopelli moniker. For example,

in response to being called "Kokopelli" by the marauding Navajo, he tells them (in *Diné* to boot!), "I am Jack Wilson Redd, I am not Kokopelli," adding (in English), "I am an American soldier and a friend to all freedom-loving peoples. Don't tread on me" (Jarrard 2012:212). Jack clearly defines himself as white, psychologically and behaviorally.

Jack's domestication also deviates from dominant characterizations of Kokopelli as eternally unattached. Jack is not the fun-loving, partying, Disneyesque figure of the tourism industry, but is nevertheless a model of potent hegemonic masculinity, although based more in the blue/white-collar crisis than in phallic virility per se. Kokopelli, functioning here as Jack's primitivist persona, is only a means to an end, a commodity to be selectively integrated with his modern self, ultimately for the purpose of negotiating modern contradictions manifested as psychological dis-ease. While his and his child's ancestry are clearly important to Jack, the possibilities offered by modern life are the ultimate end, albeit with a hybrid primitivist/blue-collar bent.

Tellingly, the last lines of the novel involve Jack's stated intent to have his son add his handprint to a rock art panel called Cave of a Hundred Hands (a real place in Fremont Indian State Park). This leads Ike, the other protagonist and a non-Native, to state, "Been thinking about doing that myself" (Jarrard 2012:311). This seemingly offhand, almost flippant, comment, as the closing line of the novel—which is titled, after all, *Petroglyph*, presumably after a mark added by a contemporary Westerner to an indigenous rock art site—emphasizes the appropriation of indigenous rock art sites in furthering white, masculine identity.

In a stark but superficial contrast to Munro's (2010) *Seeking Kokopelli* and Jarrard's (2012) *Petroglyph*, Donald Ensenbach's (2012) novel *Kokopelli: Dream Catcher of an Ancient* emphasizes the Edenic nature of the primitive as a time of simplicity, sexual innocence, and close ties with nature absent hypersexuality or overt hegemonic masculinity. In this narrative, set in southwestern, precontact North America, Kokopelli is orphaned as a young boy when a marauding band slaughters his entire village: "There is no one left but me. No family, friends or neighbors will be able to tell the story of [the village]" (Ensenbach 2012:15). Kokopelli sets out from his village to find somewhere else to live and eventually meets a trader named Koloki, who takes him under his wing as he travels, collecting and trading with various villages on a multiyear, cyclical route. Kokopelli learns to play the flute, acquires a number of animal companions, develops ongoing relationships with a number of villages, and learns skills in survival, navigation, collecting, and trading. Ensenbach's Kokopelli clearly mirrors aspects of other contemporary Kokopelli discourses: Kokopelli is free-roving, totally lacking in social ties (albeit not by choice), and a trader who plays the flute when approaching a village with which he wishes to trade.

As with the two novels discussed above, Ensenbach's (2012) Kokopelli is not a cad or sexual predator, but a character with whom readers are to identify. As an uninitiated youth, Kokopelli is a sexual innocent. As he travels to various villages, he is regularly offered the village chief's wife or daughter, or some other valued young female, to lie with him so they can, in the endlessly repeated euphemism used in the novel, "travel to the moon and stars" together. The villages Kokopelli visits have sexually open cultures, absent shame or coercion, and direct in addressing topics such as menstruation. This is indeed Eden before the Fall, characterized by an overall innocence, especially sexually, a key theme in some versions of the primitive. Accordingly, Kokopelli gradually develops a greater comfort with his sexuality and never performs a kind of Western sexual hegemonic masculinity, demonstrating instead great sensitivity as a lover, achieving his masculinity by pleasuring his partners. In a culture with no apparent sexual shame or violation of consent, there are no Squaws (Bird 1999), only Indian Princesses/Maidens and those who have become valuable wives, working as partners with their husbands. From a Western perspective on the primitive, Kokopelli's innocence is also manifested in the apparent lack of understanding of the link between intercourse and pregnancy, as he appears not to recognize his own offspring when he returns to the same village years later, nor does he seem to realize that Koloki was also likely his father given that his last visit to the village was about one year before Kokopelli was born. Koloki and Kokopelli's mother "journeyed to the moon and stars" together, and he was named after Koloki, as his parents highly respected the trader.

Ensenbach's (2012) Kokopelli also exhibits spiritual and supernatural capacities, not only in his close relationship with many animals (which can be read as spirit guides/helpers), but also in the visions he receives in his dreams, often reassuring him with forecasts of good fortune that come true or giving him valuable direction. Kokopelli eventually grows into a Wise Elder (Bird 2001), using his knowledge of the larger landscape, as well as that received through his dreams/visions, to lead the members of his favorite village to a new place to live and thrive, and to marry his favorite sexual partner. Unable to continue with the life of a trader due to his age, and in love with his wife and chosen village, he settles down to domestic life and serves as a leader in his village.

The hypermasculine Kokopelli of the tourism industry exists in a timeless state, forever unencumbered by monogamy and domesticity. However, when presented as the main character in a novel, this timelessness shifts. In the case of all three of these novels, as full-blown narratives, tensions are introduced and then resolved, ending in domesticity in the case of Jarrard's (2012) *Petroglyph* and Ensenbach's (2012) *Kokopelli: Dream Catcher of an Ancient*, and romantic, sexual, and relational consummation in the case of Munro's (2010) *Seeking Kokopelli*. While this is consistent with Western relational narratives in general, and with hegemonic masculinity specifically, it is not consistent with the "life of the party" image so often associated with Kokopelli. The lesson here seems to be the same as just about every other mainstream relational narrative: that domesticity cannot and/or should not be resisted.

However, the setting of Ensenbach's (2012) *Kokopelli* in precontact Native America does allow for his Kokopelli—of the three, the purest embodiment of the innocence and goodness of the primitive—to exist in a timeless state insofar as the novel is set entirely in the precontact, Edenic past. Like much contemporary commercial Kokopelli discourse, Ensenbach's *Kokopelli* need not address colonization, genocide, or discrimination in any way. However, tellingly, neither does Jarrard's (2012) *Petroglyph* or Munro's (2010) *Seeking Kokopelli*, both set in the present. Munro's Kokopelli, Adam, struggles with homophobia in his own tribal community and in the music industry, but not racism or the ongoing effects of assimilation and colonization. Jarrard's Kokopelli, Jack, also faces no evident discrimination due to his Native ancestry and did not grow up on a reservation, but appears to live fully integrated into his overwhelmingly white community. Colonialism and its aftereffects are barely hinted at, let alone addressed. Ironically, the ancestor for whom Jack is named, Jack Wilson, aka Wovoka, was an instigator of the Ghost Dance movement, understood as not only a resistance movement, responding to genocide and assimilation, but as a direct threat to whites. However, none of the politics of resistance, survival, and survivance (Cobb 2005) come into play in the novel because, I would argue, Jack, the author, and the implied reader all approach the novel from a white, Western standpoint.

Intersectionality, Hybridity, and Appropriation

Interpretations, appropriations, and circulations of flute player imagery can be understood as responding to and intervening in the contemporary status of Native Americans in Euro-American culture as well as, via projection and displacement, anxieties over Euro-American masculinity. In its erasure of contemporary realities, contemporary Kokopelli imagery suggests that embracing (consuming, collecting) Native cultures, myths, and/or spiritualities without acknowledging or taking action to address ongoing cultural destruction and colonization is coherent and sufficient. Kokopelli imagery represents the act implicit in films of the 1990s such as *Dances with Wolves* and *Last of the Mohicans* (Torgovnick 1996) as well as longstanding practices of "playing Indian" (Deloria 1998): Westerners legitimately inherit Native American culture because that culture contains qualities deemed in need of preservation—for the benefit of Westerners, at least. If the logic of many narratives about Native American cultures is that Westerners can, should, and must keep (what they define as) Native culture alive without concern for living Native peoples, then commercial Kokopelli imagery is the enactment of that logic. At the same time, it works to recover a potently "primitive" masculinity while obscuring the uncomfortable implications of doing so: the contradictions structured into Euro-American hegemonic masculinity.

Dynamic intersections of race, culture, gender, and neocolonialism are vital to the (re)production of systems of power and exploitation. This analysis demonstrates the importance of projection and intersectionality in the processes of commodification and consumption. The discourses that constitute Kokopelli position modern Western culture as antimasculine, hindering the expression of "natural" masculinity. Images of primitive masculinity are used to (re)construct a virile and potent masculinity, and thereby, paradoxically, maintain Western dominance. The desire for primitive spirituality and/or masculinity feeds the commodity machine and justifies the appropriation of colonized cultures, using difference (race, gender, sexuality) while erasing it. The simultaneous presence and absence of Kokopelli's sexuality and race demonstrates an important dynamic in the maintenance of hegemonic masculinity, whiteness, and neocolonialism and is vital to understanding the role of intersectionality and a variety of markers of difference.

The hybrid caricature known as Kokopelli enables and performs colonization and consumption of the Other. The visual, semiotic, cultural, and economic consumption of Kokopelli is in many ways akin to practices such as listening to rap or "world" music, eating "ethnic" food, and others described by Stanley Fish (1998) as manifestations of boutique multiculturalism. Such racialized acts of consumption are not merely liberal celebrations of diversity covering deeper dominations; the celebration of Southwest Native culture serves as a legitimating rationale for consuming the Other, in the case of Kokopelli through a primitivist and, optionally, a masculinist fantasy. In addition to its relatively obvious functions and operations (appropriation, distortion, commodification, and consumption), Kokopelli imagery enables participation in a range of fantasies—of being the life of the party; of being independent, free of social obligations; of being respected, powerful, or otherwise effective in the world; of a lack of sexual shame; of sexual virility, promiscuity, and even rape without moral misgivings—in ways that entail a range of dominations and exploitations. Such fantasies are accessed through the literal and metaphoric consumption of Kokopelli commodities, and through tourism more broadly, as they work to achieve multiple, even contradictory, ends.

This analysis demonstrates the importance of grounding discussions of the floating signifiers, polysemic symbols, and self-referential systems of meaning that seem to characterize our postmodern world, reminding us that they are not hermetically sealed in the world of the purely symbolic or ideational but are instead products and processes of material social systems. Kokopelli is a fascinating figure, a bizarre cultural hybrid: the Native American rock star. But understanding how its diverse meanings articulate, how they enable concrete social realities and systems of power, involves more than identifying pastiche, fragmentation, or multiplicity. Kokopelli imagery is certainly a product of the postmodern condition, but its role in the ongoing production of patriarchy and imperialism is what needs to be illuminated and resisted.

PLATE 1—Handprints in the vicinity of Glen Canyon, Utah/Arizona, 1983. Northern Arizona University, Cline Library, Tad Nichols Collection.

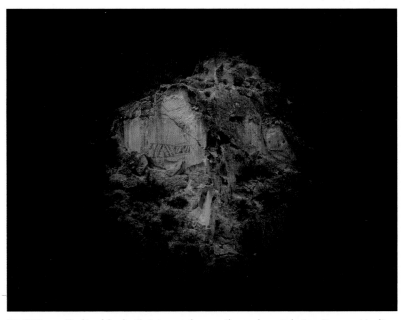

PLATE 2—"Indian blanket" pictograph seen through metal pipe, Fremont Indian State Park, Utah. The pictograph is eight feet in length (Steward 1937).

PLATE 3—Holy Ghost, Great Gallery, Horseshoe Canyon, Canyonlands National Park, Utah.

PLATE 4—Spiral petroglyph, Wupatki National Monument, Arizona. Spirals are common in rock art; large, finely-pecked, evenly-spaced, ticked petroglyph spirals such as this one, however, are less common.

PLATE 5—Rock art–decorated retail store, Castle Dale, Utah. Tourist souvenir shops, such as this one, not only sell rock art imagery, but use such imagery to attract customers.

PLATE 6—"World's Largest Kokopelli," Krazy Kokopelli Trading Post, Camp Verde, Arizona.

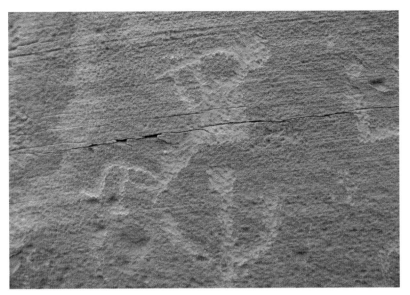

PLATE 7—Dancing flute player petroglyph, Coconino County, Arizona.

PLATE 8—*Kookopölö* and *Kokopölmana*, as drawn by Native artists (Fewkes 1903:Plate XXV). National Anthropological Archives, Smithsonian Institution INV 08547313.

PLATE 9—Bullet holes on "Wolfman" petroglyph panel, Butler Wash, San Juan County, Utah.

PLATE 10—Altered pictographs, Buckhorn Wash, Emery County, Utah. This Barrier Canyon Style panel shows pecking and painting added after the creation of the original image.

PLATE 11—Superimposed petroglyphs, Rochester Creek, Emery County, Utah. In this panel, the newer (lighter, less repatinated) petroglyphs are superimposed over older (darker, more repatinated) ones. Superimpositioning can help determine the relative ages of different petroglyphs.

PLATE 12—Superimposed pictographs, Iron County, Utah. In this composition, an orange figure was mostly painted over with yellow, creating a "canvas" for the presumably newer, red figures.

PLATE 13—Bill Key sheep panel, Death Valley National Park, California.

PLATE 14—The "Disney" panel, Joshua Tree National Park, California. The brightly colored paints on this panel of indigenous rock art were added to enhance the site's visual appeal for use in a film.

PLATE 15—Inscription Point petroglyph panels, Coconino County, Arizona. The upper right panel shows the chiseling of the snake/serpent image as well as smaller images that have been abraded. MS-372 Harold Widdison Rock Art collection. Photographer: Harold Widdison. Image title: Inscription Point (1994–1995). Image ID: MS_372_05_42_004. Courtesy Museum of Northern Arizona.

PLATE 16—The Great Gallery, Horseshoe Canyon, Canyonlands National Park, Utah.

CHAPTER 6

"YOUR GUESS IS AS GOOD AS ANY"

Indeterminacy, Dialogue, and Dissemination in Interpretations of Rock Art

At Klare Spring in Death Valley National Park, an interpretive sign titled "Petroglyphs" calls attention to the images pecked into nearby rocks but seems to offer little in the way of interpretation:

> Indian rock carvings are found throughout the western hemisphere. Indians living today deny any knowledge of their meaning. Are they family symbols, doodlings, or ceremonial markings? Your guess is as good as any. Do not deface—they cannot be replaced.

This piece of interpretive rhetoric posits the meaning of its subject matter, petroglyphs, as indeterminate, presenting three possible interpretations for the indigenous rock art at Klare Spring in the form of a question and then providing an answer: "Your guess is as good as any."

Although this statement can be interpreted as a flippant dismissal of rock art interpretation, this seems somewhat unlikely, as the sign's purpose would be to introduce the topic of rock art interpretation only to dismiss it. In addition, the sign's closing line, "Do not deface—they cannot be replaced," implies that petroglyphs are a valuable resource. A more plausible interpretation of "your guess is as good as any" is that it refers to the many potential barriers to discovering the meaning of petroglyphs in the precontact cultures that produced them. At least one of these barriers is referenced in the sign: a lack of knowledge on the part of living Native Americans due to a lack of cultural continuity with the precontact peoples who produced the petroglyphs or, possibly, reluctance on the part of contemporary Native groups to share what they do know. Most literally, "your guess is as good as any" can be interpreted as a leveling of authority, granting the interpretations of visitors a degree of validity that is equivalent to anyone else's, including affiliated Native Americans, anthropologists, and archaeologists.

Signs, pamphlets, and other materials offering information to visitors of Native American rock art sites make up an interesting body of rhetorical artifacts: a body of symbols whose subject matter is another body of symbols whose interpretation is posited as problematic. On the one hand, the Klare Spring sign licenses polysemic interpretations of rock art, taking the (apparent) indigenous lack of knowledge about rock art as a basis for empowering contemporary visitors to make their own diverse meanings. On the other, the sign announces the indeterminacy of rock art's meaning, the futility of interpretation in the face of an (apparent) indigenous denial of relevant knowledge. Examined constitutively, the sign's rhetoric establishes a particular relationship between the petroglyphs' producers and their contemporary viewers, a relationship of cultural and temporal separation that consigns the petroglyphs' meaning to the realm of the indeterminate while leveling interpretive authority, licensing a proliferation of interpretations inspired by the material traces of precontact indigenous cultures. Paradoxically, as the relationship between the rock art's ancient producers and contemporary viewers is constituted as one of profound separation, the distance between contemporary visitors and the rock art itself is collapsed through invitations to interpret the rock art through their own frameworks.

Although indigenous rock art imagery is itself an interesting case study of indeterminacy and polysemy, this chapter examines not rock art imagery, but the theme of the unknown meanings of precontact Native American rock art in interpretive materials associated with rock art sites in the southwestern United States. This focus on interpretive materials enables exploration of the rhetorical construction of indeterminacy and the licensing of diverse interpretations of the material traces of indigenous cultures. To explore the implications of this neocolonial rhetoric of indeterminacy, I begin by identifying the main claims involving the unknown meaning of rock art present in interpretive materials at rock art sites. Next, I turn to a brief discussion of polysemy and indeterminacy to clarify the operation of these claims. John Durham Peters's (1999) metatheoretical examination of dialogue and dissemination as opposed models of communication is then used to identify the complex operations of this rhetoric, specifically the rhetorical and ethical implications of posited indeterminacy and licensed polysemy in neocolonial contexts. Finally, a contrary case, in which interpretive materials do not posit indeterminacy or license diverse readings of Native American rock art, is used to further clarify the relationship between this rhetoric of indeterminacy, neocolonialism, and indigenous interiority. This analysis demonstrates how licensing non-Native readings of rock art imagery enables the remaking of the (actual) indigenous other, creating an imagined and abstracted Other that justifies and enacts neocolonial relations not only through compensatory projections but also by a refusal to access the thought worlds of indigenous peoples.

While the specific theme I focus on in this essay, the unknown and possibly indeterminate nature of rock art's meaning, would seem to bypass these projections, I argue that the lack of interpretive content in claims about rock art's indeterminacy enables a rhetorical shift in the relationship between contemporary visitors, the rock art, and the ancient cultures that produced it. This shift licenses individual interpretations of rock art that are likely to draw upon dominant cultural codes and stereotypes.

Interpretive Materials

For some visitors to rock art sites, especially those less familiar with rock art, their first or only exposure to hypotheses about the original meanings of rock art may be the interpretive signs placed at or near rock art sites, or other informational materials made available at sites or associated land management offices, visitor centers, or museums. This chapter examines these interpretive signs and related materials. Significantly, while my focus is on the unknown theme, many of these interpretive materials do offer interpretations of particular motifs or interpretative models for rock art in general, and in some cases posit singular and unqualified interpretations. The published literature, scholarly and otherwise, also contains many claims about rock art's meanings. Nevertheless, statements regarding the lack of knowledge about rock art's meaning are quite common in both the literature (see chapter 2) and interpretive materials, whether or not they are accompanied by possible interpretations.

Importantly, this analysis is not an examination of interpretive materials at rock art sites as a coherent expression of one or more specific interpretations concerning the meaning and significance of rock art, as a reflection of archaeological theory and practice, or as the product of the institutional processes of cultural resource management and interpretation. These interpretive signs are likely the result of a bewildering array of ideological, institutional, and epistemological forces, produced and placed over a long period of time (several decades), and as a result of a variety of specific institutions, ranging from the National Park Service (NPS), Bureau of Land Management (BLM), state offices of historic preservation, local or regional organizations representing avocational archaeologists, and local or regional tourism boards. I approach these interpretive materials from the perspective of visitors to rock art sites (i.e., the readers of these signs and pamphlets), for whom they form a rhetorical totality.

My focus is on how these materials potentially guide visitors' sense-making: not in terms of one interpretation versus another, but in terms of how interpretive processes and products are characterized more generally, particularly in terms of the portrayal of the relationships between the rock art, its producers and intended recipients, and contemporary visitors to rock art sites. Therefore, I am less concerned with explaining variances in these signs due to variables such as the time period any particular interpretive sign was produced, including the state of rock art research and the status of perceptions of the relevance of the knowledge of living Native peoples, or the agency responsible for its production. That is, I treat these interpretive materials as a rhetorical totality, as what is present at rock art sites, available to visitors and potentially involved in shaping their understandings and evaluations of rock art and their relationship to it. Specifically, I examine these materials in terms of their articulation of the communication processes involved in rock art interpretation as dialogue and/ or dissemination. While an analysis of these materials could usefully explore how changes over time are related to changes in archaeological theory, approaches to cultural resource interpretation, and the involvement of Native groups in rock art interpretation, my approach here is focused less on the processes that produced these materials than on their potential efficacy (their effects on audiences). Therefore, while some materials are more "defensible" than others from the standpoint of today's accepted knowledge and practices, I do not focus here on their relative validity.

Interpreting the Unknown

For many visitors to the American Southwest, one of the most exciting moments occurs when one comes face to face with a panel of rock art; executed by a people we know little of, for reasons we do not fully comprehend. . . . Significant research has resulted in the identification of numerous regional styles, common design motifs and even relative ages for certain panels. Yet, for all we know of this subject, the most compelling questions remain unanswered: Why was this work created, who was meant to see it, and for what purpose? While answers to these questions may ultimately be found, for many visitors/observers it is the mystery of the unknown that is perhaps most appealing.

—*Art on the Rocks: A Wish You Were Here Postcard Book* (Sierra Press 1993)

To explore the rhetorical construction of the indeterminate meanings of ancient indigenous rock art in contemporary contexts, I examine interpretive signs and pamphlets associated with thirteen rock art sites in the Southwest. These thirteen sites range from roadside attractions on paved roads to those accessible only by isolated dirt roads or substantial hiking or backpacking, but all are well publicized and have associated interpretive materials that posit the meaning of the rock art as unknown (see Table 6.1 for a detailed listing). Given the idiosyncratic nature of this sample, I do not claim that these interpretive materials are necessarily representative or that radically different interpretations are not present elsewhere. Nevertheless, I do hold that the theme of rock art's unknown meanings is quite prevalent in interpretive materials at southwestern rock art sites as well as in museum displays, books, and other media (such as the postcard book quoted above). Interpretive materials at some rock art sites do explicitly diverge from the theme of rock art's unknown meanings; later in the chapter I explore a major case of this divergence in order to clarify the implications of the rhetoric of indeterminacy present at the thirteen sites to which I now turn.

Five recurring themes concerning the indeterminacy of rock art's original meanings are articulated in the interpretive texts associated with these thirteen sites: unknown meanings, lost meanings, imprecise meanings, scholarly debate over meanings, and individual

Table 6.1. Public Sites with Relevant Interpretive Materials

Name and Location	Visits	Management Agency	Interpretive Materials
Hedgpeth Hills, Deer Valley Rock Art Center, Arizona	2013	Arizona State University	On-site interpretive signs (inside visitor center)
Petroglyph Plaza, Waterfall Canyon Trail, White Tank Mountain Regional Park, Arizona	2013	Maricopa County	On-site interpretive signs
Puerco Pueblo, Petrified Forest National Park, Arizona	2004	National Park Service	On-site interpretive sign
V-Bar-V Ranch, Coconino National Forest, Arizona	2002, 2005	US Forest Service	Pamphlet (available online)
Klare Spring, Death Valley National Park, California	2001, 2013, 2015	National Park Service	On-site interpretive sign
Atlatl Rock, Valley of Fire State Park, Nevada	2004	Nevada State Parks	On-site interpretive sign
Grimes Point Archaeological Area, Nevada	2002, 2012	Bureau of Land Management	On-site interpretive signs
Mount Irish Archaeological District, Nevada	2002, 2005	Bureau of Land Management	On-site interpretive sign (at district entrance)
Toquima Cave, Humboldt-Toiyabe National Forest, Nevada	2002, 2005, 2013	US Forest Service (site) and Nevada State Parks (sign)	Off-site interpretive sign (on nearest highway)
Buckhorn Wash, Utah	2003, 2006	Bureau of Land Management	On-site interpretive signs
Grand Gulch Primitive Area, Utah	2005, 2006, 2007, 2008	Bureau of Land Management	Pamphlet (available at ranger station)
Newspaper Rock, Highway 211, San Juan County, Utah	2005	Bureau of Land Management	On-site interpretive sign
Parowan Gap, Utah	2005	Bureau of Land Management	On-site interpretive signs

impressions. The first type of statement establishes the meaning of rock art as unknown. A sign at Grimes Point, Nevada, titled "Unanswered Questions" states, "Whether the artist was depicting stars in the sky, hunting, ritual practices, or something entirely different is unknown," while another at the same site titled "Ancient Artists—What Were they Saying?" concludes, "Nobody knows for sure." A sign at White Tank Mountain Regional Park, Arizona, titled "What Do the Designs Mean?" states that "rock art is almost impossible to interpret. . . . Each person looks at the same picture from a different perspective. We will never be able to climb into the head of the artist to determine what they were thinking."

Many of these statements posit possible interpretations but emphasize uncertainty as to their applicability. A sign at Parowan Gap, Utah, states, "While the meaning of the figures may never be known, they probably portray such tribal pursuits as religion, hunting and gathering trips, family history, sources of water and travel routes." A Nevada State Historical Marker for Toquima Cave states, "There are no known specific meanings attached to the particular design elements. Presumably, these people created the designs as ritual devices to insure success in the hunt." Another sign at White Tank Mountain Regional Park, titled "Petroglyphs," follows its statement that "no one is able to accurately interpret these symbols," with a list of "popular belief[s]" such as storytelling, trail markers, and clan symbols. While the signs at Parowan Gap and Toquima Cave follow statements about the lack of knowledge with probable or presumable hypotheses, a sign at Newspaper Rock, Utah, like the sign at White Tank Mountain, presents possibilities without any endorsement: "Unfortunately, we do not know if the figures represent storytelling, doodling, hunting magic, clan symbols, ancient graffiti or something else."

Second, the interpretive materials also characterize rock art's meaning as lost. A sign at Buckhorn Wash, Utah, states, "The stories are lost with the people who made the images." This invocation of loss raises the possibility of recovery, potentially relating to the need for more research. The brochure for the V-Bar-V Ranch site in Arizona explains, "These petroglyphs were made centuries ago, by people who had a culture and value system that was quite different from ours as well as those of modern Indian cultures. Consequently, we may never know exactly why they were made or what they mean." However, this statement about the possibility of a permanent lack of knowledge is followed by another implying hope: "Much research remains to be done in order to better understand the importance of petroglyphs to the people of the past." Other sites, such as the Deer Valley Rock Art Center in Arizona, also emphasize that "interpreting rock art is a challenge . . . but rock art can be studied" to learn more about its roles in the cultures that produced it.

A third type of statement references not the lack of knowledge about rock art's original meanings, but a lack of certainty or precision. Interpretive texts at rock art sites often link statements about the unknown quality of rock art's meanings with general interpretations such as hunting magic, clan markers, or doodling. As a sign at Mount Irish states, "Indian rock art in Nevada is often interpreted as having magical or religious significance. However, the precise purpose of these petroglyphs remains a mystery." Similarly, a sign at Parowan Gap states, "Although several theories have been expressed, the exact meanings of the designs is still unknown." These statements qualify interpretive models (e.g., hunting magic) as both generalizations and hypotheses; a distinction is drawn between the applicability of general interpretive models, such as clan symbols or shamanism, and the inability of those models to assign specific meanings to all rock art images. These statements indicate that some knowledge exists, thereby qualifying the universal characterization of the meaning of rock art as unknown.

The information provided at these sites is in some cases internally contradictory, with their creators apparently caught between a desire to emphasize that rock art cannot be interpreted with any certainty while still satiating visitors' appetites for answers. The "What Do the Designs Mean?" sign at White Tank Mountain uses about one-quarter of the available space to explain why "rock art is almost impossible to interpret," but begins with a relatively detailed explanation of the shamanic hypothesis and then uses the bottom half of the sign to present possible interpretations of specific motifs, such as "the concentric circle could depict the 'Sipapu'" and "the pipette . . . could possibly represent the rain god of Mesoamerican traditions." However, it qualifies these interpretations with words like "could" and "might," as well as with a statement that highlights "the caveats above" about the near impossibility of interpretation and a statement that "current archaeological interpretation relies heavily on the stories and symbols of modern Native Americans—as well as some guesses and subjective interpretation." On the same trail, another sign, which appears to be older than the one described above, forgoes any qualifications, stating that the petroglyphs "recorded events and marked locations. They were a magical way to control nature so rain would fall or mountain sheep would let themselves be caught. Some served as trail markers and maps. Others represented religious concepts." As at other sites with multiple interpretive signs, especially those placed at different points in time, visitors are left to sort out the contradictions on their own, possibly enhancing skepticism regarding the possibility of definitive interpretations, especially specific meanings of specific motifs.

An additional facet of these first three, closely related themes (unknown, lost, and imprecise meanings) is that the contemporary value and significance of rock art can be based on an understanding of its meaning and function in the ancient cultures that produced it. Therefore, emphasizing its indeterminate (unknown and possibly unknowable) nature could undermine rock art's perceived value. This potential tension is resolved in some of these interpretive materials by constituting rock art as a reflection of ancient cultures, even if we do not know what about them it reflects. A sign at Atlatl Rock in Valley of Fire State Park, Nevada, makes this compensatory move explicit: "Ancient drawings are a reflection of the past and the lifestyles of Native American cultures. Although we don't know exactly the meaning of the images, this art reflects the thoughts of these people." Such statements can be interpreted as maintaining the value of rock art in the face of a (possibly permanent) lack of knowledge about its meanings. Similarly, while some of the signs described above present lists of possibilities that include "doodling" and "graffiti," two of the three signs at White Tank Mountain that focus specifically on rock art deny the validity of these characterizations. As one states, "Rock art symbols should not be thought of as graffiti. The work of creating a petroglyph is very labor intensive and the undertaking demonstrates an obvious intent by the artists." A second sign supports its claim that the petroglyphs are "not considered to be ancient graffiti or doodling" by explaining that "the person who made them had intent and a specific purpose in their design and creation." Apparently operating under the widespread but questionable assumption that doodling and graffiti are either meaningless or simply lack any value, these statements also serve to resurrect the value of rock art in the face of barriers to interpretation. Finally, at White Tank Mountain Native Americans are also invoked to resurrect the value of rock art: "To our present day Native Americans, a Petroglyph site is a very sacred and spiritual place."

A fourth theme related to indeterminacy in these interpretive materials involves the role of scholars. At Grimes Point, two signs emphasize ongoing scholarly debate, one stating, "Scholars and archaeologists still debate the mystery and meaning of the rock engravings." Significantly, signs at Grimes Point (and many other sites I have visited) make no direct reference to knowledge gained from Native peoples, either historically or in contemporary times. The interpretive sign at Newspaper Rock states, "Scholars are undecided as to their meaning or have yet to decipher them" and links the rock art to living Native peoples only through the statement that "in Navajo, the rock is called *Tse' Hane'* (rock that tells a story)." These statements center scholars as the most suited investigators of the meaning of rock art despite their apparent lack of success. "Scholars and archaeologists *still* debate" and "have *yet* to decipher" cue a view of the knowledge of rock art's meaning as an ongoing project and leave open the possibility that its unknown status does not mean it is inherently unknowable, as in the statement from the V-Bar-V Ranch brochure that "much research remains to be done in order to better understand the importance of petroglyphs to the people of the past."

The unknown meaning of rock art culminates in the fifth theme, encouraging individual interpretations by visitors. In the face of the unknowable, unknown, or only vaguely understood meanings of rock art, these interpretive texts frequently use the lack of knowledge to license individual interpretations presumably absent any indigenous cultural knowledge or scholarly expertise. In addition to the "your guess is as good as any" sign from Klare Spring, other interpretive materials move from the unknown meanings of rock art to an appeal to individual imagination and subjective impression. The sign at Grimes Point titled "Ancient Artists—What Were They Saying?" follows its statements that "nobody knows for sure" and "the meaning of the rock art is still debated by scholars" with this question: "What stories do you see etched on the rock?" Similarly, the Newspaper Rock sign states that "scholars are undecided as to their meaning" and lists of variety of unconfirmed possibilities before concluding, "Without a true understanding of the petroglyphs, much is left for individual admiration and interpretation." The "What Do the Designs Mean?" sign at White Tank Mountain offers a variety of strongly qualified possibilities for its opening question, but ends with the statement that "interpretation of symbols continues to be an exercise in subjectivity and speculation.

Until we find the 'Rosetta Stone' of the ancient and Hohokam petro-glyphs, we will have to rely on association and our own imaginations." Similarly, at the Deer Valley Rock Art Center, a large display works through hypotheses that the Hedgpeth Hills petroglyphs are related to astronomy, religion, messages, and/or hunting, but ends up either denying the likelihood of or stating that there is a lack of supporting evidence at the site for each of the four options. Another large sign at the exhibit instructs its readers, "As you go out onto the petroglyph trail, imagine how this site would have looked to visitors thousands of years ago. Their marks are still here today and mean different things to different people. What do they mean to you?"

Naïve individual interpretations are necessary because they are all that remain; according to the rhetoric, contemporary Native Americans have no or only limited knowledge (mostly, they are just absent from the rhetoric), and scholars are engaged in ongoing debate with no foreseeable resolution. A slight difference regarding the role of Native Americans is apparent, however, at the presumably more recent signs at the Deer Valley Rock Art Center and White Tank Mountain Regional Park, both in the Phoenix, Arizona, area. At Deer Valley, one sign states, "There are many interpretations. Archaeologists and researchers propose certain answers. Native American people have other ideas." This sign not only acknowledges that Native peoples do not, across the board, "deny any knowledge of their meaning," but also places Native explanations roughly on par with those of archaeologists. At White Tank Mountain, the "What Do the Designs Mean?" sign also mentions Native Americans as a source of knowledge, but only an indi-rect one: "Current archaeological interpretation relies heavily on the stories and symbols of modern Native Americans." However, this is the same sign that states that interpretation "continues to be an exercise in subjectivity and speculation," which has the effect of negating the value of whatever information living Native peoples have given to archae-ologists. In other words, while both the Deer Valley and White Tank Mountain materials mention Native Americans as having information or opinions, the overall conclusion of these materials remains the same: We don't really know, so what do you think?

In addition to the lack of knowledge, another validation of indi-vidual interpretations is the subjective and affective nature of such engagements, as is made clear in a pamphlet provided to visitors to Utah's Grand Gulch: "Because the drawings do not represent a written language as we know it, their meaning is left to our imagination. When viewing rock art, it is important to keep in mind that the real importance is not found in literal meaning, but in the feelings that result from the viewing." In this case, individual, naïve interpretations are valued not only because they are all we have, but because they are more suited to the nonliterate/nonliteral nature of rock art, possibly reflecting the frame of the primitive in its assignation of nonrational mindsets to indigenous cultures without systems of writing (Whitley 2001b). Similarly, but less definitively linked to the primitive, both the Deer Valley and White Tank Mountain interpretive materials state that all imagery (as opposed to writing) is by its nature subjective and open to multiple interpretations, and that the only way to know what it "really" means is to crawl inside the creator's head, something we obviously cannot do even with living artists. However, in the case of White Tank Mountain at least, the explicitly stated logic remains the same: Lacking the necessary knowledge, our imagination is pretty much all we have.

Polysemy and Indeterminacy

Interpretive signs and pamphlets frequently dwell on the unknown and/or unknowable nature of the meaning of ancient, especially precontact, rock art. While potentially presented as a problem to be solved (the unknown can become known), the unknown and/or unknowable meanings of rock art can also be understood as the basis of rock art's value and appeal as well as providing a foundation for the projection of viewers' own culture(s), ideologies, fears, and fantasies onto these traces of indigenous cultures. While it is assumed that rock art had identifiable (singular or multiple) meanings in the cultural contexts in which it was produced, those originating contexts are no longer accessible or at best only partially accessible by means of oral histories and myths of affiliated contemporary cultures, historic ethnographies, archaeological research, and site visitation. In contemporary times, scholars and visitors to rock art sites bring their own contexts to the rock art, including aesthetic, ideological, and cultural systems.

Some see in rock art practical tools: maps, route and territorial markers, calendars, and astronomical observatories. Others see ceremonial, religious, and spiritual symbols. Some see symbols and enactments of social power. Others see magic, be it in support of hunting, healing, rain, or malevolent action. Some see evidence of rites of passage, gender differentiation, or clan identification. Others see evidence of human universals, such as Jungian archetypes, while some go so far as to posit that rock art evidences relationships between cultures on different continents thousands of years ago, or is a record of visitation by extraterrestrial beings. Clearly, ancient rock art in the contemporary context is polysemic. The purpose of this chapter, however, is not to explore the dynamics involved in or between each of these various interpretations, nor to examine rock art itself as inherently polysemic or indeterminate. Instead, I focus on a body of rhetoric whose subject matter and claims are about the indeterminacy of rock art in contemporary contexts in order to explore the rhetorical constitution of indeterminacy (regardless of whether the meaning of the rock art is indeed indeterminate). Therefore, I briefly turn to conceptualizations of polysemy and indeterminacy as a means of clarifying the rhetorical operation of claims to rock art's unknown meanings, specifically the relationships that are constituted by these materials between the rock art, its producers, and its contemporary viewers.

Inspired by work in the British cultural studies tradition, specifically Stuart Hall's (1980) discussions of encoding/decoding and oppositional readings, critical media and rhetorical scholars have promoted and grappled with polysemy. Polysemy refers to multiple interpretations and the operation of multiple meanings, be it in terms of a single symbol, an entire message, or even a style or genre. The primary focus of the literature on polysemy involves debates over the extent and social force of resistive readings of texts produced by the culture industry, that is, oppositional readings of mass media texts that otherwise reinforce dominant ideologies and perpetuate hegemony (see, e.g., Ceccarelli 1998; Cloud 1992; Condit 1989; Fiske 1986, 1989). John Fiske (1991b), for example, recounts how a group of homeless men enjoyed watching the film *Die Hard*, but they cheered for the terrorists rather than the police.

These scholars have primarily focused on polysemic texts and polysemic readings of texts, not on texts that posit other texts as polysemic or indeterminate. Nevertheless, of relevance to this analysis is the distinction between polysemy and indeterminacy. Leah Ceccarelli (1998) defines polysemy as divergent interpretations of a text's denotative meaning. Following Jacques Derrida's distinction, "With polysemy, distinct meanings exist for a text, and they are identifiable by the critic, the rhetor, or the audience; with dissemination, meaning explodes, and the text can never be reduced to a determinable set of interpretations" (Ceccarelli 1998:398). Polysemy involves multiple but identifiable meanings while indeterminacy, reflecting its poststructuralist origins, questions identification of any stable meaning(s), implying limitless interpretive possibilities or the impossibility of interpretation. Indeterminacy in the poststructuralist sense applies to all texts, whereas polysemy applies to specific texts in greater or lesser degrees, largely dependent on the interpretations made by diverse audiences (Condit 1989).

Both polysemy and indeterminacy are partly applicable to claims of the unknown meaning of rock art. The interpretive rhetoric examined in this chapter often posits a range of possible interpretations (e.g., hunting magic, clan identification, or doodling) followed by indications that one cannot necessarily be chosen over another with any certainty. That is, multiple interpretations are identified (polysemy), but the ability to choose between or from them is presented as problematic, as a kind of weak indeterminacy. This is expressed in the Klare Spring sign, where three possible meanings for the rock art are presented in the form of a question, immediately followed by "your guess is as good as any." However, the rhetoric of these interpretive materials can also be understood as proposing that indeterminacy exists but is potentially solvable. This latter form is reflected in the brochure for the V-Bar-V Ranch site, which states that rock art may be unknowable, but follows this with the possibility of determinacy being achieved via more research.

In this rhetoric, polysemy blurs with indeterminacy, for even if a range of possible meanings can be identified, whether or not that range of meanings is adequate is unknown, nor can one necessarily be chosen over another with confidence. Nevertheless, pure indeterminacy in the poststructuralist sense is not posited in this rhetoric: The assumption is that while "we" do not and may never know the meaning of any particular rock art motif or site, there was meaning attached to the motifs and panels in their originating contexts. The producers of the rock art are presumed in most interpretive signs and pamphlets to have encoded a single meaning in or enacted a single function through the rock art. The interpretive texts often present a list of possible interpretations in the form of "it could be x, y, or z, but we do not know for sure," implying that there is a single answer. Similarly, the emphasis on a lack of precision in contemporary knowledge of rock art's meaning presumes a precise purpose and an exact meaning. Indeterminacy, therefore, is not posited in these materials as an inherent quality of rock art but results from historical and cultural gaps between its producers and contemporary viewers, and hence the possibility of determination exists by bridging those gaps. Polysemy remains relevant, however, insofar as the unknown meaning of rock art is used as a basis for licensing diverse interpretations by visitors.

Perhaps the strongest parallel in the literature on polysemy to the texts examined here is resistive readings insofar as the form of polysemy licensed by these interpretive materials refers to interpretations by contemporary (Western) visitors, that is, audiences. However, while Western interpretations of Native cultures are certainly implicated in structures of power, it is unclear in this case how empowering non-Native audiences is resistive. Empowering Native American interpretations vis-à-vis "scholarly" knowledge could function to resist the hegemony of Western academic discourses over Native American history, culture, and identity (Smith 2004), yet with the exception of signs at Petroglyph National Monument (discussed below), the most direct and explicit reference to the knowledge of living Native peoples in these signs is that they "deny any knowledge of their meaning." So while the polysemy licensed by the interpretive materials is audience-centered, it implies non-Native audiences and is not analogous to resistive readings. Indeed, as will be demonstrated later, such an audience-centered polysemy enables neocolonial relations, specifically the appropriation of rock art for the purposes of projecting dominant meanings and ideologies onto indigenous others. This analysis, therefore, raises questions about texts that label other texts as polysemic or indeterminate, specifically those that employ indeterminacy as a basis for licensing polysemic readings of the material traces of indigenous cultures in neocolonial contexts.

Dialogue and Dissemination

Additional insight into the cultural, ethical, and political dynamics of rock art's posited indeterminacy and licensed polysemy is offered by John Durham Peters's (1999) *Speaking into the Air*. This historical analysis of the opposing ideologies of dialogue and dissemination identifies these normative models as the source of much of the modern celebration of and anxiety over communication. Through an examination of the development of the idea of communication and of historical responses to new media, Peters decenters dialogue as the normative model of communication, claiming that dissemination, more than dialogue, promotes an ability to acknowledge and address difference. The interpretive materials analyzed in this chapter articulate these two models; by analyzing this rhetoric via dialogue and dissemination, the neocolonial implications of the interpretive rhetoric are clarified and Peters's elevation of dissemination over dialogue is qualified.

"Dialogue has attained something of a holy status" (Peters 1999:33). Exemplified by face-to-face interaction, in its pure form dialogue is characterized by embodied copresence, mutuality, reciprocity, and a tight coupling between sender and receiver via messages addressed to and designed for a specific recipient. Dialogic communication, therefore, is unique, irreproducible, symmetrical, and private. Peters (1999) identifies as part of the dialogic view of communication "the dream of identical minds in concert" (241) and the "angelological tradition of instantaneous contact between minds at a distance" (24). Embedded in dialogue is the desire to access the interiority of the other, wedding two souls into a harmonious whole. With the development of means for communicating across time and distance (e.g., writing and, later, radio, telephony, and phonography), this dialogic impulse became an "expression of desire for the presence of the absent other" (Peters 1999:180). This model drives much of the anxiety over and criticism of mass media, exemplified by print and electronic broadcasting, insofar as one-way, disembodied media scatter messages, addressed to anyone, invariant in content and form, to diverse audiences who are loosely coupled with the sender. These media are dehumanizing because their messages are not fitted to individual recipients, and as such cannot achieve authentic human-to-human coupling and care for the other's soul. Peters's (1999) challenge to this model's unquestioned preeminence begins with the "tragic" but also "blessed" fact that soul-to-soul contact is a dream, that even face-to-face interaction is but the reading of the traces of a distant other.

Dissemination involves invariant and openly addressed messages indiscriminately scattered to diverse audiences (Peters 1999). Dissemination is one-way, asymmetrical, and, as exemplified by print and broadcast media, public. While dialogue centers senders as responsible for carefully coupling messages to their intended recipients, dissemination empowers recipients to determine what messages mean. Dissemination involves "uniformity in transmission but diversity in reception" (Peters 1999:52), and is closely linked to both hermeneutics, the interpretation of texts when no reply is possible, and polysemy, specifically resistive readings of mass media texts. Dissemination recognizes and affirms that all communication is action at a distance. Peters argues that while dialogue centers love, care for others' souls, dissemination centers justice, representing a fundamentally democratic impulse in its equal (indifferent) treatment of diverse recipients and its empowering of audiences to make their own meanings out of indiscriminately scattered messages.

Dialogue, with its desire for a meeting of minds, for transparency and shared meanings, sees multiple interpretations of the same message as a problem, indicating that the other has not melded with the self and the message was not sufficiently coupled with its recipient. Diverse reception of well-crafted dialogic messages indicates that messages have strayed from their intended recipients and coupled with unintended audiences (Peters 1999). Such "illegitimate couplings" are multiplied by communication media that make messages accessible to unintended audiences (Peters 1999:51). Time- and space-binding media such as writing and broadcasting lead to textual promiscuity, and polysemy can be understood as an illegitimate product of such couplings.

Peters (1999:34) points out that the dialogic ideal "can stigmatize a great deal of the things we do with words. Much of culture is not necessarily dyadic, mutual, or interactive" and the meeting of minds is not the only legitimate outcome of communication. "Much of culture consists of signs in general dispersion"; resistive readings by marginalized and oppositional audiences are enabled precisely by the processes of dissemination and media that fail to meet dialogue's "strenuous standard" (Peters 1999:34). The impersonal and dehumanizing technologies and techniques of mass media enable democratic resistance to the dominant ideology. "Once 'inscribed,' an utterance transcends its author's intent, original audience, and situation of enunciation. Such removal is not just an alienation; it is a just alienation. Inscription liberates meaning from the parochial and evanescent status of face-to-face speech" (Peters 1999:150). The flipside of this is Peters's negative evaluation of dialogue's ethical and political potential. In dialogue Peters sees not a meeting of minds, but a making over of the mind of the other in the image of the self. Dialogue demands both responsiveness and transparency, opening the interiority of the other to the potentially dominating meanings of the self. Despite widely held assumptions to the contrary, "dialogue can be tyrannical and dissemination can be just" (Peters 1999:34).

Rock Art as Dialogue and Dissemination

The models of dialogue and dissemination are integral to the framing of rock art's meaning by interpretive materials. Rock art, whatever the reasons and conditions under which it was produced, operates today as dissemination, demonstrating "the inevitable promiscuity of any intelligence committed to permanence" (Peters 1999:143). Pecked into or painted on rocks, rock art motifs can last for hundreds or thousands of years, especially in dry environments such as the southwestern United States. The repeated indication in the interpretive materials that "we" do not know what rock art means, and may never know with any certainty or precision due to temporal and cultural distance, is based on the assumption that it did mean something, that it was addressed to someone. However, the radically "loose coupling" between the sender and message of the rock art on the one hand and contemporary visitors on the other means that a "meeting of the minds" is not possible. As the Klare Spring sign states, when "Indians living today" cannot or will not provide inside knowledge about rock art's meaning, then any interpretation is as good as any other. A dialogue exists, but "we" (the presumed non-Native readers of these signs) are not part of it. Nevertheless, as a basis for rock art's appeal, its mystery and the attempted resolution thereof seems a clear case of the desire for contact with an absent and inaccessible other (Peters 1999). These interpretive materials emphasize that the dialogue is incomplete, the coupling too loose, the chasm between self and other too large.

The move these interpretive materials offer in response to this dialogic failure is individual interpretation. Since the coupling of contemporary visitors with rock art's messages is presumably unintended, the dialogic tradition would seem to encourage the marginalization of rock art interpretation: Such attempts are illegitimate, promiscuous, a kind of eavesdropping (Peters 1999). The creators of rock art as well as those for whom it was presumably intended are often assumed to be long dead or otherwise inaccessible (due to precontact extinction, postcontact genocide, assimilation, or other form of cultural discontinuity), establishing dissemination as the only applicable context for interpreting the rock art. Nevertheless, a desire for contact with the vanished primitive Other, for communication over enormous cultural and temporal distances, is strong. The broader social context of Anglo-America and Western culture—one that the ideology of dialogue characterizes as dehumanizing, alienating, and socially fragmenting due in part to the prevalence of largely one-way, disseminatory media such as radio, television, and print—shapes this desire for the primitive Other, to connect with the thoughts of an "authentic" people who presumably possess the antidote to the alienations of contemporary Western culture

(Dilworth 1996; Kadish 2004; Torgovnick 1996). This may be an exercise in hermeneutics, not dialogue, but the motivating impulse can still be a meeting of minds. Rock art, after all, "reflects the thoughts of these people." However, since we cannot know what the rock art "really" means (dialogue), the reading of traces (dissemination) is all that is left. Therefore, the solution to the (possibly unbridgeable) gap posited in the interpretive materials at rock art sites is quintessentially disseminatory: "Your guess is as good as any." For "without a true understanding of the petroglyphs," that is, due to a failure of dialogic coupling, "much is left for individual admiration and interpretation," that is, the empowered recipient of dissemination carries the burden/authority of interpretation. When dialogue fails, visitors are left with not only the unknown, but an interpretive democracy: "What stories do you see etched on the rock?"

Petroglyph National Monument: A Contrary Case

Boca Negra Canyon in Petroglyph National Monument, on the western edge of Albuquerque, New Mexico, offers interpretive texts that are quite distinct from those associated with the sites analyzed above. These signs characterize the monument's petroglyphs as largely part of a living, not a dead, tradition carried on by modern Pueblo peoples, and emphasize the need to respect these cultures and their expressions on rocks. One manifestation of the awareness of Puebloan concerns is that the phrase "rock art" is not used at Petroglyph National Monument, reflecting Pueblo cultures' (and some researchers') dis-ease with that term, due in part to the narrow Western conception of "art" (see chapter 2). As a sign at the monument explains, "Petroglyphs are more than just 'rock art,' picture writing, or an imitation of the natural world. . . . Petroglyphs are powerful cultural symbols that reflect the complex societies and religions of the surrounding tribes." Examining this contrasting interpretive rhetoric through Peters's (1999) frameworks of dialogue and dissemination helps to clarify the implications of the rhetoric of indeterminacy present at many other rock art sites and points toward an alternative interpretive framework informed, at least in part, by consultation with Native Americans.

As one Petroglyph National Monument sign explains, "There were many reasons for creating the petroglyphs, most of which are not well understood by non-Indians," implying that Indians do understand. Signs at the monument reference the knowledge of Native peoples of the region and their relationship to the petroglyphs and the landscape, indicating that some of the monument's petroglyphs "have direct meaning to modern tribes." However, any knowledge passed from Native peoples through the NPS to visitors at the monument remains rather vague, as in this direction: "Note each petroglyph's orientation to the horizon and surrounding images, as well as the landscape in which it sits," as "today's Pueblo Indians have stated that the placement of each petroglyph was not a casual or random decision." By instructing visitors about what to pay attention to, information has been provided without offering any necessary reduction in uncertainty as to the petroglyphs' original function or meaning.

The only direct explanation offered at the sites I have visited for the indigenous inability or choice not to resolve "our" lack of knowledge also occurs at Petroglyph National Monument, where visitors are told that Pueblo tribes have a direct relationship with and knowledge of some of the petroglyphs, but are constrained in revealing specific meanings. One sign reads, "Identification of some Petroglyphs is based on interpretations by today's Pueblo people. We cannot say for certain what all the images represent, nor is it appropriate for today's Pueblos to always reveal the 'meaning' of an image." These interpretive materials, therefore, offer an apparently intentional and explicitly stated vagueness about those meanings and are silent about why revealing them would be inappropriate. At Petroglyph National Monument, there are major differences from the interpretive materials examined above: The insights and debates of scholars and archaeologists are not mentioned, visitors' guesses are not as good as others', and the meaning of the rock art is not always *unknown* or *lost* but sometimes *undisclosed*.

In these interpretive signs a dialogue is posited, a meeting of the minds involving the petroglyphs, ancient indigenous peoples, and contemporary Puebloans. But visitors are not told the meaning of that dialogue because such revelations are not "appropriate," only that the petroglyphs "have deep spiritual significance to modern Pueblo groups." With the exception of Pueblo peoples, who, visitors are told, still use this "sacred landscape" for "traditional ceremonies," visitors to the monument are outsiders whose engagement with the petroglyphs is presumably an "illegitimate coupling" (Peters 1999:50). The dialogue is private and visitors are merely eavesdropping, hence its meanings "are not well understood by non-Indians." The monument licenses this eavesdropping (i.e., visitors' presence) but does not provide the code that would allow an understanding of the dialogue. Significantly, the signs at Petroglyph National Monument do not invite individual interpretations, guesses, or subjective impressions. Instead, they emphasize "respect" for other cultures. This takes the form of appeals to consider the petroglyphs' "importance to both past and present cultures" and of moral admonishments: "Degradation of the images by thoughtless visitors is a permanent reminder of the lack of respect for the legacy of another culture."

Indeterminacy and Ownership

Not only do many of the interpretive materials at the thirteen sites analyzed above encourage disseminatory interpretations, they also frame the value of rock art differently than does Petroglyph National Monument. Another type of sign present at many rock art sites (indeed this is often the only sign present at many sites, including many of those not specifically analyzed in this essay) encourages visitors to avoid behaviors that degrade the rock art, such as touching and climbing on it. They often use the stock phrases "take only photographs and leave only footprints" and "leave no trace." These "site etiquette" signs usually list relevant laws and penalties for vandalism, and often include phrases such as "please do your part in preserving our prehistoric heritage" or "please help protect your rock art." Rock art is often described as "part of our American heritage" that needs to be protected "for the benefit of all Americans." In contrast, of the interpretive materials analyzed in this chapter, only the signs at Petroglyph National Monument and White Tank Mountain emphasize respect for *other* cultures.

These different appeals for protecting rock art—as part of "our" heritage versus as part of living indigenous traditions—parallel the difference between sites where visitors are encouraged to make their own interpretations versus those where the meaning of the rock art is posited as known by Native Americans but not revealed. Whereas the dialogic rhetoric of Petroglyph National Monument is linked with appeals to respect others, the disseminatory rhetoric exemplified by "your guess is as good as any" frames the value of rock art in relation to visitors: Its value is grounded in its status as "our American heritage." The licensing of individual readings by visitors accompanies claims of those visitors' ownership of the rock art. Dialogue centers producers and intended viewers, positing rock art's value in terms of what it "reflects" about the cultures of those producers and intended viewers. Dissemination, on the other hand, centers viewers, intended or not, and therefore posits rock art's value in terms of the standpoint of contemporary visitors, their heritage, and their enjoyment. The disseminatory rhetoric at other sites typically lacks calls for respecting others and invites visitors to make their own meanings. Significantly, unlike many (if not all) of the other rock art sites in this sample, Petroglyph National Monument's interpretive materials were developed after consultations with affiliated indigenous cultures (Evans et al. 1993; Ferguson and Anschuetz 2003), and the resulting appeals to "respect" and "sensitivity" are linked to a view of the rock art grounded in dialogue.

In stark contrast, the "your guess is as good as any" sign from Death Valley uses the oft-repeated claim that "Indians living today deny any knowledge of their meaning," but, in effect, that sign involved no consultation (even via the ethnography) with affiliated Native Americans. As discussed in chapter 2, Julian Steward (1929), despite having collected ethnographic information about rock art, claimed that Indians had no relevant knowledge of rock art, for at least two possible reasons: the information provided was not easy to interpret and, in the case of the Great Basin specifically, his view of Numic groups as too primitive to have made any interesting rock art (Whitley 2001a; Whitley and Clottes 2005). In turn, Heizer and Baumhoff repeated a similar claim in their influential 1962 work, *Prehistoric Rock Art of Nevada and Eastern California*, again, due at least in part to the difficulties involved in interpreting the often nonliteral statements in the ethnographic record (Whitley 2011). This statement was picked up and repeated often, including on interpretive signs such as the one at Klare Spring in Death Valley National Park. As David Whitley summarizes the situation with the archaeological interpretation of ethnographic statements about rock art, both in general and specifically in terms of the Great Basin and Heizer and Baumhoff,

> Since they could not find what they were looking for (a complete explanation), they dismissed the ethnography as essentially valueless. This led to a pernicious inference: because historical Native Americans apparently knew nothing about rock art, these archaeologists assumed, the rock art was obviously older than the ethnographic cultures. This effectively stripped the tribes of an important part of their patrimony and heritage and

created a catastrophic (but false) cultural disjunction between past and present. (Whitley 2011:110)

The "your guess is as good as any" sign, echoing Steward (1929) and Heizer and Baumhoff (and likely dating to not long after their 1962 work), thereby perpetuates both the denial of contemporary indigenous authority over their rock art heritage and the widespread appropriation of that heritage by non-Natives, be they land management agencies, rock art scholars and enthusiasts, or the general public. In the case of the Great Basin, this is not due to a Native refusal or inability to share, but the dominant culture's refusal or inability to listen.

Dissemination, Interiority, and the Primitive

The dominant trend in the interpretive materials analyzed in this chapter is to posit a failed dialogue between the ancient producers and contemporary viewers of rock art. The dissemination theme in this rhetoric appears to be the default position; that is, when dialogue fails, viewers are invited to make their own interpretations. Dissemination, in this neocolonial context at least, is an invitation to appropriation and projection. In the case of members of subordinated groups (e.g., ethnic and sexual minorities) producing resistive readings of mass media texts made by and for dominant groups, such appropriations seem ethically justified, providing them some role in making the meanings that shape their lives in contexts of historic and contemporary subordination, exploitation, and/or marginalization. However, these invitations to appropriate rock art, to guess as to its meanings, to identify the stories seen in it from the standpoint of contemporary (and presumably Western) cultures, seem ethically problematic in a context in which widespread appropriations of Native symbols, rituals, sacred sites, and artifacts contribute directly to the felt distortion, disrespect, and exploitation of Native American cultures (Black 2002; Churchill 1994; McLeod 2002; Stuckey and Morris 1999; Whitt 1995; see chapter 3 for a more complete discussion of the appropriation of Native American cultures). The dialogic view articulated in the Petroglyph National Monument signs exhibits more concern for the other than the disseminatory licensing of individual interpretations on the part of visitors. "Your guess is as good as any," the exemplar of the disseminatory rhetoric identified here, seems grossly contrary to the concern for the other that Peters links to dissemination—"the task is to recognize otherness, not make it over in our own image" (Peters 1999:31)—yet the disseminatory licensing of individual interpretations on the part of visitors enables making the rock art over in visitors' own image, not recognizing genuine otherness. Such an audience-centered polysemy enables neocolonial relations, specifically the appropriation of rock art for the purposes of projecting dominant meanings and ideologies onto indigenous others. Following Condit (1989), there appears to be little about the rhetorical situation (e.g., Southwest tourism), other texts (e.g., dominant media representations of Native Americans), prevailing ideologies (e.g., primitivism), or the likely audiences (e.g., their access to oppositional codes such as Native American critiques of archaeology and anthropology) that would make resistive readings likely.

Polly Schaafsma (2013), a rock art scholar with far greater familiarity with the monument, its rock art, and associated cultures than I possess, assesses the interpretive materials at Petroglyph National Monument in the context of increasing concern over the public dissemination of "sensitive" information. Her assessment both converges and diverges from mine in important ways, and I therefore quote from it at length:

> Petroglyph National Monument continues to refrain from promoting petroglyphs of kachinas and other supernatural beings on their web site, eschewing mention of religion and alternative cosmologies in other promotional venues except in the most general way with interpretive information on the rock art. The fact that a highly significant proportion of the petroglyphs at the monument consists of kachinas and other figures of religious import, ignoring them has the negative effect of eviscerating the content of this rock art as it is presented to the public. The result is a puerile portrayal of Pueblo culture, as visitors are urged to discover petroglyphs along the trails in the spirit of a kind of exploratory treasure hunt. Likewise, children are urged to find their "favorite" animal. While the local Pueblos may be content with this approach as it discourages prying in regard to their religion, at the same time, it is also another form of disrespectful cultural dominance. One result of withholding background information on the complex worldviews of the Pueblos as expressed in the rock art . . . is, of course, that (1) it does not admit to or teach tolerance or respect for diversity and differences in worldviews and (2) it leads to unquestioned appropriation with

no moral barriers to alternative usages for the eye-catching
images by outsiders. (Schaafsma 2013:66)

Schaafsma and I share concerns over appropriation and projection in
neocolonial contexts of unequal power. For me, however, the key difference between the monument's interpretive rhetoric and that at most
other rock art sites is the different *relationships* the rhetorics establish
between rock art, past and present Native peoples, and contemporary
non-Natives.

I agree with Schaafsma (2013) that the interpretive materials at
the monument do not provide much meaningful information about
Pueblo cultures and their relationship to the petroglyphs that give the
monument its name: The information presented engages in cultural
interpretation with almost no content about either Pueblo culture
or the interpretation thereof. However, what is clearly conveyed in
the interpretive materials is that (1) Pueblo peoples have substantial
knowledge about the petroglyphs and their meanings, (2) they view
the petroglyphs as sacred and/or important to their culture, and (3)
a key element of Pueblo culture is nondisclosure of certain information, though the reasons for that nondisclosure are not just ambiguous,
but absent. Within the dialogic framework that gives this rhetoric its
underlying assumptions, these three pieces of "content," however general
they may be, lead to the conclusion that visitors to the monument are
outsiders—this is not their culture, their heritage, or their history, but
Pueblo culture, Pueblo heritage, and Pueblo history. Therefore, the
relationship of visitors to the petroglyphs and to Puebloans ought to be
one of "respect." The relationships are very clear, even if there is a lack
of content about the specific nature of those relationships.

This is where, at least when the monument's rhetoric is contrasted to
the other thirteen sites analyzed above, I differ with Schaafsma (2013)
about the potential outcomes of nondisclosure of insider knowledge
about the petroglyphs and Pueblo culture. One outcome identified by
Schaafsma is that a failure to provide specific cultural information (the
code to the dialogue) not only "eviscerate[s] the content" of the rock
art but encourages "unquestioned appropriation with no moral barriers
to alternative usages" (Schaafsma 2013:66). I agree that the failure to
provide visitors with specific insider information does not in itself prevent naïve but ideologically loaded projections and appropriations, and
in some cases may even enhance a desire to uncover the "mystery," to

discover the "secrets." However, unlike most other rock art sites, visitors to the monument are not told by authoritative institutions that the rock art is part of their heritage, but that it is someone else's, and guesses are not encouraged. There is a clear moral line identified in this rhetoric: This does not belong to you, it belongs to them, so respect it and them. In Peters's (1999) terms, do not pry into this (private) dialogue.

The second outcome of the lack of disclosure at the monument that Schaafsma advances is "it does not admit to or teach tolerance or respect for diversity and differences in worldviews" (Schaafsma 2013:66). Again, given the lack of specific cultural information provided, I agree that it does not "teach" about specific "differences," but that is not to say that it does not admit to such differences or that it does not "teach tolerance or respect for diversity," at least as a general rule, which this rhetoric does quite explicitly (rhetorical effectiveness is admittedly another issue). While a visitor may learn little about the "content" of either ancestral or contemporary Pueblo cultures, the monument's interpretive materials make very clear that the rock art is closely affiliated with both ancient and contemporary Native peoples (specifically, Pueblo groups), and it asks for respect of those cultures and their heritage.

What seems to be missing from Schaafsma's (2013) assessment is the agency of contemporary indigenous cultures. Via a consultation process initiated by the NPS, affiliated Pueblos and tribes provided input about a number of management issues, one being the types of information that should be shared with the public (Evans et al. 1993). While I cannot speak to the credibility of that process, it does seem clear that the interpretive materials analyzed above were developed with specific Pueblo input in mind, particularly regarding areas where disclosure was seen as problematic by those groups (e.g., Evans et al. 1993:39).

From a Western, liberal perspective, it certainly "makes sense" that groups wishing for greater tolerance and respect from the dominant culture would set about informing the dominant culture about themselves. It also "makes sense" that groups concerned about stereotypes, distortions, and inaccuracies would share knowledge about themselves with the groups holding those stereotypes and perpetuating those inaccuracies in order to reduce their negative effects. What we are talking about here, in other words, is the idea that dialogue promotes shared understanding, which, in turn, leads to tolerance and respect. If a group does not participate in that dialogue, tolerance and respect will not increase. Conclusion: The absence of Pueblo insights in the informational dialogue at Petroglyph National Monument will perpetuate misinformation, intolerance, and disrespect.

One problem with this "common sense" (i.e., Western, liberal) perspective, of course, is that it simply does not work that way. The "contact hypothesis" held so dear by Western liberals—the idea that open interaction promotes tolerance and understanding—only holds true in very particular circumstances. Interaction and sharing do not necessarily lead to positive outcomes, partially because of the dominant's ability to shape the conversation, partially because the subordinate's turns in the conversation are still filtered through the ideological lenses and investments of the dominant, and partially because the dominant still controls the overall rules of the game once the dialogue is done. Peters (1999), however, offers another take on the risks that dialogue poses for subordinate interlocutors. The Western, liberal view of dialogue and tolerance used by Schaafsma certainly may not be shared by non-Western cultures and, as Peters argues, subordinate groups within Western cultures may have a different perspective on dialogue as well.

Concerning the tyranny of dialogue, Peters writes, "The moral deficiency of the spiritualist tradition is that the hope of doubling the self misses the autonomy of the other" (Peters 1999:266). Dialogue requires participants to "open up," make their interiority (thoughts, feelings, perceptions, identities) transparent, accessible to the other. A "meeting of the minds" can take the form of one mind imposing itself onto the other. Especially in contexts of unequal power, opening up one's interiority can be a dangerous thing, making it available as "an object of power" (Peters 1999:159) and enabling its appropriation and colonization. Hence, Peters calls for attention to the "majesty . . . of nonresponsiveness" (Peters 1999:57). The nondisclosure of Native knowledge described in the interpretive materials at Petroglyph National Monument, while seeming to further enable inaccurate readings of rock art by uninformed outsiders, could be understood via Peters as a refusal to make Native interiority available to the dominant culture. It is also probable that such nondisclosures stem from complex internal divisions and the associated compartmentalization of ritual knowledge in Pueblo cultures (Geertz 1994; Glowacka 1998; Hopi Cultural Preservation Office 2009; Mills 2004; Schaafsma 2013); while Native reticence in sharing their culture with outsiders has been present in the Southwest, nothing in the rhetoric at Petroglyph National Monument indicates whether the motive for nondisclosure is internal to Pueblo cultures or a result of anthropology's colonialist history and affiliations. Nevertheless, following Peters, one could argue that providing insider knowledge about the petroglyphs could encourage additional appropriations, along with the inevitable distortions involved when not just outsiders, but powerful, dominating cultures, steeped in primitivism, appropriate indigenous cultural objects, imagery, and knowledge (for a supporting case, see Geertz's [1994] chapter on "Prophecy Rock"; for a parallel argument, see Hopi Staff [2004]).

In contrast to the possibility that Native nondisclosures could be designed to deny the colonizer access to their interiority (world view and cultural meanings), the positing of rock art's meaning as indeterminate and the licensing of polysemic interpretations by visitors can be understood as a refusal by the dominant to access the interiority of the subordinated other, a refusal disguised as a desire to access that very interiority. The projection of Western images and imaginations of the Indian Other is enabled by promoting "guessing" and "individual admiration and interpretation." Following Peters's (1999) characterization of the tyranny of dialogue (and the risks of dissemination), projecting Western fears and fantasies onto the other simply remakes the other in the image of the self. Such projections, in other words, ensure that genuine, autonomous others will not have to be engaged. The permission not to engage with actual others or even a radically alien otherness supports the reproduction of neocolonial relations with and oppressions of indigenous peoples (see, e.g., the discussion of "object hobbyists" in Deloria [1998]). As Schaafsma (2013:21) puts it, "To open up interpretation to a general public of Euro-Americans harboring foreign mental templates" is "an assertion—albeit unconscious—of cultural dominance."

The maintenance of neocolonial relations between Western and indigenous cultures requires obfuscation of the ongoing effects of colonization, genocide, dislocation, and/or assimilation (Buescher and Ono 1996). The ability of the colonizing culture to define the culture of the colonized works to quell lingering dis-ease on the part of the colonizers, creating compensatory images and meanings, a well of resources to ease their dissonance. In short, neocolonialism relies on abstracting a colonized culture into the (imagined) Other, appropriating aspects of that very culture to facilitate that abstraction while also obscuring key elements of that culture and its history (Stuckey and

Morris 1999). Neocolonialism appropriates the culture of the other to create an abstract representation, both justifying and enacting the turning of the other culture into a resource to be metaphorically mined, shipped home, and transformed into a commodity (Whitt 1995; see also chapter 3). This is what has happened with rock art imagery across the Southwest and beyond (Hays-Gilpin 2004; Lewis-Williams 1995; Welsh 1999). The rhetorically constituted indeterminacy of these material traces of ancient indigenous cultures enables the appropriation and redefinition of those cultures by dismissing what may be known about their material traces by living indigenous peoples. The implications of such appropriations, however, extend beyond the rock art and its meanings, as they function to erase contemporary indigenous subjectivity via the logic of primitivism.

The Denial of Interiority, Projection, and Neocolonialism

"The deep subtext of the adventures of 'communication' in modern thought," Peters (1999:230) argues, "is confrontation with creatures whose ability to enter into community with us is obscure." Along with case studies of communication with the dead, extraterrestrials, and machines, Peters (1999:229) includes "primitives" in his list of enigmatic others with whom communication is both desired and problematic, and the lure of both rock art and its interpretation is easily highlighted as another of the longed-for contacts with distant others that Peters deftly analyzes. In this context, primitivism is both the expression of such a longing and the means by which the other is erased (i.e., displaced by the self and its projections). The interpretive materials analyzed in the first part of this chapter symbolically kill the other, constituting the inaccessibility of both precontact and postcontact indigenous cultures and making the interpretation of rock art a case of communication with entities both unknown (mysterious) and absent (dead). Indigenous agency is rendered irrelevant while the interpretive agency of visitors is actively encouraged.

The parallels between the dominant themes in the interpretive materials analyzed here, the dominant themes in Western representations of Native Americans, and the ideology of dissemination highlight the role of interiority in neocolonial relations. The disseminatory rhetoric that licenses visitors' diverse interpretations of rock art positions Native Americans as absent—either by literal omission, by reference to their lack of knowledge or unwillingness to share it, or by the implication of their demise. Living Native Americans are either obscured or overtly dismissed as relevant authorities. Without a (necessarily political) discussion of why Native Americans may refuse to provide knowledge to non-Natives about the meaning of rock art, this fits closely with the "vanishing race" narrative that has dominated representations of Native Americans for well over one hundred years (Gidley 1998; Lyman 1982; van Lent 1996). Edward Curtis's photographic project and the salvage ethnography of the early twentieth century were predicated on the presumption that Native Americans would either literally die or be assimilated, killing their culture. Under the doctrines of primitivism and the salvage paradigm, upon contact with Westerners primitive peoples are corrupted, losing their purity and authenticity (Clifford 1987) and all that was presumed to go with it: close ties to nature, social harmony, deep spirituality, and a direct relationship with the products of their labor (Dilworth 1996; Kadish 2004). This required the invention of the ethnographic present, the study of primitive peoples soon after contact, but enacted in such a way as to filter out modern contaminants (see chapter 3 for more on primitivism, authenticity, salvage ethnography, and the ethnographic present).

The inaccessibility of primitive cultures posited by this ideological frame ignites the very dialogic longings for contact described by Peters (1999), but the cause for those longings makes clear the inevitability of dissemination: interpretation when no (authentic) response is possible. In this sense, dissemination operates in conjunction with primitivism and the salvage paradigm to deny Natives their own interiority (for such an interiority is inevitably contaminated if Westerners have access to it) while shifting the authority for determining authenticity onto non-Native observers. The denial of indigenous interiority and/or the refusal to access it (as opposed to Native refusal to provide it) shifts the locus of authority and authenticity from indigenous cultures to the tourists and rock art aficionados who consume (interpret) their material traces.

Rock art in particular is ideal for accessing the inaccessible Other while avoiding contact with living others and claiming for the self total authority about the Other. Precontact rock art is rhetorically constituted as a reflection of the thoughts of people with whom Westerners did not have direct contact. These people and their culture were pure, hence the rock art is a pure reflection of their thoughts. Rock art, as a trace, can thus serve as a bridge for the ideal of dialogic contact with a genuine other—this is its fetishized value. However, temporal and cultural gaps make accessing these thoughts problematic. The most obvious bridge for that gap—living Native people—is rejected insofar as they are constituted as degraded, contaminated, or uncooperative (see chapter 3). In most of the rhetoric at the first thirteen sites I analyzed, living Native peoples are simply absent and, due to the dominance of the vanishing-race narrative, their absence need not be explained. The disseminatory move then shifts the authority to the Western observer, much as the salvage paradigm shifted it to anthropologists and documentarians like Edward Curtis. The interiority of contemporary Native peoples is ignored, and their authority over their own cultural heritage is usurped. Rock art allows "us" to access the thoughts of ancients without contaminating their purity and authenticity through dialogic exchange. The result is the illusion of contacting otherness while only engaging the self, one's own projections onto the rock art, and one's stereotypes of the peoples imagined to have produced it. This is literally "our American heritage," not an other's heritage. The temporal/cultural gap that prohibits dialogue, therefore, is not a problem or a failure—it is rhetorically constituted in a manner that furthers neocolonial relations through the widespread appropriation of indigenous cultural elements, primitivist projections, denial of indigenous interiority and authority, and an obfuscation of the material and cultural realities of contemporary indigenous peoples.

In the materials at Petroglyph National Monument, indigenous peoples are portrayed as living cultures—cultures with continuity, not radically alienated from their past. They are granted some authority over the interpretation of their cultural heritage, including refusals to offer interpretations. Respect for others is requested while indigenous interiority is not forced open to be put on display. Significantly, the materials at Petroglyph National Monument were shaped in the context of consultation with various Native American tribes, as the monument has from its inception highlighted such consultations in its management plans (Evans et al. 1993; Ferguson and Anschuetz 2003). Indeed, many of the guidelines for interpreting cultural materials at Petroglyph National Monument that were suggested by Evans, Stoffle, and Pinel (1993) as an outcome of their consultation with related Native groups are directly reflected in the interpretive materials I have analyzed above. While indigenous input is of course filtered through the institutional and discursive systems of the NPS, and is ultimately textualized and objectified, nevertheless at some point—to put it simply—someone talked with real, living peoples. The difference between Petroglyph National Monument and the other sites analyzed here is manifested less in the types and amounts of information provided than in how the *relationships* between the rock art, living indigenous peoples, and contemporary visitors are rhetorically constituted.

Contemporary visitation of indigenous rock art sites certainly constitutes the kind of "wildly asynchronous dialogic couplings" discussed by Peters (1999:248). Time- and space-binding media not only lead to "speaking into the air" but also to painting and carving on rocks, resulting in a variety of hermeneutic moves that articulate diverse cultural politics. Dissemination is invoked when no reply is presumed to be possible, when the reading of traces is all there is. But reply *is* possible. The reply—involving interaction with living Native peoples and all the implications thereof—is precisely what the disseminatory rhetoric licenses visitors to avoid, and along with that comes the denial of authentic subjectivity and indigenous authority. What is licensed by the disseminatory rhetoric is the refusal to engage, even indirectly, with real American Indians (cf. Deloria 1998). We are offered the illusion of engaging otherness by engaging ourselves, a relatively safe project compared to engaging genuine otherness (radical difference), and an illusion fitted to further neocolonial hegemony. This is facilitated by a rhetoric of indeterminacy that embraces dissemination in its licensing of visitors' own interpretations. The appeal of rock art's mystery is not so much the possibility of engaging a radically other interiority as it is the fabrication of that interiority through projection. The rhetoric of indeterminacy analyzed here is not a rhetoric characterized by humility in the face of radical otherness, but a rhetoric that actively negates such otherness.

CHAPTER 7

OVERCOMING THE
PRESERVATION PARADIGM

Toward a Dialogic Approach to Rock Art and Culture

In preparation for one of my many drives across Nevada, I scour various maps for new routes through the state's vast expanses, routes that also take me close to rock art sites I can visit. I had recently discovered references to pictographs in Toquima Cave, and it was an easy find—one of those relatively rare rock art sites marked on widely available USGS topographic maps. Nevertheless, accessing the site was not quite as easy as the nearby Hickison Pass rock art site, incorporated into a roadside campground on US Highway 50. My journey to Toquima Cave took me a dozen miles off the highway on a dirt road that began to twist its way up into the Toquima Mountains. I discovered the empty, informal camp-ground/parking area at the trailhead, and as the light was fading I ran the half-mile to the cave's entrance, following a well-worn but small trail, as I hoped to get a good look at the cave before driving back to Highway 50 and getting closer to Reno before ending the day's driving.

My limited research into Toquima Cave had piqued my curiosity, as intact pictographs are not as common as petroglyphs, and a cave site was of additional interest as I fleshed out my range of rock art experiences. As I neared the area where I assumed I would find the cave, I began to realize what a prime location it occupied—high in the Toquima Mountains, looking eastward down a small canyon toward one of Nevada's large, long, flat, mountain-lined, and sage-filled valleys. This particular one, Monitor Valley, was one I had run across in my rock art research. I knew there was an abundance of rock art there, as well as northward at Hickison. The beauty of the piñon and juniper forest, the wonderful view eastward in the remaining light of the sunset, the contrast to the day's driving provided by my brisk walk along the trail, and the richness of the area's rock art all contributed to my eagerness to see the cave, its rock art, its immediate surroundings, and its view.

At last the trail turned upwards and I could see a dark area that was clearly the top of the cave's entrance. I could already tell this was a large cave. Not wanting to miss anything in the fading light, I picked my way slowly toward the cave's mouth, examining every rock for signs of petroglyphs and bedrock mortars, every area of open ground for potsherds. Because my eyes were in a ground-oriented scan-mode and because of the trees and boulders covering the steep slope below the cave, I was less than one hundred feet away when I looked up to see the cave's mouth—covered from side to side, from the ground to more than a dozen feet in the air, with a modern cyclone fence (see Figure 7.1).

The diamond pattern and silver color of the fence, its round metal poles thrusting upwards, its built-in gate kept in the closed position with a chain and Forest Service padlock, provided a jarring sensation, unexpected, out of sync with the natural surroundings of rough tan rock, twisted gray wood, and asymmetrical green trees, shattering my excitement at encountering another powerful rock art site. With the combination of the coming darkness and the fence keeping me several yards from the rock art, I could see relatively little, but enough to further whet my appetite. However, even if I could have seen more, I think it would have made little difference. This rock art was imprisoned, and I knew why: to protect it from vandalism as well as from the carelessness of less malicious visitors. Probably precisely because it was one of the few rock art sites in the area marked on some maps, more people visited it, and more people acted in ways that damaged the rock art. In addition, the cave itself would present a tempting target for those interested in digging up artifacts, even human remains, for their private collections or for auction on eBay.

Of course, I should be angry that the stupidity and maliciousness of some people requires such drastic actions in the name of "preservation," and I am. I do not want to see the site degraded, the glyphs covered with spray paint or scratches, the artifacts ripped from their resting place in the soil of the cave's floor. Given the treatment of archaeological sites associated with indigenous peoples, I cannot blame the Forest Service for their drastic actions, actions taken to protect the site. Of course, I should be grateful for whatever small degree of protection

FIGURE 7.1—US Forest Service fence and lock, Toquima Cave, Lander County, Nevada.

underfunded government agencies such as the Forest Service and Bureau of Land Management (BLM) manage to provide.

It reminded me of my disappointment at hiking towards the Headwaters forest in Humboldt County, California, one of those small areas of old-growth redwood forest still left due to the efforts of environmental activists. Because it was the mating season of the marbled murrelet, we were instructed not to enter the old-growth groves, and we could not even get close enough to see them. Instead, the hike ended in the midst of a massive clear-cut—hardly the experience I hiked several hours to have. But despite my disappointment, I could not be angry at the restriction. I recognized and embraced the idea that we did not save this ecosystem so that I could enjoy it—we saved this ecosystem so that it could continue to feed the streams with clear water, to allow for spawning habitat for salmon and nesting habitat for birds . . . simply, to exist. And I could accept, cognitively at least, that my presence could be contrary to these goals.

So I could also accept, on one important level, the need for the imprisonment of Toquima Cave in the name of preserving the cave

and its ancient contents. But I could also sense, feel, not just my disappointment, but the deadness of the place. It was imprisoned, despite
the justification of protection and preservation. It felt like a dead site,
not a living, breathing place. Even with more light, even if the fence
was closer to the pictographs, this would not be one of those vital,
enchanting encounters with a place touched and marked by others, a
place whose very life energy may have been the cause for its marking.

Rock Art Vandalism

As a regular visitor at rock art sites, I frequently encounter mild to
severe cases of vandalism. In addition to the familiar array of names,
initials, dates, hearts, and penises (i.e., "graffiti") applied by spray
paint, scratching, or pecking (see Figure 7.2), many sites have served
as targets, with pock-marks made by bullets marring rock art panels if
not the images themselves (see Plate 9). "Historic" graffiti (postcontact
marks made fifty or more years before the present) are also often seen,
along with paintball sprays and other "incidental" damage from activities such as rock climbing or livestock grazing. Some rock art panels
have been "chalked": Although considered vandalism today, in the past,
pictographs were sometimes outlined with chalk and the pecked areas
in petroglyphs were routinely highlighted with chalk to improve visibility
for photographs. At some rock art sites, one or more elements have
been erased or covered by scratching or abrasion. In the most severe
cases of vandalism, entire panels or sections thereof have been removed
(or attempted to be removed) by the use of chisels or power saws. The
types of vandalism described above, with some rare exceptions generally involving "historic" non-Native graffiti, are frustrating at the least,
more often maddening, as they clearly speak to thoughtlessness if not
outright disrespect for cultural resources and Native Americans. Large
rock art sites with no evident vandalism are rare, and encountering such
a site is often surprising and, in some sense, more powerful. As a result
of my interest in rock art specifically and archaeology more broadly, as
well as a desire to prevent vandalism, I serve as a volunteer site steward
for the Arizona State Historic Preservation Office and the Coconino
National Forest, visiting archaeological sites (a small minority of which
are rock art sites) in order to prevent vandalism or, more commonly, to
identify and report acts of vandalism after they have occurred.

In addition to my direct encounters with vandalism, as a subscriber
to a rock art listserve (rock-art@asu.edu), I regularly receive emails

FIGURE 7.2—Contemporary graffiti on petroglyph panel, White River Narrows, Lincoln County, Nevada.

announcing acts of vandalism at rock art sites. Though each of these acts bothers me, they hit harder when I have visited the vandalized site. At the same time, as a scholar attuned to the rhetorical and ideological operations of discourse, I also examine the coverage and discussion of the vandalism of rock art sites with an eye for key terms, themes, metaphors, systems of value, and stock narratives—for the tropes that form understandings of rock art vandalism.

In 2000, a large, prominent panel of Barrier Canyon Style pictographs in central Utah, possibly several thousand years old, was vandalized. Located high above the canyon floor, adjacent to a well-traveled road, the Temple Mountain Wash site had several large images drawn on the panel with charcoal, including antlered quadrupeds, a bow and arrow, and a possible "Kokopelli" (flute player), as well as a name and date. A member of the Utah Rock Art Research Association's conservation and preservation committee wrote in the *Salt Lake Tribune*, "The symbols drawn here indicate the perpetrator was at least familiar with Indian pictographs. . . . [T]his person knew exactly what they were doing. They were trying to emulate it" (Miller 2000). An archaeologist with the Utah Trust Lands Administration (which administers the site) stated, "We view rock art as an asset, not unlike gold, silver, gas, oil, and gravel. We intend to pursue the person who did it as vigorously as we can" (Miller 2000). A BLM law enforcement officer reacted to the vandalism by stating, "Maybe something needs to be done to eliminate access to the site. There has been quite a lot of vandalism to the panel through the years, but this last incident is horrible" (Miller 2000). Years earlier, a large anthropomorphic figure at the site had several large holes blasted in it from gunfire—one of the most common forms of vandalism I have encountered at rock art sites in the western United States. This is not exactly how one would treat "gold, silver, gas, [and] oil," although gravel may be a different story.

In 2007, Picture Canyon, the largest rock art site in the city of Flagstaff, Arizona, was repeatedly used for games of paintball, resulting in splatters of paint appearing on and around the many petroglyphs in the canyon, attributed to the Sinagua culture that inhabited the area roughly one thousand years ago (Cole 2007). The paint splatters were removed by a professional rock art conservator. Unlike the kind of vandalism described above at Temple Mountain Wash, paintball splatters may be more careless than intentional. Local rock art researchers made posters of the damage and requested local stores that sell paintball supplies to post them in order to reduce future damage through education and awareness (Cole 2007).

In 2010, a panel of petroglyphs at Keyhole Sink, west of Flagstaff, was vandalized. Someone used silver paint to place the letters "ACE" and "TJ" directly on top of several pecked images (Muller 2011). The petroglyphs at Keyhole Sink have been attributed to the Cohonina culture, which inhabited the area roughly one thousand years ago. Like the Picture Canyon paintball splatters, the graffiti were removed by a professional rock art conservator. Unlike at least some paintball splatters, however, this was clearly an intentional act. Well publicized by the Kaibab National Forest, the site is accessed by a three-quarter-mile-long foot trail. Forest Service archaeologist Neil Weintraub explains, "They had to know what they were doing, walking all the way back here and carrying paint. It had to be premeditated . . . and malicious" (Muller 2011; ellipses in original). After the relatively successful graffiti removal effort, Weintraub stated,

> Most visitors to Keyhole Sink will not be able to tell that vandalism took place here. . . . However, even though we were

largely able to repair the damage, this site will never be the same.
. . . For thousands of years and for thousands of visitors—both
recent and prehistoric—Keyhole Sink was a serene place to
make a connection with nature and with the past. . . . I feel that
all changed in late August when someone decided to hike in
three-quarters of a mile to the petroglyph panel with a bucket of
paint. (Kaibab National Forest 2010)

Like Temple Mountain Wash, this was not the first act of vandalism
at Keyhole Sink, but it was far more visible than the previous names
scratched into rocks in the area, and it occurred despite specific actions
taken to help protect the site.

Increasingly, vandalism is occurring at sites other than those in
relatively isolated, rural areas. The tremendous growth of southwestern
cities such as Phoenix, Albuquerque, and Las Vegas has created not
only conflicts between urban sprawl and the preservation of cultural/
archaeological resources, but also a substantial problem with graffiti and
other types of vandalism at rock art sites in or near large urban areas.
In 2010, just outside of Las Vegas, Nevada, in the Red Rock National
Conservation Area, three rock art panels, including both petroglyphs
and pictographs, were "tagged" by members of what local police identified as a gang called the "Nasty Habits Crew" (Valley 2010a). The
panels were completely covered with maroon paint. A BLM spokes-
person stated, "When people are doing crimes like this they are not
thinking it through" (Valley 2010b). Las Vegas Metro Police, however,
hypothesized that the location was chosen because of its "high profile,"
as "gangs of graffiti vandals . . . like a lot of shock value" (Valley 2010a).
Eventually, a seventeen-year-old "prominent graffiti vandal" who goes
by the graffiti moniker "Pee Wee" was arrested and subsequently convicted for what the American Rock Art Research Association (2011:16)
referred to as "destructive and disrespectful gang graffiti." A professional rock art conservator subsequently "restored the rock art to its
near-original condition" (ARARA 2011:16).

Over time, I have become somewhat desensitized to the shock and
sadness that result from the latest announcement of these kinds of
acts of destruction. But there is always a new twist, a quantitatively
or qualitatively more horrific act on the horizon. In the fall of 2012, I
finally managed to spend some time in the Volcanic Tablelands north
of Bishop, California, an area administered by the BLM and long

known for its petroglyph sites. I had spent a lot of time visiting rock art sites to the east, in Nevada, as well as to the south, in Death Valley National Park, and I had driven through Bishop many times, but either lacked the time or the weather was wrong to spend time in the Volcanic Tablelands. According to Leigh Marymor (1998), from the late 1920s through at least the 1950s, the rock art around Bishop, including the "Petroglyph Loop" that goes through the Volcanic Tablelands, was well publicized, including articles in popular magazines and publications by organizations such as the Automobile Club of Southern California. Despite this long history of publicity and visitation, David Whitley, in his guidebook to rock art that includes four sites as part of the Bishop "petroglyph loop" tour, explains that

> due to incidents of vandalism, the BLM has decided, with sup-
> port of local Native Americans, to control access to the Bishop
> sites . . . in part by not widely disseminating directions to them.
> They have asked that directions to the sites not be printed in this
> guide; however, you may obtain directions and a map to these
> sites from the BLM office in Bishop. . . . The BLM hopes that
> by requiring individuals to appear at its office to obtain maps it
> can prevent vandals from gaining access to the sites. (Whitley
> 1996:74)

Following these directions, I stopped at the interagency visitor center in Bishop and quickly obtained the official BLM trifold brochure with a map and clear directions to three of the major sites, as well as information about rock art, site etiquette, and relevant laws and fines, but I received no real instruction on site etiquette from the staff. In addition, without any prodding on my part, the federal employee behind the counter proceeded to tell me how to access the fourth site that was included in Whitley's 1996 guidebook but not included in the brochure. I spent three days visiting and revisiting these four sites and looking for more rock art and other archaeological sites. The rock art, other material remains of past inhabitants, wildlife, and the tablelands themselves were amazing.

Less than two weeks after my visit, visitors reported severe vandalism at a site in the tablelands. A few weeks after that, a message from the rock art listserve entered my inbox, providing a link to an *LA Times* story titled "Petroglyph Thefts near Bishop Stun Federal Authorities, Paiutes":

Ancient hunters and gatherers etched vivid petroglyphs on cliffs in the Eastern Sierra that withstood winds, flash floods and earthquakes for more than 3,500 years. Thieves needed only a few hours to cut them down and haul them away.

Federal authorities say at least four petroglyphs have been taken from the site. A fifth was defaced with deep saw cuts on three sides. A sixth had been removed and broken during the theft, then propped against a boulder near a visitor parking lot. . . .

"The individuals who did this were not surgeons, they were smashing and grabbing," U.S. Bureau of Land Management archaeologist Greg Haverstock said last week as he examined the damage. "This was the worst act of vandalism ever seen" on the 750,000 acres of public land managed by the BLM field office in Bishop.

The theft required extraordinary effort: Ladders, electric generators and power saws had to be driven into the remote and arid high desert site near Bishop. Thieves gouged holes in the rock and sheared off slabs that were up to 15 feet above ground and 2 feet high and wide. (Sahagun 2012)

The stories were vague as to the specific site within the Volcanic Tablelands that was vandalized, but a reference to a broken panel that was left behind near a visitor parking lot made clear to me that it was one of the four developed and publicized sites I had visited. My desensitization could not overcome my sadness over any of the panels I had seen the previous month being so desecrated. Two months after I first read about the vandalism on the tablelands, another *LA Times* story announced the recovery of the stolen petroglyphs as a result of an anonymous tip (Sahagun 2013). The recovered petroglyphs are being held as evidence pending identification and prosecution of the thieves. The post-prosecution fate of the panels is uncertain, but they will never be smoothly reintegrated into their native locales.

I had encountered this level of outright, machine-powered theft before, at a site north of Las Vegas on a rock art conference field trip. In that case, power saws capable of cutting through rock were hauled over rough roads, and then over much smaller trails. Multiple bedrock mortars and rock art panels had been removed, leaving behind deep saw cuts in the remaining rock as well as sections that had broken in the process of being cut or pried away (see Figure 7.3). Several other sites I have visited, such as Rochester Creek in central Utah, also show signs of successful or unsuccessful attempts at the removal of one or more petroglyphs, though rarely is there evidence of the use of power saws. These are not acts that can be explained away as thoughtless or misguided, as much modern graffiti could be, but as intentional acts of theft, with destruction being an inevitable and apparently acceptable byproduct.

But these are not the typical acts of vandalism. Names, dates, initial-filled hearts, and crude symbols of male heterosexuality are far more pervasive and highly pernicious in their own ways. For those interested in rock art, few things are more upsetting and more commonly encountered than graffiti defacing indigenous rock art sites. Such graffiti are, in effect, equivalent to many other forms of vandalism of rock art sites, such as bullet holes, paintball sprays, chalking, abrasions, or scratches on indigenous elements. Contemporary graffiti at rock art sites interferes with aesthetic appreciation, degrades the informational and archaeological value of the resource, and disrespects the cultural heritage of indigenous peoples. In short, *graffiti* and its de facto synonym, *vandalism*, operate as the paired devil terms of the rock art community. These more typical forms of vandalism are also, in some ways, more complex as to the dynamics of culture and communication, policy and interpretation, than thefts like those on the Volcanic Tablelands.

In recent years, rock art has been given increasing attention by archaeologists, artists, museums, parks, laypersons, the media, and commercial entities such as tour companies, hotels, restaurants, and souvenir shops. A widely held view in the rock art community is that this popularity has resulted in an increase in both vandalism of rock art sites and attention to the need to preserve such sites from vandalism (Dean 1998b; Marymor 2001). As both a scholar and a rock art enthusiast, I am certainly part of rock art's increasing popularity, and I share in the general outrage that comes in response to graffiti and other forms of vandalism at rock art sites. Graffiti in particular do indeed interfere with my experience of indigenous rock art, but so do invasive management efforts such as the fence over the mouth of Toquima Cave. I will admit that part of my motivation for writing this chapter is formed by my experience of *rupestrius interruptus*—of my experience of rock art being constrained, not only by acts of vandalism, but also by the attempts to preserve rock art and protect it from such acts of vandalism.

However, I believe that there is more going on here than what has been dismissively described in *Rock Art and Cultural Resource*

FIGURE 7.3—Remains of petroglyph panel removed with power saw, Clark County, Nevada.

Management as "the feeling . . . that visitors should be allowed to experience a site without restriction and enjoy the special features of the environment in an unrestrained manner" (Lee 1991:7). In other words, the issue is not simply that "some loss of freedom of action is a small price to pay when the ultimate cost may be the loss of a unique part of our heritage" (Lee 1991:7). Beyond limitations on personal freedoms when visiting rock art sites, the belief system that decries all graffiti as vandalism and that upholds various preservation efforts is based on a set of ideological assumptions that shape how we understand the nature, meaning, and function of rock art in the first place.

Questioning the Preservation Paradigm

In this book, I am exploring the contemporary status of rock art sites and motifs and interrogating the contemporary structures that mediate their interpretation, valuation, and appropriation. This chapter is an effort to think through, critically, the ways in which various marks on rock are differentially valued through the deployment of the terms *graffiti* and *vandalism*, how that process of differentially valuing various marks on rock is both grounded in and constitutive of an ideology of preservation, and how the ideology and practice of preservation limit possibilities for understanding the nature of rock art. My goal is not to argue that graffiti should be encouraged or allowed, but to uncover the assumptions and ideologies that lead to preservation efforts "making sense" and to explore the implications thereof.

I problematize the notions of *preservation* and *vandalism* that ideologically ground the discourses and practices of managing rock art sites generally and responding to graffiti specifically. The discourses and practices of preservation carry implicit and explicit systems of value by which marks on rock are deemed to constitute archaeological, cultural, and/or historic *resources* versus *graffiti* or *vandalism*. These systems of value constrain and enable the ways marks on rock can be understood, interpreted, and valued. Specifically, guided by the work of James Clifford (1987, 1988), a historian of anthropology and critical/cultural studies scholar, I critically analyze the "preservation paradigm" through the lens of the "salvage paradigm" that dominated much of twentieth-century anthropology. *Preservation*, a concept implicated in the salvage paradigm, assumes that the authenticity of a site is maintained by "freezing" it in its "prehistoric" (precontact) condition, a view that is contrary to the possible function of rock art locales as sites for dialogue, as forums for cross-cultural expression. *Vandalism* is a normative, not descriptive, category relying on presuppositions regarding the relative value of marks on rock. I explore the systems of value and ideologies that support the "preservation" of rock art sites and that define some marks as vandalism in order to identify their implications for the interpretation and evaluation of both ancient and contemporary marks on rock.

While I critically interrogate the ideologies and practices carried out in the name of preserving and protecting rock art, I am *not* engaging in a critique of the ideology and practice of preservation in order to argue for a reduction in preservation efforts. In no way are the arguments here intended to license additions or alterations to rock art sites, or to encourage any acts that would violate laws such as the Archaeological Resources Protection Act (ARPA) or ethical guidelines promulgated by organizations such as the American Rock Art Research Association (ARARA). Instead, I argue that the ideology that grounds and guides preservation efforts perpetuates a particular set of assumptions about rock art sites, the nature of their value in relation to past and present cultures, and the very nature of "culture" itself. Preservation practices materialize and perpetuate those ideologies. Those ideologies, in turn, limit how we can understand rock art.

Ultimately, I argue that preservation efforts are guided by an essentialist view of culture that constrains both indigenous cultures and nonindigenous understandings of rock art. Critical examination of the discourse of rock art preservation, along with an interrogation of the meanings, functions, and assumptions behind the labels *vandalism* and *graffiti*, offers an alternative lens for the interpretation of rock art motifs and sites, especially those containing both ancient, indigenous "rock art" (i.e., graffiti) and contemporary "graffiti" (i.e., rock art). Such a reinterpretation points to issues that are central to our understanding of communication, culture, and cultural resources: specifically, an essentialist view of culture that can affect the theorizing and analysis of cross-cultural dynamics. "Culture" is essentialized when it is presumed to be fixed, clearly bounded, and created independently of other cultures—that is, when it is treated as a thing rather than an interdependent, ongoing process that exists and is re-created in relation to other cultures. Challenging the essentialist view of culture embedded in the preservation paradigm enables the development of different models for understanding the communicative dynamics of rock art. Graffiti, despite its status as aesthetic, cultural, political, and archaeological heresy, points to a dialogic or conjunctural model of culture that may have the capacity to reveal additional significances of rock art.

To develop this argument, I begin by framing my analysis in relation to critical examinations of cultural resource management (CRM). I review common rock art preservation strategies, a rhetorical understanding of value, and then outline the preservation paradigm and its attendant ideology of cultural authenticity. With this basis, I read a variety of rock art sites in order to identify the operation of systems of value regarding precontact, "historic," and contemporary, as well as indigenous versus nonindigenous, rock art. I then use the relationships between these asymmetrically valued marks to articulate an alternative view of the value of rock art sites, a view based in the dialogic nature of culture.

Cultural Resource Management

The management of rock art sites includes activities such as site recording, site monitoring, site assessment, and development of management plans, including decisions such as whether and how to develop a site, whether and how to publicize a site, and how to manage public visitation and maximize conservation of the site (Whitley 2011). Land managers, archaeologists, and others who oversee rock art sites—however actively or passively, consciously or unconsciously—are engaged in CRM. Before discussing the management of rock art sites specifically, a review of critical approaches to CRM highlights the larger issues and implications of CRM decisions and practices.

Despite its characterization as "simply the technical processes concerned with the management and use of material culture perceived by sectors of the community as significant" (Smith 2004:6), a range of recent analyses demonstrate that CRM is an institutional practice guided by ideologies. In enacting those ideologies, CRM makes them materially consequential. Specifically, scholars have demonstrated not only CRM's relationship to archaeological theory and practice, but its social consequences, political affiliations, and implications in structures of power. Laurajane Smith (2004) examined CRM (or CHM, cultural heritage management) in the context of both the United States and Australia, demonstrating how archaeological expertise and CRM practices mediate indigenous claims to cultural identity, land, sovereignty, and nationhood (see also the essays in Mathers et al. 2005).

Joseph Tainter and Bonnie Bagley (2005:69) argue for the need for self-reflection by CRM regarding its practices because "cultural resource managers do not merely perceive, record, and evaluate the archaeological record. To the contrary, they apply a set of mostly unexamined assumptions, biases, and filters to privilege certain parts of the record, and to suppress the rest." There is a need, therefore, "to expose and debate the assumptions underlying significance evaluations" (Tainter and Bagley 2005:59). Their position is grounded in an awareness that "cultural resource managers do not so much *discover* the archaeological record as, unconsciously but actively, they *shape* and *produce* it. The archaeological record is an active construct of our assumptions and biases" (Tainter and Bagley 2005:69). In a rejection of a simplistic positivist epistemology, in which both an objective reality and our ability to directly grasp that reality are taken as givens, these authors argue that cultural resources do not simply exist as prepackaged containers of information, but are constituted as such by archaeological and CRM practices and discourses. In this view, unconscious assumptions about archaeological significance and value not only have the potential to distort our understanding of cultural resources; such assumptions, embedded in taken-for-granted ideologies, determine what will be labeled and hence treated as a valuable resource in the first place, thereby shaping the overall archaeological record and the cultural heritage of particular groups based on the unconscious assumptions of the dominant culture.

Published materials relating to protecting, preserving, and conserving rock art, many of them in *American Indian Rock Art* and other ARARA publications, reflect the idea that CRM is primarily a technical endeavor. That is, publications on rock art preservation (conservation, protection, management) in the United States focus on important, practical issues such as guidelines and techniques for site recording (ARARA 2007; Bock and Lee 1991; Mark and Billo 1999), guidelines for site visitation (Bock and Lee 1991), managing public access (Marymor 2001; Swadley 2009), balancing rock art protection with other land uses such as rock crawling (Childress 2004) and rock climbing (King 2002), research into degradation due to natural processes such as lichen (Dandridge and Meen 2003), techniques for graffiti removal (Dean 1998a; Pilles 1989), the use of public-private partnerships to reduce vandalism (Pilles 1989), and educational efforts to reduce vandalism (Pilles 1989; Sanger 1992). At least three self-contained publications also address conservation, preservation, and cultural resource management in relation to rock art in the United States (Conservation and Protection Committee 1988; Crotty 1989; Lee 1991), and the chapters by Loendorf (2001) and Loubser (2001) in the *Handbook of Rock Art Research* (Whitley 2001c) address, respectively, site recording and conservation management. Whitley's (2011) *Introduction to Rock Art Research*, the only "textbook" for rock art studies, includes a chapter on management and conservation. These publications all reflect the focus of CRM on techniques for protecting and preserving rock art, though several of them acknowledge and even highlight the nontechnical difficulties involved with balancing the sometimes competing perspectives and desires of archaeologists, indigenous peoples, tourism-related businesses, rock art enthusiasts, and other recreational users (e.g., Marymor 2001; Whitley 2011).

Given this almost exclusively technical focus, it is crucial to extend the critical examination of CRM ideologies and practices into the arena of rock art preservation, while also adding to our larger understanding of rock art by examining the implications of assumptions embedded in the discourses and practices of rock art preservation. Concerns over the infusion of contemporary, unconscious assumptions and ideologies on the interpretation of indigenous rock art are frequently mentioned in the rock art literature. Self-reflexive, critical analyses are important for the ongoing development of rock art studies, and rock art interpretation specifically. Important examples include Kelley Hays-Gilpin's (2004) work on gender, Polly Schaafsma's (1997) discussion of the impact of the secular/sacred distinction, David Whitley's (2001b) articulation of the tensions involved in using science to study the sacred, and Benjamin Smith and Geoffrey Blundell's (2004) critique of phenomenological studies of rock art and landscape. This chapter extends these and other important works by examining how the ideology and practice of preservation perpetuate certain assumptions about the nature of rock art and its meanings, assumptions that are more difficult to identify because the preservation of rock art is not explicitly understood as connected to rock art interpretation except insofar as preservation enables interpretive work in general by maintaining rock art sites. I argue, however, that the discourse and practice of rock art preservation encourage some interpretive frameworks over others. In bringing together critical examinations of CRM and the conceptualizations of culture embedded in preservation discourse and practice, I work to continue the ongoing process of critically analyzing unexamined assumptions embedded in rock art interpretation.

Strategies for Protecting Rock Art

A number of strategies are used to "conserve," "preserve," or "protect" rock art in the western United States, especially in terms of preventing vandalism (including graffiti), theft, and unintentional degradation caused by visitation. Based on my review of the literature, my experience at rock art sites, and public presentations by land managers and rock art scholars, below I outline common strategies for protecting rock art in the United States.

A variety of types of barriers to access are a primary management strategy. First, there are informational barriers. For much of the late twentieth century, and continuing to a substantial degree into the present, the approach of many archaeologists and land managers concerning rock art (and archaeological resources more broadly) has been to keep people away by not revealing site locations (Marymor 1998; Swadley 2009; Whitley 2011). Secrecy is also a key factor in the culture of rock art enthusiasts and scholars (a topic to which I shall return in chapter 8). When I became a volunteer site steward for the Coconino National Forest through the Arizona State Historic Preservation Office, I was required to sign an agreement indicating that I would not disclose the location of any archaeological sites to anyone outside of the program. Locational and some other information about some archaeological sites on federal lands is also exempt from the Freedom of Information Act. Some land management agencies, such as the National Park Service (NPS), are exceptionally strict about disclosing site locations, due in part to their distinct mission. Ask to be directed to rock art at a place like Death Valley National Park and, if you get told anything, you are likely to be directed to one or two "sacrificial sites"—sites identified for public visitation, in part because they are already highly accessible, previously vandalized, or comparatively insignificant. In terms of the official provision of information, for the general public the dozens (if not hundreds) of other rock art sites in the park simply do not exist. Other agencies, however, have a different mission, one more oriented toward promoting access and multiple use, including resource extraction. Nevertheless, even those agencies are typically tight-lipped about the location of archaeological sites unless they have been specifically identified and developed for public visitation. Most archaeological sites on federal lands are under the jurisdiction of the Forest Service and BLM, are open for visitation, and are largely unmonitored—the main (if not sole) barrier to access is simply not telling people where they are. In the age of GPS, the internet, and geocaching, however, this lack of provision of information by land management agencies is likely far less effective than in the past (if it was effective then).

A second type of barrier involves access to the general area where the rock art is located. The V-Bar-V rock art site in the Verde Valley, Arizona, for example, is not only fenced off so that a volunteer docent must be present to approach the rock art, but the entire V-Bar-V historic ranch site is closed to access outside of regular visiting hours. On a much larger scale, in the 1990s the entirety of Arizona's Wupatki National Monument outside of four developed sites was closed to unaccompanied access in response to instances of vandalism. Most of the monument had previously been open for pedestrian exploration to anyone who showed up at the visitor center to get a "backcountry permit," which involved signing in and getting a pamphlet and mini-lecture on site etiquette. Even "back in the good old days," however, monument staff likely would not have told you where rock art (or any other cultural resource) is located, or that it even exists, but it was nevertheless possible to go out to try to find it if one were so inclined. Currently, only a tiny portion of these backcountry areas, including rock art and other archaeological sites, are accessible via infrequent guided walks. Road closures can also be used, making access to a site still possible but far more arduous than driving down a road, pulling into a parking lot, and walking a few hundred yards to the site. Road closures can also be used with the intent of preventing the kind of mechanized looting that occurred in the Volcanic Tablelands. Remote sensors are also sometimes used to monitor closed areas and roads.

Third, within a site, physical barriers may also be used to prevent people from getting close to the rock art, such as the cyclone fences found at Toquima Cave in Nevada or at Sand Island along the San Juan River in southeastern Utah. At Atlatl Rock in Valley of Fire State Park outside of Las Vegas, Nevada, a large stairway and viewing platform were constructed to stop people from climbing up the rock to see the petroglyphs clustered near the top (see Figure 7.4). In addition, large pieces of Plexiglas were placed on the edge of the viewing platform to prevent people from touching the petroglyphs or hopping on the rock itself; however, the Plexiglas became a surface for graffiti—protecting the rock art, but severely degrading anyone's view of the petroglyphs. This exceptionally intrusive and obtrusive effort at preservation is rare in the western United States, whether due to limited budgets or wise judgments by land managers.

Fourth, in an effort to preserve the natural and aesthetic setting, as well as to maximize limited resources, passive or psychological barriers are frequently employed. Marymor (2001:5) argues that unobtrusive barriers are generally preferred because "obtrusive barriers may antagonize visitors thereby encouraging increased vandalism." Low, open fences, well-positioned interpretive signs, and clearly defined trails discourage but do not prevent people from getting closer to the rock art (Swadley 2009). A variant of this strategy involves the use of prohibitionist signs, ranging from the more direct "area closed" or "off-trail hiking prohibited in this area" to the more polite "please stay on trail" or "please do not climb on rocks." Intentional misdirection is also employed, such as posting a "rattlesnake habitat" sign to keep people out of areas intended to be off-limits to the public (Lee 1991). On the Waterfall Trail in White Tank Mountain Regional Park outside of Phoenix, for example, petroglyphs are clustered in several places along

FIGURE 7.4—Viewing structure, Atlatl Rock, Valley of Fire State Park, Nevada. This kind of elaborate structure, designed to enable viewing while constraining climbing on and touching the rock and petroglyphs, is rare in the western United States.

the one-mile trail. The greatest concentration is at the end, however, and in this area multiple signs state, "area closed—poisonous snakes and insects inhabit the area." The signs also include color pictures of a scorpion and rattlesnake. I have no doubt that these creatures inhabit this area, but I think they inhabit many other areas along the trail as well. It is difficult not to suspect that these signs are either duplicitous or at least have a secondary function of restricting access to areas with potentially fragile cultural resources such as petroglyphs. Of course, no one should ignore such a sign under the possibly false presumption that it may be a case of misdirection!

There are other strategies beyond these various barriers to access, however. Site monitoring, be it by the staff of land management agencies, volunteer site stewards, tour guides, or others, is a key component in site preservation (Hyder and Loendorf 2005), but the large number of rock art sites (let alone the far larger number of archaeological sites in general) makes monitoring alone far too resource-intensive to protect sites. Volunteer site steward programs, however, provide far greater coverage without straining limited agency budgets. Some sites, determined to have particular value and to be at particular risk for looting or vandalism, are monitored with motion sensors and other remote surveillance technologies.

Another strategy is education, which can be provided on site either in person or through pamphlets or signs, at visitor centers, or through schools or community organizations. There is a strong assumption that the more people understand about rock art, the less likely they are to vandalize it. Publicized and developed sites often have a variety of signage indicating the value and irreplaceable nature of rock art, often identifying specific actions that degrade rock art (e.g., touching and chalking). The most commonly used signs emphasize the need to protect and preserve "our" past while at a minority of sites the emphasis is on respect for the past and present cultures who produced the sites and/ or hold them as sacred (see chapter 6 for a discussion of these two rhetorical strategies). Site monitoring efforts also have educational components, and archaeological education in schools offers another avenue (Sanger 1992). Signs and other forms of education, while focusing on the value of rock art as both archaeological resource and cultural heritage, also emphasize relevant laws and potential penalties for defacing rock art. Education about these laws, as well as direct efforts at enforcement and prosecution, also contribute to site preservation.

Beyond education, outright advocacy is also part of rock art preservation efforts, but not due to the acts of vandals or careless visitors. Many rock art sites are endangered by off-road vehicles (ORVs) and other recreational activities (e.g., rock climbing), mineral exploration and extraction, and urban sprawl. Individual members of the rock art community and rock art organizations participate in educating and pressuring government agencies, private companies, and the public at large regarding such issues, as with Utah's Nine Mile Canyon, which remains threatened by fossil fuel extraction (Utah Rock Art Research Association 2004), and Albuquerque, New Mexico's Petroglyph

National Monument, where, after a prolonged battle, a new four-lane highway was built for accessing new suburban areas, threatening the integrity of the monument's boundaries and requiring the removal and relocation of a small number of petroglyphs (Schaafsma 2013).

Sixth, graffiti removal and other forms of restoration serve, in part, to deter further vandalism. An explicitly stated assumption of rock art conservation is that a clean, well-maintained site with no visible graffiti is far less likely to be vandalized than when graffiti is clearly present and allowed to remain (e.g., Marymor 2001; Swadley 2009). In addition to isolated acts of graffiti at remote or rural sites such as Temple Mountain Wash and Keyhole Sink, graffiti has become a particular problem in urban areas, such as Phoenix's South Mountain Park (Bostwick and Krocek 2002), Albuquerque's Petroglyph National Monument (Dean 1998a), and Las Vegas's Red Rock National Recreation Area (Valley 2010a, 2010b). While stories of horribly failed efforts at restoration by untrained land managers are part of the mythic reservoir of the rock art community (Dean 1998b), restoration practices and techniques have improved over the last several decades. Recent restoration efforts by trained conservators have included covering and removing contemporary graffiti and filling bullet holes.

Finally, an important part of site conservation is site recording, thoroughly documenting rock art sites via maps, drawings, verbal descriptions, and photographs. Site documentation preserves the "database" before vandalism occurs and can be used to document the extent or nature of vandalism when it does occur. Involving regional rock art organizations, avocationalists, and enthusiasts in rock art recording projects also has educational and research benefits and provides structured, monitored access to sites for enthusiasts (Hyder and Loendorf 2005). A few ambitious examples include the recording of the Lagomarsino site in Nevada (Nevada Rock Art Foundation 2012), South Mountain Park in Phoenix (Bostwick 2008), and the rock art at Baby Canyon Pueblo in Agua Fria National Monument, Arizona (Huang 2010).

The drive to protect rock art sites from senseless destruction is a strong one among members of the rock art community. At a 2004 regional rock art conference attended by archaeologists, land managers, volunteer site stewards, and avocationalists, one speaker presented a crudely drawn cartoon-like slide of a rock art vandal, spray paint can in hand, being shot by another person with a gun, presumably a land manager or rock art enthusiast. A member of a federal land management agency later reiterated a similar visual "joke" but in this case the intended target was a person driving their ORV into an area rich in archaeological resources. While everyone understood these cartoons as jokes, the very fact that such presentations were considered funny—a cause for laughter, signs of affirmation, and increased energy throughout the audience—is indicative of the strength of feeling in operation. These reactions and the commitment to site preservation, especially in terms of deterring vandalism generally and graffiti specifically, point to the positive value ascribed by this community to precontact, indigenous marks on rock in particular, and the negative value associated with "graffiti." I turn next to a brief discussion of the nature of value to set up a more systematic analysis of how different marks on rock are ascribed radically different values.

The Rhetorical Nature of Value

A naïve understanding of value assumes that value inheres in an object, that it is an inherent property of things. However, as rock art itself makes abundantly clear, value is relational and variable, not an objective, intrinsic, or fixed quality of a thing. For some, the value of rock art resides in its aesthetic properties. For some, unfortunately, its value is as a target. For others, the value of rock art is in its status as part of their own or others' cultural heritage, identity, and/or spirituality. For others still, its value resides in its status as an archaeological resource, a container of information about past cultures awaiting our ability to unlock its significance. As Peter Welsh (1999) put it in his discussion of the commodification of rock art, objects do not have inherent value; value is constructed through social relations, however abstract or obscured those may be through the process of commodification (see chapter 3).

The value of something can therefore vary from person to person, social position to social position, discipline to discipline, culture to culture. In addition, value is rhetorical: Value is attributed to objects through discourse, and different discourses can assign competing or contrary values to the same object. For example, archaeologists may decry the "looting" of sites by "pot hunters." In turn, for some Native Americans what archaeologists call "excavation" may be considered "looting" or "desecration" (Smith 2004). In addition, these differential value judgments are interrelated: The use of discourse that clearly differentiates "pot hunters" from "archaeologists" and "looting" from "careful and systematic excavation" serves to affirm the value of what archaeologists do through opposition and negation. While value is relative, and therefore debatable, certain systems for assigning value are taken as more authoritative than others. Legal and other institutional forces use specific value systems as a basis for material practices (such as prosecuting vandals)—hence, in pragmatic terms value is not "simply" relative or subjective but is socially produced, maintained, and contested. This is made painfully clear in attempts at prosecuting those who steal rock art, as ARPA requires that the item have a minimum monetary value, but professional archaeological ethics prohibit the identification of what such a monetary value would be (Woody 2005). In 2006, two men convicted of stealing petroglyph boulders near Reno, Nevada, had their convictions overturned by the Ninth U.S. Circuit Court of Appeals due to the prosecution's failure to provide evidence that the rock art had a *market* value of over $1,000. The prosecution's strategy of relying on the items' *archaeological* value, a term used in ARPA and for which they provided supporting testimony, was rejected by the court as not applicable to ARPA-based prosecutions (*United States v. Ligon* 2006).

The rhetorical processes involved in assigning (constituting) value to marks on rock can be easily illustrated through an examination of the interpretive signs located at the Buckhorn Wash pictograph site in the San Rafael Swell in central Utah. One interpretive sign, titled "Look at the Holes in Their Chests!" points, with a tone of excitement and curiosity, to later additions to the original pictographs (see Plate 10 for the pictograph panel being discussed in the text below):

> The holes in the chests of these figures were <u>INTENTIONALLY PECKED</u>. Did someone ceremonially release the power of the art? Were the beings ritually killed? Notice the yellow paint on some of these figures. Someone painted over the original red paint. Why? When? Did people change their beliefs, artistic tastes or fashion? Did the later artists have a different culture?

In this case, marks added to the pictographs (holes and paint) are constituted as potential sources of meaningful archaeological/historical/cultural information. Regardless of whether these changes were done by members of the same or another culture, these additions are perceived as having value in shedding light on precontact events and/or cultures. Yet these same two actions—the production of holes and the addition of paint on the top of rock art—are denounced as "vandalism" if carried out in the last several decades. This is made clear by another sign at the same site titled "It Only Takes Seconds to Vandalize Rock Art." This sign provides two sets of before-and-after photographs to illustrate the damage done by vandals, explaining that

> these photographs and boulder before you show <u>VANDALISM</u>. People damage rock art with: Chisels, Brushes & Gouges; Fingers, Bullets, & Fire; Charcoal, Crayon & Chalk; Paint, Pencil & Pen. Vandalizing this site in any way violates the Archaeological Resources Protection Act of 1979 (16 USC 470 ee), punishable by up to $250,000 fine and/or 5 years imprisonment.

The potential contradiction between these two signs is not directly addressed, presumably because it is not understood in any way as a contradiction: Taken-for-granted assumptions are in play here, assumptions that make the radically different value attached to roughly similar types of marks seem simply "common sense." In this case, these assumptions primarily involve *when* the marks are made, which is closely related to *who* made them: Marks placed by precontact indigenous peoples are valuable, marks made by contemporary (and perhaps even historic, depending on one's point of view) Westerners are not valuable, and in turn detract from the value of the indigenous marks.

More potential contradictions are evidenced by a third sign, explaining the restoration efforts at the site and titled "How Was The Damage Treated?":

> Sadly, much damage is permanent and we cannot "repaint" lost art. However, the Buckhorn Panel was greatly improved in 1995. Bullet holes and gouges were filled to match the sandstone. Paint, charcoal, crayon and chalk were removed with special erasers and jewelers' tools. Scraped and chiseled areas were disguised with watercolors and pastels.

Ironically, many of the techniques for vandalism identified in the second sign appear here again, but in the context of actions taken to "greatly improve" the site. Fillers, erasers, jewelers' tools, watercolors, and pastels are described differently but are basically illustrative of the list of vandals' tools from the second sign. This sign indicates particular conditions under which contemporary additions to an indigenous rock art site are "improvements" rather than "vandalism" and can therefore be assigned positive rather than negative value. The underlying system for assigning value that is operating in these signs allows for one type of contemporary addition/alteration that can be considered of value by the combination of the following three conditions:

1. The intent to restore: the actions "improved" the site and were designed to "match" the natural surface, "remove" illegitimate marks and materials, and "disguise" those that could not be removed.
2. The expertise to restore: while vandalism "takes only seconds," the use of such phrases on the restoration sign as "filled to match," "special erasers and jewelers' tools," and "disguised with watercolors and pastels" lend a sense of legitimacy to the act, tinged as they are with references to artistic expertise (in addition, an accompanying photograph shows a person restoring the site using a small power tool and wearing white gloves).
3. The authority to restore: the main "welcome" sign at the site thanks the Emery County Centennial Committee, Utah State Centennial Commission, and the BLM "for restoring this site," complete with each entity's logo.

My point is not to critique restoration efforts such as this one, but to give a clear example of how value does not reside in a mark, but is assigned to a mark through discourse based on a usually implicit value system. In particular, the nature of the value assigned to marks on rock is closely linked to the concept of "authenticity" and the discourse of "preservation."

Authenticity and the Preservation Paradigm

Two terms generally used to refer to the contemporary addition of graphic or linguistic elements to rock art sites are *graffiti* and *vandalism*. Graffiti, while defined by Merriam-Webster in neutral terms as "inscription[s] or drawing[s] made on some public surface (as a rock or wall)," is generally used in contemporary discourse with a negative connotation, as graffiti are often associated with gangs, juveniles, or others who "deface" property. In this sense, this common usage of "graffiti" is roughly equivalent to the second term, "vandalism," defined by Merriam-Webster as the "willful or malicious destruction or defacement of public or private property." However, the dominant assumption in the case of rock art sites is that (almost) any contemporary addition to a site constitutes "vandalism": Despite the dictionary definition's focus on destructive intent ("willful or malicious destruction or defacement"), in the case of rock art it is the act itself which constitutes vandalism, generally regardless of intent (with exceptions such as the Buckhorn Wash restoration discussed above, though such restorations are problematic from a strict archaeological, as opposed to an aesthetic, perspective). Educational efforts, for example, presume that at least some rock art vandalism is not malicious but is instead based in ignorance or misdirected excitement in response to the rock art—as in the story of a woman who inscribed her name and the date on a rock art site near Sedona, Arizona, making the initiation of legal prosecution relatively easy.

This view of rock art vandalism holds that intent is largely irrelevant to the loss or damage of cultural resources, focusing instead on the addition of (almost) any mark to a rock art site. This view is consistent with the ideology of preservation that guides rock art protection efforts. The outlines of this ideology are identified by Clifford (1987, 1988) in his discussion of the "salvage paradigm." The salvage paradigm in Anglo-American anthropology includes the salvage ethnography of the late nineteenth and early twentieth century, museum collections, parks and monuments, and, I argue, efforts to protect and preserve rock art sites. The salvage paradigm reflects and enacts "a desire to rescue 'authenticity' out of destructive historical change" (Clifford 1987:121). The paradigm's central preoccupation is with authenticity, which "is produced by *removing objects from their current historical situation*— a present-becoming-future" (Clifford 1988:228; emphasis added). Preservation seeks to "freeze" rock art sites in their current condition, with particular attention to minimizing human impacts on motifs, panels, and sites. Transforming something that was dynamic into a static "resource" is necessary because "authenticity in culture or art exists just prior to the present—but not so distant or eroded as to make collection or salvage impossible" (Clifford 1987:122). Preservation of rock art is often presented as driven by threats both imminent and increasing: The overriding need is to preserve the record before even more damage is done. As discussed in chapter 3, the underlying assumption is that indigenous cultures cannot survive contact with the "modern" (Western, industrial) world; therefore, as soon after contact as possible, these cultures must be "collected" and thereby "preserved" in their "authentic" state, a state that by definition must be precontact. The essence of the culture must be preserved, an essence that begins to erode upon contact with the Western world. "Artifacts and customs are saved out of time" (Clifford 1988:231). In the case of precontact rock art, taken by many as direct reflections of the thoughts, feelings, and ideas of otherwise uncontactable, ancient peoples (see chapter 6), preserving rock art sites means reducing degradation, mostly human but also natural, to as close to zero as possible. The degradation of indigenous peoples may be seen as inevitable, but the degradation of rock art sites can be prevented through proper management, maintaining a record of the pure and authentic culture of the precontact primitive.

In order for this view of authenticity to work, the precontact primitive must be essentialized, defined as singular and unchanging. Both the primitive/civilized (traditional/modern) duality and the ideology of primitivism, along with the salvage paradigm and the notion of the ethnographic present, require the essentializing of primitives in dualities defined by the civilized West: mind/body, spirit/matter, rational/emotional, culture/nature, and so forth. The primitivist notion of authenticity and the essentializing of indigenous peoples articulate with both colonialism (e.g., indigenous people as a fixed Other, while also representing the West's own past) and neocolonialism (e.g., the function of primitivist nostalgia in assuaging modern anxieties, white guilt, and anomie). Ultimately, living indigenous peoples are held to this standard of authenticity, demonstrating that the standard is based on objectifying a group of people for others' interests (Archuleta 2005). This paradigm does not protect the autonomy and dynamism of living Native cultures (Cobb 2005), but confines them to a primitivist and neocolonialist straight jacket, specifically via the trope of the "degraded" Indian (see chapter 3).

Clifford (1988:233) argues that this paradigm is predicated on a particular understanding of culture: "Expectations of wholeness, continuity, and essence have long been built into the linked Western ideas of culture and art." "Culture" is a dead metaphor—one that has become so conventional that it is not recognized as a metaphor—but a metaphor nonetheless: The modern, Western notion of culture is based on the source domain of the tilling of the land and the cultivation of plants, as well as practices of modern biology such as growing cultures in petri dishes, meanings that are unconsciously transferred to the target domain, resulting in the notion of human culture as the growing, tending, and shaping of its members. Grounded in this organic metaphor, culture is reified, viewed metaphorically as an organism that cannot survive radical environmental shifts, loss and/or replacement of substantial elements, or radical hybridization. Fragmentation and disjuncture are incompatible with this view of culture—their presence therefore signifies the death of the organism (culture):

> The culture concept accommodates internal diversity and an "organic" division of roles but not sharp contradictions, mutations, or emergences. . . . Groups negotiating their identity in contexts of domination and exchange persist, patch themselves together in ways different from a living organism. A community, unlike a body, can lose a central "organ" and not die. All the critical elements of identity are in specific conditions replaceable: language, land, blood, leadership, religion. . . . Metaphors of continuity and "survival" do not account for complex historical processes of appropriation, compromise, subversion, masking, invention, and revival. (Clifford 1988:338)

As an alternative, Clifford (1988:11) argues that "identity is conjunctural, not essential." Identity and culture are not essences, discrete things, but relationships, intersections, formed amidst multiple lines of power and difference. As an early work in what has come to be known as postcolonial theory, Clifford grapples with the complexities of identity formation and cultural maintenance in postcolonial and neocolonial—not to mention postmodern and globalized—contexts. The implications of this kind of inevitable cultural hybridity are central to conceptualizations of globalization (Appadurai 1990; Lull 2000), but can be argued to extend to previous eras, not just the late twentieth and early twenty-first centuries (Rogers 2006), and have profound implications for the authority of living Native cultures over their own cultural heritage and self-definition (Clifford 1998; Torgovnick 1996). Similar conceptualizations of culture as both conflictual and hybridized are applied in the context of Native American studies, as in Mary Lawlor's (2006) examination of tribal casinos and museums and Michelle Raheja's (2010) history of the participation of Native Americans in Hollywood's construction of the "Indian," as well as wider applications of the notion of "survivance" (e.g., Cobb 2005). Such conceptualizations of culture are in direct, critical opposition to the essentialism of primitivism and the salvage paradigm, which emphasize traditional cultures' fundamental conservatism: static, unchanging, and lacking in the dynamism and agency attributed to Western cultures. The essentialist foundations of both primitivism and the salvage paradigm, therefore, articulate deeply with evolutionary, racist, and (neo)colonialist ideologies.

While rock art preservation differs from salvage ethnography (insofar as the rock art can persist long after the originating culture vanishes or is forgotten) and collecting (literally, insofar as rock art is generally not portable, though a metaphoric sense of collecting certainly applies), I argue that the same ideology operates in rock art preservation. In addition, Clifford's (1988) replacement of "essence" with "conjuncture" provides an alternative frame, not just for culture and identity, but for understanding rock art sites as forums for spatially grounded, asynchronous dialogues. When material culture is treated (constituted) as an informational resource that can provide insight into the culture that produced and used it, and culture itself is understood as a fixed and singular essence analogous to an organism, then the meaning and significance of material culture is also fixed and singular. Therefore, following Boyd, Cotter, Gardiner, and Taylor (2005), in order to create possibilities for new interpretations, notions of essentialism should be rejected in cultural resource management. As Robert Layton and Julian Thomas (2001) argue, "preservation" is intimately linked to the notion of an archive—that is, of material culture as an archaeological resource. Questioning the essentialism embedded in dominant Western conceptions of culture—the notion of cultures as pure, clearly bounded, and organic—also questions the very foundation on which the authenticity of cultural resources is based. As Layton and Thomas (2001:18) put it, in a formulation that will be important for the impact of preservation discourses on conceptualizations of the nature of rock art sites, "questioning the notion of authenticity appears scandalous to an archaeology that . . . privileges entities over relationships." While some discussions (e.g., Smith 2004) have focused on the important differences between cultural or archaeological "resources" and cultural "heritage" (the first representing the archaeological view, the second those communities affiliated with the material culture in question), both of these labels/concepts perpetuate the essentialist view of culture that is embedded in the discourse and practice of rock art preservation.

Valuing Marks on Rock: Drawing Lines, Preventing Dialogue

The lines drawn in the preservation of archaeological resources are ideological and rhetorical distinctions based in particular systems of value. Systems for assigning value to various forms of expression on rock, in operating from the essentialist view of culture outlined above, generally deny value to postcontact marks at rock art sites regardless of who made them or with what intent. Through this discussion, I hope to clarify the (potentially) conjunctural quality of rock art sites as unique locales for dialogues between various cultures and different historical periods. To do so, I work through a crude typology of rock art dialogues, places where marks from different times coexist and interact. Under each type of dialogue, I use a number of rock art sites and motifs for illustration. I do not advance my interpretation of these sites and motifs as definitive; their purpose is heuristic, to think through the implications and possibilities of our valuations of diverse marks on rock.

Precontact Indigenous Marks from Different Time Periods

Many indigenous rock art sites, panels, and even individual elements are not constructions of singular points in time (e.g., Bernardini 2009; Bostwick and Krocek 2002; Christensen et al. 2013; Weaver et al. 2001; Young 1988). Rock art motifs that build from existing imagery are not rare, with the most obvious case being superimpositioning, wherein newer motifs have been placed, in whole or in part, over older motifs (see Plate 10). In their study of rock art in the Grand Canyon region, Christensen, Dickey, and Freers (2013) point to evidence that the Paiute occasionally outlined or repainted images associated with earlier cultural groups or traditions. In their take on Numic versus pre-Numic rock art in the Great Basin, Angus Quinlan and Alanah Woody (2003:385) hypothesize that Numic populations, upon entering the Great Basin, created the scratched rock art often found on or near the presumably older, pre-Numic, pecked petroglyphs, doing so as a means of "socializing the landscape through reuse of the monuments of preceding populations." Christensen, Dickey, and Freers (2013:173) also identify the "inclination to replicate the rock art of earlier cultural groups." In the Great Basin, for example, the common assumption that the presence of atlatl images means that the marks date prior to the introduction of the bow and arrow overlooks the possibility that the relatively frequent presence of highly stylized, abstracted atlatls in pre–bow-and-arrow rock art could have led later populations, of the same culture or another one, to reproduce the image, with or without understanding the original imagery's presumed referent.

The first case of rock art dialogue, therefore, is the coexistence of multiple elements from significantly different points in time on a single panel or in the immediate vicinity, but all the elements are presumably precontact or perhaps "historic" (postcontact) but still indigenous in origin. Superimpositioning is the strongest form of this general case (sometimes moving to the point of obliteration); the newer elements directly "degrade" or "interfere" with the older ones in ways not dissimilar to some acts of contemporary graffiti and vandalism (see Plates 11 and 12). However, there is no theme of loss in the rock art literature with regard to superimposition. Instead, cases of superimpositioning become rich sources of data for relative dating and the relationship between multiple cultures or rock art styles. Superimpositioning, combined with relative repatination or other factors, can enable conclusions not only about which image was placed first, but of the possibility that the superimposed image is indeed significantly younger than the original. As Schaafsma (2010:28) puts the value of superimpositioning, "new carvings and paintings—even figures made on top of earlier ones—compound and thus enhance the significance of place." This is largely consistent with the preservation paradigm insofar as the superimposed elements are indigenous (and preferably precontact or early in the postcontact period). That is, a rock art panel may represent (or "contain") more than one culture, but the cultures involved are constituted as authentic by the preservation paradigm because they are "pure"—that is, uncontaminated by the civilized West or the forces of modernity.

Precontact Indigenous and Postcontact Nonindigenous Marks

Some disjunctions between the preservation paradigm and the legal and bureaucratic practices of CRM can be illustrated through the examination of sites that constitute the second case of rock art dialogue, those involving both precontact indigenous elements and "historic" (postcontact but not "contemporary") nonindigenous elements.

One such site is on the west side of Death Valley National Park (DVNP). In the transition zone between a small mountain range and a Joshua tree–covered flat, several rock outcrops along a wash are peppered with indigenous, presumably precontact rock art. Images of bighorn sheep predominate (see Figure 7.5). Searches of other canyons and suitable rock outcrops in the immediate vicinity failed to reveal additional rock art—that is, the petroglyphs appear to be localized. This could be for a number of reasons: perhaps this was a favored route for those groups who made the rock art, perhaps the wash was used by game animals (and therefore hunters), perhaps a small seep was the only water in the vicinity, perhaps there were nearby habitation areas (although no habitation caves or house rings were found, there were a few grinding slicks), and/or perhaps it was selected as a focused site for ritual activity.

As with many other rock art sites, there are also historic signatures in the same area, in very close proximity to indigenous motifs. In this case, one small rock near the wash bottom contains a name dated "9/20 1905" followed by the initials of the 1905 name and the date "8/15 1908," presumably indicating repeated visitation by the same person. Another small rock has two sets of initials followed by "05" and a large rock surface contains a set of initials dated 1916. These [19]05 and 1916 inscriptions are superimposed on visible, presumably precontact petroglyphs. On the top of a boulder are two signatures dated "7-18-47," with a third signature dated 1994 right above them. Other historic marks in the area include a set of initials dated 1897 and a full name dated "7/07," with an accompanying skull and crossbones image.

The largest panel of presumably historic inscriptions is on a boulder in the middle of the wash (see Figure 7.6). Three prominent signatures are each individually dated "July 4th, 1907" or "July 4th 07." The third signature's date is followed by "Portland, ORE." A fourth and fifth signature on this same boulder are separated from the other three by either a vertical, pecked line or an angular shift in the aspect of the rock face as well as a different date: "May 18 -08." In between the first two "July 4th" signatures on the left and the two "08" and the "Port-land" "07" signatures on the right, written vertically and following the angular shift in the aspect of the rock face, is the phrase "UBEHEBE BUNCH." Ubehebe, reportedly a Paiute word, is a place name used elsewhere in the Death Valley area, including for a mine. Three or four small, repatinated, indigenous motifs appear above these signatures, as well as a large but unidentifiable shape that appears, given the lack of repatination and the nature of the dents, to have been made at or after the time of the historic signatures. Three of the letters in one of the "July 4th" signatures have been obscured by additional pecking.

FIGURE 7.5—Bighorn sheep petroglyphs, Death Valley National Park, California.

Finally, a little farther up the wash, at the upper extent of the second concentration of indigenous rock art, is another signature, Bill Key, dated 1895, this one accompanied by a well-made mountain sheep motif, clearly different in style from the indigenous sheep motifs and produced with a tool similar to the one used to produce the signature and date (see Plate 13). The second obvious occurrence of contemporary graffiti (i.e., less than fifty years old) in the area is just below this historic sheep motif, separated from it by a crack in the rock: "TG 1995." Both the name and style of the 1994 signature described above match these 1995 initials, also indicating repeat visitation by the same person.

My reactions to these historic and contemporary signatures in DVNP are far different than, for example, my reaction to the "Steve 1977" and "Ricky '76'" inscriptions on a large rock art panel in the White River Narrows (WRN) in eastern Nevada (see Figure 7.2). However, setting aside matters of the degree of direct interference/destruction and aesthetic impact, both historic and contemporary signatures are violations of the integrity of the indigenous rock art sites. Nevertheless, as historic resources (defined roughly as fifty or more years old), the 1895–1916 and the 1947 "graffiti" in DVNP could be granted the same

FIGURE 7.6—Ubehebe Bunch panel, Death Valley National Park, California.

protection as the precontact, indigenous rock art in the same area or even on the same rock (Lee 1991; Price 1989).

The 1995 vandalism (contemporary graffiti) at the DVNP site (Plate 13), however, does not seem to me as much of a violation as the 1970s WRN inscriptions (Figure 7.2). This is certainly due in part to the relative size and visual prominence of the inscriptions. The 1970s WRN inscriptions are crudely made, large, and right across the top of a long, horizontal panel while the 1995 initials in DVNP are small, neatly pecked, and to the lower-right of the historic signature and sheep motif, separated by a natural crack. In addition, the 1995 initials are close to the 1895 signature and sheep motif, but not to any (visible) indigenous rock art, so it directly violates a historic, presumably Euro-American panel, not an indigenous one. Similarly, the 1994 signature (not pictured), presumably created by the same person as the 1995 initials, is also seemingly not in close proximity to any indigenous marks, only historic signatures from 1947. While the 1994 signature seems aesthetically more intrusive than the 1995 initials, my subjective emotional response is not highly negative given that it appears with signatures from 1947; based on the principle that things increase in value as they recede in time from the present, the 1947 signatures are less valuable resources, hence less has been "lost" by the addition of the 1994 signature on the same panel.

Given all of the wonderful rock media in the immediate and broader vicinity, why has this particular area become a concentration for historic signatures? If the indigenous choice of this locale was formed by environmental factors—natural travel routes, water sources, and/or game activity—then the presence of nonindigenous historic peoples in the same area can be explained. But the historic signatures were not made casually or in passing, and in at least two cases it appears that twentieth-century visitors returned and marked the site a second time. Even with modern, metal tools, such as a miner's hand pick, substantial time and effort was put into the 1895, 1907, and 1908 signatures in particular. A choice was made to invest time in marking this particular spot in a prominent way. In this sense, the role of the indigenous rock art in the production of the historic signatures seems readily apparent. Whether these historic marks were made in conscious and specific response to the indigenous marks is unknown, but it seems clear to me that these inscriptions were produced, broadly speaking, in response to the older, indigenous inscriptions. It seems even clearer, of course, that the "TG 1995" inscription was made in response to the 1895 signature. In this case, the immediate proximity and date parallel provide additional indications of responsiveness. Setting this aside, however, I would argue that the earliest historic inscriptions (Bill Key's 1895 signature and sheep) might well have never been made in this place if it were not for the indigenous rock art already present. This interpretation is made clearer by the producer's choice to peck a mountain sheep motif, as mountain sheep are by far the most frequent motif at the entire site, where there are at least 150 sheep petroglyphs.

Marks on rock seem to invite the placement of more marks on the same or nearby rocks. A well-known maxim regarding graffiti prevention—whether in urban areas or at rock art sites—is that the best way to stop more graffiti from occurring is to remove the graffiti as soon as possible (Dean 1998a; Lee 1991; Marymor 2001; Swadley 2009). When one person leaves a mark, others choose the same spot to leave their mark (Silver 1989). There seems to be something about such marks that invites or encourages additional marks. One way to interpret this, in the context of contemporary graffiti or vandalism, is that existing vandalism seems to send the message that the place is somehow "primed" for more vandalism. Graffiti removal (or, more directly, the actual or apparent lack of graffiti) sends the "message" that the place has value and should be respected, whereas the presence of graffiti sends the "message" that the preservation of the place is not valued. This rationale is consistent with the efforts of those who wish to preserve a place—be it archaeological or natural—to keep it "pure" or "intact."

However, I think there is a broader, less loaded interpretation of this phenomenon: Marks invite marks, statements invite response. That is, setting aside particular judgments about the value of one mark on rock versus another type of mark on rock, one could hypothesize that the motivation for placing marks where others have been placed is dialogue, which can include both hostile and friendly relations between the various utterances that make up that dialogue. As Constance Silver (1989:12) states in her discussion of graffiti at rock art sites, "When one really studies the graffiti, one finds that people start to answer each other, just as they do in public restrooms." This broad sense of responsiveness is evident in all-indigenous panels as well, when one group superimposes its images on older images, repaints or repecks existing images, reproduces existing images, or incorporates existing images into larger compositions. The result of this ongoing set of responses to existing inscriptions is a fascinating and localized (as well as mysterious) dialogue: traces of conversation over time between multiple groups occupying the same place. Dialogues of this type are somewhat unique in that, like unmediated face-to-face conversation, the interlocutors must occupy the same physical space though, unlike face-to-face conversation, not at the same time.

Precontact Indigenous Marks and Contemporary Nonindigenous Marks

This notion of place-bound (spatially but not temporally grounded) cultural dialogues may be more palatable when confined to the second case, in which indigenous and nonindigenous but "historic" elements occur together at a rock art site. The third case, however, seems an equally valid case of such a dialogue: contemporary additions to precontact indigenous rock art sites.

The rhetorically constituted distinction between contemporary acts of vandalism ("graffiti") and historic, nonindigenous marks points to some clear disjunctions between the preservation paradigm, which would see any postcontact marks, nonindigenous but indigenous as well, as lacking value, and the legal and bureaucratic practices of CRM, which assigns value to anything "historic." For example, at the Rochester Creek site in central Utah, a panel includes presumably precontact images, two quadrupeds and two anthropomorphs, with one of the anthropomorphs possibly partially superimposed on one of the quadrupeds; however, the levels of patination on these four images are all roughly the same, making any inferences about relative ages problematic (see Figure 7.7). The panel also includes historic graffiti directly superimposed over the indigenous images: the initials "LA," the date Nov. 6 1928, and a quadruped. The quadruped (reflecting the content of the indigenous imagery) and the choice to place the graffiti directly on top of existing images are both indications of responsiveness. In terms of the preservation paradigm, predicated upon an essentialist view of precontact cultures, these graffiti are clear and direct degradations of this cultural resource. In legal, institutional, and CRM terms, however, the age of the graffiti, being well over fifty years, positions it as a historic resource, and thereby deserving of protection—not because of its responsiveness to the indigenous art, but simply due to its age. In other words, these 1928 marks are both graffiti—in the evaluative sense of inappropriate, unauthorized marks that degrade the value of what they are placed upon—*and* they are historic resources.

Here, in one sense, the arbitrariness of the relevant laws and their underlying logics comes into play. Graffiti of a certain age becomes "historic" and its perceived/ascribed value changes, at least in institutional (CRM) terms. However, while the specific line is arbitrary, the general concept motivating it is still grounded in a system whereby increasing value adheres to objects as they recede in time from the present. They become "historic resources" rather than "graffiti." How are such lines enacted by those engaged in rock art preservation and restoration? One horrific (and not necessarily representative) example comes from the White River Narrows in eastern Nevada, at what is sometimes called the "Shoshone frog" site. Today, this panel contains a few visible elements that are presumably indigenous. The majority of the panel, however, is dominated by several large amorphous splotches of white, presumably the byproduct of an attempt to remove contemporary graffiti (an effort about which I have been unable to locate

FIGURE 7.7—Historic graffiti superimposed on petroglyphs, Rochester Creek, Emery County, Utah.

any information). The method used appears to have been successful in obscuring the graffiti, but also bleached the rock surfaces where it was applied (see Figure 7.8). This crude obliteration of graffiti carefully avoided not only some indigenous elements, but also a few cases of presumably older graffiti. Specifically, the following marks are completely surrounded, but not directly affected, by the graffiti-removal effort: "Wallace Thorley, Roe Thorley} March 11 1933" (see Figure 7.9). Another name and date (1936) was also apparently intentionally avoided. Aside from the fact that this is one case in which doing nothing would have been far better, and aside from who did it under what authority, it is clear that the removal choices were guided by some kind of "fifty-year rule" (Christensen et al. 2013). This is reinforced by Peter Pilles's (1989) discussion of graffiti removal at rock art sites in northern Arizona, in which everything post-1940 was removed, everything pre-1920 was left untouched, and graffiti from 1920 to 1940 were judged on a case-by-case basis with the names of early pioneers and their family members left intact.

FIGURE 7.8 —"Shoshone frog" panel, White River Narrows, Lincoln County, Nevada. This panel presumably shows the results of a disastrous graffiti removal effort.

This third case involves the coexistence of contemporary marks (graffiti/vandalism) and precontact, indigenous marks (and possibly historic, nonindigenous marks as well). This, of course, is the paradigm case of graffiti as vandalism, the circumstance that causes the greatest concern among those interested in the preservation of rock art and which garners the most press attention. While I do not advocate the addition of contemporary marks to rock art sites, my argument is that it is myopic to dismiss or devalue these marks as simply or only vandalism. Instead, there are reasonable cases in which the contemporary marks are clearly made in response to indigenous marks, perpetuating a dialogue that is not necessarily radically dissimilar to that involved in cases of indigenous or historic nonindigenous additions to indigenous rock art sites. Despite its illegal and immoral status, contemporary graffiti, therefore, can help us learn something about the nature of cross-cultural dialogue at rock art sites.

A comparison of two marks added to the Land Hill (aka "Anasazi Ridge") petroglyph area near St. George, Utah, demonstrates relative

FIGURE 7.9—Selective graffiti removal, "Shoshone frog" panel, White River Narrows, Lincoln County, Nevada. A close-up of the panel shown in figure 7.8, the application of the "fifty year rule" is evidenced by the postcontact, presumably non-Native, signatures that were intentionally left while other, more recent graffiti on the panel were presumably removed.

degrees of responsiveness to the indigenous elements in the area. The first example received much press attention, where it was depicted as one of many acts of vandalism carried out by a group of partying teens, described as "irresponsible, immature brats," who subsequently plead guilty to their offenses (Winslow 2006). In one specific graffito from their vandalizing spree, the initials "LB" were lightly but broadly scratched into the patina just above an indigenous element, geometric in design, which is itself possibly an echo of ceramic or textile designs (see Figure 7.10). Close attention to the "LB," however, shows that its general form—the "B" is nestled inside the "L" and is made with two triangles, not curves—strongly parallels the indigenous geometric design just below it. Whether this was a conscious design or not, there is a kind of responsiveness going on here, if for no other reason than the technique used to produce the LB graffito encourages angular over curved shapes. Importantly, even if the element was made without destructive intent, as a nonhostile response to the indigenous mark, it still constitutes destruction of the aesthetic and archaeological resource values of the panel and merits negative moral judgment and possible legal action.

However, what we potentially miss by dismissing this mark as simply or only vandalism, or as the destructive action of a drunken and possibly ignorant teen, is the way in which elements at rock art sites call forth responses from others, and in doing so possibly shape those responses. Rock is a relatively unique medium: Like writing, for example, it is a time-binding medium but, unlike writing on portable materials, it is not a space-binding medium. It is, in a sense, the opposite of many electronic media, such as the telegraph and telephone, which allow for synchronous conversation across great distances (space-binding but not time-binding). Rock art sites, therefore, can be understood as sites for dialogue between people separated by days, months, years, decades, centuries, or even millennia, but the turns in those dialogues all occur in the same place. Those who visit a rock art site share

FIGURE 7.10 —Petroglyph and modern graffiti, Land Hill, Washington County, Utah. Near a presumably precontact, indigenous petroglyph, a set of modern initials visually echoes the original petroglyph's design.

(in some sense) the same spatial context but occupy different temporal contexts, and hence different cultural contexts. In this sense, rock art sites can be understood as locations for dialogues between peoples and cultures separated by time. If we understand rock art locales as sites for such ongoing dialogues, their "essence" becomes not *the* culture or cultures that made the rock art, but the *relationship* between these peoples, cultures, and temporal periods. This is not simply an argument that rock art sites can "contain" information about more than one culture: I am suggesting that an important, even defining, trait of some rock art sites may be that they are both a record of, and an ongoing site for, dialogues, and hence relationships, between cultures. The preservation paradigm, focused on notions such as purity, essence, wholeness, and continuity, both guides and is perpetuated by efforts at rock art preservation, and works against a full recognition and positive valuation of this dialogic/relational quality of rock art sites as well as the cultures themselves. As Clifford (1988), Bakhtin (1981), and many others have argued, both individuals and cultures come into being in dialogue with others, by borrowing from and adapting the cultural forms of others, by both responding to and being responded to. While we have enough unknowns to keep us going for quite some time, the mystery of rock art deepens even more when we move from "What does this element or panel from culture X mean?" to "What were (and are) the relationships among the peoples and cultures who engaged in such a place-bound, long-term dialogue?"

Another contemporary graffito at Land Hill is a painted design composed of three pointed ovals which extend outward, symmetrically, from a central point, around which is drawn a single circle that bisects each oval (see Figure 7.11). I would loosely categorize this mark as "New Age" in nature and spirit; it is likely a triquetra, a neo-Pagan/Wiccan symbol for the female trinity (maiden/mother/crone) that was also featured prominently in the opening credits for the witch-themed television show *Charmed* (1998–2006). Unlike the "LB" mark, this graffito appears not to share a common surface with any indigenous marks, though there are indigenous petroglyphs on nearby boulders. It also appears not to share any design parallels with the indigenous marks, and is also differentiated by being painted, not pecked, chiseled, or scratched. I imagine that the mark was placed with some care, and that it is possibly a response to the perceived sacred nature of the location; that is, its responsiveness to the indigenous marks is not in terms of the qualities of the marks themselves but in relation to what the indigenous marks are presumed to mean: This is a sacred or spiritual site. While still potentially dialogic, this, I would argue, is a dialogue grounded not in marks, but in what those marks are imagined to mean, as well as in what Native Americans/Indians have come to mean for many Westerners: a people grounded in both nature and spirituality, representing what many Westerners feel they themselves lack (aka primitivism). Unlike many other modern graffiti, such as the range of names and initials already discussed, this mark appears not to stress personal identity (Murray 2004). Such "New Age" graffiti has been a problem at other rock art sites as well (ARARA 1995).

Another effort at taking graffiti seriously as a valuable form or record of cultural expression is William Breen Murray's (2004) essay "Marking Places." In this attempt to value contemporary marks as a form of cultural expression and marking of the landscape, Murray rightly points out that today's graffiti will become tomorrow's (valuable) archaeological record. However, my point is not simply that contemporary marks at

FIGURE 7.11—Modern "Pagan" graffito, Land Hill, Washington County, Utah. This modern graffito, possibly a neo-Pagan symbol, does not demonstrate the kind of graphic responsiveness shown in figure 7.10.

rock art sites will themselves become tomorrow's "rock art," but that the *relationships* among and between these marks is a valuable cultural resource that suggests a different way of looking at cultures: not as slowly changing, integrated, organic wholes, but as defined by their intersections and relationships, by conjuncture and dialogue.

The "Disney" panel near Barker Dam in Joshua Tree National Park can help clarify this distinction (see Plate 14). The information in circulation about this panel varies in many of the details, but the best information I have obtained indicates that in the late 1950s this cave-like rock formation containing indigenous rock art was "enhanced" by adding both modern petroglyphs and bright, modern paints for use in a film being shot in the area (Daniel McCarthy, personal communication, 2006). Directed by Walter Perkins, *Chico, the Misunderstood Coyote* was subsequently aired on *Walt Disney's Wonderful World of Color* in 1961 and was released theatrically outside the United States in 1962 (IMDb 2015). Although not entirely consistent with the information otherwise available about this panel (i.e., whether the petroglyphs absent the paint were indigenous or modern), the official NPS interpretive sign at the site states that the petroglyphs "have been traced over with paint. This type of vandalism prevents others from seeing the petroglyphs in their original form. Please help us by reporting any vandalism you observe."

In spite of inconsistent or vague information regarding the extent and nature of the indigenous versus contemporary motifs at this site, as well as the Park Service's role in and reaction to the additions, all accounts agree that there was some indigenous rock art at the site before it was altered for the film. Any such use of cultural resources and cultural heritage evidences enormous disrespect for Native Americans. But it is a response and, therefore, dialogue (dialogue is not always warm and fuzzy). This site could be seen as a valuable historic resource (the defacement is now over fifty years old) that records something about the culture that produced it, including attitudes toward indigenous cultures and their material traces.

This panel is not simply a record of two or more cultures that marked the same place in different ways for different reasons. It is a place-bound dialogue between these groups. This site is a material record of the interaction between multiple cultures: at a minimum, the culture(s) that produced the indigenous rock art and the culture that added to and/or painted them over for the purpose of producing a film.

Is that record of cultural interaction, and of the attitudes of one culture towards the material traces of another, a resource of lower value than a "pristine" (indigenous only) site? More importantly, how are these cultures interrelated, made interdependent by this ongoing exchange of marks? Clearly, the contemporary marks demonstrate a dependence on others' marks, of the use of others' marks to define, shape, and perpetuate one's own culture and/or identity—a central quality of dialogue (Bakhtin 1981).

Contemporary Indigenous Marks and Precontact Indigenous Marks

A fourth type of rock art dialogue is contemporary indigenous additions to precontact sites (and perhaps "historic" indigenous sites). These acts would be considered vandalism if not for the Native status of their makers, or, depending on one's point of view and the tribal affiliation of the "vandal," are considered acts of vandalism (a case with legal dimensions, e.g., the American Indian Religious Freedom Act of 1978). Inscription Point, on the Navajo Nation near Wupatki National Monument, provides an example, as documented by Weaver, Mark, and Billo (2001). Here, in addition to contemporary graffiti, several individual petroglyphs have been abraded and thereby practically obliterated, including masks and potential copulation scenes (see Figure 7.12), although, significantly, not all masks and copulations scenes at the site have been so erased. Most visibly, a particularly large snake or "serpent" image was altered sometime after 1976 with what appears to have been a metal chisel (Mark and Billo 1999; see Plate 15). Various possibilities suggested in published literature (Bock 1989; Weaver et al. 2001), as well as by staff of nearby Wupatki National Monument and local rock art researchers and enthusiasts, include the obliteration of ancestral Puebloan motifs by non-Puebloan Native Americans (i.e., Navajo), the obliteration of sexual and serpent imagery by Christians (Native or otherwise), and the intentional obliteration of specific images by or at the instruction of a local Native healer for some ceremonial/ritualistic purpose. Without assuming that any of these or other explanations are correct or incorrect (none are presented as definitive or confirmed), the general case provides the opportunity to identify and discuss other forms of dialogue, in this case not necessarily including non-Natives but members of multiple indigenous groups, some or all of whose

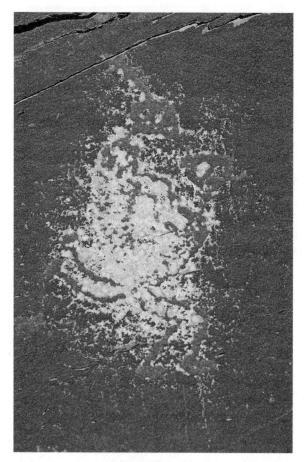

FIGURE 7.12—Abraded anthropomorphic couple, Inscription Point, Coconino County, Arizona. This possible copulation scene is one of several images specifically targeted for abrasion at Inscription Point. For a preabrasion photograph of the petroglyph, see Mark and Billo (199:166, Figure 12). MS-372 Harold Widdison Rock Art collection. Photographer: Harold Widdison. Image title: Inscription Point (1994–1995). Image ID: MS_372_05_44_010. Courtesy Museum of Northern Arizona.

cultural ancestors produced rock art at Inscription Point. As with the other cases discussed here, however, my purpose is to use the site as a heuristic, not to make definitive claims about specific marks.

In the eyes of many, these acts would clearly constitute vandalism. Weaver, Mark, and Billo (2001:149) describe the acts as "scratching, abrading or chiseling out specific motifs in an attempt to completely destroy the images," an attribution of intent clearly consistent with the definition of vandalism but not necessarily, I would argue, a conclusion warranted by the physical evidence itself or entirely consistent with some of the stories circulating about the nature and intent of these acts. These acts are clearly utterances in an ongoing dialogue both within and between the various indigenous groups who have produced (and possibly continue to produce) rock art at Inscription Point. As Weaver, Mark, and Billo (2001) conclude, the marks at Inscription Point have been made for at least two thousand years by at least three, if not many more, cultural groups.

In particular, while abrasions have completely obscured several motifs, such as masks and copulation scenes, the chiseled serpent is a potentially different story (see Figure 7.13). The serpent image, while heavily chiseled and missing any previous internal detail, retains its

FIGURE 7.13—Portion of snake/serpent with recent chiseling, Inscription Point, Coconino County, Arizona. This photograph shows a close-up of part of the chiseled snake seen in Plate 15. For a photograph of the panel prior to these additions, see Mark and Billo (1999:165, Figure 11). MS-372 Harold Widdison Rock Art collection. Photographer: Harold Widdison. Image title: Inscription Point (1994–1995). Image ID: MS_372_05_44_003. Courtesy Museum of Northern Arizona.

basic shape and outline, as evidenced in Robert Mark and Evelyn Billo's (1999:165, Figure 11) before and after photographs. Weaver, Mark, and Billo (2001:149) describe the large serpent as having "been chiseled out of the rock" and include this act under the umbrella of "recent vandalism and destruction of rock art" at Inscription Point. However, as discussed earlier, cases of superimposition as well as the repecking of petroglyphs or repainting of pictographs have been identified at many ancient rock art sites, and in these instances these acts are considered valuable dimensions of the archaeological record "contained" in these sites. Indeed, in some cases, repetitive pecking has created very large holes in petroglyphs, as in the case of a female anthropomorph (see Figure 7.14) and a zoomorph at the Chevelon Steps/Rock Art Ranch site in northern Arizona (Kolber 2000). Again, this is a valuable record of cultural practices, and in some cases may involve the actions of more than one culture. These acts, in one sense, also "destroy" or "degrade" (pre)historic motifs but are positively valued, whereas the chiseling of the serpent image at Inscription Point is not presented as a case of repecking or other form of (destructive) alteration—it is simply destruction, vandalism.

North of Inscription Point, at the Tutuveni (Willow Springs) site near Tuba City, Arizona, Wesley Bernardini (2009:7) compared historic and contemporary photographs of the site, demonstrating "that many petroglyphs have been repecked or 'renovated' at least once over the past century." While Tutuveni is in many ways not a typical Puebloan rock art site (see below), this evidence points to ongoing alterations of rock art in the historic period and into contemporary times, alterations that could be defined today as vandalism and, if continued, theoretically prosecuted under the Archaeological Resources Protection Act (Schaafsma 2013).

In a severe example, large anthropomorphs at a Basketmaker petroglyph site along the San Juan River in southeastern Utah were obscured by chiseling at what is commonly called the "desecration" panel. Local Navajos reportedly chiseled over the images in the 1950s in response to a flu epidemic. In a Navajo worldview, such images contain power, which can be appropriated by malicious individuals to cause illness; hence, the "destruction" of these specific petroglyphs was intended to neutralize the power within the images, protecting members of the community from danger (Schaafsma 2013). It seems unsurprising, therefore, that some Navajo have objected to the use of "desecration" to describe the

FIGURE 7.14—Deeply pecked holes in anthropomorph, Chevelon Steps/Rock Art Ranch, Navajo County, Arizona. This large female anthropomorph evidences deeply pecked holes, possibly placed long after the image was created (or not), potentially over a long period of time (or not), and perhaps by people who were not of the same culture or group as the original creators of the figure (or not).

site. By analogy, this story suggests a potentially different spin on the "vandalism" and "destruction" at Inscription Point.

What the Inscription Point example highlights is that "vandalism," in some sense at least, is determined not by the nature of the mark itself, but by its meaning, social function, and/or the intentions of the person adding the mark. This is the "willful or malicious" element of vandalism. A related example is provided by Jane Young (1988) in her study of contemporary Zuni perceptions of rock art. As a result of her Zuni partners' reports of practical uses of rock art (e.g., creating an image of a hump-backed flute player in order to bring rain), she explored the possibility that hunting magic applied to Zuni rock art. In addition to identifying a number of instances of imagery that could fit the hypothesis, she cites Stevenson's early twentieth-century ethnographic account that Zuni hunters would shoot arrows at rock art depictions of game animals before setting out to hunt. Knowing that some contemporary Zunis were known to shoot bullets at rock art, she analyzed the rock art motifs at Zuni that were impacted by bullets, concluding that images related to game animals were targeted far more often than others:

> When I initially undertook the project of recording rock art at Zuni, I assumed that bullet holes, like spray-painted, chalked, and carved graffiti, were examples of vandalism. Now I have come to believe that, at least in some cases, the bullet holes are visible remains of the modern version of the sort of ritual activity described by Stevenson rather than the result of vandalism. (Young 1988:176)

Significantly, however, hunting magic may not be the only reason some Zunis shoot at rock art, and not all Zunis condone the practice, seeing it as vandalism (Young 1988).

A final example that demonstrates the tensions between Western, archaeological notions of preservation and vandalism versus ongoing efforts at cultural continuity among indigenous cultures in (post)colonial contexts comes from Australia, but relates directly to the potential issues involved with the renovation, alteration, and obliteration of rock art by indigenous peoples in the contemporary United States. In the west Kimberley region in 1987, a grant-funded project involving a group of Ngarinyin elders and youth retouched, freshened, and repainted some *wandjina* paintings (Mowaljarlai et al. 1988; Mowljarlai and Peck 1987). This act led to a controversy, both in the popular press and in archaeological and cultural heritage management circles. Many nonindigenous peoples, including a white landowner and some researchers, criticized this action on several grounds, which can be roughly divided into three groups: that the work was done improperly (in terms of technique, skill, and materials), that there is a lack of cultural continuity between the painted images and those who did the repainting, and that the art is a cultural resource belonging to all of humanity (e.g., Bowdler 1988; O'Connor et al. 2008).

Setting aside some of the "factual" disagreements involved in the first two groups of criticisms (see the above sources for more detail on these issues), the more fundamental issues are differences in the understanding of art and the ownership/control over cultural heritage/

resources. The repainting of *wandjina* imagery is not only part of the cultural heritage of the Ngarinyin, it is specifically called for by the role of such imagery in the cosmologies of the cultures that produced, and that have continued to retouch and repaint, them. In other words, it is not just that the paintings are part of Ngarinyin cultural *heritage*; the retouching and repainting of the images is part of Ngarinyin cultural *continuity* (Mowaljarlai et al. 1988). In Western aesthetic, scientific, and archaeological frameworks, the "art" or "resource" is an object containing value, be it aesthetic or archaeological, and hence repainting destroys the valued object as well as the information about the past contained within it. In a Ngarinyin perspective, however, the images are living beings, part of a living culture, and are understood in terms of an ongoing (not to mention nonlinear) *process*, not a static *thing* (Mowaljarlai et al. 1988). Both the imagery and their cultural traditions are living, not dead objects, requiring efforts to insure regeneration and continuation (O'Connor et al. 2008).

The center of much of the larger debate is whether the *wandjina* images in question belong to the Ngarinyin as part of their cultural heritage or whether they are more properly understood as "the cultural heritage of all mankind" (Bowdler 1988:521). The dominant Western "common sense" regarding cultural heritage sees the labeling of something as part of the history of all humanity as an effective and logical way to ensure its protection. However, such a claim has the symbolic and actual effect of alienating living indigenous groups from their specific cultural heritage, furthering colonialism and inhibiting cultural continuity. "Defining something as belonging to that transcendent category is a means of excluding anyone who might have a particular interest in it" (Bowdler 1988:521). Universalization is a form of involuntary appropriation, wherein those who define the "universal" usurp control from those whose claims are based in particularities. This is a clear case of the operation of hegemony, wherein those engaged in acts of cultural appropriation operate in a structure of belief that emphasizes preservation of the past, making it "common sense" to actively oppose efforts by colonized peoples to retain and re-create their cultural traditions and identities. The ideology of preservation works, in effect, to deny the possibility of the cultural continuity of indigenous groups based on the ongoing use of the material traces of their ancestors.

Significantly, unlike the Ngarinyin repainting project, not all ongoing dialogues at rock art sites are in affinity with the existing imagery.

Dialogues can be conflictual as well as harmonious. In the cases of precontact superimpositioning, repecking, repainting, abrasion, and obliteration, such acts may have been in harmony or hostility with the original glyph, or they may have been appropriations with malevolent, benevolent, or more neutral motives. From the traces on rock alone, as in the case of the chiseled serpent at Inscription Point, I am not confident we can determine the nature of the relationship between the original and the imposed marks, their meanings, and their affiliated cultures. But the existence of the dialogue seems clear. A focus on preservation, grounded as it is upon a model of cultural essence, diverts our attention away from these dialogues, at least as they have recently occurred and will continue to do so in the future, and in doing so may blind us to dialogic or relational, as opposed to essential or self-contained, qualities of rock art, including at exclusively precontact rock art sites.

The Inscription Point case makes evident that existing rock art not only encourages historic and contemporary graffiti, it appears to have encouraged additional rock art by indigenous groups as well. These relationships are a part of the dynamics involved in rock art, but the discourses and practices of preservation divert our attention away from the value or centrality of those relationships for both the rock art and the cultures involved. A clear example of how an essentialist, not conjunctural, view of culture operates in evaluating rock art vandalism is found in the following comment made during a panel discussion about rock art protection in relation to the issue of contemporary Native peoples making marks at rock art sites:

> I would have to look at it in terms of what indigenous group was there and whether these are the descendants of that particular group who are doing it in terms of some sort of a ritual associated with their traditional religion. . . . But if they're doing it to some other descendants' rock art, then I think they're basically vandalizing it." (Bock 1989:84)

However, if done in the precontact period, such acts of superimpositioning are cast positively in terms of their value as a resource, a repository of knowledge.

Contemporary (or historic) graffiti also occurs at Inscription Point. On one patinated but heavily spalled boulder surface, a partial remnant of a likely precontact, indigenous spiral is accompanied by two words in English. To the extreme left is the spiral. Just to its right is the word

"Indian," although distortion of the last few letters makes that less than definitive. To the right of "Indian" is a large gap in the patina left by spalling. Just to the right of the spall, separated from "Indian" by the unpatinated stone surface, are two letters: "U.S." Who left these marks? Why? What did they mean? I am not certain, of course, but I do take this as evidence that the dialogues between cultures that have occurred at this site for a long time are ongoing.

Similar to Inscription Point, but on a much greater scale, the Tutuveni (Willow Springs) petroglyph site records dialogues taking place over long periods of time, both between members of the same culture (Hopi) as well as between different indigenous cultures (Hopi and Navajo). Bernardini (2009:2) explains, "The area around Tutuveni has been the subject of a longstanding dispute over land claims and reservation boundaries between the Hopi Tribe and the Navajo Nation." Although the site is recognized as a Hopi shrine, it is located on Navajo land:

> Tutuveni's location, combined with the unusually clear expressions of Hopi cultural identity which are materialized at the site, have made it a target of those who take issue with Hopi historical claims on the surrounding area. The site has suffered from vandalism, especially the targeted destruction of symbols perhaps deemed by visitors to tell the wrong version of history. (Bernardini 2009:2–3)

Specifically, Bernardini's documentation of the site showed that 51 of the 235 boulder faces with one or more rock art elements had been vandalized. Datable graffiti ranged from 1872 to 2005 (the year of Bernardini's recording), with the bulk of it appearing to be from the 1970s or later. Distinct from "casual graffiti" and the "renovation of petroglyphs" are instances of obliteration, where a particular motif from among dozens or hundreds on a panel was selected and then erased by either pecking or chiseling (Bernardini 2009:51), much like the elements at Inscription Point. Bernardini identified 109 obliterated motifs on 28 panels. Using historic photos, 88 of the 109 obliterated motifs were identified. Katsina symbols, the images most publicly recognizable as associated with the Hopi, were disproportionately targeted, as they were at Inscription Point. Further evidence of the intertribal tensions being played out at the site is provided by the large, scratched words "Damn Hopi Drawing" on one panel (Bernardini 2009:54). Whereas the Hopi elements at the site are an expression of Hopi cultural and clan identities, many of the more recent acts of obliteration and graffiti can be understood as an expression, not just of hostility to the Hopi, but of a Navajo cultural identity, constructed in part by its opposition to Hopi.

Indigenous views of what it means to "preserve" or "protect" rock art sites or other types of material culture do not always converge with those of archaeologists and cultural resource managers. For example, excavating cultural objects to put them in climate-controlled museum collections, actions that flow from the preservation paradigm, often clash with indigenous views of preservation, which may involve leaving the items in situ—items that may be viewed, in indigenous terms, as entities, not objects (Colwell-Chanthaphonh and Ferguson 2006; White Deer 1997). Vandalism of rock art sites certainly disturbs many Native peoples (e.g., Arrillaga 2012; Sahagun 2012; Young 1988), and many conventional (Western) efforts to protect sites make sense from indigenous perspectives as well. In the case of Tutuveni, the overlapping interests and perspectives of archaeologists, preservationists, the Hopi Cultural Preservation Office, the Navajo Nation Historic Preservation Department, and an electric utility company resulted in a cooperative effort to help protect the site, including a fence enclosing the site, surveillance equipment (Arrillaga 2012), and further in-depth digital recording (CyArk 2013).

Abstracting and Commodifying Rock Art

In preserving the traces of cultures past, what constitutes preservation depends on how culture is understood. If we view culture as an essence, and especially indigenous culture as a thing whose purity is endangered by interaction with other (Western, modern) cultures, then efforts to "freeze" sites in their current condition make sense. That is, the view of culture embedded in the preservation paradigm is one of the "conditions of possibility" (Foucault 1972) for the discourses and actions taken in rock art preservation efforts, which range from secrecy to education, from the imprisonment of vandals to the imprisonment of rock art sites themselves. If, on the other hand, we view culture as conjunctural, as defined by the relations between various groups and worldviews, then culture's essence is those relationships, the dialogues within and between various cultures. In this sense, rock art sites function as forums for dialogues between cultures separated by years, decades, centuries, and even millennia. As with individual interlocutors, the identities and qualities of cultures can only be constituted in dialogue with others (Bakhtin 1981). In "preserving" rock art sites, these past dialogues are maintained for ongoing access, but are at the same time transformed into something that should not be engaged in their place. Sites that have, for whatever reason, served as the locale for such dialogues are frozen and localized rejoinders to the dialogue are prohibited. While this retains the precontact and perhaps historic dialogue, it also functions to halt that dialogue by prohibiting additional utterances at that site and, of particular relevance for rock art scholars, thereby encourages a view of a single rock art motif, panel, site, or style as a container of information about a culture as opposed to traces of the relations and interactions among and between various cultures—relations and interactions that are part of constituting those very cultures. Cultures are conjunctural, not fixed and bounded essences (Clifford 1988; Rogers 2006).

Put differently, the preservation paradigm functions to abstract the value of rock art, replacing the specificity of any particular glyph or site or locale with the general idea of "cultural resources" and/or "cultural heritage." Rock art is valued for the knowledge it can provide, the questions it can help answer, about "other" cultures as well as the universal history of humanity as a whole. Rock art is thus constituted by the discourse of the preservation paradigm as a container of historical knowledge to be preserved until it can be "mined" or "decoded" by experts. In this sense, rock art is clearly commodified, its specificity replaced by an abstract sense of value as a "cultural resource" (see chapter 3), furthering implicit assumptions that encourage rock art to be viewed in one set of ways as opposed to others. In addition to shedding light on embedded assumptions and thereby opening up possibilities for interpretation within rock art studies by reframing the significance of rock art as part of a relationship rather than as a thing, working with the specificity of rock art as a relatively unique genre of discourse can also help develop conjunctural models of culture.

The addition of contemporary graffiti to indigenous rock art sites is vandalism. But its illegality, its violation of the ethical codes of organizations like American Rock Art Research Association, and its interference with what we each value about rock art sites should not lead us to see it *only* as a detraction from the knowledge to be gained from a rock art site. A careful examination of contemporary marks added to rock art sites can teach us something about the nature of rock art as a medium, about cross-cultural dialogue and the very nature of culture, and about the places where rock art occurs. We should be explicit and conscious about why we want to protect and preserve rock art, and at the same time conscious of how the very same assumptions that lead us to denounce graffiti—something we experience as interfering with our appreciation or understanding of indigenous rock art—may interfere with our ability to make sense of a variety of rock art's dimensions and functions.

CHAPTER 8

SEARCHING FOR FLUTE PLAYERS, FINDING KOKOPELLI

Reflections on Authenticity, Appropriation, and Absent Authorities

In the time I have been immersed in the rock art literature, I have seen significant advances in relation to some of the issues I raise in this book. There is a comparatively greater sensitivity to gender, at least in terms of not automatically presuming that anthropomorphs without obvious sex indicators are male and that rock art was made by men unless there is direct information to the contrary. However, much more remains to be tackled, such as attending to the sex/gender distinction and the ways in which contemporary, dualistic gender ideologies drive our constructions of the past. There have been repeated calls for an increase in Native Americans in research and the inclusion of indigenous perspectives in rock art interpretation and research, and while there have also been significant advances in this area they are still rather limited. Rock art research increasingly evidences post-processualist influences, such as a recognition of internal diversity within cultures, the granting of agency to precontact indigenous peoples, and the recognition of multiple, sometimes incompatible, epistemologies. If nothing else, NAGPRA has pushed researchers and land managers to interact more with indigenous peoples and to at least record their perceptions. Finally, while I don't think the rock art community's complicity in the commodification of rock art has really been taken to heart, the issue is at least being raised (Dickey 2012; Quinlan 2007a; Welsh 1999).

While I have advanced a series of arguments about the impact of Anglo-American gender ideologies, neocolonialism, primitivism, and essentialism on the interpretation, appropriation, and management of rock art, my goal has been to offer rock art enthusiasts, land managers, and rock art researchers more tools for engaging in self-reflexive and self-implicative analyses of their engagement with rock art: self-reflexive in the sense of looking back on our own interest in, appetite for, and sense-making of indigenous rock art; self-implicative in the sense of building on reflexivity to examine our own participation in perpetuating certain systems of meaning, such as views of Native peoples both past and present, as well as the attendant power relations and systems of privilege. We need to look to our complicity in these views and their implications, much as NAGPRA and postcolonial theory encouraged an archaeological self-examination regarding the removal of archaeological artifacts and sites from the patrimony of Native American cultures.

In this final chapter, I use impressionist narratives and reflections to weave together the central themes of this book while focusing my critical eye more on myself, my practices, my motivations, and my complicities. As I indicated in chapter 1, the critical, constitutive view of communication to which I subscribe compels a shift from linear, strategic questions—How do I get my audience to believe X and do Y?—to reflexive questions (Pearce 1989)—What kind of a world am I creating by communicating in this way? What relationships with Native Americans am I establishing by my visitations, documentations, collections, discussions, reproductions, representations, interpretations, and appropriations of rock art? What identities am I creating for myself and for others? What work do those identities do? How are they complicit in dominant ideologies, systems of power, and exploitative relations? How can I best wind my way through the mysteries, complexities, and consequences of engaging the marks on rock left by other cultures, cultures that continue to exist, but in a postmodern, neocolonial context not of their own choosing? What story am I (are we) telling and what story am I (are we) living out (Pearce 1989)?

Decontextualization and Abstraction

Among rock art enthusiasts, certain sites are positioned as penultimate exemplars of indigenous expressions on rock that should be visited ("collected") if possible. Some of these remain largely invisible, absent from publications or with only vague locational descriptions, though the number of such little-known sites has decreased dramatically due to the internet. Others are and in some cases have long been widely

publicized: They have already been "sacrificed" to the graffiti and vandalism that follows widespread public knowledge of their location, or
they are well protected by personnel, gates, fences, or other barriers,
including distance. For example, a well-publicized list-topper of southwestern US petroglyph sites is found in the Coso Range of southeastern
California, and the Coso sites are widely discussed as well as reproduced photographically. Located not far from Death Valley, inside the
boundaries of the China Lake Naval Weapons Station, they are well
protected, inaccessible to the general public except through tours
organized by the Maturango Museum.

Arguably, the "Holy Grail" of pictograph sites in the Southwest is
the Great Gallery, the type site for the Barrier Canyon Style, located in
Horseshoe (formerly Barrier) Canyon, an island unit of Canyonlands
National Park in southern Utah. Perhaps the most reproduced panel
at the site features the "Holy Ghost" figure (see Plate 3), a name that
unfortunately overwhelms any purely visual, nonverbal experience of
the panel. It is readily accessible, requiring no permit. The site's location
is well publicized in many guidebooks and websites, and the park itself
provides extensive, if incomplete, information about the site's location
and archaeological features. Granted, visiting Horseshoe Canyon is not
a small task. Access is not from the more popular east side of Canyonlands, near the hiking, ORV, mountain-biking, and rock-climbing mecca
of Moab, Utah, but a fairly remote area on the park's west side. After
leaving paved highways, there is over thirty miles of mostly well-graded
if horribly wash-boarded dirt road, so it is somewhat off the beaten path.
A well-marked trail down into the canyon and up its flat bottom requires
over six miles of roundtrip hiking, in conditions that can range from
extreme heat to extreme cold, extreme dryness to intense thunderstorms
and flash floods. But given enough time and good weather, people with
a typical two-wheel-drive passenger vehicle and a modicum of physical
fitness and common sense can make the trip.

After a fairly quick, switchback descent into the canyon, the trail
winds up the canyon's smooth, level bottom, following the meandering curves around one corner and the next. A typical—that is, awe-
inspiring and soul-easing—southern Utah locale: red sand, curving red
sandstone walls, green cottonwoods, blue sky, and white clouds. On
my first and only visit, which I involuntarily think of as a pilgrimage, I
stopped at smaller rock art sites along the way. It was all amazing stuff,
from the Barrier Canyon Style pictographs for which the canyon lent

its previous name, to petroglyphs and crude charcoal drawings, along with some—but not too much—historic graffiti. But when I turned a corner and saw the huge sandstone alcove that holds the Great Gallery (see Plate 16), even in the instant before I cognitively realized this was the Great Gallery and I could consciously pick out the long line of life-size figures from several hundred yards away, I was struck by a physical-affective response, a kind of relief like that which accompanies a large, involuntary sigh. I followed my impulse to look up, past the top of the alcove, to the top of the canyon wall, and then down to the bottom of the alcove—which is when I recognized the rock art itself, leading to another layer of physical-psychic-affective responses that are quite distinct from those that came in response, later, to examining the figures close-up.

The close examination was fascinating. Typically visitors are requested to keep their distance from the panels themselves via a long, light-weight, single-rope barrier, so I was glad a volunteer ranger was there to allow me and the other two visitors who were present to climb right up to the panels, alleviating any internal tension over respecting the passive barrier. Approaching the panels with the ranger and other visitors, things went all cognitive: Lots of talking . . . various ideas and hypotheses . . . bits of physical evidence . . . radiocarbon dating . . . later additions to figures . . . faded elements. . . . I sucked it all up, but more in my mind than my body. In between the talking, there was lots of obsessive photographing, not the least by me. This was all in stark contrast to the holistic affective-sensorial response to the site as a whole, its setting, and its placement, that I experienced during my solitary approach to the site.

My first conscious memory of seeing the Great Gallery and other pictograph panels from Barrier Canyon is the opening scene from Godfrey Reggio's 1983 film *Koyaanisqatsi*. As I discussed in chapter 3, the "Holy Ghost" image remains on the screen for an extended period, only to be "burned" away as a close-up shot of the exhaust cones of a launching rocket is imposed over it. In the larger context of the film, the Holy Ghost image functions as a stand-in for indigenous peoples and their superior relationship with the earth—superior, at least, to the modern way of life portrayed in the film, a life of mechanistic insanity characterized as "life out of balance." When I first saw it, I was sucked into the film's primitivist message (and I still am, though with a self-implicative slap to my face). After I returned home from Horseshoe

Canyon, I popped *Koyaanisqatsi* into the DVD player to review the scenes featuring the Great Gallery.

The opening and closing scenes of *Koyaanisqatsi*, as powerful as they are within the larger context of the film, cannot do the Great Gallery justice, choosing to focus tightly in on two panels, one at a time, with the physical, natural setting completely absent from the frame. Such decontextualization works to abstract the pictographs' meaning into a worshipping of the primitive, but it misses what for me were major elements of the site's impact: the canyon, the bend in the canyon where the alcove is located, the alcove itself, the blue sky above, and the cottonwoods below the alcove in the canyon's bottom; the smell of the air, the feeling of the sand underfoot and on my skin, the sounds of the wind and birds, the echoes of the ranger's voice bouncing back from inside the Great Gallery itself. This concrete, material, sensorial setting, and the rock art's role in that setting, constitutes something way beyond aesthetic and archaeological details, something way beyond objects and resources, in the realm of relationship and the ineffable combination of somatic, affective, and cognitive experiences. Unlike the more extreme diagnoses of the postmodern condition, in which reproductions come to serve as indicators of the real, my direct experience of the Great Gallery managed to overcome (or at least build upon) the many preexisting representations of it that I had seen, including in *Koyaanisqatsi*. It may well be that the "aura" (Benjamin 1989 [1936]) that I experienced was the result of those representations and the cultural and ideological resonances that I share with them, but at an experiential level the site's aura seemed an outcome of the relationships between the images, the setting, and my sensing body and its consciousness.

Collecting and Secrecy

Amidst my specific experiences in Horseshoe Canyon and the complex of motivations that led me to go there, there is no doubt that among them was collecting. Like an avid birder, I have a growing list of sites I've visited. Barrier Canyon Style: Buckhorn Wash—check. Horseshoe Canyon—check. Temple Mountain Wash—check. Head of Sinbad—check. Moki Queen—check. Black Dragon Canyon—check. Thompson Wash—check. I have photographed the sites and logged the photos into a database, organized geographically and marked with keywords to make them searchable. I selectively reproduce some of these images for my research and teaching, and even more selectively as "art" for my walls or those of my friends. I don't display my rock art collection in the way my mother displayed her Seraphim Angel figurines in a glass cabinet in her living room. That is, I don't make the collection itself publicly visible outside of research and educational presentations and a handful of photos in my home and office. The collection is there when I need it for a presentation or a research question, but its function goes further, constituting my identity as a rock art scholar and aficionado amidst a complex array of ideologies, stereotypes, institutions, motivations, anxieties, fantasies, and academic and cultural capital.

Criticizing elements of the rock art culture is easy; more difficult is acknowledging the degree to which I participate. I make it a point of principle to not purchase any Kokopelli kitsch, except for the books used in my research. Admittedly, my students continue to bring me Kokopelli gifts on a regular basis, and I can't bring myself to reject them, instead adding them to my "specimens," but not my decor. Despite my weak Kokopelli embargo, I nevertheless have a collection of not only photographs of rock art, both my own and those of others, but also reproductions of rock art made from papier-mâché or carved into or painted onto rock, not to mention a library of books and articles on rock art. To pretend that my academic orientation to the subject somehow inoculates me against the draw of commodity fetishism or in some way inhibits the hegemonic functions of these appropriations would be foolish. The act of collecting may be more fulfilling to me than the collection itself, and my (conscious) goals may be noble, but I am clearly an active participant in the neocolonial relationships implicated in being an Anglo-American rock art aficionado and scholar, including deep ties to primitivism and investments in a variety of identities that help compensate for my ambivalence and dis-ease with elements of my Anglo-American (Western, colonialist, capitalist, industrial, postmodern) culture.

The role of collecting sheds an important light on the issue of secrecy in the rock art community, which includes land managers, archaeologists, avocationalists, and enthusiasts. As I indicated earlier, my experience of the rock art community, broadly defined, points to a fairly pervasive tone of secrecy. From the exemption of archaeological information from the Freedom of Information Act to the often-feigned ignorance of park personnel as to the existence and/or location of rock art sites, not to mention open criticism of those who directly or indirectly publicize site locations via websites, guidebooks, or academic publications (Dickey 2012; Marymor 1998), members of the rock art community are, understandably, cautious in sharing information about the location of rock art sites. While perhaps not the intention, this attitude of secrecy often adopts a tone of "we are the privileged insiders, guardians of coveted knowledge." The stated goal is to create barriers to access, thereby protecting the rock art. At the same time, many (if not most) enthusiasts join rock art organizations and attend conferences with at least one of their goals being access to rock art sites via field trips or obtaining locational information, even just hints, about sites (Dickey 2012). I am personally implicated in that characterization.

In discussions of secrecy and publicizing site locations in the rock art community, three themes are present: protection vs. access, efficacy, and elitism. The first is a series of tensions between protecting sites and providing access. The primary strategy used to protect rock art sites on public lands has traditionally been inhibiting visitation through informational barriers—keeping site locations secret (Dickey 2012; Whitley 2011). The more significant the site, the more fragile it is, and the less developed it is, the greater the need to protect it by withholding location information. Certainly, some dedicated enthusiasts will still find the sites, but the harder it is, the fewer visitors there will be, and sites will be better preserved.

On the other side of this first theme is access, which has several dimensions. First, land management agencies operate institutionally, often with mandates to both protect sites and make public land "resources" available to users (Dickey 2012), though with different weighting attached to each side, as in the NPS versus the Forest Service and BLM. While the overall mandate of the Forest Service, for example, may be promoting access for multiple uses, archaeological resources such as rock art fall under a distinct set of institutional mandates and procedures. Second, there are potential educational benefits to promoting access to cultural resources, possibly increasing awareness and motivating further protection (Whitley 2011). Third, despite all of the justifications that can be offered (e.g., greater knowledge and awareness), can we as rock art researchers or aficionados really claim that we should be able to visit these sites, while others should not? For many, however, there is no real tension between access and preservation: access is not really a weighty factor given the overriding challenge of protecting sites (as long as *I* can still go, of course).

The second theme in discussions of secrecy is whether it works. It does indeed seem to be an assumption that secrecy reduces visitation, which in turn reduces vandalism and other forms of anthropogenic degradation. While there are many anecdotes of sites being vandalized after their locations were publicized, I am not aware of empirical support for the generalization (and none ever seems to be cited except anecdotally). Indeed, some archaeologists, land managers, and others having been arguing that increased visitation at some sites, if managed correctly, can reduce vandalism, with some test cases offering support for that claim (e.g., Pilles 1989; Whitley 2011). In his guidebook, David Whitley cites BLM archaeologist Russ Kaldenberg's claim that "the simple presence of responsible and informed visitors, especially at remote sites, will serve as a deterrent to vandals who may intentionally or inadvertently harm the art" (Whitley 1996:xiii; see also Marymor 1998). Whitley (2011:186) argues that the secrecy "approach has not worked," stopping neither enthusiasts nor looters from findings sites. There is agreement, however, that if sites are to be publicized, several conditions must first be met: the sites must be thoroughly documented, a management plan must be completed, the sites must be developed to minimize impacts from visitation and include an educational or interpretive component, and sites should be monitored (Marymor 1998; Whitley 2011). Nevertheless, despite some trends to the contrary (Marymor 1998), the secrecy approach, being passive in nature and without direct budgetary impact (Whitley 2011), remains the default condition for the vast majority of rock art sites.

The third theme, albeit not always explicit, is elitism: being an insider, a member of the club, with the required capital—having visited valued sites—to demonstrate one's status and receive more sites to add to one's list in return. To justify restricting site location information while avidly seeking out more rock art sites to visit, be it for one's own enjoyment, artistic inspiration, commercial benefit, documentation, monitoring, or research, strikes many (including those advocating secrecy) as a bit undemocratic, perhaps not unlike the liberal, Western critiques of restricting information about Pueblo cultures and cultural heritage (Brown 1998, 2003; Schaafsma 2013). Nevertheless, it has long been the practice to pass sites around like trading cards while also decrying increased visitation. The issue of elitism is occasionally named, indicating recognition of the tensions related to public access even if they are ultimately subordinated to the need for research, documentation, and preservation (e.g., Christensen et al. 2013).

Given the emphasis on secrecy in both institutional practices and the culture of enthusiasts, despite indications of ideological tensions over such exclusionary and restrictive practices, and given the lack of clear evidence that secrecy works to achieve the stated goal of site protection, perhaps the topic needs to be reframed: not in terms of whether it works (to protect sites), but in terms of the work it does do. What is the function of secrecy, especially for rock art insiders? What kind of identities, relationships, and values are we creating through the communicative practice of secrecy?

Prior to the mixture of affordable GPS devices and easily accessed internet, rock art site locations that were not widely publicized (i.e., the vast majority of them) were guardedly passed from person to person, usually only after the person with knowledge of the site's location and content was satisfied that the other could be trusted with the information, that they had in some sense earned the "right" to see it. Beyond sites "collected" via these kinds of contact, sites were located by nonprofessionals such as myself through painstaking research in sometimes-obscure rock art publications, random sources (e.g., depression-era WPA publications, nature writing, and travelogues), and maps, not to mention lots of time in the field—and, of course, through rock art conferences and by volunteering as a site steward. The GPS-internet-hobbyist assemblage has not eliminated such word-of-mouth access to sites, but sites are easier to find than ever before. Khota Circus, Lion's Mouth, the Shooting Gallery, White Cliffs, and many that I still will not name in public for fear of increased visitation: Sites that I once gained access to only by getting "in" with the right person, or by extensive and painstaking research involving repeated visits to libraries, notoriously slow interlibrary loans, and hours poring over USGS maps are now accessible via the information gained in minutes via a multitude of websites.

I enjoy finding sites by these "old school" methods. The search is much of the fun. I like having to look around, not just blindly following a GPS unit leading me to accurate and precise coordinates. I like finding references to a site, poring over USGS maps (though I'm happy I can now access these from home on my computer), and heading into the field to orient myself and seek out the site I had researched or others I would stumble on in the process. In the years since I began actively seeking out rock art sites, the number of guidebooks has increased and it seems as if the BLM in particular has diverged somewhat from the secrecy strategy, making my searches easier. But far more pernicious than either of those sources is the often indiscriminate dissemination of locational information about rock art on web pages ranging from geo-caching sites to travelogues to sites devoted to rock art. While a part of me is jealous, I mostly feel deflated, for two reasons: (1) the sites I had to work so hard to find can now be visited by any yahoo with a GPS unit, and (2) fear for the sites' preservation. Whereas tracking down rock art sites such as the White River Narrows, Mount Irish, and the Shooting Gallery in eastern Nevada required poring over numerous publications and maps, and a lot of driving and hiking, Lincoln County now pub-lishes a fifty-page pamphlet with detailed maps, directions to seven major rock art locales, and GPS coordinates for each individual panel (Lincoln County Nevada 2014a) along with a website (Lincoln County Nevada 2014b) complete with a "Pahrangat Man" rock art mascot, the tagline "get primitive," and detailed directions.

My point here is not to hearken back to the good old days (at least not entirely). The point is that my experience highlights something about secrecy and its function vis-à-vis collecting. For whatever reason, there is clearly a zero-sum mindset operating here, in which secrecy (which may or may not actually protect sites) functions to maintain the perceived value of a site in a system that privileges sites that are less visited, presumably because of barriers to access, be they informational and/or geographical. Secrecy about rock art site locations, in other words, functions to maintain the perceived (ascribed, fetishized) value of the rock art collection, as opposed to the pretense that the secrecy strategy is driven by the value and fragility of the sites. My identity as a rock art aficionado is not as effectively constructed by visiting the likes of Newspaper Rock along the highway into Canyonlands National Park, Petroglyph Plaza on the Waterfall Canyon Trail in White Tank Mountain Regional Park near Phoenix, or Atlatl Rock in Valley of Fire State Park near Las Vegas. I am not arguing that all sites should be widely publicized; indeed, in this book I have been consciously and strategically selective about what I reveal about sites. I am suggesting that there is not only a need for the rock art community to fess up to its role in the increasing degradation of rock art sites through our own high-minded activities (Dickey 2012; Quinlan 2007a), but also to reflect upon the work we *are* doing—as opposed to the work we *say* we are doing—through the withholding and sharing of site location infor-mation. For example, I am careful about what information to reveal about sites and I tell myself and others that is driven by concern for the site's preservation, but I'd be dishonest if I didn't admit that it isn't also about maintaining the psychological value of my collection based on exclusion.

The issue of secrecy points to some of the ways in which rock art sites are valued, in this case by their "scarcity" due to informational barriers and other restrictions on access. However, the widespread reproduction, commercialization, and commodification of rock art points to a related but broader hierarchy of value for rock art imagery.

Authenticity

For me, Toquima Cave's metal cage offers more than the metaphor of imprisonment (see chapter 7 and Figure 7.1). Rock art imagery has proliferated throughout the Southwest and beyond, extending from the realm of tourism into the broader consciousness and economy of the West. Spirals clearly designed to imitate petroglyphs adorn banks and t-shirts. Petroglyph-inspired bighorn sheep mark not only the sign for a Colorado River rafting company, but giant towers of concrete supporting freeways in Southwest megalopolises. Rock art imagery is plastered over the walls of visitor centers from southeastern California to southwestern Colorado. Kokopelli is not only ubiquitous in the tourism-scapes of the Southwest and beyond, operating as a symbol for "the Southwest," "[long-dead] Indians" or "ancient ruins—this way"; Kokopelli has entered wider commercial realms as a mascot for housing developments and wineries. The image can be bought on jewelry, t-shirts, pottery, coasters, mugs, socks, shower curtains, mailboxes, and more.

Of course, this commercial Kokopelli image has become so abstracted from its origins that its meanings resonate as strongly with those of the rock star, the roving minstrel, the traveling salesman, Mickey Mouse, and Casanova as they do with the real indigenous peoples and cultures who did and in many cases still inhabit the Southwest (see chapter 5). There are, however, what some rock art aficionados, archaeologists, anthropologists, and others rather insistently call "flute players." Flute players can be found as petroglyphs, pictographs, and in other visual media across the Colorado Plateau and beyond. These rock art images vary widely, some of them sharing traits with the Hohokam-inspired commercial image of Kokopelli. Some are simple stick figures, some highly ornate; some small, some large; some stand while others recline; some appear more like insects than humans; some have large, erect phalluses. While I am derisive toward Kokopellis, I seek out flute players along with other rock art imagery. The difference, as I have come to articulate it, is finding Kokopellis "in the wild." Any form of rock art is better "in the wild" than when found in museums, coffee-table books, or the local tourist kitsch store. And not just as a roadside attraction with a paved path—the harder to find, the more isolated, the more unknown the better. In my first encounters with rock art in and around Canyonlands, the roadside attraction of Newspaper Rock was certainly impressive in its size, complexity, and number of images— but those simple handprints, appearing unexpectedly while exploring the Needles District, totally unmarked, unsigned, and uninterpreted, were in many ways far more powerful and exciting (see chapter 1).

So while commercial rock art imagery has been mutated and enslaved, and places like Toquima Cave have been imprisoned in an attempt to freeze them in time, it is that rock art out there—not marked on the map, known to a relative few, requiring extensive research, luck, and travel to find—that appeals to me most. And finding flute players is a bonus—in some sense, each flute player I encounter in the wild psychologically counterbalances the millions of Kokopellis littering the Southwest. Seeking out rock art in general, and flute players in particular, enacts an attempt at recovery, a desire for purity—even though I know that such a recovery is impossible and that any sense of purity is a product of my dis-eased Western (not to mention postmodern) imagination.

Similarly, each time I find a photograph of a rock art site that I have visited and presumed to be unpublicized displayed on a web page or in a coffee-table book, a bit of the mystique is lost. Ancient, indigenous rock art sites are nonrenewable resources, but finding rock art is not necessarily a zero-sum game. Another visitor's experience of a rock art site need not degrade my own: If they leave no marks and are not present at the site when I am, no value need be detracted from my experience. But my experience *is* shaped by a zero-sum frame, one that subtracts value and excitement when the knowledge arises of the presence of others who are really not that unlike myself. My brain knows it need not be so, but my spirit yearns to recover the unrecoverable: that which is not commodified, that which has not been sullied by the presence of (contemporary, non-Native) others, that which awaits "discovery."

This is why I recognize that I am no better than the various others I imagine to have visited the same rock art sites that I have. I collect rock art—not literally, as physical collection is often impossible and even if it is possible would require violations of both laws and a code of ethics to which I subscribe. But I collect rock art sites in a way not greatly dissimilar to those who collect Kokopelli kitsch, Precious Moments figurines, or stamps. I obsessively photograph every rock art site I visit. Sometimes I become so fixated on photographing a site that I don't really see it, and fail to notice the power of the site itself as both a natural and as a culturally marked place. I catalog these photographs for their easy retrieval. I keep lists of rock art sites I have visited and rock art sites I want to visit. Through such collecting I bring an identity into being. I embody a primitivist nostalgia, working to counteract the guilt over what I, my ancestors, my culture have done: to indigenous peoples, to humanity as a whole, to the natural world. I seek out something that seems more real to me than my daily life even though I know it isn't more real, more pure, more authentic. I know that I, too, see in these ancient images more that is about me than about their creators; that I, too, "collect" such objects to satisfy my own hunger; that I, too, engage in commodification, attributing to objects a powerful magic capable of transforming my banal existence. But such awareness does not lessen the pull of rock art in the wild, does not diminish the sense of awe I experience when I find or stumble upon a "new" (to me) rock art site.

In looking for flute players, I seek to escape Kokopelli, knowing that he cannot be escaped and that my relationship with flute players in the wild is not necessarily fundamentally different than the person whose house is filled with Kokopelli commodities. Nevertheless, I still seek such an escape, such a recovery, such wholeness, and I find a mirage-like glimpse of it with almost every rock art site I visit. But maybe it's all a hoax of sorts.

A common concern about non-Natives interpreting indigenous rock art is that such interpretations can feed back into the living cultures affiliated with the rock art, potentially distorting Native self-understandings. In terms of the preservation of rock art sites, there is a similar "feedback loop" in operation: not simply the alteration of sites by the addition of graffiti, but the addition of images to rock art sites based on widely reproduced, commercially propagated rock art imagery. Here, we re-enter the historical condition of postmodernity and commodity capitalism, in which representations, especially images, overcome the "original" and function as the "real," often in tandem with commodification (see chapter 3). Kokopelli, of course, is an exemplar. Indeed, Kokopelli—not flute players and not *Kookopölö*, but the contemporary commercial figure—is a hybrid creation, a piece of postmodern pastiche, not in itself a "real" or "genuine" figure from any ancient culture (see chapter 5). What is the "original" upon which Kokopelli is built? Yes, the imagery itself is based on the Hohokam plate and other ancient flute player images. Yes, the name is based on the Hopi *katsina Kookopölö* and stories about that and related Pueblo beings. But the gestalt "thing"—the commodity—called "Kokopelli," known by so many, at least visually if not verbally, is itself, and has always been, a representation, a manufactured image attached to a nonrandom collage of myths and stories with tenuous connections to anything Hohokam, ancestral Puebloan, or otherwise. "Kokopelli" is like "Anasazi" (see chapter 1): a (post)modern, Western, primitivist, abstracted re-creation of an ancient culture. When most people visit a rock art site and see a flute player, if they recognize the image, they will likely recognize it as Kokopelli, that is, as the commercial image. They probably don't see a "flute player," they see "Kokopelli," overshadowing the original. The representation feeds back into the experience of the original imagery. Nevertheless, visitors to rock art sites can still see flute players and even know that they are flute players (at least if they think they know enough to know that they aren't Kokopellis).

I have seen two instances of what are clearly modern Kokopellis pecked into ancient rock art sites: one at Hickison Pass, a roadside attraction just off US Highway 50 in central Nevada (not far north of Toquima Cave), and another in Bullet Canyon, Grand Gulch, southeastern Utah. The Hickison Kokopelli is a stylized, simple stick figure, clearly recognizable as playing a flute and having a humped back, two antennae, and a possible penis (see Figure 8.1). At least four factors point to its contemporary manufacture: flute players are not known in that region, the image is not repatinated, the image was made with a different technique and in a different style than the indigenous elements at the site, and it is next to another clearly con-temporary graffito, a cartoon-like bear. As with many other instances of contemporary graffiti at the site, it appears someone has tried to cover the image with more marks.

The Bullet Canyon Kokopelli (see Figure 8.2) looks more like the predominant version of Kokopelli based on the Snaketown plate (see

FIGURE 8.1—Hickison Pass Kokopelli graffito, Lander County, Nevada.

Figure 5.8) than the Hickison Kokopelli. It includes the "antennae" and flute, but is upright and without an apparent humped back or backpack. Although the image is ambiguous on this count, it appears to have an erect penis, although this could have been added later or be a natural feature of the rock surface. Pecked in an area absent a dark patina, the image is actually darker than the surrounding rock, whereas the indigenous petroglyphs in the area are placed in areas with dark patina, creating light-colored images. As with the Hickison Kokopelli, the image is clearly different from those around it in terms of technique and style, being deeply etched as opposed to pecked. Unlike Hickison, however, flute players are very common in the Grand Gulch area and southeastern Utah in general, and the site is anything but a roadside attraction, requiring several hours of hiking to access and evidencing little contemporary graffiti. This site, in other words, meets my criteria for rock art "in the wild."

In the case of both of these images, I hope no one has been fooled. To me, it seems obvious that they are both contemporary and unrelated to the indigenous rock art at the sites. That does not mean, however,

FIGURE 8.2—Bullet Canyon Kokopelli graffito, San Juan County, Utah.

that others have not been fooled—or put more appropriately, that they are susceptible to the postmodern condition, in which representations of Kokopelli become the basis for judging the reality and authenticity of flute players, as opposed to "real" rock art sites anchoring the representations thereof.

A case in point is "reported" by Coyote True (1995), a pseudonym, in an *Edging West* article titled "Kokopelli Krime." The author reports that in 1976 (far in advance of the popular advent of the Kokopelli craze) he pecked a dancing, insect-like flute player complete with hunched back, erect penis, and flute into a boulder in a rock shelter in the Escalante area of southern Utah. As the tale unfolds, the author recounts confessing his crime (there were indigenous petroglyphs on the boulder) to several individuals who were initially taken in by his forgery. Not only were others fooled, but they published photographs of his flute player petroglyph in *High Country News*, *Audubon* magazine, and a book presenting a pictorial essay on southern Utah, all under the presumption of it being an authentic (ancient and Native) petroglyph. Some of those who were fooled should have known better, as the image clearly lacked repatination and was stylistically out of its territory (True 1995). As the author clarifies, his crime was not creating a Kokopelli image, but doing so in close proximity to indigenous petroglyphs. He characterizes his motives as originating with another trickster figure in Native American mythology, coyote, and he chose the pseudonym "Coyote True," leading me to question whether the entire story is itself a bit of tricksterism. Regardless of its veracity, the story rings true, seeming entirely plausible to me. Among those who were fooled was one who indicated that he recognized the particular style of Kokopelli from Frank Waters's *Book of the Hopi*, further demonstrating the operation of the postmodern condition: Waters's representation came to serve as evidence that the petroglyph is authentic. Here, quite literally, representations of Kokopelli feed back into rock art sites themselves, not only making flute players harder to find, but pulling the presumed foundation of authenticity—precontact indigenous rock art—out from underneath representations thereof.

Theorists respond ambivalently to this dimension of the postmodern condition: for some, the loss of a foundation initiates a kind of nihilism, bemoaning the loss of absolute truth; for others, the loss of a foundation opens up new possibilities in identity, meaning, truth, and culture. Postmodernity is characterized by a pervasive irony, a kind of perpetual wink, in that we seek out representations, we collect fetishized commodities, all in the service of an authenticity that we know does not exist.

On a visit to Zion National Park many years ago, I hiked to the Emerald Pools, stopping at the top of a waterfall for lunch. Sitting and looking out over the waterfall and into the main canyon, I turned around to get something from my pack, and there behind me I saw a panel of petroglyphs (see Figure 8.3). Before even processing what the petroglyphs were exactly, I reached into my pack for my camera and started snapping photos. At this point, I noticed two things: Three of the petroglyphs looked relatively authentic in terms of their content and style, but the fourth was clearly a contemporary graffito. Despite being crudely scratched, I interpreted it as a fairly clear representation of a camera. I cannot help but think that the artist of this fourth image was making a commentary on exactly the kind of practice I was engaged in: I was apparently so worried about missing another rock art panel to add to my collection (and a surprise discovery at that), that I reached for my camera to capture the panel before I fully registered what it was. Upon recognizing the camera graffito, I began to question the age of the other three petroglyphs. A spiral, a plant-like object, and a possible partial anthropomorph are not unusual subjects, nor do they stylistically stand out too starkly from indigenous petroglyphs in the region, but their location, levels of patination, placement next to the camera graffito, and other factors leave me in doubt to this day as to their age and their makers. They could well be fakes, in which case the joke played on me by the camera graffito is even more ironic, as the petroglyphs I rushed to capture for my collection are anything but authentic.

This tension and uncertainty between representations of rock art, "fake" rock art, and "authentic" rock art may explain my joy in proving that David Muench violated expectations of photographic realism in pursuit of aesthetic impact. Muench's coffee-table book focusing on rock art, *Images in Stone* (Muench and Schaafsma 1995), includes a photograph of the San Francisco Peaks (in northern Arizona) as seen through a natural rock window, with a petroglyph panel immediately above the rock window (to see the image without accessing the original book, see Muench 1995). Upon seeing this photograph in 2007, I was a bit surprised that I had not heard of this kind of unusual site so close to home, in an area where I had spent so much time and where many colleagues of mine had spent even more time. Based on careful study of USGS maps and the photo, especially the high-capacity power lines visible in front of the peaks, and using my familiarity with the landscape, including the route of the power lines, I was able to determine that the photo was taken outside of Wupatki National Monument—not in it, thankfully, as that would have hindered my search. I wanted to find the site, to experience this phenomenal combination of rock art, a natural window, and a wonderful view in person, embodied, and with all the senses, not just a preframed visual representation. I wanted to experience the "real" behind the photograph, never questioning the illusion of photographic realism from which I was operating.

After a couple of days of driving around various dirt roads in the area without finding the panel, my colleague Mark Neumann joined me in the search. For a few more days, we moved around several miles to the north and south, east and west, trying to line up the natural and artificial features on the landscape in a way that would match the photo, all the while looking for likely or even possible rock art sites, places where both a window and petroglyphs could exist. Finally, we located a relatively low red sandstone ridge that included both the window and the petroglyph panel. The window does indeed offer a beautifully

FIGURE 8.3—Emerald Pools petroglyphs and/or graffiti, Zion National Park, Utah.

framed view of the San Francisco Peaks, consistent with the photo. But the petroglyph panel is not above, or even near, the window. The image is a composite, inserting the petroglyph panel to make it appear as if it is just above the window, not several dozen yards away. I understand that Muench's book is not a piece of archaeological research and that his photographic oeuvre, often with highly saturated colors, is far more about aesthetics than documentation. Three things nevertheless fed my disillusionment: Muench's failure to note his photographic sleight of hand, my culture's deep investment in photographic realism, and rock art scholar Polly Schaafsma's provision of the written text for the book, lending it an aura of scholarly authority.

My disappointment with Muench quickly passed, but not my emotional attachment to the discovery. I know he is a commercial photographer with a focus on aesthetics. I have been familiar with his photography since 1983, and what I learned about photography in the years since made clear that his work is more about aesthetics than realism (that tension that has haunted photography almost from its inception, based on an opposition that I do not even buy into). And to top it off, Muench himself was avowedly primitivist: "This portfolio of color images will help us see and remember a beauty and harmony that went before. . . . . We hope . . . the photographs will convey a rich, primal power" (Muench and Schaafsma 1995:9). Any disillusionment turned quickly into a reaffirmation of my identity: a sense of both moral superiority in response to Muench's unacknowledged fabrication and informational superiority because of my on-the-ground efforts to seek out the "original." Indeed, at least one review of an exhibit including this photo indicates that the combination of two separate photographs went unnoticed: "Some fancy lens work, and perhaps even a split-focus adapter, was necessary to give us this image" (Huff 2000).

Most importantly, for me, on an affective level, "authenticity" has been restored . . . at least for this site, for me. I experienced the site firsthand. I invested my knowledge, skills, and labor in the search. I not only know its locale, its setting, and its multisensorial qualities—things I could never know through a photograph—but I also know that it is not what has been represented to the public, to those who haven't taken the time and effort to seek out the site. Once again, authenticity seems to be at least as much about cultural capital, about the construction, maintenance, and repair of identity, about a sense of exclusive and exclusionary superiority, as it is about a grounding in objective reality. Yes, I know the "truth" of the site, but the question is not simply "what is the truth?" but, pragmatically, "what work does that 'truth' do?"

Appropriations, Theirs and Mine

Everyone who views, collects, interprets, or reproduces rock art employs and deploys rock art strategically, with particular intentions and purposes, from different underlying motivations and ideological orientations. One cannot represent, appropriate, or communicate about rock art and not do so. All acts of communication, representation, and appropriation are done from some standpoint, through some frame, for some purpose, from certain motivations, and with a variety of functions and consequences.

My work, which functions in part to critique what I see as illegitimate appropriations and representations of rock art, functions, in many ways, like the identifications and characterizations of the crackpots and crazies of the rock art world (see chapter 2). Like those who criticize the lunatic fringe, my intent is to point out what I see as legitimately illegitimate. But also like those who criticize the lunatic fringe, the function of the act is, at least in part, to reinforce my own sense of legitimacy and avoid uncomfortable questions and reflections on my own practices, assumptions, biases, and underlying motivations.

In 1924, Samuel Hubbard embarked on the Doheny Scientific Expedition to the Grand Canyon, specifically the Havasu region (Menkes 2007). Hubbard claimed to have definitively identified a petroglyph of a dinosaur, which he presented (along with other seemingly bizarre findings) as proof of the coexistence of humans and dinosaurs and the invalidity of the theory of evolution. Hubbard's claims and evidence are still frequently cited today by "young earth" creationists as evidence supporting the creation of the earth about six thousand years ago (Menkes 2007). Phil Senter (2012) has presented a conventionally convincing argument that the "dinosaur" is likely a bird with a J-shaped extension, based on examination of other bird images in similar rock art styles, along with debunking several other claims of dinosaur depictions in rock art. Of course, as an "educated" and "liberal" person who opposes the creationist fight against the teaching of evolution as part of a larger fundamentalist social movement, I can easily get on board with the debunking as well as gain a sense of superiority by opposition to Hubbard's clearly uniformed and highly skewed interpretation.

In chapter 1, I presented a mid-nineteenth-century LDS translation of a Manti, Utah, rock art panel (see Figure 1.3) as a passage from the Book of Mormon, as reported by Garrick Mallery (1894). Such interpretations cannot simply be dismissed as the product of a time where we didn't know better, as in seeing rock art as a kind of written language, proto or otherwise, or of excessive religious zeal. But such interpretations continue, and not just as the sensationalistic claims used to draw in audiences to reality TV shows of the archaeological variety, but as serious belief systems (to those who hold them, at least).

The American Indian Research Press (based in Hurricane, Utah) promotes its interpretation and translation of southwestern petroglyphs, consistent with the same basic LDS theology that guided the nineteenth-century interpretation reported by Mallery (1894). They explain that "an American Indian Prophet, called Hoh, existed in the First Century AD and wrote petroglyphic stories in stone found in the SW USA that describe in minute detail Judeo/Christian teachings in Egyptian-like hieroglyphs" (AIR Press 2015). They present "copyrighted proof" of this in the form of a colored drawing of a petroglyph panel (the colors being part of their decoding system) produced by their Decipherment Antiquities Team, along with its translation, which is from the New Testament (John 3:16): "For God so loved the world, that he gave his only begotten Son, that whosoever believeth in him should not perish, but have everlasting life" (AIR Press 2015).

American Indian Research Press also offers translations and photographs of a large panel on top of a boulder at the Little Black Mountain site in the Arizona strip, which they call "Crucifixion Rock." The petroglyphs are interpreted as depicting the crucifixion: "The Large Bird laying down is the symbolic representation of the self-sacrificing dead Lord. The Rising Bird represents his resurrection" (AIR Press 2015). Two connected circles "depict the two churches, the top being already established in the Eastern Hemisphere and the other newer church, in the Western Hemisphere" (AIR Press 2015). Richard Marquardt explains in the site's "Scientific Statement" that he is an "independent Archaeologist" who, as a result of "direct empirical evidence" found in the petroglyphs of Utah and Arizona, has determined that "most of the stories are from one artistic and intelligent source who is now identified as a sage named Ho" (AIR Press 2015). The petroglyphs "accurately emanate the Hebrew language stories of Moses in Genesis and other Bible books" and were "created in a very similar format to the older style of the Egyptian Hieroglyphic language containing full figures of gods, persons, animals, events, places and things" (AIR Press 2015). Concerned about the degradation of the petroglyphs, AIR Press calls out to those interested in helping to "create a special museum called JESUS CHRIST IN AMERICA where everyone can come freely to see and touch models of the ancient Petroglyphs and other wonderful objects from the time of Jesus in the American Indian Southwest" (AIR Press 2015).

Another contemporary LDS interpretation of Southwest rock art brings us back to the inescapable Kokopelli. On an LDS discussion forum about the "Location of the Book of Mormon Lands," Benjamin Harrison (2012) explains that Kokopelli "was a figure who played a type of flute or a trumpet and had a humped back." Whereas novelist Shelley Munro (2010) gave her Kokopelli a saxophone instead of a flute to make him more consistent with the "rock star" figure (see chapter 5), here we see the move from flute to trumpet, enabling an easier link to LDS imagery. Stories from Joseph Smith are used to establish that the angel Moroni, who is portrayed as playing a trumpet (as in the statue on the top of LDS temples in Salt Lake City and elsewhere), was known to have carried a backpack containing the gold plates from which the Book of Mormon was translated. Moroni was also known to have traveled to Utah to, among other things, dedicate the ground where the Manti Temple would later be built. Moroni was in Utah back in the day, carried a heavy backpack, and played a trumpet, leading Harrison to suggest that the rock art images popularly known as Kokopelli are in fact Moroni.

Harrison (2012), however, goes beyond appropriating the imagery itself, citing "traditions among the Hopi that Kokopelli was a spiritual teacher and signaled the people by playing his flute, making it known he was in the area and was going to teach them the gospel that night." In this version, the image of Kokopelli is transformed into Kokopelli/Moroni as the bearer of the good news of the Lord Jesus Christ. Once again, the image of flute players and supposed Hopi stories about Kokopelli are combined to present a different story about the pre-Columbian peoples of the Americas. Translations and interpretations of precontact indigenous rock art in terms of the Bible and the Book of Mormon are consistent with the LDS belief that Jesus was in ancient North America and that at least some Native Americans are the descendants of the lost tribes of Israel. This can be perceived as an attempt to appropriate Native Americans, their histories, and their cultures in support of LDS theology.

Religion is of course by no means the only driving force behind strategic, rhetorical appropriations of rock art imagery. On Nevada Highway 376, just south of its intersection with US Highway 50, is the Nevada State Historical Marker for Toquima Cave. Sometime between May 2002 and September 2005, an unofficial addition was made to the sign, and sometime since was removed. The following message was written in black marker at the bottom of the sign: "These petroglyphs make [*sic*] have been make [as] early as 1958 when local high school kid painted these designs no [*sic*] the walls of the cave as [a] prank. The Forest Service soon desided [*sic*] that they could make hay out of these drawings and used them to withdraw more land from use of the general public." This statement was followed by the initials USFS (US Forest Service), BLM, and EPA (Environmental Protection Agency), each with its own circle and line through the acronym. This is clearly a statement against federal control of public lands, a common sentiment in rural Nevada, where hostility toward federal land management agency employees has a long history and is linked to right-wing, antifederal, antigovernment sentiments and ideologies (such as the Sagebrush Rebellion of the 1980s and 1990s and the 2014 stand-off involving Clark County, Nevada, rancher Cliven Bundy). This statement (technically, vandalism) symbolically appropriates the rock art in Toquima Cave as the creation of a teenager, expropriating the rock art from living Native peoples with affiliations to it, in order to argue for free and unregulated access, use, and exploitation of public lands in the western United States. In direct contention with this claim, the National Register of Historic Places Registration Form for Toquima Cave (Kumiega and Walter 2001) clearly indicates the cave's long-term habitation, the continuity between this and other pictograph sites in the region, and direct affiliations with living Native peoples, specifically the Western Shoshone, who regard it as a sacred site.

My point here is not simply to identify more instances of what are deemed "the lunatic fringe"—a popular pastime among rock art scholars and one in which I participate—but to clarify two things about the rôle of rock art in the contemporary cultural landscape. First, all interpretations, representations, and appropriations are positioned and interested; few if any are driven by evidence alone. Evidence is selected and interpreted in particular frames, which enables these interpretations to "make sense" to audiences who are invested in the underlying assumptions or to seem "crazy" to those who do not. Second, it is almost always easier to identify those assumptions and investments in others' interpretations as opposed to our own.

In the harsh terms that Bancroft (1875) reserved for the Mormons, in the course of this book and my previous research and teaching, I have admittedly, and I think obviously, "made [these] aboriginal inscription[s] subservient to" (as quoted in Mallery 1894:118) my ideological investments, political commitments, identities, and scholarly goals. Even if done in order to critically examine others' interpretations for noble ends, I have nevertheless selected, represented, appropriated, and to some degree interpreted indigenous rock art. In the cases of hunting magic, shamanism, and Kokopelli, I have used rock art to advance my feminist politics through the interrogation of white masculinities. While criticizing open invitations to interpret rock art, I have presented yet more material that others can use to advance more interpretations. In the context of examining the preservation of rock art, I appropriated the precontact, postcontact, and contemporary rock art of Inscription Point and Tutuveni/Willow Springs to advance a theoretical and political argument about the nature of culture. While I do so in order to identify, and hopefully counter, the operation of the primitivist prison into which living indigenous peoples are placed, this does not mean that living peoples associated with these sites concur with my assessments and objectives.

Absent Authorities: What about the Natives?

As I reflect in a serious, self-implicative manner on the nature of my work in this book, perhaps the most obvious and troubling pattern is the overall absence of Native voices and perspectives on rock art itself. I could easily lay the responsibility for this on rock art studies, whose literature contains few Native American researchers and authors; in my experience, when they do appear they are most often late in a list of coauthors, seemingly confined to the role of collaborator and/ or consultant. Certainly, between these coauthors, Native participants interviewed by rock art scholars, and the use of historic ethnography, there is some degree of Native input into rock art research, but my (and some others') overall assessment would have to be that it is quite limited (Loendorf et al. 2005). In the era of NAGPRA, there is certainly a large amount of consultation taking place with Native communities about rock art sites in the context of CRM, which includes substantial information about the rock art's uses, meanings, affiliations, and values (e.g., Gilreath et al. [2011] on Black Canyon, eastern Nevada; Kumiega and Walter [2001] on Toquima Cave, central Nevada; Evans et al. [1993] and Ferguson and Anschuetz [2003] on Petroglyph National Monument, New Mexico). However, this information is often not incorporated into the literature, whether due to bureaucratic or budgetary constraints, Native concerns about inappropriate dissemination (Schaafsma 2013), or just a failure to write it up. Substantial exceptions exist and are on the rise, however, constituting a definite trend, including direct consultations with affiliated Native American groups, Native American coauthors, inclusion of oral histories alongside traditional archaeological evidence, and revisiting previously dismissed ethnographies (e.g., Bernardini 2005; Colwell-Chanthaphonh and Ferguson 2006; Stoffle et al. 2000; Whitley 1994a, 1998c; Young 1988).

I could also justify the relative absence of Native perspectives on rock art in this book by pointing to the focus and purpose of my project. This is not a traditional piece of archaeological, anthropological, or rock art research; its focus is not on using rock art to gain insights into traditional indigenous cultures. That is a perfectly valid research purpose, but it isn't mine—I am not a credentialed archaeologist, and there are plenty of rock art researchers tackling those kinds of questions. My focus is on the role of rock art in the contemporary cultural landscape. While this by no means excludes Native American cultures and perspectives, my primary focus is on how and why outsiders (non-Natives, Westerners) visit, reproduce, interpret, appropriate, and manage rock art. Put another way, while the general topic of this book is indigenous rock art, the book is more about whiteness: how whiteness is constructed, maintained, repaired, transformed, and contested through interpretations and appropriations of rock art. It is also a book about neocolonialism, which of course necessarily involves indigenous cultures, but mostly in the role of resources from which the colonizing culture appropriates as it deems fit. Of course, even given this focus on white appropriations and interpretations, Native American perspectives on neocolonialism and appropriation are highly relevant, especially in terms of the implications for living Native peoples, and I have included those perspectives when relevant and available—although, again, when it comes to rock art specifically, there isn't much, even if many indigenous authors have directly addressed broader issues related to the representation and appropriation of Native American cultures.

In terms of rationalizing the relative absence of Native voices in my work, the third point is perhaps the most valid, or perhaps it is just the easiest dodge. Much of the work that I do focuses on regions where the bulk of the rock art is attributed to various ancestral Puebloan groups, such as the Kayenta and Sinagua. These groups are arguably ancestors of today's Acoma, Hopi, Laguna, Tiwa, Zia, Zuni, and other Pueblo peoples. In the case of the northern Sinagua, for example, there is strong evidence of cultural continuity with the Hopi, ranging from early twentieth-century identifications and interpretations by Hopi people of artifacts from excavated sites (McGregor 1943) to Hopi place names and oral histories linked to northern Sinagua sites (Kuwanwisiwma et al. 2012). While this doesn't mean that every interpretation of affiliated rock art from a Hopi person should automatically be accepted without question, it is difficult to deny that contemporary Pueblo peoples, among others, have much that is meaningful to say about ancient rock art. At the same time, however, as my discussions of Pueblo perspectives on Petroglyph National Monument (chapter 6) and Hopi views on the sharing of religious and spiritual information (chapter 5) clearly indicate, Pueblo groups have adopted a cautious stance when it comes to sharing some types of cultural information with outsiders, have sought control over the distribution of information shared previously, and to some degree have asked outsiders to just stop asking (Brown 1998; Hopi Cultural Preservation Office 2009; Hopi Staff 2004; Schaafsma 2013). Taken in the light of Peters's (1999) discussion of dialogue and dissemination (chapter 6), this can be understood as a refusal to make Native interiority available for colonization by the dominant. It becomes very easy for me, therefore, to justify not even knocking on Native people's doors. I am not trying to dig into rock art's "real" meanings; I am trying to understand the nature, origin, function, and implications of non-Native reproductions, representations, interpretations, and appropriations. Native peoples certainly have insight into those topics, but the line between "tell me about your spiritual beliefs and practices" and "tell me about how you feel about the interpretation and use of those beliefs and practices by Anglos" seems awfully thin.

This all still seems too convenient, a decent justification that also suspiciously gives me an easy way out. I am not only a critical/cultural studies scholar who is particularly attuned to the forces of primitivism, essentialism, neocolonialism, and appropriation. I am also a rock art enthusiast, and I share with many rock art enthusiasts the social positions of white, Anglo-American, and white-collar. With many of those, I also share the social positions of heterosexual, cisgender, and male. My critical stance toward primitivism and essentialism, for example, does not mean that the appeal of rock art to me is not deeply shaped by those standpoints. I, too, am shaped by the New Age, by the stereotype of the Ecological Indian, and by a profound dis-ease with my culture's relationship to nature, labor, community, and spirituality.

So I really need to ask myself, am I, too, refusing to access the interiority of living Native peoples, choosing to live instead in a fantasy world of the "primitive" via my relationship with rock art? Or am I really respecting the request to not dig into their cultures, to discontinue the tradition of forcing their interiority open for the colonial gaze? I am deeply uncomfortable going beyond the relatively little that has been published or publicized on Native American perspectives on rock art. Is that out of genuine respect, or am I just another "object" hobbyist of the variety that Deloria (1998) describes—wanting to make precise, historically accurate indigenous artifacts (or collections thereof) while avoiding contact with living indigenous peoples? Is my desire to "collect" rock art sites that different from the suburban

Phoenix home decorated throughout with Kokopelli kitsch or high-end Native arts? Am I invested in avoiding the perspectives of living Native peoples out of genuine respect, or fear of confronting my own investments in the cultural heritage of others? If I did seek out such information and obtained it, what would I do with it? Whose interests would I be serving in doing so?

Frankly, beyond general moves toward greater reliance on ethnography, compliance with legal and regulatory requirements for consultation, and an attunement to elements of indigenous ontologies, epistemologies, and spiritualities—all of which are extremely important—I am still not very optimistic about the future of indigenous perspectives in rock art studies and the broader rock art community. There are still very strong tendencies to treat Native Americans as relics, as abstracted fetishes of authenticity, or as barriers to access and interpretation. The absence of indigenous voices—especially as represented in their own terms, under their own authorship—remains in the literature. The single largest and longest running publication in the United States devoted to rock art, *American Indian Rock Art*, includes very few American Indian authors. Whether that is due to a lack of Native interest in the topic, a lack of Native interest in participating in such a forum, epistemological and related stylistic barriers to Native participation, broader issues related to educational access and credentialing, or some combination of these and other factors, the fact remains that rock art tourism, rock art hobbyism, and rock art research remain demographically and ideologically white.

There Are Some Indians Still Around

On an autumn trip through Nevada and eastern California to visit some rock art sites that I had never seen or had visited only briefly, I found myself heading south and dropping in elevation as the temperatures dropped almost daily. This trajectory took me to Death Valley National Park, home to the lowest elevations and highest temperatures on the continent. But I also had another reason for heading to Death Valley: to revisit the Klare Spring petroglyph site, which had helped launch my scholarly reflections on rock art fifteen years earlier.

Klare Spring is a relatively modest rock art site, and far from pristine. In Death Valley National Park, there are many rock art sites ranging from a few to hundreds of motifs. However, as a general rule, when it comes to the archaeology of indigenous peoples, park personnel provide information about only a few, select sites, and Klare Spring is number one on that list. Secrecy—not access—is the norm in the NPS and sacrificial sites such as Klare Spring are the exceptions that prove the rule. It is widely publicized by the park, with information available to visitors both orally and in writing, along with a host of non-NPS publications that also provide detailed directions, and it sits only a few feet off the most popular "backcountry" road in the park, Titus Canyon Road.

After a gradual climb through creosote-covered desert, the one-way road enters the Grapevine Mountains and eventually traverses Red Pass, dropping into Titus Canyon near the site of Leadville, a short-lived, lead-driven boomtown not unlike dozens of other mining towns in the park and surrounding areas. Below Leadville, the road passes through a mile and a half of narrows, where the canyon walls rise almost vertically on both sides of the road, before exiting into Death Valley itself. After Leadville and before the narrows lies Klare Spring, a substantial spring for Death Valley, with several hundred square yards of dense vegetation and visible pools of water.

Adjacent to the spring, a large boulder displays dozens of petroglyphs, including the bighorn sheep motifs found throughout the Great Basin and beyond. Another boulder presents more historic and contemporary scratches than indigenous petroglyphs. However, what pulls me to return to Klare Spring is not the rock art per se, but the large NPS interpretive sign positioned in between these two boulders, facing the road (see Figure 8.4). When I first read this sign some fifteen years earlier, some random thoughts I had been having about the contemporary cultural use and interpretation of rock art began to congeal:

Petroglyphs
Indian rock carvings are found throughout the western hemisphere. Indians living today deny any knowledge of their meaning. Are they family symbols, doodlings, or ceremonial markings? Your guess is as good as any. Do not deface—they cannot be replaced.

For some aficionados and scholars of rock art, the obvious problem with this sign, probably erected four or five decades ago, is the claim that "Indians living today deny any knowledge of their meaning." This statement is demonstrably inaccurate, and I often stress in presentations to rock art scholars, archaeologists, and land managers that I

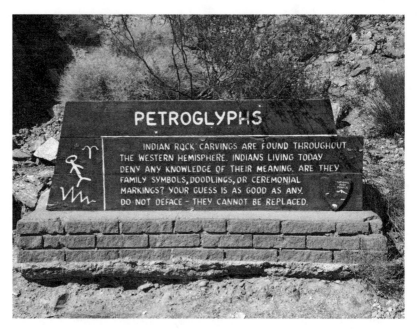

FIGURE 8.4—Klare Spring interpretive sign, Death Valley National Park, California.

understand that this sign's text would in all likelihood read very differently were it written today. David Whitley and Jean Clottes (2005) trace the history of this claim, which was and is often made about Great Basin rock art in particular, in published works, websites, and interpretive materials. As I discussed in chapter 2, the second major synthetic publication about North American rock art was Julian Steward's 1929 *Petroglyphs of California and Adjoining States.* Somewhat ironically, Steward, a cultural anthropologist (i.e., not an archaeologist), severely downplayed the ethnography on rock art. Despite including specific statements about specific aspects of rock art by a variety of tribes, his chapter on the "Meaning and Purpose" of rock art opens by declaring not only the complete "failure" of ethnographic work on the subject, but that "the Indians disclaim all knowledge of their meaning or origin" (Steward 1929:224). The same basic claim was repeated by Heizer and Baumhoff (1962) directly in relation to the Great Basin, probably not long before this sign was erected. Certainly Steward (1929), Heizer and Baumhoff (1962), and/or others citing their work are the origin of the sign's claim that "Indians living today deny any knowledge of their meaning." In a post-NAGPRA world, this statement undeniably operates not as a factual claim but as an overt denial of indigenous authority. Of even more interest to me, however, is the conclusion drawn from the proclaimed indigenous denials of knowledge, which is the authorization of a new interpretive regime: "Your guess is as good as any." For me, this statement serves as the constellation of the colonization of indigenous cultures (in this case, their rock art), a bizarrely "democratic" licensing of interpretive authority over the traces of indigenous cultures by Anglo-Americans and other non-Natives (see chapter 6).

I have returned to Klare Spring, at least in part, to confirm the continued existence of this sign, a sign whose content was both outdated and politically questionable when I first saw it in the late 1990s. Indeed, not only is the sign still present, but it has clearly been repainted, a conclusion I draw from both photographs from my previous visit and careful inspection of the sign itself, which reveals new paint bubbling and peeling off to make visible the older, stained wood surface underneath.

Having revisited the site, checked out the sign, explored the petroglyphs and spring, and of course obsessively photographed it all, I decide to spend the rest of the afternoon right there, observing the canyon and the petroglyphs as the sun moved toward the west. During the three or so hours I had been on the Titus Canyon road thus far, I had not heard or seen anyone else. Not long after stopping at Klare Spring, however, cars begin to occasionally drive by and I start to keep track of who stops, who doesn't, and what they do if they stop. Most cars roll by without even slowing down. A few others slow down long enough to look at the sign and the surrounding boulders, but without getting out of their cars they cannot really see the petroglyphs. A few stop and spend a few minutes quickly examining the rock art. Out of a dozen cars, only two, traveling together, spend more than five minutes at Klare Spring in general or engaged in a close examination and discussion of the petroglyphs.

I am sitting on my tailgate in the shade of the rear hatch, facing the petroglyph boulders and sign from just across the narrow gravel road. Two black sport-utility vehicles pull up, and the inhabitants remain in their vehicles for a short minute before eight doors pop open to disgorge four adults and six children, Anglo and seemingly middle class, apparently comprising an extended family: a grandfather, mother, two fathers, and two related groups of siblings. As the doors open, I pick up a conversation already in progress between a father and his son:

"Why did they make them only here?" asks the son.

"We don't know—no one is around to ask," replies the father.

I presume that the father's answer has been provided by the sign, readily visible and readable from where they parked, but also, or instead, from the broader cultural narrative that the "real Indians" are all dead or degraded, either absent or living without meaningful connection to their cultural heritage.

Almost without pause, the son emphatically retorts, "There are *some* Indians around still." At this point, I am somewhat in shock hearing this preteen boy overtly resisting not only the authority of the NPS sign and his father, but the pervasive Euro-American myth of the actual and inevitable disappearance of Indians (at least "real" ones), be it through genocide, assimilation, integration, or the Inevitable Progression of Western Civilization. Perhaps not surprisingly, however, given both the complexity of the issue of the presence of Native Americans in the contemporary United States and the physical commotion of ten people getting out of two cars, the father manages a barely audible "well . . ." and that particular conversation ends.

As the rest of the family heads up to examine the petroglyphs, the grandfather decides he will not be climbing, opting instead to shout periodic statements of concern that the kids are climbing too high. At one point he turns to me and asks, "Did they put you out here to make sure no one defaces them?" Again, I presume he has possibly been cued by the sign, whose last words are "do not deface—they cannot be replaced." I laugh heartily at his question, shake my head no, and explain that I'm just hanging out here for the afternoon. The adults in the group seem a bit perplexed about why someone is just sitting at a site that most see as a roadside attraction, not a destination per se, but Grandpa is the only one who asks me what I'm up to.

Meanwhile, up around the larger and more petroglyph-covered boulder, the kids and one of the dads are not only looking at the petroglyphs but are also following the sign's instruction, though I never hear them mention "your guess is as good as any" specifically. One of the older boys, perhaps in his early to mid-teens, posits that the petroglyphs indicate what "tribe" claims this territory and "how many men you had," concluding that the overall message is to "stay the hell out of here." I laugh inside at this fairly typical interpretative inclination—hegemonic masculinity—though most masculinist interpretations are focused more on hunting than warfare per se, especially since this site doesn't appear to depict shields or other weapons. For a young American male, an interpretation grounded in territoriality and potential conflict seems cliché. Images of young boys playing war from the opening scenes of Oliver Stone's *Born on the Fourth of July* pop into my head along with my own childhood memories of playing Cowboys and Indians, the Alamo, and World War II.

After a few minutes of looking, pointing, and conversing that is primarily focused on identifying specific images, such as bighorn sheep, one of the fathers announces that he thinks it's "peyote on the rocks." Some of the seemingly more abstract and geometric images might have sparked this implication of hallucinatory inspiration, or perhaps he has encountered the increasingly widespread altered-states-of-consciousness, neuropsychological, or, more popularly, shamanic view of rock art at other sites, a museum or visitor center, or in a guidebook (see chapter 4). Regardless, just like the boy's comment about territoriality, this specific interpretation was not one offered by the NPS sign, but nevertheless followed the invitation to guess openly.

One of a host of ironies embedded in this interaction is that despite the sign's (false) denial of indigenous knowledge, the son's initial question—"Why did they make them only here?"—is both a really good question and one for which there's even a pretty good answer, though admittedly one not necessarily reflecting an indigenous point of view per se nor directly identifying what the petroglyphs mean.

As the family begins to move back to their cars to head down the road, the mother is standing nearby and I make an active intervention in their visit, telling her that if they walk a few hundred feet down the road, there is a large spring with lots of plant life and algae-filled pools of water to look at. *We are in the driest place in North America, so don't miss the spring!* While I didn't articulate that thought, it wasn't necessary, as the mom began enthusiastically coordinating the movement of ten people and two cars to the bottom end of the spring.

I directed them to the spring for another reason. Given what I have read and heard about Great Basin rock art and given all my visits to Great Basin rock art sites, I believe that the spring is the rather obvious (though admittedly incomplete) answer to the son's question about why "they" made them "here." Certainly not all Great Basin rock art sites are by springs, but in my experience many springs in the Great Basin have rock art nearby. The correlation is there, along with many others, although the meaning of those correlations is another matter altogether, and that's part of why I do not explicitly mention the connection between the petroglyphs and the spring. While I find "your guess is as good as any" to be both belittling and colonizing, I also have no desire to put myself in the position of telling people what a particular piece of rock art does or does not mean. My guess isn't as good as any, and while perhaps it would be more informed than most, I am not comfortable with presuming to know more than those far more connected to a particular motif, panel, or style than I, be it through heritage or thoughtful ethnographic research.

In this sense, this is the best I can do: acknowledging and recognizing that Native peoples do have relevant insights into rock art, that rock art is their heritage, and that it is up to them if they want to share their views of it, while at the least not overtly colonizing it with my interpretations. Inevitably, I deploy rock art in my work; I use it to my own ends. However narrow and self-serving or broad and genuinely liberatory my interests may be, it is a power-laden appropriation. It is not my heritage, despite the government signs posted at so many sites telling me otherwise. Given this, I was understandably heartened to hear this young boy challenge his father and the NPS, loudly proclaiming that "there are *some* Indians around still." There are, and I believe they have much more knowledge about rock art's meanings than I do. I am more than happy to listen to whatever they choose to say, and content if they choose not to say anything at all.

REFERENCES CITED

Abram, David
    1996 *The Spell of the Sensuous.* Vintage, New York.
Adams, Carol J.
    2003 *The Sexual Politics of Meat: A Feminist-Vegetarian Critical Theory.* 10th anniversary ed. Continuum International, New York.
AIR Press
    2015 American Indian Research Press. Electronic Document, http://air7. yolasite.com, accessed July 17, 2015.
Althusser, Louis
    1971 *Lenin and Philosophy and Other Essays.* Monthly Review, New York.
American Rock Art Research Association (ARARA)
    1995 New-Age Petroglyphs Create Management Problems. *La Pintura* 21(4):16.
    2007 *A Basic Guide for Rock Art Recording.* Electronic document, www. arara.org, accessed January 11, 2017.
    2011 Red Rock Canyon: A Conservation Update. *La Pintura* 37(3):16.
Appadurai, Arjun
    1990 Disjuncture and Difference in the Global Cultural Economy. *Public Culture* 2:1–24.
Archuleta, Elizabeth
    2005 Gym Shoes, Maps, and Passports, Oh My!: Creating Community or Creating Chaos at the NMAI? *American Indian Quarterly* 29:426–449.
Arrillaga, Pauline
    2012 Indian Tribes Join Forces to Save Petroglyph Site. *The Seattle Times* 28 January. Electronic document, http://www.seattletimes.com/nation-world/indian-tribes-join-forces-to-save-petroglyph-site/, accessed April 8, 2017.
Ashcraft, Karen Lee, and Lisa A. Flores
    2000 "Slaves with White Collars": Persistent Performances of Masculinity in Crisis. *Text & Performance Quarterly* 23:1–29.
Associated Press
    2000 Indian Band Applies for Trademark on Ancient Petroglyphs. 16 February. Electronic document, http://www.oocities.org/aeissing/00252. html, accessed January 11, 2017.
Aujoulot, Norbert
    2014 Lascaux. French Ministry of Culture and Communication. Electronic

document, http://www.lascaux.culture.fr/#/en/02_00.xml, accessed March 24, 2015.

Austin, Don
2013 Petroglyphs.us. Electronic document, http://www.petroglyphs.us, accessed July 10, 2015.

Bakhtin, M. M.
1981 *The Dialogic Imagination*. Translated by Caryl Emerson and Michael Holquist. University of Texas Press, Austin.

Bancroft, Hubert Howe
1875 *Native Races of the Pacific States of North America*, Vol. IV, *Antiquities*. Longmans, Green, London.

Banks, Leo W.
1999 Cuckoo for Kokopelli: The Ancestry of the Southwest's Hottest New Star Is Shrouded in the Dim Past. *Tucson Weekly* 14 October. Electronic document, http://www.tucsonweekly.com/tucson/cuckoo-for-kokopelli/ Content?oid=1065426, accessed January 12, 2017.

Barnes, F. A.
1989 *Canyon Country Prehistoric Rock Art*. Rev. ed. Wasatch, Salt Lake City, Utah.

Bass, Patricia M.
1994 A Gendered Search through Some West Texas Rock Art. In *New Light on Old Art: Recent Advances in Hunter-Gatherer Rock Art Research*, edited by David S. Whitley and Lawrence L. Loendorf, pp. 67–74. Institute of Archaeology, University of California, Los Angeles.

Baudrillard, Jean
1983 *Simulations*. Translated by Paul Foss, Paul Patton, and Philip Beitchman. Semiotext(e), New York.

Beauchamp, Douglas
2013 Context Interrupted: The Displacement and Re-Situation of Four Unique Petroglyph Boulders in Oregon. In *IFRAO 2013 Proceedings, American Indian Rock Art*, Vol. 40, edited by Peggy Whitehead, pp. 685–688. American Rock Art Research Association, Glendale, Arizona.

Bederman, Gail
1995 *Manliness and Civilization: A Cultural History of Gender and Race in the United States, 1880–1917*. University of Chicago Press, Chicago.

Belk, Russell W.
1995 *Collecting in a Consumer Society*. Routledge, New York.

Benjamin, Walter
1989 [1936] The Work of Art in the Age of Mechanical Reproduction. In *The Critical Tradition: Classic Texts and Contemporary Trends*, edited by David H. Richter, pp. 571–588. St. Martin's, New York.

Benson, Larry V., E. M. Hattori, J. Southon, and B. Aleck
2013 Dating North America's Oldest Petroglyphs, Winnemucca Lake Subbasin, Nevada. *Journal of Archaeological Science* 40(12):4466–4476.

Berger, Peter, and Thomas Luckman
1966 *The Social Construction of Reality: A Treatise in the Sociology of Knowledge*. Anchor/Doubleday, New York.

Berkhofer, Robert F.
1978 *The White Man's Indian: Images of the American Indian from Columbus to the Present*. Vintage, New York.

Bernardini, Wesley
2005 *Hopi Oral Tradition and the Archaeology of Identity*. University of Arizona Press, Tucson.
2009 *Hopi History in Stone: The Tutuveni Petroglyph Site*. Arizona State Museum, University of Arizona, Tucson.

Bertola, Max
1996 Kokopelli: Anasazi Casanova. *Max Bertola's Southern Utah*. Electronic document, http://www.so-utah.com/feature/kokopeli/homepage.html, accessed August 24, 2005.

Bettinger, Robert L., and Martin A. Baumhoff
1982 The Numic Spread: Great Basin Cultures in Competition. *American Antiquity* 47:485–503.

Bicknell, Robin Scott
2001 *Images from the Past: A Self-Guided Tour of Petroglyphs and Pictographs of the American Southwest*. Patrice, Tucson, Arizona.
2009 *Arizona's Rock Art: Guide to Rock Art Sites*. Outskirts, Denver, Colorado.

Bird, S. Elizabeth
1999 Tales of Difference: Representations of American Indian Women in Popular Film and Television. In *Mediated Women: Representations in Popular Culture*, edited by Marian Meyers, pp. 91–109. Hampton, Cresskill, New Jersey.
2001 Savage Desires: The Gendered Construction of the American Indian in Popular Media. In *Selling the Indian: Commercializing and Appropriating American Indian Cultures*, edited by Carter Jones Meyer and Diana Royer, pp. 62–98. University of Arizona Press, Tucson.

Bjork, Carl
2013 Carl Bjork's Rock Art Site. Electronic document, http://home.comcast.net/~carlbjork, accessed July 10, 2015.

Black, Jason Edward
2002 The "Mascotting" of Native America: Construction, Commodity, and Assimilation. *American Indian Quarterly* 26:605–622.

Bock, A. J., and Georgia Lee
1991 Footsteps to Destruction: A Guide for Visiting and/or Recording

Rock Art Sites. In *American Indian Rock Art*, Vol. 18, edited by Frank G. Bock, pp. 23–26. American Rock Art Research Association, Las Vegas, Nevada.

Bock, Frank (moderator)

1989 Conservation and Protection Symposium Panel Discussion. In *Preserving Our Rock Art Heritage: Proceedings from the Symposium on Rock Art Conservation and Protection*, edited by Helen K. Crotty, pp. 75–86. Occasional Paper 1. American Rock Art Research Association, San Miguel, California.

Bordo, Susan

1999 *The Male Body: A New Look at Men in Public and in Private*. Farrar, Straus & Giroux, New York.

Bostwick, Todd W.

2008 The South Mountains Rock Art Project: A Collaborative Effort in Recording Rock Art as Archaeology in a City Park. In *Set in Stone: A Binational Workshop on Petroglyph Management in the United States and Mexico*, compiled by Joseph P. Sánchez, Angelica Sánchez-Clark, and Edwina L. Abreu, pp. 82–97. Petroglyph National Monument, Albuquerque, New Mexico.

Bostwick, Todd W., and Peter Krocek

2002 *Landscape of the Spirits: Hohokam Rock Art at South Mountain Park*. University of Arizona Press, Tucson.

Bousé, Derek

1996 Culture as Nature: How Native American Cultural Antiquities Became Part of the Natural World. *The Public Historian* 18(4):75–98.

Bowdler, Sandra

1988 Repainting Australian Rock Art. *Antiquity* 62:517–523.

Boyd, W. E., Maria M. Cotter, Jane Gardiner, and Gai Taylor

2005 "Rigidity and a Changing Order . . . Disorder, Degeneracy and Dae-monic Repetition": Fluidity of Cultural Values and Cultural Heritage Management. In *Heritage of Value, Archaeology of Renown: Reshaping Archaeological Assessment and Significance*, edited by Clay Mathers, Timothy Darvill, and Barbara J. Little, pp. 89–113. University Press of Florida, Gainesville.

Brady, Liam M., and Paul S. C. Taçon (editors)

2016 *Relating to Rock Art in the Contemporary World: Navigating Symbolism, Meaning, and Significance*. University Press of Colorado, Boulder.

Brown, Michael F.

1998 Can Culture Be Copyrighted? *Current Anthropology* 39:193–222.

2003 *Who Owns Native Culture?* Harvard University Press, Cambridge.

Brummett, Barry

2004 *Rhetorical Homologies: Form, Culture, Experience*. University of Alabama Press, Tuscaloosa.

Brunk, Conrad G., and James O. Young
2012 "The Skin off Our Backs": Appropriation of Religion. In *The Ethics of Cultural Appropriation*, edited by James O. Young and Conrad G. Brunk, pp. 93–114. Wiley-Blackwell, Malden, Massachusetts.

Bsumek, E. M.
2008 *Indian-made: Navajo Culture in the Marketplace, 1868–1940*. University Press of Kansas, Lawrence.

Buescher, Derek T., and Kent A. Ono
1996 Civilized Colonialism: *Pocahontas* as Neocolonial Rhetoric. *Women's Studies in Communication* 19:127–153.

Burke, Kenneth
1966 *Language as Symbolic Action*. University of California Press, Berkeley.
1973 *The Philosophy of Literary Form: Studies in Symbolic Action*. 3rd ed. University of California Press, Berkeley.

Bury, Rick
1999 Too Many Shamans: Ethics and Politics of Rock Art Interpretation. In *American Indian Rock Art*, Vol. 25, edited by Steven M. Freers, pp. 149–154. American Rock Art Research Association, Tucson, Arizona.

Butler, Judith
1990 *Gender Trouble: Feminism and the Subversion of Identity*. Routledge, New York.

Cannon, William J., and Alanah Woody
2007 Toward a Gender-Inclusive View of Rock Art in the Northern Great Basin. In *Great Basin Rock Art: Archaeological Perspectives*, edited by Angus R. Quinlan, pp. 37–51. University of Nevada Press, Reno.

Carey, James W.
1988 *Communication as Culture*. Routledge, New York.

Castleton, Kenneth B.
1984 *Petroglyphs and Pictographs of Utah, Volume One: The East and Northeast*. 2nd, enlarged ed. Utah Museum of Natural History, Salt Lake City.
1987 *Petroglyphs and Pictographs of Utah, Volume Two: The South, Central, West and Northwest*. Rev. ed. Utah Museum of Natural History, Salt Lake City.

Ceccarelli, Leah
1998 Polysemy: Multiple Meanings in Rhetorical Criticism. *Quarterly Journal of Speech* 84:395–415.

Charon, Joel M.
1998 *Symbolic Interactionism: An Introduction, An Interpretation, An Integration*. 6th ed. Prentice Hall, Upper Saddle River, New Jersey.

Cheeks, Lawrence W.
2004 *Kokopelli*. Rio Nuevo, Tucson, Arizona.

Childress, Jane P.
2004 Rock Art and Rock Crawling in Central Arizona. In *American Indian*

Rock Art, Vol. 30, edited by Joseph T. O'Connor, pp. 103–110. American Rock Art Research Association, Tucson, Arizona.

Childs, Craig
2006 *House of Rain: Tracking a Vanished Civilization across the American Southwest.* Back Bay Books, New York.

Chippindale, Christopher
2001 Studying Ancient Pictures as Pictures. In *Handbook of Rock Art Research*, edited by David S. Whitley, pp. 247–272. AltaMira Press, Walnut Creek, California.

Christensen, Don D., Jerry Dickey, and Steven M. Freers
2013 *Rock Art of the Grand Canyon Region.* Sunbelt, San Diego, California.

Church, Lisa
2005 Hopi Group Disputes Popular Perception of the Flute Player. *The Salt Lake Tribune* 28 November. Electronic document, http://archive.sltrib.com, accessed July 2, 2013.

Churchill, Ward
1994 *Indians Are Us?* Common Courage Press, Monroe, Maine.

Clifford, James
1987 Of Other Peoples: Beyond the "Salvage Paradigm." In *Discussions in Contemporary Culture*, edited by Hal Foster, pp. 121–130. Bay, Seattle, Washington.

1988 *The Predicament of Culture: Twentieth-Century Ethnography, Literature, and Art.* Harvard University Press, Cambridge, Massachusetts.

Cloud, Dana L.
1992 The Limits of Interpretation: Ambivalence and Stereotype in *Spencer: For Hire. Critical Studies in Mass Communication* 9:311–324.

Cobb, Amanda J.
2005 The National Museum of the American Indian. *American Indian Quarterly* 29:361–383.

Cockburn, Patrick
1993 US Indian Tribe Enjoys the Fruits of Its "Best Windfall Since Buffalo": The Pequots Are Bigger than Donald Trump in the World of Gambling. *The Independent* 20 December. Electronic document, http://www.independent.co.uk, accessed January 14, 2017.

Coel, Margaret
2007 *The Drowning Man: A Wind River Reservation Mystery.* Berkeley, New York.

Cole, Cyndy
2007 Paintballers Target Picture Canyon. *Arizona Daily Sun* 19 January. Electronic document, azdailysun.com, accessed June 14, 2014.

Cole, Sally J.
1990 *Legacy on Stone: Rock Art of the Colorado Plateau and Four Corners Region.* Johnson Books, Boulder, Colorado.

Colton, Mary Russell F., and Harold S. Colton
1931 Petroglyphs, the Record of a Great Adventure. *American Anthropologist* n.s. 33:32–37.

Colwell-Chanthaphonh, Chip
2010 *Living Histories: Native Americans and Southwestern Archaeology.* AltaMira, Lanham, Maryland.

Colwell-Chanthaphonh, Chip, and T. J. Ferguson
2006 Memory Pieces and Footprints: Multivocality and the Meanings of Ancient Times and Ancestral Places among the Zuni and Hopi. *American Anthropologist* 108:148–162.

Condit, Celeste Michelle
1989 The Rhetorical Limits of Polysemy. *Critical Studies in Mass Communication* 6:103–122.

Connell, Raewyn
1995 *Masculinities.* Polity, Sydney, Australia.

Conservation and Protection Committee
1988 *Conservation Guidelines of the American Rock Art Research Association.* American Rock Art Research Association, San Miguel, California.

Crotty, Helen K. (editor)
1989 *Preserving Our Rock Art Heritage: Proceedings from the Symposium on Rock Art Conservation and Protection.* Occasional Paper 1. American Rock Art Research Association, San Miguel, California.

CyArk
2013 Hopi Petroglyph Sites. Electronic document, http://www.cyark.org/ projects/hopi-petroglyph-sites/in-depth, accessed April 8, 2017.

Dandridge, Debra E., and James K. Meen
2003 The Degradation of Rock Art by Lichen Processes. In *American Indian Rock Art*, Vol. 29, edited by Alanah Woody and Joseph T. O'Connor, pp. 43–52. American Rock Art Research Association, Tucson, Arizona.

Dean, J. Claire
1998a Grappling with Graffiti at Petroglyph National Monument. In *American Indian Rock Art*, Vol. 22, edited by Steven M. Freers, pp. 111–117. American Rock Art Research Association, Tucson, Arizona.
1998b The Kokopelli Dilemma: The Use, Abuse, and Care of Rock Art. *La Pintura* 25(5):1, 6–12.

Debord, Guy
1983 *Society of the Spectacle.* Black and Red, Detroit, Michigan.

Delabarre, Edmund Burke
1928 *Dighton Rock: A Study of the Written Rocks of New England.* Walter Neale, New York. Electronic document, https://archive.org/details/ dightonrockstudy00dela, accessed March 15, 2017.

Deloria, Philip J.
1998 *Playing Indian.* Yale University Press, New Haven, Connecticut.

Deloria, Vine
1995 *Red Earth, White Lies: Native Americans and the Myth of Scientific Fact.* Scribner, New York.
2003 *God Is Red: A Native View of Religion.* 30th anniversary ed. Fulcrum, Golden, Colorado.

DeLuca, Kevin Michael, and Anne Teresa Demo
2000 Imaging Nature: Watkins, Yosemite, and the Birth of Environmentalism. *Critical Studies in Media Communication* 17:241–260.

Dickey, Jerry
2012 Rock Art Organizations, Visitation, and the Destruction of Rock Art Sites. *La Pintura* 38(3):5–7, 13.

Dilworth, Leah
1996 *Imagining Indians in the Southwest: Persistent Visions of a Primitive Past.* Smithsonian Institution Press, Washington, DC.

Dowson, Thomas A.
1999 Off the Rocks, onto T-Shirts, Canvasses, etc. . . . Power and the Popular Consumption of Rock Art Imagery. In *Rock Art and Ethics: A Dialogue,* edited by William D. Hyder, pp. 1–19. Occasional Paper 3. American Rock Art Research Association, Tucson, Arizona.
2001 Queer Theory and Feminist Theory: Toward a Sociology of Sexual Politics in Rock Art Research. In *Theoretical Perspectives in Rock Art Research,* edited by Knut Helskog, pp. 312–329. Institute for Comparative Research in Human Culture, Oslo, Norway.

Draper, Scottie
2014 Kokopelli Finds a New Home in Price. ETV 10 News 5 July. Electronic document, http://etv10news.com/kokopelli-finds-a-new-home-in-price/, accessed January 14, 2017.

Earth Studio
2005 Earth Studio, Tucson, Arizona. Electronic document, http://www.earthstudiomoab.com/home/es1/page_55_17, accessed July 5, 2005.

Ensenbach, Donald L.
2012 *Kokopelli: Dream Catcher of an Ancient.* Tate, Mustang, Oklahoma.

Evans, Michael J., Richard W. Stoffle, and Sandra Lee Pinel
1993 *Petroglyph National Monument Rapid Ethnographic Assessment Project.* University of Arizona Bureau of Applied Research in Anthropology, Tucson. Electronic document, https://arizona.openrepository.com/arizona/bitstream/10150/272097/1/azu_stoffle_new_mexico_petroglyph_nm_w.pdf, accessed January 14, 2017.

Fabian, Johannes
1983 *Time and the Other: How Anthropology Makes Its Object.* Columbia University Press, New York.

Faludi, Susan
1999 *Stiffed: The Betrayal of the American Man*. HarperCollins, New York.
Farnsworth, Janet Webb
2006 *Rock Art along the Way*. Rio Nuevo, Tucson, Arizona.
Ferber, Abby L.
2004 Racial Warriors and Weekend Warriors: The Construction of Masculinity in Mythopoetic and White Supremacist Discourse. In *Feminisms and Masculinities*, edited by Peter F. Murphy, pp. 228–243. Oxford University Press, Oxford, England.
Ferguson, T. J., and K. F. Anschuetz
2003 Ethnographic Landscapes in the Petroglyph National Monument: Working with Traditionally Associated Peoples in New Mexico. In *Traditionally Associated Peoples and Ethnographic Resources*. National Park Service, US Department of the Interior. Electronic document, http://www.nps.gov/ ethnography/training/TAPS/petro.htm, accessed January 14, 2017.
Fewkes, Jesse Walter
1903 Hopi Katcinas, Drawn by Native Artists. In *Twenty-First Annual Report of the Bureau of American Ethnology*, J. W. Powell, pp. 3–126. Government Printing Office, Washington, DC.
Fine, Michelle, Lois Weis, Judi Addelston, and Julia Marusza
1997 (In)Secure Times: Constructing White Working-Class Masculinities in the Late 20th Century. *Gender & Society* 11:52–68.
Firnhaber, Michael Paul
2007 *Experiencing Rock Art: A Phenomenological Investigation of the Barrier Canyon Tradition*. Doctoral dissertation, Department of Anthropology, University College of London, London.
Fish, Stanley
1998 Boutique Multiculturalism. In *Multiculturalism and American Democracy*, edited by Arthur Melzer, Jerry Weinberger, and Richard Zinman, pp. 69–88. University Press of Kansas, Lawrence.
Fiske, John
1986 Television: Polysemy and Popularity. *Critical Studies in Mass Communication* 3:391–408.
1989 *Understanding Popular Culture*. Unwin Hyman, Boston.
1990 *Introduction to Communication Studies*. 2nd ed. Routledge, New York.
1991a Writing Ethnographies: Contributions to a Dialogue. *Quarterly Journal of Speech* 77:330–335.
1991b For Cultural Interpretation: A Study of the Culture of Homelessness. *Critical Studies in Mass Communication* 8:455–474.
Forsyth, Bob
2015 Southern Nevada Rock Art: Petroglyph/Rock Art Sites in the Southwest, with a Focus on Southern Nevada. Electronic document, www. nevadarockart.info, accessed July 10, 2015.

Foucault, Michel

1970 *The Order of Things: An Archaeology of the Human Sciences.* Vintage, New York.

1972 *The Archaeology of Knowledge & the Discourse on Language.* Translated by A. M. Sheridan Smith. Pantheon, New York.

Francis, Julie

2005 Pictographs, Petroglyphs, and Paradigms: Rock Art in North American Archaeology. In *Discovering North American Rock Art*, edited by Lawrence L. Loendorf, Christopher Chippindale, and David S. Whitley, pp. 181–195. University of Arizona Press, Tucson.

Galloway, Patricia

1998 Where Have All the Menstrual Huts Gone? The Invisibility of Menstrual Seclusion in the Late Prehistoric Southeast. In *Reader in Gender Archaeology*, edited by Kelley Hays-Gilpin and David S. Whitley, pp. 197–211. Routledge, New York.

Garb, Yaakov Gerome

1990 Perspective or Escape? Ecofeminist Musings on Contemporary Earth Imagery. In *Reweaving the World: The Emergence of Ecofeminism*, edited by Irene Diamond and Gloria Feman Orenstein, pp. 264–278. Sierra Club Books, San Francisco, California.

Geertz, Aarmin W.

1994 *The Invention of Prophecy: Continuity and Meaning in Hopi Indian Religion.* University of California Press, Berkeley.

Geertz, Clifford

1973 *The Interpretation of Cultures.* Basic Books, New York.

Gidley, Mick

1998 *Edward S. Curtis and the North American Indian, Incorporated.* Cambridge University Press, Cambridge, England.

Gilchrist, Roberta

1999 *Gender and Archaeology: Contesting the Past.* Routledge, New York.

Gilman, Sander L.

1985 *Difference and Pathology.* Cornell University Press, Ithaca, New York.

Gilreath, Amy J., Ginny Bengston, and Brandon Patterson

2011 *Ethnographic and Archaeological Inventory and Evaluation of Black Canyon, Lincoln County, Nevada, Volume 1: Report and Appendices A–F.* Far Western Archaeological Research Group, Davis, California. Submitted to US Fish and Wildlife Service, Portland, Oregon.

Gladwin, Harold Sterling

1957 *A History of the Ancient Southwest.* Bond Wheelwright, Portland, Maine.

Gladwin, Harold S., Emil W. Haury, E. B. Sayles, and Nora Gladwin

1937 *Excavations at Snaketown: Material Culture.* Medallion Papers No.

XXV. Privately printed for Gila Pueblo, Globe, Arizona, by Lancaster Press, Lancaster Pennsylvania.

Glover, Wayne
1995 *Kokopelli: Ancient Myth/Modern Icon*. Camelback/Canyonlands, Bellemont, Arizona.

Glowacka, M. D.
1998 Ritual Knowledge in Hopi Tradition. *American Indian Quarterly* 22:386–392.

Gonzales, Gloria
1997 Archeologist Leads Viewers to Pictographs; Guidebook Casts Light on Area Cave Art. *Daily News* 10 August. Electronic document, www.thefreelibrary.com, accessed January 14, 2017.

Good, Leslie
1989 Power, Hegemony, and Communication Theory. In *Cultural Politics in Contemporary America*, edited by Ian Angus and Sut Jhally, pp. 51–64. Routledge, New York.

Goodwin, Andrew, and Joe Gore
1990 World Beat and the Cultural Imperialism Debate. *Socialist Review* 20(3):63–80.

Gramsci, Antonio
1971 *Selections from the Prison Notebooks of Antonio Gramsci*. Edited and translated by Quintin Hoare and Geoffrey Nowell Smith. International, New York.

Grant, Campbell
1967 *Rock Art of the American Indian*. Thomas Y. Crowell, New York.
1968 *Rock Drawings of the Coso Range*. Maturango Museum, China Lake, California.
1978 *Canyon de Chelly: Its People and Rock Art*. University of Arizona Press, Tucson.

Greer Services
2015 Rock Art Research. Electronic document, http://greerservices.com/html/RockArtFrameset.html, accessed July 10, 2015.

Gronemann, Barbara
2014 Rock Art at Taliesin West. *La Pintura* 40(4):7–9.

Gruber, Jacob W.
1970 Ethnographic Salvage and the Shaping of Anthropology. *American Anthropologist* 72:1289–1299.

Guest, Richard A.
1995/1996 Intellectual Property Rights and Native American Tribes. *American Indian Law Review* 20:111–139.

Hall, Stuart
1980 Encoding/Decoding. In *Culture, Media, Language: Working Papers in*

Cultural Studies, 1972–79, edited by Stuart Hall, pp. 128–138. Hutchinson, London.

1985 Signification, Representation, Ideology: Althusser and the Post-Structuralist Debates. *Critical Studies in Mass Communication* 2:91–114.

Hampson, Jamie

2013 Rock Art Heritage and the (Re)Negotiation of Post-Colonial Identities. In *Heritage Studies: Stories in the Making*, edited by Meghan Bowe, Bianca Carpeneti, Ian Dull, and Jesse Lipkowitz, pp. 141–170. Cambridge Scholars Publishing, Cambridge, England.

Harding, Sandra

1991 *Whose Science? Whose Knowledge? Thinking from Women's Lives.* Cornell University Press, Ithaca, New York.

Harris, Rick

1995 *Easy Field Guide to Rock Art Symbols of the Southwest.* American Traveler Press, Phoenix, Arizona.

Harrison, Benjamin

2012 Location of the Book of Mormon Lands. 11 November. Discussion thread. LDS Freedom Forum. Electronic document, http://www.ldsfreedomforum.com/viewtopic.php?f=14&t=24264&start=60, accessed January 14, 2017.

Haury, Emil W.

1976 *The Hohokam: Desert Farmers and Craftsmen, Excavations at Snaketown, 1964–1965.* University of Arizona Press, Tucson.

Hawley, Florence

1937 Kokopelli, of the Prehistoric Southwestern Pueblo Pantheon. *American Anthropologist* n.s. 39:644–646.

Hays-Gilpin, Kelley A.

2004 *Ambiguous Images: Gender and Rock Art.* AltaMira Press, Walnut Creek, California.

2005 From Fertility Shrines to Sacred Landscapes: A Critical Review of Gendered Rock Art Research in the Western United States. In *Discovering North American Rock Art*, edited by Lawrence L. Loendorf, Christopher Chippindale, and David S. Whitley, pp. 196–216. University of Arizona Press, Tucson.

Hedges, Ken

1985 Rock Art Portrayals of Shamanic Transformation and Magical Flight. In *Rock Art Papers*, Vol. 2, edited by Ken Hedges, pp. 83–94. San Diego Museum Papers No. 18. San Diego Museum of Man, San Diego, California.

2001 Traversing the Great Gray Middle Ground: An Examination of Shamanistic Interpretation of Rock Art. In *American Indian Rock Art*, Vol. 27, edited by Steven M. Freers and Alanah Woody, pp. 123–136. American Rock Art Research Association, Tucson, Arizona.

Heizer, Robert F., and Martin A. Baumhoff
1962 *Prehistoric Rock Art of Nevada and Eastern California*. University of California Press, Berkeley.

Heyd, Thomas
2003 Rock Art Aesthetics and Cultural Appropriation. *The Journal of Aesthetics and Art Criticism* 61:37–46.

Heyser, Doak
2015 Southwestern United States Rock Art Gallery. Electronic document, net.indra.com/~dheyser/rockart.html, accessed July 10, 2015.

Hinsley, Curtis M.
1996 The Promise of the Southwest. In *The Southwest in the American Imagination: The Writings of Sylvester Baxter, 1881–1889*, edited by Curtis M. Hinsley and David R. Wilcox, pp. 181–206. University of Arizona Press, Tucson.

Hollimon, Sandra E.
2001 The Gendered Peopling of North America: Addressing the Antiquity of Systems of Multiple Genders. In *The Archaeology of Shamanism*, edited by Neil Price, pp. 123–134. Routledge, New York.

Hopi Cultural Preservation Office
2009 Traditional Knowledge. Electronic document, http://www8.nau. edu/~hcpo-p/knowledge.html, accessed June 30, 2015.

Hopi Staff
2004 Cultural Theft and Misrepresentation. The Hopi Tribe. 22 August. Electronic document, http://www.hopi.nsn.us/view_article.asp?id=20 &cat=1, accessed July 2, 2015.

Huang, Jennifer K. K.
2010 *Petroglyphs of Baby Canyon Pueblo, Agua Fria National Monument, Arizona: Archaeological Contributions to the Human Geographical Perspective*. OCRM Report No. 98. Arizona State University Office of Cultural Resource Management, Tempe.

Huff, Dan
2000 Sharp Shooters: A Trio of Legendary Landscape Photographers Celebrates "Arizona Highways" and Byways at the Center For Creative Photography. *Tucson Weekly* 16 March. Electronic document, http:// www.tucsonweekly.com/tucson/sharp-shooters/Content?oid=1066068, accessed January 14, 2017.

Huhndorf, Shari M.
2001 *Going Native: Indians in the American Cultural Imagination*. Cornell University Press, Ithaca, New York.

Hurst, Winston B., and Joe Pachak
1989 *Spirit Windows: Native American Rock Art of Southeastern Utah*. Spirit Windows Project, Blanding, Utah.

Hyder, William D., and Lawrence L. Loendorf
2005 The Role of Avocational Archaeologists in Rock Art Research. In

Discovering North American Rock Art, edited by Lawrence L. Loendorf, Christopher Chippindale, and David S. Whitley, pp. 228–239. University of Arizona Press, Tucson.

IMDb

2015 *Chico, the Misunderstood Coyote*. IMDb. Electronic document, http://www.imdb.com/title/tt0205814/, accessed January 14, 2017.

Indian Arts and Crafts Board

2015 The Indian Arts and Crafts Act of 1990. US Department of the Interior. Electronic document, http://www.iacb.doi.gov/act.html, accessed January 14, 2017.

Jameson, Fredric

1991 *Postmodernism, or, the Cultural Logic of Late Capitalism*. Duke University Press, Durham, North Carolina.

Jandt, Fred, and Heather Hundley

2007 Intercultural Dimensions of Communicating Masculinities. *The Journal of Men's Studies* 15:216–231.

Jarrard, G. M.

2012 *Petroglyph*. Preservation Books. Self-published.

Kadish, Lesley V.

2004 Reading Cereal Boxes: Pre-packaging History and Indigenous Identities. *Americana: The Journal of American Popular Culture (1900–present)* 3(2). Electronic document, http://www.americanpopularculture.com/journal/articles/fall_2004/kadish.htm, accessed January 14, 2017.

Kaibab National Forest

2010 Vandalized Keyhole Sink Petroglyph Panel Receives Restoration Work. Press release 19 November. Forest Service, United States Department of Agriculture. Electronic document, http://www.fs.usda.gov/detail/kaibab/news-events/?cid=STELPRDB5226821, accessed January 14, 2017.

Kaplan, Ann (editor)

1988 *Postmodernism and Its Discontents: Theories, Practices*. Verso, New York.

Kehoe, Alice B.

1999 Where Were Wovoka and Wuzzie George? In *Julian Steward and the Great Basin*, edited by Richard O. Clemmer, L. Daniel Myers, and Mary Elizabeth Rudden, pp. 164–169. University of Utah Press, Salt Lake City.

2002 Emerging Trends *Versus* the Popular Paradigm in Rock-Art Research. *Antiquity* 76:384–385.

Kelen, Leslie, and David Sucec

1996 *Sacred Images: A Vision of Native American Rock Art*. Gibbs-Smith, Salt Lake City, Utah.

Kelly, Isabel T.

1936 Chemehuevi Shamanism. In *Essays in Anthropology: Presented to A. L.*

Kroeber in Celebration of His Sixtieth Birthday June 11, 1936, edited by
Robert H. Lowie, pp. 129–142. University of California Press, Berkeley.
1939 Southern Paiute Shamanism. *Anthropological Records* 2(4):151–167.
University of California Press, Berkeley.
2016 *Isabel T. Kelly's Southern Paiute Ethnographic Field Notes, 1932–1934,
Las Vegas.* Compiled and edited by Catherine S. Fowler and Darla
Garey-Sage. The University of Utah Anthropological Papers No. 130.
University of Utah Press, Salt Lake City.

Kent, Susan
1999 Egalitarianism, Equality, and Equitable Power. In *Manifesting Power:
Gender and the Interpretation of Power in Archaeology*, edited by Tracy L.
Sweely, pp. 30–48. Routledge, New York.

Keyser, James D., and Michael A. Klassen
2001 *Plains Indian Rock Art.* University of Washington Press, Seattle.

Keyser, James D., and David S. Whitley
2006 Sympathetic Magic in Western North American Rock Art. *American
Antiquity* 71:3–26.

Kimmel, Michael S.
1987 Rethinking "Masculinity": New Directions in Research. In *Changing
Men, Changing Men: New Directions in Research on Men and Masculinity*, edited by Michael S. Kimmel, pp. 9–24. Sage, Newbury Park,
California.

King, C. Richard
1998 *Colonial Discourses, Collective Memories, and the Exhibition of Native
American Cultures and Histories in the Contemporary United States.*
Garland, New York.

King, Larry
2002 Conservation and Management Concerns in the Development of
Rock Climbing Areas at Three Central Oregon Pictograph Sites. In
American Indian Rock Art, Vol. 28, edited by Alanah Woody, pp. 63–72.
American Rock Art Research Association, Tucson, Arizona.

King of the Hill Wiki
2013 John Redcorn. Electronic document, http://kingofthehill.wikia.com/
wiki/John_Redcorn, accessed October 7, 2017.

Kitchell, Jennifer A.
2010 Basketmaker and Archaic Rock Art of the Colorado Plateau: A
Reinterpretation of Paleoimagery. *American Antiquity* 75:819–840.

Kloor, Keith
2009 Insider: Who Were the Anasazi? *Archaeology* 62(6). Electronic document, http://archive.archaeology.org/0911/etc/insider.html, accessed
January 14, 2017.

Knaak, Manfred
1988 *The Forgotten Artist: Indians of Anza-Borrego and Their Rock Art.*

Anza-Borrego Desert Natural History Association, Borrego Springs, California.

Kokopelli Kingdom
2005 Welcome to Kokopelli Kingdom. Electronic document, http://www.angelfire.com/ny4/HOMEPAGE/kokokingdom.html, accessed October 7, 2017.

Kokopelli.com
2001 Electronic document, http://www.kokopelli.com/kokopellidotcom/kokdec.html, accessed July 5, 2005.

Kolber, Jane
2000 Variations of Human Figures through Time and Space at Baird's Chevelon Steps. In *1999 International Rock Art Congress Proceedings*, Vol. 1, edited by Peggy Whitehead and Lawrence Loendorf, pp. 67–74. American Rock Art Research Association, Tucson, Arizona.

Kroeber, A. L.
1925 *Handbook of the Indians of California*. Smithsonian Institution Bureau of Ethnology Bulletin 78. Government Printing Office, Washington, DC.

Krupp, E. C., Evelyn Billo, and Robert Mark
2010 Star Trek: Recovery and Review of the First Alleged Supernova Rock Art. *Archaeoastronomy* 23:35–43.

Kumiega, Karen, and Gwen Walter
2001 Toquima Cave National Register of Historic Places Registration Form. 29 June. National Park Service, United States Department of Interior.

Kuwanwisiwma, Leigh J., Stewart B. Koyiyumptewa, and Anita Poleahla
2012 Pasiwvi: Place of Deliberations. In *Hisat'sinom: Ancient Peoples in a Land without Water*, edited by Christian E. Downum, pp. 7–9. School for Advanced Research Press, Santa Fe, New Mexico.

Lacroix, Celeste C.
2011 High Stakes Stereotypes: The Emergence of the "Casino Indian" Trope in Television Depictions of Contemporary Native Americans. *The Howard Journal of Communications* 22:1–23.

Lawlor, Mary
2006 *Public Native America: Tribal Self-Representation in Museums, Powwows, and Casinos*. Rutgers University Press, New Brunswick, New Jersey.

Layton, Robert, and Julian Thomas
2001 Introduction: The Destruction and Conservation of Cultural Property. In *Destruction and Conservation of Cultural Property*, edited by Robert Layton, Peter G. Stone, and Julian Thomas, pp. 1–21. Routledge, New York.

Lee, Georgia
1991 *Rock Art and Cultural Resource Management*. Wormwood Press, Calabasas, California.

Lekson, Stephen H.
2008 *A History of the Ancient Southwest*. School for Advanced Research Press, Sante Fe, New Mexico.

Lewis-Williams, J. David
1995 Some Aspects of Rock Art Research in the Politics of Present-Day South Africa. In *Perceiving Rock Art: Social and Political Perspectives*, edited by Knut Helsog and Bjomar Olsen, pp. 317–337. Instituttet for Sammenlignende Kulturforskning, Oslo, Norway.
2001 Brainstorming Images: Neuropsychology and Rock Art Research. In *Handbook of Rock Art Research*, edited by David S. Whitley, pp. 332–357. AltaMira Press, Walnut Creek, California.
2002 *The Mind in the Cave: Consciousness and the Origins of Art*. Thames & Hudson, London.
2003 Putting the Record Straight: Rock Art and Shamanism. *Antiquity* 77:165–170.
2006 The Evolution of Theory, Method and Technique in Southern African Rock Art Research. *Journal of Archaeological Method and Theory* 13:343–377.

Lewis-Williams, J. David, and Thomas A. Dowson
1988 The Signs of All Times: Entoptic Phenomena in Upper Palaeolithic Art. *Current Anthropology* 29:201–245.
1990 Through the Veil: San Rock Paintings and the Rock Face. *South African Archaeological Bulletin* 45:5–16.

Lincoln County Nevada
2014a *Rock Art Guide*. LincolnCountyNevada.com. Electronic document, www.birdandhike.com/Glyphs/LincolnCo/LincolnCoRockArtGuide. pdf, accessed July 28, 2014.
2014b LincolnCountyNevada.com. Electronic document, http://lincoln countynevada.com, accessed January 14, 2017.

Loendorf, Larry
2001 Rock Art Recording. In *Handbook of Rock Art Research*, edited by David S. Whitley, pp. 55–79. AltaMira Press, Walnut Creek, California.

Loendorf, Lawrence L., Christopher Chippindale, and David S. Whitley
2005 The Discovery of North American Rock Art and Its Meanings. In *Discovering North American Rock Art*, edited by Lawrence L. Loendorf, Christopher Chippindale, and David S. Whitley, pp. 3–7. University of Arizona Press, Tucson.

Loubser, Johannes
2001 Management Planning for Conservation. In *Handbook of Rock Art Research*, edited by David S. Whitley, pp. 80–115. AltaMira Press, Walnut Creek, California.

Lowe, Sam
2001 World's Largest Kokopelli in Camp Verde. *Arizona Oddities* 18 October. Electronic document, http://arizonaoddities.com/2011/10/ worlds-largest-kokopelli-in-camp-verde/, accessed June 2, 2014.

Lull, James

2000 *Media, Communication, Culture: A Global Approach.* 2nd ed. Columbia University Press, New York.

Lyman, Christopher. M.

1982 *The Vanishing Race and Other Illusions: Photographs of Indians by Edward S. Curtis.* Smithsonian Institution Press, Washington, DC.

McCreery, Patricia, and Ekkehart Malotki

1994 *Tapamveni: The Rock Art Galleries of Petrified Forest and Beyond.* Petrified Forest Museum Association, Petrified Forest National Park, Arizona.

McGregor, John C.

1943 Burial of an Early American Magician. *Proceedings of the American Philosophical Society* 86(2):270–298.

McLeod, C. (producer/director)

2002 *In the Light of Reverence.* Videocassette. Bullfrog Films, Oley, Pennsylvania.

McPeak, Tamara

2004 *The Educational Function of Native American Art Shops in Flagstaff, Arizona.* Master's thesis, Department of Anthropology, Florida State University, Tallahassee. Electronic document, http://diginole.lib.fsu.edu/islandora/object/fsu%3A180798, accessed January 14, 2017.

Mallery, Garrick

1894 *Picture-Writing of the American Indians.* Extract of the Tenth Annual Report of the Bureau of Ethnology, Smithsonian Institution. Government Printing Office, Washington, DC. Electronic document, http://library.si.edu/digital-library/book/picturewritingofoomall, accessed February 12, 2017.

Malotki, Ekkehart

2000 *Kokopelli: The Making of an Icon.* University of Nebraska Press, Lincoln.

2003 Liminal Animals in the Archaic/Basketmaker II Rock Art Iconography of the Palavayu Anthropomorphic Style (PASTYLE), Arizona. In *American Indian Rock Art,* Vol. 29, edited by Alanah Woody and Joseph T. O'Connor, pp. 139–154. American Rock Art Research Association, Tucson, Arizona.

2007 *The Rock Art of Arizona: Art for Life's Sake.* Kiva, Walnut, California.

Malotki, Ekkehart, and Donald E. Weaver

2002 *Stone Chisel and Yucca Brush: Colorado Plateau Rock Art.* Kiva, Walnut, California.

Mancini, Salvatore

1996 *On the Edge of Magic: Petroglyphs and Rock Paintings of the Ancient Southwest.* Chronicle Books, San Francisco, California.

Marcom, Geron

2006 Death Valley's Other Moving Rocks: A Brief Look at Some Rock Art

Boulders That Have Been Purposely Moved from Their Original Sites. Electronic document, http://www.petroglyphs.us/article_death_valley's_other_moving_rocks.htm, accessed June 2, 2014.

Mark, Robert, and Evelyn Billo
1999 A Stitch in Time: Digital Panoramas and Mosaics. In *American Indian Rock Art*, Vol. 25, edited by Steven M. Freers, pp. 155–168. American Rock Art Research Association, Tucson, Arizona.

Martin, Emily
1991 The Egg and the Sperm. *Signs* 19:485–501.

Martineau, LaVan
1973 *The Rocks Begin to Speak*. KC Publications, Las Vegas, Nevada.

Marubbio, M. Elise
2006 *Killing the Indian Maiden: Images of Native American Women in Film*. University Press of Kentucky, Lexington.

Marx, Karl
1986 *Karl Marx: The Essential Writings*. 2nd ed. Edited by Frederic L. Bender. Westview Press, Boulder, Colorado.

Marymor, Leigh
1998 Promoting Visitation to Rock Art on Public Lands. *La Pintura* 25(2):13–14.
1999–2000 We Get Letters . . . Publication of a Guide to Rock Art Sites. *La Pintura* 26(3):9–10.
2001 *ARARA Guidelines for Managers of Rock Art on Public Lands: Public Access*. ARARA Conservation and Protection Committee. American Rock Art Research Association. Electronic document, www.arara.org, accessed January 14, 2017.

Mathers, Clay, Timothy Darvill, and Barbara J. Little (editors)
2005 *Heritage of Value, Archaeology of Renown: Reshaping Archaeological Assessment and Significance*. University Press of Florida, Gainesville.

Meighan, Clement W.
1982 Rock Art and Archaeology. In *American Indian Rock Art*, Vols. 7–8, edited by Frank G. Bock, pp. 225–229. American Rock Art Research Association, El Toro, California.

Menkes, Dove
2007 Giants and Dinosaurs in the Grand Canyon: Samuel Hubbard and the 1924 Doheny Scientific Expedition. *The Journal of Arizona History*, 48(1):53–88.

Miller, Autumn, and Susan Dente Ross
2004 They Are Not Us: Framing of American Indians by the *Boston Globe*. *The Howard Journal of Communications* 15:245–259.

Miller, Layne
2000 Vandal Disfigures Popular Pictograph in San Rafael Reef—Vandal

Scrawls on Pictograph in Emery County. *Salt Lake Tribune* 28 March. Electronic document, newsbank.com, accessed June 2, 2013.

Mills, Barbara J.

2004 The Establishment and Defeat of Hierarchy: Inalienable Possessions and the History of Collective Prestige Structures in the Pueblo Southwest. *American Anthropologist* 106:238–251.

Mirabel, Robert Wayne

2007 Introduction. In *Kokopelli: The Magic, Mirth, and Mischief of an Ancient Symbol*, by Dennis Slifer, pp. xii–xiv. Gibbs Smith, Salt Lake City, Utah.

Molyneaux, Brian Leigh

1998 The History of Rock Art as a History of Perception in Archaeology. Paper presented at the 63rd Annual Meeting of the Society for American Archaeology, Seattle, Washington.

Monteleone, Sue Ann

1998 Great Basin Rock Art: Numic Tradition or Multicultural Diversity? In *American Indian Rock Art*, Vol. 22, edited by Steven M. Freers, pp. 19–28. American Rock Art Research Association, Tucson, Arizona.

Monteleone, Sue Ann, and Alanah Woody

1999 Changing Light on the Cosos. In *American Indian Rock Art*, Vol. 25, edited by Steven M. Freers, pp. 57–68. American Rock Art Research Association, Tucson, Arizona.

Moore, Sabra

1998 *Petroglyphs: Ancient Language/Sacred Art*. Clear Light, Santa Fe, New Mexico.

Mowaljarlai, David, Patricia Vinnicombe, Graeme K. Ward, and Christopher Chippindale

1988 Repainting of Images on Rock in Australia and the Maintenance of Aboriginal Culture. *Antiquity* 62:690–696.

Mowljarlai, David, and Cyril Peck

1987 Ngarinyin Cultural Continuity: A Project to Teach the Young People the Culture, Including the Re-painting of Wandjina Rock Art Sites. *Australian Aboriginal Studies* 2:71–78.

Muench, David

1995 San Francisco Peaks through Petroglyph (F-6246.jpg). Photoshelter and Muench Photography. Electronic document, http://muench.photoshelter.com/gallery-list, accessed July 16, 2015.

Muench, David (photographer), and Polly Schaafsma (writer)

1995 *Images in Stone*. BrownTrout, San Francisco, California.

Muller, Seth

2011 Rock Art Rebound. *Arizona Daily Sun* 9 February. Electronic document, azdailysun.com, accessed March 13, 2013.

Munro, Shelley

2010 *Seeking Kokopelli*. Electronic book. Samhain, Macon, Georgia.

Murray, William Breen
2004 Marking Places: Graffiti, Inscriptions, and Rock Art in Northeast Mexico (and Elsewhere). In *American Indian Rock Art*, Vol. 30, edited by Joseph T. O'Connor, pp. 129–136. American Rock Art Research Association, Tucson, Arizona.
2011 Rock Art? Or Graphic Rock Manifestations. *La Pintura* 37(1):12.
Museum of Northern Arizona
2013 Easton Collection Center. Electronic document, http://musnaz.org/collections/easton-collection-center/, accessed January 14, 2017.
Nakai, R. Carlos
2007 Foreword. In *Kokopelli: The Magic, Mirth, and Mischief of an Ancient Symbol*, by Dennis Slifer, pp. ix–xi. Gibbs Smith, Salt Lake City, Utah.
Nakayama, Thomas K., and Robert L. Krizek
1995 Whiteness: A Strategic Rhetoric. *Quarterly Journal of Speech* 81:291–309.
Nelson, John, Allan Megill, and Donald N. McCloskey (editors)
1987 *The Rhetoric of the Human Sciences: Language and Argument in Scholarship and Public Affairs*. University of Wisconsin Press, Madison.
Nelson, Sarah Milledge
1997 *Gender in Archaeology: Analyzing Power and Prestige*. AltaMira Press, Walnut Creek, California.
2006 Introduction: Archaeological Perspectives on Gender. In *Handbook of Gender in Archaeology*, edited by Sarah Milledge Nelson, pp. 1–27. AltaMira Press, Lanham, Maryland.
Neumann, Mark
1999 *On the Rim: Looking for the Grand Canyon*. University of Minnesota Press, Minneapolis.
Nevada Rock Art Foundation
2012 *Lagomarsino Canyon: 10,000 Years of Art*. Public Education Series No. 1. Nevada Rock Art Foundation. Electronic document, http://www.nvrockart.org, accessed January 14, 2017.
2014 The Nevada Rock Art Foundation. Electronic document, www.nvrockart.org, accessed January 14, 2017.
New Mexico Department of Cultural Affairs
2014 Report to the Indian Affairs Committee of the New Mexico Legislature: Zia Pueblo. Electronic document, https://www.nmlegis.gov/handouts/IAC%20092914%20Item%206%20FINAL%20REPORT%20Zia%20Sun%20Symbol%20ekm%209%2029%202014.pdf, accessed March 18, 2017.
Nicholas, George P., and Alison Wylie
2012 Archaeological Finds: Legacies of Appropriation, Modes of Response. In *The Ethics of Cultural Appropriation*, edited by James O. Young and Conrad G. Brunk, pp. 11–54. Wiley-Blackwell, Malden, Massachusetts.

Norman, V. Garth
    2007 *The Parowan Gap: Nature's Perfect Observatory.* Rev. ed. CFI,
    Springville, Utah.
O'Connor, Sue, Anthony Barham, and Donny Woolagoodja
    2008 Painting and Repainting in the West Kimberley. *Australian Aboriginal
    Studies* 1:22–38.
Ono, Kent A., and Derek T. Buescher
    2001 *D*eciphering Pocahontas: Unpackaging the Commodification of a
    Native American Woman. *Critical Studies in Media Communication*
    18:23–43.
Park, Willard Z.
    1934 Paviotso Shamanism. *American Anthropologist* n.s. 36:98–113.
Patterson, Alex
    1992 *A Field Guide to Rock Art Symbols of the Greater Southwest.* Johnson
    Books, Boulder, Colorado.
Pearce, W. Barnett
    1989 *Communication and the Human Condition.* Southern Illinois University
    Press, Carbondale.
Pearson, James L.
    2002 *Shamanism and the Ancient Mind: A Cognitive Approach to Archaeology.*
    AltaMira Press, Walnut Creek, California.
Peña, Anthony L.
    1996 Kokopelli—Pueblo Native American Indian Archetype of The
    Trickster. *The Zodiac Master.* Electronic document, http://thezodiac.
    com/koko.htm, accessed October 7, 2017.
Pendegraft, Signa W.
    2007 Grinding Stone and Pecking Rock: Rock Art of the High Basins, Spanish
    Springs, Nevada. In *Great Basin Rock Art: Archaeological Perspectives,* edited
    by Angus R. Quinlan, pp. 52–68. University of Nevada Press, Reno.
Peters, John Durham
    1999 *Speaking into the Air: A History of the Idea of Communication.* Univer-
    sity of Chicago Press, Chicago.
Petry, Bill
    2013 *Petroglyphs in Your Pocket: A New Field Guide to Rock Art.* Bill Petry,
    Forestville, California.
Pilles, Peter J.
    1989 Public Education and the Management of Rock Art Sites on the
    Coconino National Forest. In *Preserving Our Rock Art Heritage: Proceed-
    ings from the Symposium on Rock Art Conservation and Protection,* edited
    by Helen K. Crotty, pp. 23–34. Occasional Paper 1. American Rock Art
    Research Association, San Miguel, California.
Plumwood, Val
    1993 *Feminism and the Mastery of Nature.* Routledge, New York.

Poor, Martin, and Hannah Rachel Bell
2012 "Rock-art," "Animism" and Two-way Thinking: Towards a Complementary Epistemology in the Understanding of Material Culture and "Rock-art" of Hunting and Gathering People. *Journal of Archaeological Method and Theory* 19:161–205.

Price, Nicholas Stanley
1989 What Makes a Conservation Treatment Acceptable or Not? In *Preserving Our Rock Art Heritage: Proceedings from the Symposium on Rock Art Conservation and Protection*, edited by Helen K. Crotty, pp. 17–22. Occasional Paper 1. American Rock Art Research Association, San Miguel, California.

Prokos, Anastasia, and Irene Padavic
2002 "There Oughta Be a Law against Bitches": Masculinity Lessons in Police Academy Training. *Gender, Work and Organization* 9:439–459.

Quinlan, Angus R.
2000 The Ventriloquist's Dummy: A Critical Review of Shamanism and Rock Art in Far Western North America. *Journal of California and Great Basin Anthropology* 22:92–108.
2007a Rock Art as an Artifact of Religion and Ritual: The Archaeological Construction of Rock Art's Past and Present Social Contexts. In *Great Basin Rock Art: Archaeological Perspectives*, edited by Angus R. Quinlan, pp. 140–149. University of Nevada Press, Reno.
2007b Integrating Rock Art with Archaeology: Symbolic Culture as Archaeology. In *Great Basin Rock Art: Archaeological Perspectives*, edited by Angus R. Quinlan, pp. 1–8. University of Nevada Press, Reno.

Quinlan, Angus R., and Alanah Woody
2003 Marks of Distinction: Rock Art and Ethnic Identification in the Great Basin. *American Antiquity* 68:372–390.

Raheja, Michelle H.
2010 *Reservation Reelism: Redfacing, Visual Sovereignty, and Representations of Native Americans in Film*. University of Nebraska Press, Lincoln.

Reggio, Godfrey (director)
1983 *Koyaanisqatsi*. Motion picture. Pacific Arts.

Ricks, Mary F.
1999 With an Open Mind: The Place of Rock Art in Northern Great Basin Prehistoric Cultural Systems. In *Models for the Millennium: Great Basin Anthropology Today*, edited by Charlotte Beck, pp. 192–199. University of Utah Press, Salt Lake City.

Roberts, David
1996 *In Search of the Old Ones: Exploring the Anasazi World of the Southwest*. Touchstone, New York.

Robinson, David W.
2013 Drawing upon the Past: Temporal Ontology and Mythological Ideol-

ogy in South-Central Californian Rock Art. *Cambridge Archaeological Journal* 23:373–394.

Robinson, Sally
2000 *Marked Men: Masculinity in Crisis.* Columbia University Press, New York.

Rogers, Richard A.
1993 Pleasure, Power and Consent: The Interplay of Race and Gender in *New Jack City. Women's Studies in Communication* 16(2):62–85.
1998 Overcoming the Objectification of Nature in Constitutive Theories: Toward a Transhuman, Materialist Theory of Communication. *Western Journal of Communication* 62:244–272.
2006 From Cultural Exchange to Transculturation: A Review and Reconceptualization of Cultural Appropriation. *Communication Theory* 16:474–503.
2008 Beasts, Burgers, and Hummers: Meat and the Crisis of Masculinity in Contemporary Television Advertisements. *Environmental Communication: A Journal of Nature and Culture* 2:281–301.

Rosaldo, Renato
1989 *Culture and Truth.* Beacon, Boston.

Ross, Mairi
2001 Emerging Trends in Rock-Art Research: Hunter-Gatherer Culture, Land and Landscape. *Antiquity* 75:543–48.

Rotundo, E. Anthony
1993 *American Manhood: Transformations in Masculinity from the Revolution to the Modern Era.* BasicBooks, New York.

Rowe, Marvin W.
2005 Dating Studies of Prehistoric Pictographs in North America. In *Discovering North American Rock Art*, edited by Lawrence L. Loendorf, Christopher Chippindale, and David S. Whitley, pp. 240–263. University of Arizona Press, Tucson.

Rupestrian CyberServices
2015a RCS Homepage. Electronic document, http://www.rupestrian.com, accessed July 10, 2015.
2015b Panoramas. Electronic document, http://www.rupestrian.com/panoramas.html, accessed July 10, 2015.

Sahagun, Louis
2012 Petroglyph Thefts near Bishop Stun Federal Authorities, Paiutes. *Los Angeles Times* 18 November. Electronic document, http://www.latimes.com, accessed June 15, 2015.
2013 Petroglyphs Stolen from Sacred Eastern Sierra Site Recovered. *Los Angeles Times* 31 January. Electronic document, http://www.latimes.com, accessed June 15, 2015.

Said, Edward W.
1983 *The World, the Text, and the Critic.* Harvard University Press, Cambridge, Massachusetts.

Salvador, Michael, and Tracey Lee Clark
1999 Native Americans and the Environment: Cultural Representation in *Sierra* Magazine. *World Communication* 28:27–44.

Sanders, Ronald D.
2005 *Rock Art Savvy: The Responsible Visitor's Guide to Public Sites of the Southwest.* Mountain Press, Missoula, Montana.

Saner, Reg
1998 *Reaching Keet Seel: Ruin's Echo and the Anasazi.* University of Utah Press, Salt Lake City.

Sanger, Kay Kenady
1992 Making Our Work in Rock Art Count. In *American Indian Rock Art*, Vol. 18, edited by Frank G. Bock, pp. 19–22. American Rock Art Research Association, San Miguel, California.

Santa Fe New Mexican
2014 Legislative Roundup, Feb. 13, 2014. 12 February. Electronic document, http://www.santafenewmexican.com/news/legislature/legislative-round-up-feb/article_f939d8ec-58df-577d-b8fe-055b52df562c.html, accessed January 14, 2017.

Sapir, Edward
1924 Culture, Genuine and Spurious. *The American Journal of Sociology* 29:401–429.

Schaafsma, Polly
1971 *The Rock Art of Utah.* University of Utah Press, Salt Lake City.
1980 *Indian Rock Art of the Southwest.* University of New Mexico Press, Albuquerque. .
1985 Form, Content, and Function: Theory and Method in North American Rock Art Studies. *Advances in Archaeological Theory and Method* 8:237–277.
1994 Trance and Transformation in the Canyons: Shamanism and Early Rock Art on the Colorado Plateau. In *Shamanism and Rock Art in North America*, edited by Solveig A. Turpin, pp. 45–71. Rock Art Foundation, San Antonio, Texas.
1997 Rock Art, World Views, and Contemporary Issues. In *Rock Art as Visual Ecology*, edited by Paul Faulstich, pp. 7–20. IRAC Proceedings, Vol. 1. American Rock Art Research Association, San Miguel, California.
2010 Landscape and Painted Walls: Images in Place. In *Painting the Cosmos: Metaphor and Worldview in Images from the Southwest Pueblos and Mexico*, edited by Kelley Hays-Gilpin and Polly Schaafsma, pp. 19–40. Bulletin No. 67. Museum of Northern Arizona, Flagstaff.
2013 *Images and Power: Rock Art and Ethics.* Springer, New York.

Schmader, Matt
2008 On the Rocks: Albuquerque and Its Petroglyph Past. In *Set in Stone: A Binational Workshop on Petroglyph Management in the United States and Mexico*, compiled by Joseph P. Sánchez, Angelica Sánchez-Clark, and Edwina L. Abreu, pp. 1–9. Petroglyph National Monument, Albuquerque, New Mexico.

Scholes, Robert
1989 *Protocols of Reading*. Yale University Press, New Haven, Connecticut.

Schott, Robin May
1988 *Cognition and Eros: A Critique of the Kantian Paradigm*. Beacon Press, Boston.

Schwinning, Susan, Jayne Belnap, David R. Bowling, and James R. Ehleringer
2008 Sensitivity of the Colorado Plateau to Change: Climate, Ecosystems, and Society. *Ecology and Society* 13(2). Electronic document, http://www.ecologyandsociety.org/vol13/iss2/art28/, accessed January 14, 2017.

Senter, Phil
2012 More "Dinosaur" and "Pterosaur" Rock Art That Isn't. *Palaeontologia Electronica* 15(2):1–14. Electronic document, http://palaeo-electronica.org/content/pdfs/321.pdf, accessed January 14, 2017.

Shugart, Helene A.
1997 Counterhegemonic Acts: Appropriation as a Feminist Rhetorical Strategy. *Quarterly Journal of Speech* 83:210–229.

Sierra Press
1993 *Art on the Rocks: A Wish You Were Here Postcard Book*. Sierra Press, Mariposa, California.

Silver, Constance
1989 Rock Art Conservation in the United States: Wish or Reality? In *Preserving Our Rock Art Heritage: Proceedings from the Symposium on Rock Art Conservation and Protection*, edited by Helen K. Crotty, pp. 3–15. Occasional Paper 1. American Rock Art Research Association, San Miguel, California.

Simms, Steven R., and François Gohier
2010 *Traces of Fremont: Society and Rock Art in Ancient Utah*. University of Utah Press, Salt Lake City.

Simons, Herbert W. (editor)
1990 *The Rhetorical Turn: Invention and Persuasion in the Conduct of Inquiry*. University of Chicago Press, Chicago.

Slifer, Dennis
2000a *Guide to Rock Art of the Utah Region*. Ancient City Press, Santa Fe, New Mexico.
2000b *The Serpent and the Sacred Fire: Fertility Images in Southwest Rock Art*. Museum of New Mexico, Santa Fe.
2007 *Kokopelli: The Magic, Mirth, and Mischief of an Ancient Symbol*. Gibbs Smith, Salt Lake City, Utah.

Slifer, Dennis, and James Duffield
   1994 *Kokopelli: Flute Player Images in Rock Art*. Ancient City Press, Santa
   Fe, New Mexico.
Sloop, John M.
   2005 In a Queer Time and Place and Race: Intersectionality Comes of Age.
   Quarterly Journal of Speech 91:312–326.
Smith, Andrea
   2005 *Conquest: Sexual Violence and American Indian Genocide*. South End
   Press, Cambridge, Massachusetts.
Smith, Benjamin W.
   2016 Rock Art in South African Society Today. In *Relating to Rock Art in
   the Contemporary World: Navigating Symbolism, Meaning, and Signif-
   icance*, edited by Liam M. Brady and Paul S. C. Taçon, pp. 127–156.
   University Press of Colorado, Boulder.
Smith, Benjamin W., and Geoffrey Blundell
   2004 Dangerous Ground: A Critique of Landscape in Rock-Art Studies.
   In *Pictures in Place: The Figured Landscapes of Rock-Art*, edited by
   Christopher Chippindale and George Nash, pp. 239–262. Cambridge
   University Press, Cambridge, England.
Smith, Laurajane
   2004 *Archaeological Theory and the Politics of Cultural Heritage*. Routledge,
   New York.
Stecopoulos, Harry
   1997 The World According to Normal Bean: Edgar Rice Burroughs's Pop-
   ular Culture. In *Race and the Subject of Masculinities*, edited by Harry
   Stecopoulos and Michael Uebel, pp. 170–191. Duke University Press,
   Durham, North Carolina.
Steward, Julian H.
   1929 Petroglyphs of California and Adjoining States. *University of California
   Publications in American Archaeology and Ethnology* 24(2):47–238.
   1937 Petroglyphs of the United States. *The Smithsonian Report for 1936*, pp.
   405–425. Publication 3437. United States Government Printing Office,
   Washington, DC.
Stewart, Susan
   1984 *On Longing: Narratives of the Miniature, the Gigantic, the Souvenir, the
   Collection*. Johns Hopkins University Press, Baltimore, Maryland.
Stoffle, Richard W., Lawrence Loendorf, Diane E. Austin, David B. Halmo,
   and Angelita Bulletts
   2000 Ghost Dancing the Grand Canyon: Southern Paiute Rock Art,
   Ceremony, and Cultural Landscapes. *Current Anthropology* 41:11–24.
Stokes, William Michael, and William Lee Stokes
   1980 *Messages on Stone: Selections of Native Western Rock Art*. Starstone, Salt
   Lake City, Utah.

Stuckey, Mary E., and Richard Morris
1999 Pocahontas and Beyond: Commodification and Cultural Hegemony. *World Communication* 28:45–67.

Sublette, Mark
2013 *Hidden Canyon: A Charles Bloom Murder Mystery.* Just Me Publishing, Tucson, Arizona.

Sundstrom, Linea
2002 Steel Awls for Stone Age Plainswomen: Rock Art, Religion, and the Hide Trade on the Northern Plains. *Plains Anthropologist* 47:99–119.
2004 *Storied Stone: Indian Rock Art of the Black Hills Country.* University of Oklahoma Press, Norman.
2008 Buffalo Gals: Images of Women in Northern Great Plains Rock Art. In *American Indian Rock Art*, Vol. 34, edited by James D. Keyser, David A. Kaiser, George Poetschat, and Michael W. Taylor, pp. 167–179. American Rock Art Research Association, Tucson, Arizona.

Swadley, Ben H.
2009 Actively Managing Rock Art Sites. In *American Indian Rock Art*, Vol. 35, edited by James D. Keyser, David A. Kaiser, George Poetschat, and Michael W. Taylor, pp. 219–235. American Rock Art Research Association, Tucson, Arizona.

Taçon, Paul S. C., and Christopher Chippindale
1998 An Archaeology of Rock-Art through Informed Methods and Formal Methods. In *The Archaeology of Rock Art*, edited by Christopher Chippindale and Paul S. C. Taçon, pp. 1–10. Cambridge University Press, Cambridge, England.

Tainter, Joseph A., and Bonnie Bagley
2005 Shaping and Suppressing the Archaeological Record: Significance in American Cultural Resource Management. In *Heritage of Value, Archaeology of Renown: Reshaping Archaeological Assessment and Significance*, edited by Clay Mathers, Timothy Darvill, and Barbara J. Little, pp. 58–73. University Press of Florida, Gainesville.

Taylor, Michael W., James D. Keyser, and Phillip Cash Cash
2008 The Role of Women in Columbia Plateau Rock Art. In *American Indian Rock Art*, Vol. 34, edited by James D. Keyser, David A. Kaiser, George Poetschat, and Michael W. Taylor, pp. 133–154. American Rock Art Research Association, Tucson, Arizona.

Tisdale, Shelby J.
1993 From Rock Art to Wal-Mart: Kokopelli Representations in Historical Perspective. *Papers of the Archaeological Society of New Mexico* 19:213–223.

Titiev, Mischa
1937 A Hopi Salt Expedition. *American Anthropologist* n.s. 39:244–258.
1939 The Story of Kokopele. *American Anthropologist* n.s. 41:91–98.

Toffelmier, Gertrude, and Katharine Luomala
   2006 [1936] Dreams and Dream Interpretation of the Diegueño Indians of Southern California. *Journal of California and Great Basin Anthropology* 26:215–228.

Torgovnick, Marianna
   1996 *Primitive Passions: Men, Women, and the Quest for Ecstasy.* University of Chicago Press, Chicago.

Trimble, Stephen, and Terry Tempest Williams
   1996 *Testimony: Writers of the West Speak on Behalf of Utah Wilderness.* Milkweed Editions, Minneapolis, Minnesota.

Trocolli, Ruth
   1999 Women Leaders in Native North American Societies. In *Manifesting Power: Gender and the Interpretation of Power in Archaeology*, edited by Tracy L. Sweely, pp. 49–61. Routledge, New York.

True, Coyote [*pseud.*]
   1995 Kokopelli Krime. *Edging West.* August/September:16–19.

Trujillo, Nick
   1991 Hegemonic Masculinity on the Mound: Media Representations of Nolan Ryan and American Sports Culture. *Critical Studies in Mass Communication* 8:290–308.

Turner, Christy G., II
   1963 *Petroglyphs of the Glen Canyon Region.* Museum of Northern Arizona Bulletin 38, Glen Canyon Series No. 4. Northern Arizona Society of Science and Art, Flagstaff.

Turpin, Solveig A. (editor)
   1994 *Shamanism and Rock Art in North America.* Texas Rock Art Foundation, San Antonio.

Twin Rocks Trading Post
   2013 Native American Legends and Culture. Electronic document, http://www.twinrocks.com/legends/, accessed June 2, 2014.

United States v. Ligon, No. 04-10495. No. 04-10524. 440 F.3d 1182 (9th Cir. Mar. 21 2006). Electronic document, http://openjurist.org/440/f3d/1182/united-states-v-ligon, accessed January 14, 2017.

Upton, Reed
   2005 Zia Pueblo Receiving Money for Use of Sun Symbol. KOBTV.com 2 December. The National Association of Tribal Historic Preservation Officers. Electronic document, http://www.nathpo.org/News/Legal/News-Legal_Issues27.html, accessed January 14, 2017.

Utah Rock Art Research Association
   2004 Nine Mile Canyon News. Electronic document, http://www.utahrockart.org, accessed July 2, 2015.

Valley, Jackie
    2010a Vandals Hit Ancient Art at Red Rock. *Las Vegas Sun* 29 November.
        Electronic document, https://lasvegassun.com, accessed January 14, 2017.
    2010b Police: Ancient Red Rock Art Vandalized for "Shock Value." *Las
        Vegas Sun* 9 December. Electronic document, https://lasvegassun.com,
        accessed January 14, 2017.
Van Lent, Peter
    1996 "Her Beautiful Savage": The Current Sexual Image of the Native
        American Male. In *Dressing in Feathers: The Construction of the Indian
        in American Popular Culture*, edited by S. Elizabeth Bird, pp. 211–227.
        Westview Press, Boulder, Colorado.
Van Tilburg, Jo Anne, Gordon E. Hull, and John C. Bretney
    2012 *Rock Art at Little Lake: An Ancient Crossroads in the California Desert.*
        University of California Los Angeles Cotsen Institute of Archaeology
        Press, Los Angeles.
Vološinov, V. N.
    1973 [1929] *Marxism and the Philosophy of Language.* Translated by Ladislav
        Matejka and I. R. Titunik. Harvard University Press, Cambridge,
        Massachusetts.
Vuncannon, Delcie H.
    1985 Fertility Symbolism at the Chalfant Site, California. In *Rock Art
        Papers*, Vol. 2, edited by Ken Hedges, pp. 119–126. San Diego Museum
        Papers No. 18. San Diego Museum of Man, San Diego, California.
Walker, Dave
    1998 *Cuckoo for Kokopelli.* Northland, Flagstaff, Arizona.
Wallis, Roger, and Krister Malm
    1984 *Big Sounds from Small Peoples: The Music Industry in Small Countries.*
        Constable, London.
Walsh, Andrea N., and Dominic McIver Lopes
    2012 Objects of Appropriation. In *The Ethics of Cultural Appropriation*,
        edited by James O. Young and Conrad G. Brunk, pp. 211–234.
        Wiley-Blackwell, Malden, Massachusetts.
Walters, Harry, and Hugh C. Rogers
    2001 Anasazi and 'Anaasází: Two Words, Two Cultures. *Kiva* 66:317–326.
Wander, Philip C., Judith N. Martin, and Thomas K. Nakayama
    1999 Whiteness and Beyond: Sociohistorical Foundations of Whiteness and
        Contemporary Challenges. In *Whiteness: The Communication of Social
        Identity*, edited by Thomas K. Nakayama and Judith N. Martin, pp.
        13–26. Sage, Thousand Oaks, California.
Warburton, Miranda, and Richard M. Begay
    2005 An Exploration of Navajo-Anasazi Relationships. *Ethnohistory*
        52:533–561.

Watson, Patty Jo, and Mary C. Kennedy
   1998 The Development of Horticulture in the Eastern Woodlands of North
      America: Women's Role. In *Reader in Gender Archaeology*, edited by Kelley
      Hays-Gilpin and David S. Whitley, pp. 173–190. Routledge, New York.
Weaver, Donald E., Robert Mark, and Evelyn Billo
   2001 Inscription Point: Too Little Too Late? In *American Indian Rock Art*,
      Vol. 27, edited by Steven M. Freers and Alanah Woody, pp. 137–150.
      American Rock Art Research Association, Tucson, Arizona.
Welsh, Elizabeth C.
   1995 *Easy Field Guide to Southwestern Petroglyphs*. American Traveler Press,
      Phoenix, Arizona.
Welsh, Liz, and Peter Welsh
   2000 *Rock-Art of the Southwest: A Visitor's Companion*. Wilderness Press,
      Berkeley, California.
Welsh, Peter H.
   1999 Commodification of Rock Art: An Inalienable Paradox. In *Rock Art and
      Ethics: A Dialogue*, edited by William D. Hyder, pp. 29–37. Occasional
      Paper 3. American Rock Art Research Association, Tucson, Arizona.
Western Rock Art Research
   2010 Western Rock Art Research. Electronic document, www.westernrock-
      artresearch.com, accessed July 10, 2015.
Wharton, Tom
   2008 Fertility God Kokopelli Moved from View in State Park. *The Salt
      Lake Tribune* 2 October. Electronic document, www.sltrib.com, accessed
      October 3, 2008.
White Deer, Gary
   1997 The Return of the Sacred: Spirituality and the Scientific Imperative.
      In *Native Americans and Archaeologists: Stepping Stones to Common
      Ground*, edited by N. Swidler, K. Dongoske, R. Anyon, and A. Downer,
      pp. 37–43. AltaMira Press, Walnut Creek, California.
Whitley, David S.
   1994a Ethnography and Rock Art in the Far West: Some Archaeological
      Implications. In *New Light on Old Art: Recent Advances in Hunter-
      Gatherer Rock Art Research*, edited by David S. Whitley and Lawrence L.
      Loendorf, pp. 81–93. Institute of Archaeology, University of California,
      Los Angeles.
   1994b Shamanism, Natural Modeling and the Rock Art of Far Western
      North American Hunter-Gatherers. In *Shamanism and Rock Art in
      North America*, edited by Solveig A. Turpin, pp. 1–43. Rock Art Foundation,
      San Antonio, Texas.
   1996 *A Guide to Rock Art Sites: Southern California and Southern Nevada*.
      Mountain Press, Missoula, Montana.

1998a By the Hunter, for the Gatherer: Art, Social Relations and Subsistence Change in the Prehistoric Great Basin. In *Reader in Archaeological Theory: Post-Processual and Cognitive Approaches*, edited by David S. Whitley, pp. 257–274. Routledge, New York.

1998b New Approaches to Old Problems: Archaeology in Search of an Ever Elusive Past. In *Reader in Archaeological Theory: Post-Processual and Cognitive Approaches*, edited by David S. Whitley, pp. 1–28. Routledge, New York.

1998c Finding Rain in the Desert: Landscape, Gender and Far Western North American Rock-Art. In *The Archaeology of Rock Art*, edited by Christopher Chippindale and Paul S. C. Taçon, pp. 11–29. Cambridge University Press, Cambridge, England.

2000a *The Art of the Shaman: Rock Art of California*. University of Utah Press, Salt Lake City.

2000b Use and Abuse of Ethnohistory in the Far West. In *1999 International Rock Art Congress Proceedings*, Vol. 1, edited by Peggy Whitehead and Lawrence Loendorf, pp. 127–154. American Rock Art Research Association, Tucson, Arizona.

2001a Rock Art and Rock Art Research in a Worldwide Perspective: An Introduction. In *Handbook of Rock Art Research*, edited by David S. Whitley, pp. 7–51. AltaMira Press, Walnut Creek, California.

2001b Science and the Sacred: Interpretive Theory in U.S. Rock Art Research. In *Theoretical Perspectives in Rock Art Research*, edited by Knut Helskog, pp. 124–151. Institute for Comparative Research in Human Culture, Oslo, Norway.

2003 What Is Hedges Arguing About? In *American Indian Rock Art*, Vol. 29, edited by Alanah Woody and Joseph T. O'Connor, pp. 83–104. American Rock Art Research Association, Tucson, Arizona.

2008 The Long View of Old Art: Rock Art in the 22nd Century. In *Set in Stone: A Binational Workshop on Petroglyph Management in the United States and Mexico*, compiled by Joseph P. Sánchez, Angelica Sánchez-Clark, and Edwina L. Abreu, pp. ix–xvi. Petroglyph National Monument, Albuquerque, New Mexico.

2011 *Introduction to Rock Art Research*. 2nd ed. Left Coast Press, Walnut Creek, California.

Whitley, David S. (editor)

2001c *Handbook of Rock Art Research*. AltaMira Press, Walnut Creek, California.

Whitley, Davis S., and Jean Clottes

2005 In Steward's Shadow: Histories of Research in the Far West and Western Europe. In *Discovering North American Rock Art*, edited by Lawrence L. Loendorf, Christopher Chippindale, and David S. Whitley, pp. 161–177. University of Arizona Press, Tucson, Arizona.

Whitley, David S., and Lawrence L. Loendorf
    1994 Introduction: Off the Cover and into the Book. In *New Light on Old Art: Recent Advances in Hunter-Gatherer Rock Art Research*, edited by David S. Whitley and Lawrence L. Loendorf, pp. xi–xx. Institute of Archaeology, University of California, Los Angeles.
Whitt, Laurie Anne
    1995 Cultural Imperialism and the Marketing of Native America. *American Indian Culture and Research Journal* 19(3):1–31.
Williams, Raymond
    1977 *Marxism and Literature*. Oxford University Press, New York.
Winslow, Ben
    2006 Five Teens Who Vandalized Petroglyphs Are Sentenced. *Deseret News* 1 February. Electronic document, deseretnews.com, accessed October 7, 2017.
Wood, Julia T.
    1992 From "Woman's Nature" to Standpoint Epistemology: Gilligan and the Debate over Essentializing in Feminist Scholarship. *Women's Studies in Communication* 15:1–24.
Woody, Alanah
    2005 Reply to Dorn. *La Pintura*, 31(2):12–14.
Woody, Alanah, and Alvin R. McLane
    2000 The Distribution of Vulviforms on White Tuff in Nevada. In *American Indian Rock Art*, Vol. 24, edited by Frank G. Bock, pp. 29–48. American Rock Art Research Association, Tucson, Arizona.
Young, James O., and Conrad G. Brunk
    2012 Introduction. In *The Ethics of Cultural Appropriation*, edited by James O. Young and Conrad G. Brunk, pp. 1–10. Wiley-Blackwell, Malden, Massachusetts.
Young, John V.
    1990 *Kokopelli: Casanova of the Cliff Dwellers*. Filter Press, Palmer Lake, Colorado.
Young, M. Jane
    1988 *Signs from the Ancestors: Zuni Cultural Symbolism and Perceptions of Rock Art*. University of New Mexico Press, Albuquerque.
Ziff, Bruce, and Pratima V. Rao
    1997 Introduction to Cultural Appropriation: A Framework for Analysis. In *Borrowed Power: Essays on Cultural Appropriation*, edited by Bruce Ziff and Pratima V. Rao, pp. 1–27. Rutgers University Press, New Brunswick, New Jersey.
Zoll, Kenneth J.
    2008a *Understanding the Rock Art of Sedona*. Sunwatcher, Sedona, Arizona.
    2008b *Sinagua Sunwatchers: An Archaeoastronomy Survey of the Sacred Mountain Basin*. Sunwatcher, Sedona, Arizona.

INDEX

Page numbers printed in *italics* refer to graphs, illustrations, or tables.